EXPORTING THE EUROPEAN CONVENTION ON HUMAN RIGHTS

This book explores how the European Convention on Human Rights (ECHR) operates and influences on the global stage. The ECHR and its interpretation by the European Court of Human Rights (ECtHR) have considerable influence inside and outside Europe. To what degree has that influence translated into its norms, doctrines and methods of interpretation being exported into equivalent systems which also enact the protection of fundamental rights? This book answers that question by exploring the judicial dialogue of the ECHR system with comparable legal orders.

Through a horizontal and multifaceted study of regional and global systems, the book identifies the impact of the ECHR within the confines of their jurisprudence to provide scholars in the field of international human rights law with an essential text. Discussing the extent to which the ECHR penetrates into the judicial production of the most affected legal systems, the book mostly focuses on the case law of the Court of Justice of the European Union, the Inter-American Court of Human Rights and the UN Human Rights Committee. It also investigates whether there is room for cross-fertilisation between them and, finally, moves on to explore the legal consequences of the interplay of these mechanisms with the ECtHR and what it means for the overall functioning of international human rights law.

Volume 112 in the Series Modern Studies in European Law

Modern Studies in European Law

Recent titles in this series:

Law and Judicial Dialogue on the Return of Irregular
Migrants from the European Union
Edited by Madalina Moraru, Galina Cornelisse and Philippe De Bruycker

Framing Convergence with the Global Legal Order: The EU and the World
Edited by Elaine Fahey

EU Citizenship at the Edges of Freedom of Movement
Katarina Hyltén-Cavallius

The Internal Market 2.0
Edited by Sacha Garben and Inge Govaere

New Directions in European Private Law
Edited by Mateja Durovic and Takis Tridimas

Standing to Enforce European Union Law before National Courts
Hilde Ellingsen

The Relative Authority of Judicial and Extra-Judicial Review: The EU Courts,
the Boards of Appeal and the Ombudsman
Michal Krajewski

Responsive Human Rights: Vulnerability and the ECtHR
Corina Heri

The Architecture of Fundamental Rights in the European Union
Šejla Imamovic

The EU and its Member States' Joint Participation in International Agreements
*Edited by Nicolas Levrat, Yuliya Kaspiarovich, Christine
Kaddous and Ramses A Wessel*

The UN Convention on the Rights of Persons with
Disabilities and the European Union: The Impact on Law and Governance
Carmine Conte

EU Criminal Law, Second Edition
Valsamis Mitsilegas

The EU as a Global Digital Actor:
Institutionalising Global Data Protection, Trade, and Cybersecurity
Elaine Fahey

Exporting the European Convention on Human Rights
Maria-Louiza Deftou

**For the complete list of titles in this series
see www.bloomsbury.com/uk/series/modern-studies-in-european-law/**

Exporting the European Convention on Human Rights

Maria-Louiza Deftou

• HART •
OXFORD • LONDON • NEW YORK • NEW DELHI • SYDNEY

HART PUBLISHING

Bloomsbury Publishing Plc

Kemp House, Chawley Park, Cumnor Hill, Oxford, OX2 9PH, UK

1385 Broadway, New York, NY 10018, USA

29 Earlsfort Terrace, Dublin 2, Ireland

First published in Great Britain 2022

A catalogue record for this book is available from the British Library.

A catalogue record for this book is available from the Library of Congress.

Library of Congress Control Number: 2022940275

ISBN: HB: 978-1-50995-243-4
ePDF: 978-1-50995-245-8
ePub: 978-1-50995-244-1

Typeset by Compuscript Ltd, Shannon

To my little sister, Aspasia

FOREWORD

There is an ocean of ink spent on discussing the impact of the European Convention on Human Rights. This is only fitting as the importance of the ECHR, as interpreted by the European Court of Human Rights and implemented in the domestic legal order of all European States parties to it, cannot be overstated: in the past 70 years it has shaped institutions and administrative practices, has informed our understanding of both what is the essence of human rights protection and how we best achieve it, has in fact set the standard of human rights protection worldwide.

The present monograph concentrates on this last point: the impact of the ECHR beyond the shores of Europe, onto other legal worlds. Dr Deftou attempted a veritable *tour de force* in the human rights world at large – and she succeeded admirably. She did not just select diverse yet comparable legal orders: the European Union, the protection system created by the American Convention on Human Rights; or indeed similar but not identical protection mechanisms: the Human Rights Committee, as a typical example of the increasingly influential work done by treaty bodies. Moving away from what could have been a descriptive exercise, she immersed herself into the intricacies of each one of these separate universes and produced a critical examination of their inherent strengths and deficiencies to better illustrate the means and ways one could detect and identify the impact of the European Convention on Human Rights. Her insights on the jurisprudence of the Court of Justice of the European Union on matters pertaining to data protection and procedural guarantees before a court of law or the manner in which social rights or asylum cases are handled in Luxembourg showcase the subtle but very solid ways in which ECHR serves both as part of the European Union legal order in direct application and as a restraining mechanism for the precepts of the European Union law.

Perhaps the most ground-breaking part of the monograph lies in the exploration of the horizontal interrelation between regional human rights protection regimes. Dr Deftou has gifted us with an in-depth analysis of the Inter-American legal system with an impressive level of detailed information and understanding of its strong points and peculiarities – and then took her analysis a giant step further, identifying the areas of both convergence and separate development with an eye to the debate that rages, tacit and inaudible but undoubtedly real and effective, between them. The same feat is repeated between the regional and the global, with emphasis on the workings of the Human Rights Committee and a keen understanding of the limitations the difference in their nature poses upon the two regimes.

Dr Deftou has undertaken a massive work, tracing an impact that could easily be qualified – and denigrated – as a prime example of legal imperialism. Her careful selection of the issues to be highlighted and her honest yet sensitive to cultural nuances approach has enabled her to produce excellent research of immediate usefulness to the research community and rare insight into difficult issues. For this is a book that starts where difficult questions are being asked – and for that alone, she should be congratulated.

On a personal note, it is always a moment of immense satisfaction and contentment to watch young scholars to grow and mature and produce innovative work of great value. I owe thanks to Mariliza for the long hours of discussion and the many moments of thoughtful contemplation as well as the myriad instances of hard work, personal kindness and joined effort and I look forward to more in the future.

Professor Maria Gavouneli
National & Kapodistrian University of Athens

PREFACE

This monograph is based on a PhD thesis awarded by National and Kapodistrian University of Athens (School of Law) in December 2019. It reflects the law and jurisprudence as they stood, to the best of the author's knowledge, in June 2021. An earlier draft of part of Chapter 4 was published as 'Tracing Strasbourg's Standards of Protection in Geneva: Poles apart or Secret Sweethearts?' (2021) 4 *European Human Rights Law Review* 407.

ACKNOWLEDGEMENTS

The present monograph started as a PhD thesis defended at the School of Law of the National and Kapodistrian University of Athens in December 2019, and was written with love and pure interest for research. As far as possible, the text has been updated as of June 2021, although in some instances the reader is alerted to cases where judgments have been delivered after this date. Looking back on all these years of exhaustive work, I realise that the way was full of bitter-sweet souvenirs of an unforgettable time which is now gone and is never coming back in my life: the unstoppable bibliographic research, the conferences, the long working hours at the library, the stimulating discussions with friends, colleagues, librarians. Since a part of my research was funded by the Greek State Scholarships Foundation (IKY), the financial support I received was absolutely crucial for the completion of my work.

My first words of immense gratitude are profoundly owed to my supervisor, Professor Maria Gavouneli, for her generosity, indispensable guidance and most importantly, for being a constant inspiration. I am also sincerely grateful to Professor Photini Pazartzis and Professor Revekka-Emmanouela Papadopoulou for their availability and for their insightful comments, as well as to the examiners for their challenging questions and thought-provoking observations. At this point, I should particularly thank Emeritus Professor Antonios Bredimas, with whom I often shared my PhD-related worries at the library, for being constantly willing to provide a valuable piece of advice.

My sincere thanks and appreciation also go to Dr Akis Papastavridis for his useful comments on my work and his encouragement, and Dr Nikolas Giannopoulos for the stimulating discussions and his precious assistance throughout the research process whenever needed. I must warmly thank all friends and colleagues from the Department of International Studies and AthensPIL for their support along this way. Many thanks are also owed to Mrs Myrto Stavridi for her valuable assistance with style editing when preparing the manuscript.

Of course, I am extremely indebted to my family and my best friend Nicky, who always stand by me, support every endeavour I undertake and believe in me so passionately.

CONTENTS

PART II
EXPORTING THE ECHR TO THE INTERNATIONAL LEGAL ORDER

LIST OF ABBREVIATIONS

ACHR	American Convention of Human Rights
AComHPR	African Commission of Human and Peoples' rights
ACRWC	African Charter on the Rights and Welfare of the Child
ACtHPR	African Court of Human and Peoples' rights
AFDI	Annuaire Français de Droit International
AFSJ	Area of Freedom, security and Justice
AG	Advocate General
Art	Article
ASIL Insights	American Society of International Law Insights
CAT	Committee Against Torture
CEAS	Common European Asylum System
CEDAW	Committee on the Elimination of Discrimination Against Women
CERD	Committee on the Elimination of Racial Discrimination
CETS	Council of Europe Treaty Series
CFI	Court of First Instance
CFR	Charter of Fundamental Rights of the European Union
CFSP	Common Foreign and Security Policy
CISA	Convention Implementing the Schengen Agreement
CJEU	Court of Justice of the European Union
CoE	Council of Europe
CRC	Committee on the Rights of the Child
DAA	Draft Accession Agreement
DPD	Data Protection Directive
EAW	European Arrest Warrant

ECHR	European Convention on Human Rights
ECJ	European Court of Justice
ECLI	European Case Law Identifier
ECommHR	European Commission of Human Rights
ECR	European Court Reports
ECRE	European Council on Refugees and Exiles
ECtHR	European Court of Human Rights
EEC Treaty	Treaty establishing the European Economic Community
ETS	European Treaty Series
EU	European Union
EUCFR	Charter of Fundamental Rights of the European Union
FD	Framework Decision
FRY	Federal Republic of Yugoslavia
GDPR	General Data Protection Regulation
HRC	Human Rights Committee
IACommHR	Inter-American Commission of Human Rights
IACtHR	Inter-American Court of Human Rights
IAHRS	Inter-American Human Rights System
ICCPR	International Covenant of Civil and Political Rights
ICJ	International Court of Justice
ICTY	International Criminal Tribunal for the former Yugoslavia
ILC	International Law Commission
ILO	International Labour Organisation
JHA	Justice and Home Affairs
Legal Issues of Econ. Integration	Legal Issues of Economic Integration
LGBTQI community	Lesbian, gay, bisexual, transgender, queer or intersex community
MoA	Margin of Appreciation

MS	Member State(s)
NATO	North Atlantic Treaty Organization
NGO	Non-Governmental Organisation
OASTS	Organization of American States Treaty Series
OAS	Organization of American States
PNR	Passenger name record
PWD	Posted Workers Directive
TCNs	Third Country Nationals
TEU	Treaty on European Union
TFEU	Treaty on the Functioning of the European Union
UNTS	United Nations Treaty Series
UN	United Nations
UNGA	United Nations General Assembly
UNHCR	United Nations High Commissioner for Refugees
UNSC	United Nations Security Council
VAT	Value-Added Tax
VCLT	Vienna Convention on the Law of the Treaties
VEA	Veteran Entitlement Act

TABLE OF CASES

Courts and Tribunals

Permanent Court of International Justice (PCIJ)

International Court of Justice (ICJ)

International Criminal Tribunal for the former Yugoslavia (ICTY)

European Court of Human Rights

European Commission of Human Rights

Court of Justice of the European Union

General Court of the European Union

Inter-American Court of Human Rights

Inter-American Commission of Human Rights

African Court of Human and Peoples' Rights

UN Treaty Bodies

Human Rights Committee (ICCPR)

Committee on the Elimination of Discrimination against Women (CEDAW)

National Courts

German Constitutional Court

TABLE OF TREATIES

UN Conventions and Treaties

Council of Europe

EU Treaties

Other Regional Instruments

America

Africa

TABLE OF DOCUMENTS

United Nations

UN Treaty Bodies

Human Rights Committee (HRC)

European Union

Regulations

Directives

EU Documents

Organization of American States (OAS)

Miscellaneous

Introduction

Following World War II and during the Cold War years, human rights discourse was heralded as the ultimate counterweight to the lack of political stability and the impunity of state actors. Numerous regional regimes of human rights protection operating in radically diversified socio-political and legal settings were mandated to guide national jurisdictions when implementing shared human rights norms. Under the global spread of human rights instruments, the European Convention on Human Rights (hereinafter ECHR)[1] has stood the test of time and still remains the ultimate beacon for the protection of human rights worldwide. It is interpreted as a *living instrument* by its supervisory organ, the European Court of Human Rights (hereinafter ECtHR or Strasbourg Court), which has elaborated on the constant evolution of the entire system and has built upon the enrichment of its normative force outside Europe.

The continuing enrichment of the Convention through its 16 Protocols[2] has permitted the oldest text in the context of international human rights law to reorient itself towards new legal fields that merit its guidance, keeping up with contemporary challenges and thus, remaining at the forefront of the effective observance of human rights universally. All 46 Contracting Parties to the ECHR are obligated to enforce and guarantee the peaceful enjoyment for their nationals of a wide collection of core, non-derogable rights (eg, right to life, prohibition of torture and inhuman or degrading treatment) and civil and political rights and freedoms, which need to be balanced with competing interests. National jurisdictions are guided in this task by the ever-evolving jurisprudence of the Court, whose interpretative toolkit and famous doctrines have hammered out common

[1] Convention for the Protection of Human Rights and Fundamental Freedoms (ECHR) (Rome, 4 November 1950). The Convention was drafted and adopted under the auspices of the Council of Europe (CoE). The Convention entered into force in September 1953 and its implementation was, at first, monitored by two organs; namely the European Commission of Human Rights (ECommHR) and the European Court of Human Rights (ECtHR). The right of individual application came into force in 1955. Due to the emerging complexity of the system, the Commission was abandoned pursuant to Protocol No 11 which entered into force in November 1998: ECHR, Protocol No 11 to the Convention for the Protection of Human Rights and Fundamental Freedoms restructuring the control machinery established thereby (Strasbourg, 11 May 1994).

[2] E Bates, *The Evolution of the European Convention on Human Rights: From Its Inception to the Creation of a Permanent Court of Human Rights* (Oxford, Oxford University Press, 2011) 49; E Steiner, 'Some Reflections on the Process which Led to the Preparation of the European Convention on Human Rights (ECHR)' in D Spielmann, M Tsirli and P Voyatzis (eds), *La convention européenne des droits de l'homme, un instrument vivant: mélanges en l'honneur de Christos Rozakis* (Brussels, Bruylant, 2011) 597–623; WA Schabas, *The European Convention on Human Rights: A Commentary*, Oxford Commentaries on International Law (Oxford, Oxford University Press, 2015) 3–32.

European standards in the spirit of the Universal Declaration on Human Rights (hereinafter UDHR).[3]

Being an unusual construction of international law,[4] the mere text of the ECHR and the entire Strasbourg architecture inspired the formulation and pattern of equivalent regional regimes such as the Inter-American and African Human Rights systems. In the wake of the atrocities of World War II, European states were ready to accept the supranational authority of a body, the binding judgments of which would urge them to observe their international obligations. In its 63 years of life, the Strasbourg Court was confronted with political constraints, severe workload and remarkable hardships which derived from the system's expansion eastwards, raising warranted doubts on the effectiveness and the future of the entire CoE system.[5]

Generating an abundant jurisprudence which covered – and still covers – numerous areas of legal practice, the ECtHR influences all of its counterparts both at the global and at the regional levels. It is upon this premise that the research question of this monograph was built. How are Strasbourg-made human rights norms, doctrines and methods of interpretation *exported* to equivalent systems also entitled to enact the protection of fundamental rights?

The book's title is intentionally provocative. The word 'exporting' inevitably brings to mind the legal imperialism of the major European colonial powers and their respective families of law during the colonial era.[6] That is not the approach

[3] Universal Declaration of Human Rights (10 December 1948) UNGA Res 217A (III) (UDHR).

[4] Compared with other treaties of traditional international law, the special nature of the ECHR has been repeatedly confirmed over time. See especially: A van Aaken, I Motoc and JJ Vasel, 'Introduction: The European Convention on Human Rights and General International law' in A van Aaken and I Motoc (eds), *The European Convention on Human Rights and General International law* (Oxford, Oxford University Press, 2018) 3.

[5] The CoE today consists of 46 members, 27 of which are EU Member States. Founded in the wake of World War II, its mandate was, at that time, to foster the democratisation and rule of law on the Continent through the supranational enforcement of human rights. The enormous caseload, however, was not easily manageable and further reform of Strasbourg's arsenal was urged. Protocol 14 was adopted to alleviate these difficulties, provoking, however, a severe political backlash: ECHR, Protocol No 14 to the Convention for the Protection of Human Rights and Fundamental Freedoms, amending the control system of the Convention (Strasbourg 13 May 2004). See, eg: B Bowring, 'Russia and Human Rights: Incompatible Opposites' (2009) 1 *Göttingen Journal of International Law* 257; P Leuprecht, 'Innovations in the European system of Human Rights Protection: Is Enlargement Compatible with Reinforcement?' (1998) 8 *Transnational Law and Contemporary Problems* 313; B Bowring, 'Russian Federation, Protocol No. 14 (and 14bis), and the Battle for the Soul of the ECHR' (2010) 2 *Göttingen Journal of International Law* 589; M Antonov, 'Conservatism in Russia and Sovereignty in Human Rights' (2014) 39 *Review of Central and East European Law* 1; L Caflisch, 'The Reform of the European Court of Human Rights: Protocol No. 14 and Beyond' (2006) 6 *HRLR* 403.

[6] For instance, this might bring to mind France's colonial empire, where it 'exported' its civil law tradition; or the expansion of English common law during the eighteenth and nineteenth centuries. The same goes for other families of law, which significantly expanded their legal culture on the basis of military dominance, colonial infliction, and/or economic conquest. See eg, J Schmidhauser, 'Legal Imperialism: Its Enduring impact on Colonial and Post-Colonial Judicial Systems'(1992) 13 *International Political Science Review* 321; A Anghie, 'The Evolution of International Law: colonial and postcolonial realities' (2006) 27 *Third World Quarterly* 739.

taken in this monograph. In other words, besides the tremendous significance of the law-production of the ECtHR, the notion of 'exporting' is not understood as an 'imperialist' export of the ECtHR's unequivocal wisdom to other legal regimes, nor are its normative and judicial constructions conceived by the author as the 'absolute truth'. Instead, given the underlying role of the ECHR in international human rights adjudication, Strasbourg's human rights norms are used as a point of reference by which to explore the extent to which the work of the ECtHR has influenced other legal regimes. This study goes on to map out the shapes or forms that the judicial – or quasi-judicial – dialogue of the ECHR system with comparable legal orders is taking. Indeed, even in instances in which other regimes have exceeded the ECHR levels of protection (see eg, Part II, Chapter 3 section II) and/or 'export' is not easily traceable (see eg, Part II, Chapter 4), the analysis takes stock via the parallel analysis of the mechanisms' protection standards in common human rights topics, with the view to reveal whether the ECHR system has influenced or gained from each peer system.

Given the already extensive academic literature on the theoretical foundations and the judicial practice of the most fundamental human rights court of our time, the present monograph aims to contribute to the whole academic discussion around fragmentation of international human rights law. Through a horizontal and holistic – but not exhaustive – study of regional and global systems it seeks to document the unequivocal influence of the Strasbourg Court within the confines of their jurisprudence. The present analysis sets out not only to discuss whether, how and with what legal consequences the ECHR norms, as interpreted by the Strasbourg Court, affect other regional or global legal orders, but also to explore what this indicates about the overall functioning of the international human rights law discourse.

To this end, the main focus remains on the judicial or quasi-judicial mechanisms enforcing civil and political rights. This study could not but concentrate on the systems presenting the most vivid or creative interaction with the ECtHR, particularly assessing the characteristics of the endorsement of Strasbourg's loans by each mechanism.

Hence, three particular legal systems mainly triggered my investigation of the influence of the ECtHR to their judicial production: the Court of Justice of the European Union (hereinafter CJEU or Luxembourg Court) with regard to human rights cases, the Inter-American Court of Human Rights (hereinafter IACtHR or San José Court), and finally the work of the UN Human Rights Committee (hereinafter HRC). All the above legal regimes share some common features: the adjudication of individual complaints, a mandate that mainly covers civil and political rights and, finally, a wealth of case law cutting across common types of disputes, allowing the author to draw safe conclusions on the basis of the research question. In this spirit, the author does not extensively or separately discuss how the ECHR is 'exported' to the younger African Court of Human and Peoples' Rights due to its limited judicial production hitherto, or to other UN human rights treaty bodies whose specialised mandate is neither equivalent nor comparable to the

ECtHR, albeit without overlooking potential traces of the ECtHR's impact on their (quasi-) jurisprudence. Therefore, in this second part of the study, although the focus is mainly on the work of the San José Court and the HRC, useful analogies to the case law of the African Court or the UN treaty bodies are drawn whenever significant points of convergence or divergence with ECHR law are documented.

Both parts of the proposed monograph begin with an introductory note aiming to introduce the reader to the special regime that is subsequently examined. This approach was deemed particularly necessary in the first part of the monograph which addresses the interplay between the ECtHR and the CJEU. The latter interrelationship cannot be comprehensively assessed without touching upon the *sui generis* features of the EU system, particularly relevant to the on-going negotiations over the EU's accession to the ECHR. The same goes for the second part of the monograph, which commences with an introduction setting the scene with regard to the specificities of the Inter-American system and the HRC. Thus, the reader will be guided to explore their *modus operandi* and outputs through the prism of the transferability of the ECtHR's patterns to their respective judicial contexts. Alongside these introductory remarks in each part, due to the horizontal assessment of the impact of the Strasbourg Court to other legal systems, particular emphasis is also given to the particularities of each system whenever this is dictated by legal analysis.

Accordingly, the themes selected by the author in each chapter represent the main legal territories covered by the relevant jurisdictions in which the interrelationship with the ECHR system is well-established, leaving aside others for which extensive literature already exists. Given the horizontal perspective of the present study, particular emphasis and priority was given by the author to the legal areas hitherto underexplored in literature. Since human rights jurisdictions have inevitably relied upon Strasbourg's standards of human rights protection by design, the purpose of this monograph is not to provide an exhaustive treatment of all these influences; rather, using the ECtHR as a point of departure, its purpose is to map the main areas of interaction between the judicial and quasi-judicial bodies under examination that present original scientific interest, contain instances of progressive development of human rights law, and thus, give rise to some critical remarks and shrewd reflections on the room actually left for judicial dialogue among the relevant institutions.

Part I therefore examines the exportation of the ECHR to the EU legal order and addresses the interrelationship of the ECtHR with the CJEU, which has constituted an issue of considerable controversy for some time now. Post-Lisbon, the academic and institutional conversation concerning the ambitious accession of the EU to the ECHR has marked the recent jurisprudence of both mechanisms. Chapter 1 sheds light on the manner with which the latter makes recourse to the Convention's provisions or ECtHR jurisprudence with regard to the right to private and family life, the interpretation of the procedural principles within the EU system, and the application of the *ne bis in idem* principle. Having mapped the direct dialogue between the two bodies, this study continues with exploring the CJEU's judgments in which human rights are prioritised over EU rules and the occasions on which this Court has treated the ECHR as a restriction mechanism of EU law. Hence, Chapter 2 revolves around the restriction of internal market freedoms of the European Union, data protection legislation, UN sanctions as well as application of the ECHR when it comes to the Dublin Regulation.

In Part II, the research aims to ascertain the form that the normative and jurisprudential influence of the ECHR to regional and global human rights systems has taken. Inevitably, the IACtHR and the HRC loom large among the judicial mechanisms borrowing from the long-standing experience of the Strasbourg system. Modelled on the structure and function of the Convention's legal order, the IACtHR has applied extensively the aspirations of the European Convention in order to draw legitimacy from the latter and enforce core human rights in a region plagued with the brutalities of totalitarian regimes. Nevertheless, the mere particularities witnessed in the Americas forced the Court to outreach the European paradigm and offer adequate protection of human rights.

Chapter 3 addresses the direct application of Strasbourg human rights norms by the IACtHR and the convergence or the divergence that occurs. The analysis here is both horizontal and vertical. The first section addresses the IACtHR's direct import of the ECtHR's standards that extend horizontally across the entire compendium of the IACtHR's cases, including the use of positive obligations, the principle of subsidiarity as well as the protection in emergency cases, while the vertical perspective covers the legal treatment of freedom of expression and the rights of irregular migrants. The second section traces the legal fields in which the IACtHR has broken new ground and has successfully expanded the protection correspondingly offered by its European peer. In this realm, we also seek to detect whether there is room for cross-fertilisation in terms of mutual citation of each other's judgments. Here, the main focus is on the novelty of the IACtHR, which increasingly denotes *jus cogens* norms and the pioneer approach of the Court regarding reparations.

Subsequently, Chapter 4 is devoted to the uneasy interplay between the ECtHR and the HRC. The central argument put forward here is as follows: notwithstanding the persistence of the Committee in remaining true to its lonely road by not citing external legal sources and its apparent reluctance to embrace Strasbourg's understanding of specific human rights, obscure signs of quasi-judicial dialogue with the ECtHR can be still traced. The first section of the chapter is about the horizontal dimension of this interaction and concerns in particular, the procedural point of interaction which impedes the Committee from ruling on a case if the 'same thing' has already been examined by the Strasbourg Court, and the margin of appreciation within the jurisprudence of the Committee. Finally, the second section discusses the specific areas of law where an implied dialogue between the two institutions can be discerned, providing mostly conflicting interpretations of equivalent standards. These areas are, first, religious freedom, second, women's reproductive rights, and finally, the rights of migrants. Throughout this part of the book, some references are also made, as appropriate, to the African Court on Human and Peoples' Rights and the rest of the UN human rights treaty bodies.

This monograph concludes that the examination of the methodology of the judicial dialogue between the ECtHR and its partners in human rights adjudication substantiates the undoubted impact of the Court's ubiquitous output on international law-making. Local particularities shaping the strengths and weaknesses of each system are also building upon this methodology, which varies accordingly. Yet, even in instances where only conflicting interpretations and inconsistencies are witnessed, a court-to-court dialogue in realistic terms can be achieved and competition between human rights systems can eventually be retrieved. To be functional, such a dialogue requires due respect of the specificities of each jurisdiction often dictating diverse legal responses and, hence, vindicates the complementarity of human rights fora instead of their fragmentation.

PART I

Exporting the ECHR to the EU Legal Order

Introduction

Despite the fact that the European Union does not constitute a Contracting Party to the Convention, the interplay between the two European judicial mechanisms, namely the CJEU and the ECtHR has, notably, strengthened over time. In view of the CJEU's strong persistence to preserve the *sui generis* features of the common market within the EU from the 1970s onwards, the Luxembourg Court has progressively incorporated fundamental rights into the EU legal order as it repeatedly acknowledged that the ECHR has 'special significance', which 'must be taken into consideration in Community law'.[1] However, there is no 'formal linking' between the two legal orders, and the Treaties remained silent on the matter of human rights. As such, the CJEU initially used the Convention as 'a point of orientation'[2] to 'inspire' and guide the EU protection of fundamental rights, rather than directly applying the ECHR. It did so through the general principles of EU law[3] on the grounds of the protection of the *direct effect* doctrine[4] as a manifestation of the supremacy of EU law.

The CJEU, therefore, indirectly applied the ECHR by extrapolating this instrument and applying the Convention's provisions as EU principles, in an attempt to interpret the vague text[5] of the ECHR in order to develop its own autonomous protection through its rich and dynamic jurisprudence. It is due to the absence of a formal link, that the two European jurisdictions have gradually established a relationship based on informal comity and co-operation. However, this informal judicial dialogue between the two courts has not ensured the same interpretation of human rights, as overlapping jurisdiction and divergent interpretations have inevitably occurred in several fields of EU law.

[1] Case 4/73 *Nold v Commission* [1974] ECR 491.

[2] M Dauses, 'The Protection of Fundamental Rights in the Community Legal Order' (1985) 10 *EL Rev* 398, 401.

[3] Case 29/69 *Stauder v City of Ulm* [1969] ECR 419; Case 11/70 *Internationale Handelsgesellschaft v Einfuhr- und Vorratstelle for Getreide und Futtermittel* [1970] ECR 1125.

[4] The direct effect doctrine was introduced by the CJEU in its landmark decision Case 26/62 *Van Gend & Loos v Nederlandse Administratie der Belastingen* [1963] ECR 1.

[5] ADJ Balfour, 'Application of the European Convention on Human Rights by the European Court of Justice' (2005), *Harvard Law School Student Scholarship Series*, Paper 4.

At the outset, the Court acknowledged the necessity of respect for human rights in a rather loose, undefined, way in which most rights were recognised as meriting protection by the EU. Direct effect and supremacy were the initial fundamental principles of the EU, which had the common market as its vision. However, as the common market was gradually achieved, human rights started to become a guiding principle as well.[6] At the same time, its Strasbourg peer has also drawn inspiration from EU legal sources to interpret Convention rights, and intensified even more this mutual cross-referencing. From Strasbourg's perspective, in the 1990s the ECtHR famously introduced its *equivalent protection* principle in its *Bosphorus* ruling[7] presuming that the EU legal system provides human rights protection which is considered equivalent to that of the ECHR, in the sense of 'comparable' rather than 'identical' protection. Citing each other, both the Luxembourg and the Strasbourg Courts have progressively fortified their legitimacy and supremacy *vis-à-vis* national jurisdictions.[8]

It is in this context that the relationship between the two European systems has surprisingly evolved over the decades, from parallel and separate development in the 1950s to the institutional and political endeavour pursuing the EU's accession to the ECHR.[9] The question around the latter is not a recent one. It has been discussed in great detail and depth in academic circles, as a long-awaited advancement which is anticipated to bridge the gaps between the two regimes in the field of human rights protection. By scrutinising national actions within the scope of EU law, the ECtHR might be competent to exercise an external, indirect review of primary or secondary EU law. Furthermore, EU citizens would be allowed to challenge EU actions before the Strasbourg Court.[10] On the long road to the ambitious accession,[11] numerous political and legal issues stood out.[12] The first such issue was Opinion 2/94 of the Luxembourg Court on the Union's legal competence to accede to the ECHR.[13] The judges of the CJEU, having repeated that 'fundamental rights form an integral part of the general principles of law', and that the Convention has 'special significance' within the context of the EU legal architecture, cast doubt on

[6] See especially S Douglas-Scott, 'A Tale of Two Courts: Luxembourg, Strasbourg and the Growing European Human Rights Acquis' (2006) 43 *CML Rev* 629.

[7] *Bosphorus Hava Yollari Turizm ve Ticaret Anonim Şirketi v Ireland* [GC], Merits, ECHR 2005-VI 107.

[8] S White, 'Accession of the European Union to the European Convention on Human Rights' (2011) 86 *Amicus Curiae* 7, 8.

[9] G de Búrca, 'The Road not Taken: The European Union as a Global Human Rights Actor' (2011) 105 *Am J Int'l L* 649.

[10] See especially A Torres Pérez, 'Too Many Voices? The Prior Involvement of the Court of Justice of the European Union' (2013) 4 *Journal européen des droits de l'homme* 565, 566–7.

[11] European Commission, 'Memorandum on the accession of the European Communities to the Convention for the Protection of Human Rights and Fundamental Freedoms' COM (79) 210 final.

[12] JP Jacqué, 'The Accession of the European Union to the European Convention on Human Rights and Fundamental Freedoms' (2011) 48 *CML Rev* 995, 1002; T Lock, 'Walking on a Tightrope: The Draft Accession Agreement and the Autonomy of the EU Legal Order' (2011) 48 *CML Rev* 1025.

[13] Opinion 2/94 [1996] ECR I-1759.

the legality of the accession, due to the lack of treaty provisions conferring, at the time, competence to enact legislation on human rights.[14]

The ECtHR responded to this sign of the CJEU's restraint on the occasion of the *Matthews* litigation.[15] The case concerned the alleged violation of the right of a resident of Gibraltar to vote in the European Parliamentary elections under the 1976 EC Act that excluded Gibraltar from suffrage. The ECtHR famously reaffirmed that a human rights violation could be attributable to states even though they had transferred sovereign power in that particular field to an international organisation.[16] Commonly understood as having introduced the possibility of a certain review exclusively for those EU acts with the status of international treaties, *Matthews* constituted a decisive step towards the idea that an action of the EU could be subject to a test of compatibility with the ECHR. The Strasbourg Court definitely has a word to say – even if it is not the last one – when it comes to application of the ECHR by EU institutions, notwithstanding the fact that the EU is not a Contracting Party to the ECHR.

Originally drafted to promote economic integration within the EU, the Treaties did not provide for the possibility of an accession. Their modification appeared to be the solution to remove all the legal impediments, and thus the requested legislative amendments were provided by the Treaty of Lisbon: Article 6(2) TEU laid down that the EU 'shall accede' to the Convention.[17] From the CoE perspective, after the entry into force of Protocol No 14 ECHR, Article 59 ECHR was also modified to leave the door open for the EU's accession. Numerous meetings and exhaustive negotiations amongst the representatives of the Committee of Ministers and the European Commission – the so-called ad hoc '47+1' group – resulted in the elaboration of a Draft Accession Agreement (DAA) incorporating the final consensus of the two institutions in 2013.[18]

The agreement sought to enunciate coherently the means and the legal parameters of the EU's accession to the Convention, paying meticulous attention to the EU's respect for human rights and the special features of the EU legal order. Its main institutional innovation is the *co-respondent mechanism* under Article 3, which also provided for the prior involvement of the CJEU in cases brought before the ECtHR against the EU. In this context, the EU and one or more of its Member States may constitute parallel parties to the proceedings before the Strasbourg Court, following either an invitation of the latter or the Court's decision upon a

[14] ibid para 5.

[15] *Matthews v the United Kingdom* [GC], Merits, ECHR 1999-I 251. See also *M & Co v Federal Republic of Germany* (dec) (1990) 64 DR 138.

[16] *Matthews* (n 15) para 32.

[17] Article 6 para 2 of the Consolidated Version of the Treaty on European Union [2012] OJ C326/13.

[18] See, eg T Lock, 'End of an Epic? The Draft Agreement on the EU's Accession to the ECHR' (2012) 31 *Yearbook of European Law* 162; F Fabbrini and J Larik, 'The Past, Present and Future of the Relation between the European Court of Justice and the European Court of Human Rights' (2016) 35 *Yearbook of European Law* 145.

request by the Member State, when a question arises of the compatibility of EU law provisions with ECHR rights.[19] The practical repercussion of such a mechanism is to allow the EU to enjoy all the prerogatives of being a party to the judicial proceedings to preserve the proper interpretation of the contested provisions of EU law and of ECHR.[20]

Bearing in mind that a third-party intervention mechanism under Article 36 ECHR already exists, it passes without surprise that this novel scheme raised a chorus of criticism with regard to its complexity and the mere necessity of establishing a brand-new mechanism. Its incorporation in the DAA was, nonetheless, legitimised by the autonomous and *sui generis* character of the EU, clothed as a means to deter the ECtHR from interpreting the EU Treaties and ruling upon competences.[21] Article 3(6) DAA also provides for a prior involvement of the CJEU before the final pronouncement of the Strasbourg Court in cases in which the compatibility of EU law with the ECHR is under discussion. This mechanism would be triggered in cases where the Union is a co-respondent and national measures strictly implementing EU law and affecting individuals' rights are called into question. The basic rationale of this procedure is to ensure that the CJEU may carry out an internal review of the EU actions before the ECtHR carries out its external compatibility review.[22] This *prior involvement mechanism* was initially suggested in the Joint Communication of former President Jean-Paul Costa (ECtHR) and former President Vasileios Skouris (CJEU) in 2011 so that the principle of subsidiarity of the ECtHR – built upon the idea that the supreme responsibility for human rights protection lies with the MS – cannot also be undermined in the context of the accession.[23]

However, individuals who have challenged Member State authorities' acts in the enforcement of EU provisions on the basis of their human rights complaints cannot have direct access to judicial redress before the EU Courts, as it depends on the national courts to make – or not make – a preliminary reference before the CJEU, and EU citizens have no way of putting pressure on the domestic courts to trigger the EU's ex ante supervisory judicial instrument. Logically, if this was not the case, individuals would be likely to lodge an application before

[19] P Craig, 'EU Accession to the ECHR: Competence, Procedure and Substance' (2013) 36 *Fordham Int'l LJ* 1114, 1122–23.

[20] See especially G Gaja, 'The 'Co-respondent Mechanisms' According to the Draft Agreement for the Accession of the EU to the ECHR' in V Kosta, N Skoutaris and V Tzevelekos (eds), *The EU Accession to the ECHR*, Modern Studies in European Law 48 (Oxford, Bloomsbury, 2014) 341–7.

[21] S Andreadakis, 'Problems and Challenges of the EU's Accession to the ECHR: Empirical Findings with a View to the Future' in S Morano-Foadi and L Vickers (eds), *Fundamental Rights in EU: A Matter for Two Courts*, Modern Studies in European Law 53 (Oxford, Bloomsbury, 2015) 60.

[22] R Baratta, 'Accession of the EU to the ECHR: The Rationale for the ECJ's Prior Involvement Mechanism' (2013) 50 *CML Rev* 1305.

[23] The concept was recently reinforced as evidenced by the Copenhagen Declaration on the reform of the European Convention on Human Rights system which was adopted by all CoE Member States following a high-level conference in Copenhagen on 12–13 April 2018, www.echr.coe.int/Documents/Copenhagen_Declaration_ENG.pdf.

the Strasbourg Court without the Luxembourg Court having had the chance to pronounce on the validity or the corrrect interpretation of the EU law provisions at stake. That is exactly the *lacuna* that the prior involvement mechanism came to fill. Nonetheless, former Presidents Costa and Skouris had already, interestingly, declared in their Joint Communication that the preliminary reference cannot be regarded as a legal remedy to be exhausted by the applicant.[24] Hence, the paradox of a two-speed application of subsidiarity emerges: while the EU would participate in the proceedings as a co-respondent without the exhaustion of local remedies requirement, if the co-respondent were a Member State, local remedies would not need to be exhausted within the state and no prior involvement of the supreme national courts would be foreseen.[25] This is exactly the situation that touches upon the most significant criticism to this mechanism, which is based on the privileged position granted to the CJEU in comparison to the national supreme or constitutional courts.[26] Be that as it may, the subsidiarity concept gives the only convincing explanation to the incorporation of the prior involvement formula to the DAA concluded by the two European institutions in 2013.

Besides the subsidiarity argument, this insistence on the need for a prior involvement mechanism is undoubtedly deep-rooted to the autonomy concept, intimately linked to the *sui generis* nature of the EU. The mere institutionalisation of this mechanism implies the reluctance of the Luxembourg Court to accept the competence of the Strasbourg Court as the last instance court to rule on human rights issues arising in the context of EU law. This question around the principle of autonomy within the Union's legal order brings us to the second ground of justification of this mechanism. On the one hand, in the post-Lisbon era, the level of EU human rights protection was enhanced not only by the removal of barriers offered by the modification of the Treaties, but also by the entry into force of the Charter of Fundamental Rights of the EU (EUCFR or CFR).[27] On the other hand, having overcome the tensions of judicial politics, the long negotiation procedure purporting to the elaboration of the famous DAA also revealed the ever-growing concern about the post-accession autonomy of the EU legal order.

To this end, Protocol No 8 Relating to Article 6(2) of the Treaty on European Union on the Accession of the Union to the European Convention on the Protection of Human Rights and Fundamental Freedoms[28] laid down in Article 1 that this agreement 'shall make provision for preserving the specific characteristics

[24] Joint communication of Presidents JP Costa (ECtHR) and V Skouris (CJEU) of 17 January 2011, www.curia.europa.eu/jcms/upload/docs/application/pdf/2011-02/cedh_cjue_english.pdf.

[25] A Torres Pérez, 'Too Many Voices? The Prior Involvement of the Court of Justice of the European Union' in V Kosta, N Skoutaris and V Tzevelekos (eds), *The EU Accession to the ECHR*, Modern Studies in European Law 48 (Oxford, Bloomsbury, 2014) 36.

[26] ibid 40–41.

[27] Charter of Fundamental Rights of the European Union [2012] OJ C326/391.

[28] Protocol (No 8) relating to Article 6(2) of the Treaty on European Union on the accession of the Union to the European Convention on the Protection of Human Rights and Fundamental Freedoms [2012] OJ C326/273.

of the Union and Union law'. The notion of the Union's autonomy is rather multidimensional. The autonomy concept of the EU system, firstly, revolves around the idea that the validity of EU law relies solely on the Treaties as interpreted by the CJEU, irrespective of the rules of any other national or international legal order. This perception of autonomy leads us to the interpretive autonomy, which means that the competence to interpret the constitutional and legal rules of EU legislation belongs exclusively to EU institutions and ultimately to the Luxembourg Court. Last but not least, the principle of autonomy suggests that the allocation of powers between the EU and MS cannot be determined by any other judicial mechanism outside the Union's legal order.

The main objection to this autonomy-based justification of the prior involvement mechanism is the fact that accession would not impinge upon the monopoly of the CJEU: the ECtHR would only rule on the compatibility of EU legislation with the Convention's provisions, and not on the validity of EU legislation.[29] Even if the ECtHR declared an EU provision to be contradictory to the ECHR, embarking – perhaps – on a soft review or a minimal interpretation of EU law, it would be up to the EU organs to proceed to all the legislative amendments necessary for enforcement of the Strasbourg ruling. Therefore, it is highly unlikely that any constraint on the CJEU's exclusive role to rule on the EU's acts or omissions could be imposed.[30]

Notwithstanding the technical complexities and the significant concern regarding the increasing risk of open confrontation between the two judicial *fora* in the event of interpretative inconsistency, the Draft Agreement aimed to guarantee the primary role of both institutions in their respective fields focusing on complementarity, not competition.[31] Nevertheless, the good intentions paving the way to accession have proven insufficient, as the Draft Agreement was famously dropped by the CJEU's Opinion 2/13,[32] delivered in December 2014. Having found a number of flaws in the agreement which regulated the particular aspects of the accession process, the Court provoked severe controversy and left numerous issues open, mostly grounded on the supremacy of the EU legal system *vis-à-vis* the Strasbourg jurisdiction.

At this point, it seems necessary to take a step back from this analysis and expound the overall landscape in which the CJEU's Opinion was delivered.

[29] CoE, Draft Agreement on the Accession of the EU to the European Convention on Human Rights, 'Fifth Negotiation Meeting between the CDDH Ad Hoc Negotiation Group and the European Commission on the Accession of the EU to the ECHR – Final report to the CDDH' (Strasbourg, 10 June 2013) 47+1(2013)008rev2, para 62.

[30] Torres Pérez, 'Too Many Voices?' (n 25) 33.

[31] Baratta, 'Accession of the EU to the ECHR' (n 22) 1332.

[32] Opinion 2/13 [2014] ECLI:EU:C:2014:2454. Yet, in its 2016 Report on the application of the EU Charter of Fundamental Rights, the European Commission declared the EU's commitment to the accession plan. Ever since, the latter appears in several EU documents. See, eg European Commission, '2016 Report on the Application of the EU Charter of Fundamental Rights' (Communication) COM (2017) 239 final.

Besides the amendment of the Treaties, the Treaty of Lisbon entered into force and therefore, the Charter was granted binding force, elevating it to primary EU law. Following the example of the ECHR and incorporating the MS legal traditions, the codification of the rights and principles as guaranteed under EU legislation and the CJEU emphasised that the protection of human rights was henceforth a priority within the Union's system. As such, it clearly constituted the legal foundation of legality not only for the Member States but also for the EU institutions and bodies when it comes to the elaboration of important policies in several legal fields or to the mere implementation of EU law.[33] Notably, as Louise Halleskov Storgaard observed, 'fundamental rights protection in Europe today is made up of a "crowded house" of profoundly overlapping national, international and supranational human rights norms each of which is supervised by its own authoritative judicial body.'[34] The CJEU has also developed high protection standards after the entry into force of the Charter, as it opted all the more for using the latter as a legal basis reinventing the relationship with its Strasbourg peer. It is noteworthy that, in this new legal framework, Article 6(3) TEU now acknowledges the human rights enshrined in the ECHR as general principles of EU law, which have direct effect in the domestic legal orders of Member States. In addition, Article 52(3) CFR provides the scope for EU law to offer more extensive protection than the Strasbourg Court.

Opinion 2/13 occurred in the post-Lisbon era, which was marked by a multilevel human rights protection and the use of the EU Charter as the main legal source of fundamental rights protection within the EU legal order. This is probably the reason why the CJEU felt that the accession presented a clear danger for the *sui generis* autonomous dimension of the Union. At the outset, the Court set the scene as it observed for the first time that the EU is not a state, as well as the importance of guaranteeing the primacy and *effet direct* of EU law. Regardless of its famous *Melloni* jurisprudence[35] leaving no room for national courts to apply higher human rights standards than those ones provided by the EU Charter, the Court held that the DAA failed to preserve the primacy and unity of EU law,[36] since there is a similar provision under the ECHR, namely Article 53 ECHR.[37] However, since the Strasbourg Court is engaged in enforcing the Convention's standards and not those applied by the domestic legal orders, the concern of the Court seems unrealistic, as it appears to be unlikely that the ECtHR will promote,

[33] See G Di Federico (ed), *The EU Charter of Fundamental Rights: From Declaration to Binding Instrument*, Ius Gentium: Comparative Perspectives on Law and Justice 8 (Dordrecht, Springer, 2011).

[34] L Halleskov Storgaart, 'EU Law Autonomy versus European Fundamental Rights Protection– On Opinion 2/13 on EU Accession to the ECHR' (2015) 15 *HRL Rev* 485, 486.

[35] Case C-399/11 *Stefano Melloni v Ministerio Fiscal* [2013] ECLI:EU:C:2013:107.

[36] S Peers, 'The CJEU and the EU's Accession to the ECHR: a Clear and Present Danger to Human Rights Protection' (*EU Law Analysis*, 18 December 2014), www.eulawanalysis.blogspot.gr/2014/12/the-cjeu-and-eus-accession-to-echr.html.

[37] Opinion 2/13 (n 32) para 189.

in practice, the application of national standards of protection that are higher than the Convention's, especially when the Member State involved is already bound by the Charter's level of protection.

The Court subsequently focused on the specificities of EU law which, in its view, were disregarded by the Draft Agreement starting from the *mutual trust* principle in Area of Freedom, Security and Justice (AFSJ) matters. Within this context, mutual trust found its clearest expression as the mutual recognition of national judgments in civil and criminal matters are considered apt to foster borderless, yet automatic, enforcement of decisions among Member States.[38] As a presumption originally conceived to achieve harmonised integration and judicial cooperation within the EU, *mutual trust* is mostly understood as the presumption that all Member States observe the international human rights obligations upon which the mutual recognition of decisions is grounded.[39] It is the constitutional character[40] and the near-automaticity of the judicial recognition that mutual trust entails that rendered the principle a powerful harmonisation tool that endangered the post-Lisbon EU fundamental rights *acquis* and unbalanced its interrelationship with its Strasbourg peer.[41] In this respect, the CJEU assessed that, under the *mutual trust* principle, only in 'exceptional circumstances' are the national authorities of a Member State allowed to evaluate whether another Member State sufficiently safeguards fundamental rights as guaranteed by the EU. Additionally, the CJEU observed with regard to Protocol 16 to the ECHR, which offers the opportunity to national courts to address questions to the ECtHR concerning the interpretation of the Convention's provisions, that this newly instituted mechanism would result in side-stepping the similar preliminary ruling procedure of the Union's legal order. In the Court's view, this would allow the ECtHR to adjudicate claims in relation to EU law, before its Luxembourg counterpart.

[38] The fact that mutual recognition is based upon the principle of mutual trust is reaffirmed by EU secondary law and jurisprudence. See Case C-403/09, *Detiček*, ECLI:EU:C:2009:810, para. 45; Case C-168/13 PPU, *Jeremy F.*, ECLI:EU:C:2013:358, para. 50. See also Recitals 16 and 17 of Council Regulation (EC) No 44/2001 on jurisdiction and the recognition and enforcement of judgments in civil and commercial matters [2001] OJ L12/1 (hereinafter Brussels I Regulation); Recital 21 of Regulation (EC) 2201/2003 of the Council of 27 November 2003 concerning jurisdiction and the recognition and enforcement of judgments in matrimonial matters and the matters of parental responsibility, repealing Regulation (EC) 1347/2000, OJ L338/2003 (hereinafter Brussels II Regulation); Recital 10 of Council Framework Decision 2009/299/JHA amending Framework Decisions 2002/584/JHA, 2005/214/JHA, 2006/783/JHA, 2008/909/JHA and 2008/947/JHA, thereby enhancing the procedural rights of persons and fostering the application of the principle of mutual recognition to decisions rendered in the absence of the person concerned at the trial [2009] OJ L81/24.

[39] See V Mitsilegas, 'The Limits of Mutual Trust in Europe's Area of Freedom, Security and Justice: From Automatic Inter-State Cooperation to the Slow Emergence of the Individual' (2012) 31 *Yearbook of European Law* 319; E Xanthopoulou, *Fundamental Rights and Mutual Trust in the Area of Freedom, Security and Justice-A Role for Proportionality?* (Bloomsbury Publishing, 2020).

[40] Opinion 2/13, n 4, para 168.

[41] See inter alia G Anagnostaras, 'The Common European Asylum System: Balancing Mutual Trust Against Fundamental Rights Protection' (2020) 21 *German Law Journal* 1180.

Subsequently, the Court examined the compatibility with EU law of the previously analysed mechanisms, namely the *co-respondent* and the *prior involvement mechanisms*. As for the former, the Court fears that it would allow the Strasbourg Court to proceed to an interpretation of EU law when ruling on the admissibility of requests to trigger the said mechanism. It also underlined that the possibility of a Strasbourg decision on the joint responsibility of both the Union and its Member States would impinge on Member States' reservations to the Convention under Article 57 ECHR and would also violate Article 2 Protocol 8 on the accession providing the duty to ensure that nothing affects the situation of Member States in relation to the ECHR. For the CJEU, the ECtHR should not interfere with the allocation of responsibilities between the EU and Member States even when the issue at stake touches upon an infringement of the Convention seeing the fact that only the CJEU can decide on matters related to EU law.[42] Moving, then, to the *prior involvement* formula, the Court found it similarly incompatible with the Union's law on two grounds. First, it fails to give to the EU the power to pronounce on whether the Luxembourg Court has already delivered a judgment on an issue, and secondly, it hinders the CJEU from deciding for the interpretation, not just the validity, of EU law.[43] Lastly, the provisions of the DAA regarding the Common Foreign and Security Policy (CFSP) also run counter to EU law as it is not acceptable for the CJEU, a judicial body which is outside the institutional and the judicial framework, to scrutinise EU acts in this field, notwithstanding the fact that the CJEU has no such jurisdiction itself as regards a number of CFSP issues.[44]

Hence, the Court famously concluded that the said agreement is not compatible with Article 6(2) TEU or with Protocol (No 8) relating to Article 6(2) of the Treaty on EU to the ECHR. For some scholars, the Court's judgment was considered an 'unmitigated tragedy'.[45] The EU accession to the ECHR intended to safeguard an effective external control of the EU acts and Member States acts when implementing EU law, without, though, complicating EU human rights law. Integrating the Union in the ECHR system with a clear recognition of the direct effect of the Convention would contribute to constantly keeping the focus of EU human rights law on what matters: the effective protection of EU citizens' rights. However, it flows from the spirit of Opinion 2/13 that it is one thing to refer or even directly apply the Convention and the ECtHR's jurisprudence in a legal context in which neither the former nor the latter have binding force; it may be another to acknowledge that the EU judicial system is actually bound by Strasbourg's jurisprudence. And that is exactly what brings us to the Court's major fear: a relationship of equals suddenly turning into an 'unwelcome

[42] ibid para 234.
[43] ibid paras 236–48.
[44] ibid paras 249–57.
[45] Against see T Isiksel, 'European Exceptionalism and the EU's Accession to the ECHR' (2016) 27 *EJIL* 565.

hierarchical constellation',[46] seriously destabilising the autonomous architecture of the EU system.

It is in this context that a generalised chorus of criticism was raised in the aftermath of the Court's ruling. Looking back, even from a very early stage, the CJEU started, in its famous *Costa v ENEL* case,[47] founding the supremacy of the EU legal order on the autonomy concept establishing the distinction of the EU system from both the international legal order and the domestic legal orders. In its Opinion 1/91 regarding the first draft agreement on the European Economic Area, the Court emphasised the autonomy of the EU *vis-à-vis* international law.[48] However, in parallel with the development of the autonomy doctrine, the CJEU also developed its judicial dialogue concept in relation not only with the domestic courts but also, and most significantly, with the Strasbourg Court.

Seen in this light, the Court's robust objections appear highly problematic as this Opinion clearly halted the fruitful judicial dialogue of the CJEU with its peer. It appears to express great difficulty in digesting the possibility to allow, post-accession, the external control of EU actions from the ECtHR. This reasoning seems rather ironic, if we recall the *Matthews* or the *Bosphorus* litigation, which strikingly prove that the Strasbourg Court was never deterred from reviewing the EU's interference with the rights of individuals when these rights, as embodied in the Convention, were in danger of being violated.

As for the Court's appraisal regarding the power given to the ECtHR to make pronouncements on the allocation of competences between the EU and its Member States, it comes as an after-effect of the accession that, within the confines of Strasbourg's external review function, the latter will naturally dig into EU law in order to guarantee the most effective observance of human rights and the proper redress for victims of confirmed violations. This in no way can be construed as a green light to the ECtHR to substantially determine this division of powers. Even if the Strasbourg Court concludes that EU law is somehow incompatible with the Convention, it cannot modify this problematic provision. The exclusive authority for the interpretation of EU law or the amendment of the Treaties remains that of the CJEU and cannot be transferred to a non-EU Court. This is actually the *raison d'être* of the co-respondent and the prior-involvement mechanisms which may be triggered when the Luxembourg Court is prompted to pronounce on these puzzling issues. As for the CJEU's concerns in view of the CFSP and AFSJ areas,

[46] P Eeckhout, 'The European Convention on Human Rights and Fundamental Freedoms as an Integral Part of EU Law–Some Reflections on Status and Effect' in I Govaere, E Lannon, P van Elsuwege and S Adam (eds), *The European Union in the World: Essays in Honour of Marc Maresceau* (Leiden, Brill, 2013).

[47] Case 6/64 *Flaminio Costa v ENEL* [1964] ECR 585.

[48] Opinion 1/91 Draft agreement between the Community, on the one hand, and the countries of the European Free Trade Association, on the other, relating to the creation of the European Economic Area [1991] ECR I-6079, para 35.

these reveal the Court's 'indifference' regarding the guidance that the Strasbourg Court has to offer in the controversial field of irregular migration and asylum, particularly following the Dublin Regulation.[49] Post-accession, the key role of the Strasbourg Court's guidance remains of the utmost importance, as litigation before the ECtHR relating to contentious CFSP and AFSJ areas of EU law has simply increased, as was logically expected. Therefore, despite its character as a cornerstone of European integration, *mutual trust* should not impede the fundamental rights protection within the Union.

Yet, the most recent developments in this field signal that the entire accession project is not abandoned once negotiation of the relevant documents (Draft agreement and Explanatory Report) is *de nouveau* launched.[50] In December 2020, a Chair's paper saw the light of day as a leaked document summarising the proposed amendments which purport to ease the negotiations on autonomy-related fears of the EU system and to remedy some of the thorny issues that curtailed the project.[51] Specific propositions are currently being discussed during the latest negotiating meetings and are codified in the relevant meeting reports.[52] Such propositions mainly touch upon the EU-specific mechanisms of the proceedings before the ECtHR, operation of inter-party applications and of references for an advisory opinion by the ECtHR (ECHR Article 33 and Protocol 16), the principle of mutual trust, the area of CFSP, the inter-party applications and references for an advisory opinion by the ECtHR and EU participation before the CoE organs. Of course, all these points are yet to be further negotiated and approved, both by the EU Member States and the State Parties to the ECHR, and most importantly, by the CJEU.

Regardless of how long the accession road is at this juncture, and the ongoing *bras de fer* between the two judicial mechanisms, it remains undeniable that the exportation of the Convention and the Strasbourg Court's case law to the EU legal order offered to the latter the power to observe more successfully the rights of

[49] Regulation (EU) No 604/2013 of the European Parliament and of the Council establishing the criteria and mechanisms for determining the Member State responsible for examining an application for international protection lodged in one of the Member States by a third-country national or stateless person (recast) (Dublin III Regulation) [2013] OJ L180/31. For more information on the operation of The Dublin system, see Chapter 4, section IV.

[50] See especially European Council of the EU, 'Accession of the European Union to the European Convention for the Protection of Human Rights and Fundamental Freedoms (ECHR)' (EU restricted note, 20 September 2019), www.statewatch.org/media/documents/news/2019/sep/eu-council-acession-coe-12349-19.pdf.

[51] CoE, 'Sixth Meeting of the CDDH Ad Hoc Negotiation Group ('47+1') on the Accession of the European Union to the European Convention on Human Rights – Paper by the Chair to Structure the Discussion at the sixth Meeting of the CDDH Ad Hoc Negotiation Group ('47+1') on the Accession of the European Union to the European Convention on Human Rights' (Strasbourg, 31 August 2020) 47+1(2020)2.

[52] Follow the progress made in this field 'EU accession to the ECHR', Official website of the Council of Europe, www.coe.int/en/web/human-rights-intergovernmental-cooperation/accession-of-the-european-union-to-the-european-convention-on-human-rights.

individuals submitted to EU law. Post-Lisbon, if we zoom in closer, we can argue that the ECtHR jurisprudence maintains its position in the EU system due to the new provisions of Article 6(3) TEU and Article 52(3) of the EU Charter and the mere jurisprudence of the CJEU notwithstanding the tensions developed in view of the failed accession project. In this context, Part I will focus on the fertile dialectic relationship between Luxembourg and Strasbourg in order to monitor how the influence of the Convention and the ECtHR marked the development of the EU human rights law, initially, through the direct application of the ECHR by the CJEU (Chapter 1) and secondly, through the 'restriction' of EU rules in the name of the Convention's provisions (Chapter 2).

1

The Direct Application of the ECHR by the Luxembourg Court

I. Article 8 ECHR in CJEU Case Law: Overlapping and Divergent Jurisprudence

As for the right to protect one's private and family life, as enshrined in Article 8 ECHR, the CJEU provided the very first explicit reference to the ECHR in *Rutili v Minister for the Interior*.[53] *In casu*, the Convention was conceived as a source of inspiration as well as a human rights standard for determining the legality and legitimacy of the acts of Member States applying EU law. Therefore, the CJEU applied the ECHR as a clear human rights standard to also interpret the 'public policy' exception to the free movement of workers, justifying Member States to restrict this freedom only to the extent authorised by the ECHR, that is, when it is necessary for the protection of the interests of national security or public safety 'in a democratic society'.[54] This landmark case illustrates how the CJEU has progressively shaped its autonomous human rights case law, inspired, though, by the ECHR and by the common constitutional traditions of EU Member States.[55] The Luxembourg Court established a much broader human rights review over their actions and paved the way for a much clearer reference to the Convention's provisions as a material source of EU legal order, rather than a source of inspiration.[56] Nonetheless, besides the consensus in this field, conflicts and inconsistencies between the two European jurisdictions have not been sidestepped. The main preoccupation of the following section is thus to unveil the extent to which the CJEU has directly referred to ECHR norms to protect private and family life[57] with regard to the most controversial fields of data protection and migration/asylum cases.

[53] Case 36/75 *Rutili v Minister for the Interior* [1975] ECR 1219.

[54] See also Case 118/75 *Lynne Watson and Alessandro Belmann* [1976] ECR 1185, Opinion of AG Trabucchi.

[55] RA García, 'The General Provisions of the Charter of Fundamental Rights of the European Union' (2002) 8 *European Law Journal* 492.

[56] S Denys, 'Des influences réciproques entre CJCE et CEDH: 'je t'aime, moi non plus'?' (2001) 96 *Pouvoirs – Les Cours européennes:Luxembourg et Strasbourg* 31.

[57] The ECtHR clarified the criteria of interpretation of Article 8 of ECHR stating in its *Silver and Others v the United Kingdom* judgment: *Silver and Others v the United Kingdom*, Merits, Series A no 61 (1983), para 97.

A. The Right to Private Life and EU Data Protection

European data protection is, arguably, the most luminous example of creative legal evolution in recent decades. In response to emerging developments in the field of information technology in the 1960s, the concept of privacy under Article 8 of the ECHR, formulated in 1950, needed to be revisited to meet with the new technological challenges and to guarantee the protection of individuals' personal data. As a response to this growing need, the Council of Europe[58] adopted various resolutions with reference to Article 8 ECHR and then, in 1981, adopted the Convention on Personal Data[59] (Convention 108), a legally binding instrument providing for specific safeguards against abuses from private actors or state authorities concerning the fair and lawful collection, storage and automatic processing of personal data. The ECtHR applied the notion of private life broadly, expanding the ECHR protection, at first, to cases related to interception of telephone communications in *Klass*[60] in 1978 and in its *Malone*[61] judgment in 1984, and progressively to cases with regard to video-surveillance in *Peck*[62] or data storage to secret registers, as was the case in *Leander*[63] and *Rotaru.*[64]

At this point, it should be highlighted that the Strasbourg Court also found the provisions of Article 8 ECHR applicable in cases with no relevance to the private home and the intimate sphere. The notion of 'private life' might embrace the development of interpersonal relationships and protect not only the domestic sphere; it might also concern data related to personal actions taking place in the public sphere, which might amount to a clear intrusion to the individual's *inner circle*. For instance, in *Peck*, the disclosure to the media of footage filmed in public by a closed-circuit television camera, showing the applicant committing suicide was deemed a violation of Mr Peck's right to private life.[65]

The Strasbourg Court's evolutive interpretation of the 'private life' concept along with the regulatory transformations of EU Member States created the

[58] CoE Committee of Ministers, Resolution (73) 22 on the protection of the privacy of individuals *vis-à-vis* electronic data banks in the private sector (26 September 1973); CoE Committee of Ministers, Resolution (74) 29 on the protection of the privacy of individuals *vis-à-vis* electronic data banks in the public sector (20 September 1974).

[59] Convention for the Protection of Individuals with regard to Automatic Processing of Personal Data (Convention 108) (Strasbourg, 28 January 1981). The recently adopted Protocol amending the Convention for the Protection of Individuals with regard to Automatic Processing of Personal Data aims to modernise the provisions of this Convention in the light of ever-evolving technological advances. Convention 108, Protocol amending the Convention for the Protection of Individuals with regard to Automatic Processing of Personal Data (Convention 108+) (Strasbourg, 10 October 2018).

[60] *Klass and Others v Germany*, Merits, Series A no 28 (1978).

[61] *Malone v the United Kingdom*, Merits, Series A no 82 (1984).

[62] *Peck v the United Kingdom*, Merits, ECHR 2003-I 123.

[63] *Leander v Sweden*, Merits, Series A no 116 (1987).

[64] *Rotaru v Romania* [GC], Merits, ECHR 2000-V 61.

[65] *Peck v the United Kingdom*, Merits, ECHR 2003-I 123, paras 62–63.

conditions under which the EU adopted several legal instruments with the aim of harmonising the national data protection legislations of its Member States. To this end, the EU Data Protection Directive,[66] adopted in 1995, was seen as 'the leading force of globalizing data protection'[67] incorporating most of the principles and the requirements of the CoE system.[68] The Directive was later followed by EU Regulation 45/2001[69] addressing EU legal bodies, and by two more Directives covering specified fields of the legal protection of personal data, namely the Directive on Privacy and Electronic Communications[70] and the Data Retention Directive.[71] Under this legal framework, the CJEU enlarged the scope of application especially of the Data Protection Directive and went so far as to apply its provisions outside the area of the internal market.[72] *Rechnungshof*[73] concerned the applicability of the Directive to the disclosure of data on employees' salaries,[74] elucidating that the guiding light for the implementation of the Directive remains the normative force of right to private life as applied by the Strasbourg Court.[75]

[66] Directive 95/46/EC of the European Parliament and of the Council on the protection of individuals with regard to the processing of personal data and on the free movement of such data (Data Protection Directive) [1995] OJ L281/31.

[67] M Birnhack, 'The EU Data Protection Directive: An Engine of a Global Regime' (2008) 24 *Computer Law & Security Report* 508, 512.

[68] For the connection between the Convention 108 and the Data Protection Directive see CoE, ECtHR, European Data Protection Supervisor and EU Agency for Fundamental Rights, *Handbook in European Data Protection*, 2018 edition (Luxembourg, Publications Office of the EU, 2018) 18.

[69] Regulation (EC) No 45/2001 of the European Parliament and of the Council on the protection of individuals with regard to the processing of personal data by the institutions and bodies of the Community and on the free movement of such data [2001] OJ L8/1. Regulation (EC) 45/2001 was repealed by the Regulation (EU) 2018/1725, which came into force in 11 December 2018. Regulation (EU) 2018/1725 of the European Parliament and of the Council on the protection of natural persons with regard to the processing of personal data by the Union institutions, bodies, offices and agencies and on the free movement of such data, and repealing Regulation (EC) No 45/2001 and Decision No 1247/2002/EC [2018] OJ L295/39.

[70] Directive 2002/58/EC of the European Parliament and of the Council concerning the processing of personal data and the protection of privacy in the electronic communications sector (Directive on Privacy and Electronic Communications) [2002] OJ L201/37.

[71] Directive 2006/24/EC of the European Parliament and of the Council on the retention of data generated or processed in connection with the provision of publicly available electronic communications services or of public communications networks and amending Directive 2002/58/EC (Data Retention Directive) [2006] OJ L105/54. This Directive was declared invalid by the Court on 8 April 2014.

[72] P De Hert and S Gurtwirth, 'Data Protection in the Case Law of Strasbourg and Luxemburg: Constitutionalisation in Action' in S Gutwirth, Y Poullet, P De Hert, J Nouwt and C De Terwangne (eds), *Reinventing Data Protection?* (Dordrecht, Springer, 2009) 18–19.

[73] Joined Cases C-465/00, C-138/01 and C-139/01 *Rechnungshof v Österreichischer Rundfunk and Others and Christa Neukomm and Joseph Lauermann v Österreichischer Rundfunk* [2003] ECR I-4989.

[74] See especially M Tzanou, 'Data Protection in EU Law: An Analysis of the EU Legal Framework and the ECJ Jurisprudence' in C Akrivopoulou and A Psygkas (eds), *Personal Data Privacy and Protection in a Surveillance Era: Technologies and Practices* (Hershey, IGI Global, 2010) 285–87.

[75] Joined Cases C-465/00, C-138/01 and C-139/01 *Rechnungshof v Österreichischer Rundfunk and Others and Christa Neukomm and Joseph Lauermann v Österreichischer Rundfunk* [2003] ECR I-4989, para 72.

Moreover, in *Lindqvist*,[76] the CJEU ruling took further steps to establish a more flexible interpretation of the Directive. *In casu*, for reasons concerning a charity, a Swedish citizen published on the Internet personal data – some of it sensitive – of her colleagues without their consent. The Luxembourg Court reiterated that it 'cannot depend on whether the specific situations at issue in the main proceedings have a sufficient link with the exercise of the fundamental freedoms guaranteed by the Treaty'.[77] Clearly influenced from the margin of appreciation doctrine of the ECtHR, in its attempt to weight up the main objective of the Directive, namely the free movement of personal data within the context of the internal market with the protection of private life, the Court stated that Member States are also entitled to expand the scope of application of the national legal framework enforcing Directive 95/46 'to areas not included in the scope thereof provided that no other provision of Community law precludes it'.[78] Put differently, despite the requirement of complete harmonisation deriving from the Directive, national regimes enjoy a wide margin for manoeuvre while implementing this legal instrument to areas not included in the scope of the internal market, always taking into serious consideration the maintenance of the balance between the conflicting rights of individuals.[79] It is clear that the Luxembourg Court refused to deem the fundamental right to the protection of private life as a secondary purpose or means for the achievement of the objectives of the Directive 95/46. As Maria Tzanou maintained, the *Lindqvist* judgment could be positively appreciated 'for succeeding in making the "successful marriage" between fundamental rights and fundamental freedoms, as established by the Community legislator in the Data Protection Directive, even more solid and stronger'.[80]

Apart from the guarantees provided by EU secondary law regarding data protection, its explicit recognition as a fundamental right of equivalent value within the EU legal framework came with the adoption of the EU Charter, which not only contained a provision pertaining to respect for private and family life, but also established independently the right to data protection. Drafted a few years after the adoption of the Data Protection Directive, Article 8 of the Charter must be deemed as mirroring pre-existing EU data protection law and relevant jurisprudential principles.

As previously analysed, the right to data protection does not constitute an 'absolute prerogative and can be subject to restrictions in the general interest'.[81]

[76] Case C-101/01 *Bodil Lindqvist* [2003] ECR I-12971.

[77] ibid para 42.

[78] ibid para 99.

[79] See also on whether the application of the Directive infringes Article 10 ECHR (freedom of expression) ibid, para 90.

[80] See, eg M Tzanou, 'Balancing Fundamental Rights: United in Diversity? Some Reflections on the Recent Case Law of the European Court of Justice on Data Protection' (2010) 6 *Croatian Yearbook of European Law and Policy* 53, 63.

[81] S Peers, 'Taking Rights Away? Limitations and Derogations' in S Peers and A Ward (eds), *The EU Charter of Fundamental Rights: Politics, Law and Policy, Essays in European Law*' (Oxford, Hart Publishing, 2004) 141.

Along these lines, data protection needs to be enforced in the EU system with respect for the scope of other competing rights. The Luxembourg Court, even though it incorporated the lessons learned from the ECtHR jurisprudence, found it difficult to carry out this balancing task, as outlined in the *Promusicae*[82] and *Satamedia*[83] cases.

Firstly, in *Promusicae*, in 2008, the Court was asked to reconcile the right to property and the right to an effective remedy with the data protection rules using as a source of inspiration the provisions of the Charter, since the latter lacked legally binding effect at that time. Subsequent to the refusal of Telefonica, a telecom network, to disclose to Promusicae, an NPO of holders of intellectual property rights, personal data of a number of persons against whom Promusicae intended to initiate civil actions, the Spanish Court asked for a preliminary ruling, and particularly, whether the required data must be communicated under not only the provisions of the EU data protection secondary law but also of Articles 17 and 47 of the Charter. The CJEU ruled that the relevant directives do not create an obligation of Member States 'to communicate personal data in order to ensure effective protection of copyright in the context of civil proceedings'. Instead, the Court clarified that the only obligation emanating from EU law in the field relates to the balanced interpretation of conflicting fundamental rights protected by EU law, when transposing EU secondary legislation into the domestic legal order.[84] As for the implementation of the Directives, the Luxembourg Court underlined that national courts apply national law reconciling the requirements of the EU Directives with the EU human rights law or general principles of EU law (ie, the proportionality principle).[85]

Having sought a clear response within the EU legal regime,[86] the Court showed a strong reluctance to provide the national court with an assessment on how the equilibrium between the conflicting human rights should be accomplished in practice, leaving enormous discretion to the Member States. The 'blank cheque' approach of the margin of appreciation doctrine was also criticised on the basis of its future implications specifically in a field heavily regulated by the EU legislation.[87] This *laissez-faire* approach of the CJEU was reiterated in the *Satamedia* case. The Court attempted to resolve the conflict between data protection and freedom of expression and more particularly, freedom of the press under Article 9 of the Data Protection Directive. The issue at stake was Markkinapörssi

[82] Case C-275/06 *Productores de Música de Espana (Promusicae) v Telefónica de Espana SAU* [2008] ECR I-271, paras 54, 60.

[83] Case C-73/07 *Tietosuojavaltuutettu v Satakunnan Markkinapörssi Oy and Satamedia Oy* [2008] ECR I-9831.

[84] *Productores de Música de Espana* (n 82) para 70.

[85] ibid.

[86] Tzanou, 'Balancing Fundamental Rights' (n 80) 68. See also M Dougan, 'The Treaty of Lisbon 2007: Winning Minds, not Hearts' (2008) 45 *CML Rev* 617, 661–62.

[87] Tzanou, 'Balancing Fundamental Rights' (n 80) 68. See also V Kosta, *Fundamental Rights in EU Internal Market Legislation*, Modern Studies in European Law 58 (Oxford, Bloomsbury, 2015).

and Satamedia's dissemination of the tax data of 1.2 million natural persons, made publicly available by the Finnish tax authorities. These personal data related to the tax returns of the persons involved, and were collected to be published by the regional Veropörssi newspaper, or distributed using a text-messaging system through mobile phones.

After concluding that the activities of Markkinapörssi and Satamedia fall within the notion of processing of personal data as set ouy in the Directive, the Court overly expanded the notion of journalistic purposes apt to result in an exception or derogation in relation to the protection of personal data according to Article 9, albeit whenever is strictly necessary.[88] Moreover, the Court adopted the position of AG Kokott that these rules are not only applicable to media undertakings but also to every person engaged in journalism and the journalistic activities may be undertaken for profit-making reasons.[89] The AG's assertion *in casu* provided a solid human rights reasoning[90] indicative of the guidance that the ECtHR's case law has to offer in such contentious cases. She reminded that, in light of the standards of protection under Article 8(2) and Article 10(2) and the ECtHR case law, the EU has extended data protection to processing by individuals and it is upon that legal basis that the interferences with human rights must be read by the CJEU.[91]

Bearing in mind the broad discretion conferred to national authorities by the Directive while balancing freedom of expression and the protection of personal data, the failure of the Court to confine the concept of journalism solely to matters of public interest raised questions with regard to its compatibility with the invoked Strasbourg's case law[92] and the spirit of the Directive.

The case law left unanswered questions concerning the effective implementation of EU harmonisation measures such as the Data Protection legislation since the CJEU has conferred large room for manoeuvre to Member States.[93] A similar approach was confirmed in the ECtHR judgment on the same case[94] in which the latter concluded that the Finnish authorities struck a fair balance between

[88] Case C-73/07 *Tietosuojavaltuutettu v Satakunnan Markkinapörssi Oy and Satamedia Oy* [2008] ECR I-9831, para 58.

[89] ibid para 61.

[90] ibid Opinion AG Kokott, paras 38–44.

[91] ibid paras 41–42.

[92] Recently the ECtHR reaffirmed its well-established criteria in the field, namely whether the event that the published article concerned was of general interest, the arrest and conviction of a person was a public judicial fact and therefore of public interest, whether the person concerned was a public figure, how the information was obtained and whether it was reliable. *Axel Springer AG v Germany* [GC], Merits, App no 39954/08 (ECtHR, 7 February 2012), paras 90–91.

[93] See especially FJ Mena Parras, 'From Strasbourg to Luxembourg? Transposing the Margin of Appreciation Concept into EU law' (2015) Centre Perelman de Philosophie du Droit Working Paper 2015/7, 15–16, www.academia.edu/17852645/From_Strasbourg_to_Luxembourg_Transposing_the_margin_of_appreciation_concept_into_EU_law.

[94] *Satakunnan Markkinapörssi Oy and Satamedia Oy v Finland*, Merits, App no 931/13 (ECtHR, 21 July 2015).

the data protection legislation and the freedom of expression as it ruled that no violation of Article 10 ECHR had occurred. Having referred to the preliminary ruling of the CJEU, the Court reaffirmed the criteria of its case law applicable in cases in which fundamental rights enshrined in the Convention come into conflict with each other.[95] Confirming explicitly the wide margin of appreciation afforded to the domestic courts, the ECtHR accepted the pronouncement of the national court that the publication of personal tax data by the applicants could not be considered journalistic activity, due to a rather narrow and strict interpretation required by the exceptions for journalistic purposes under the Personal Data Act and Article 9 of the Data Protection Directive.[96] Nevertheless, given the Court's previous position and the availability – *in casu* – of personal data in the public domain, the ECtHR failed to offer helpful guidance to national authorities as regards the specific boundaries of lawful publication of taxation data.[97]

Another case brought before the CJEU, in which the reconciliation of conflicting human rights was at issue,[98] is the seminal *Bavarian Lager* case.[99] The Court pronounced on a Commission's appeal seeking annulment of the General Court judgment.[100] The latter, having applied the Article 8 ECHR test, annulled the Commission's decision denying Bavarian Lager, a company importing German beer into the UK, access to a copy of the full minutes of a meeting organised by the Commission including personal data of the attendees, on the basis of Article 4(1)(b) of the Access to Documents Regulation.[101] AG Sharpston's Opinion[102] highlighting the use of the necessity and proportionality test under Article 8 ECHR deserves our attention: in order to determine which EU Regulation is applicable in case of request for access to documents, he distinguished two separate categories of documents.[103] The first (B-1) contains documents with an incidental mention of personal data, where the primary purpose of compiling the document has little to do with personal data, since the aim of such documents is to store information in which personal data are of little

[95] *Von Hannover v Germany* (no. 2) [GC], Merits, ECHR 2012-I, para 351; *Armellini and Others v Austria*, Merits, App no 14134/07 (ECtHR, 16 April 2015), para 42.

[96] *Satakunnan Markkinapörssi Oy* (n 94), para 70.

[97] D Voorhoof, 'ECtHR accepts strict application of data protection law and narrow interpretation of journalistic activity in Finland' (*Strasbourg Observers*, 12 August 2015), www.strasbourgobservers.com/2015/08/12/ecthr-accepts-strict-application-of-data-protection-law-and-narrow-interpretation-of-journalistic-activity-in-finland/.

[98] See also the CoE Committee of Ministers (2002), Recommendation Rec (2002) 2 to Member States on access to official documents (21 February 2002); Council of Europe Convention on Access to Official Documents (Tromsø, 18/06/2009).

[99] Case C-28/08 P *European Commission v The Bavarian Lager Co Ltd* [2010] ECR I-6055.

[100] T-194/04 The *Bavarian Lager Co Ltd v Commission* [2007] ECR II-4523.

[101] Regulation (EC) No 1049/2001 of the European Parliament and of the Council regarding public access to European Parliament, Council and Commission documents [2001] OJ 2001 L145/43.

[102] Case C-28/08 P *European Commission v The Bavarian Lager Co Ltd* [2010] ECR I-6055, Opinion of the AG Sharpston.

[103] ibid paras 163–66.

importance. Along with Regulation No 1049/2001, the Article 8 ECHR test on a precautionary basis should be also applied since these documents might contain personal data. The second category consists of documents incorporating – by nature – a large number of personal data, as the aim is to actually collect such personal data, and therefore Regulation No 45/2001 is applicable.[104]

As the accomplishment of an equilibrium between the Access to Documents Regulation and the Data Protection Regulation was actually being sought, the CJEU did not seem to adopt the AG's appraisal, set aside the judgment of the General Court[105] and particularly held that the Access to Documents Regulation provided 'a specific and reinforced system of protection of a person whose personal data could, in certain cases, be communicated to the public'.[106] Emphasising the consent of five participants at that meeting, it finally ruled that the company had failed to provide express and legitimate justification ample to demonstrate the necessity for the data transfer. For the CJEU, 'the Commission has not been able to weigh up the various interests of the parties concerned. Nor was it able to verify whether there was any reason to assume that the data subjects' legitimate interests might be prejudiced.'[107]

As freedom of expression is nowadays applied in the modern media environment, balancing this right with the right to private life of individuals interacting in the digital world is constantly causing severe hardships to both European legal mechanisms. It is in this context that the *Google Spain* case[108] should be examined with regard to the applicability of data protection legislation to internet search engines. In the light of post-Lisbon CJEU jurisprudence recognising the *valeur juridique* of the EU Charter and strictly implementing EU data protection legislation,[109] this milestone ruling was seen[110] as conferring on data subjects the right to be forgotten and to control their online reputation. Particularly, M Gonzalez who asked for the deletion of published information in the online version of *La Vanguardia* newspaper regarding personal data relating to his participation in a real-estate auction held in 1998, alleged inter alia that when an internet user searched for his full name in the Google search engine, he would obtain access to such data. As the publisher of *La Vanguardia* and Google Spain, which in

[104] ibid para 165.

[105] The Court of First Instance (now General Court) adopted the threshold theory, specifically inspired from the ECtHR reasoning in similar cases. Case C-28/08 P *European Commission v The Bavarian Lager Co. Ltd* [2010] ECR I-6055, Opinion of AG Sharpston, para 123. Unlike *Osterreichischer Rundfunk*, the disclosure of the names of persons acting as members of a collective body, whose personal opinions cannot be identified does not necessarily amount to a violation to the right to protection of private life.

[106] Case C-28/08 P *European Commission v The Bavarian Lager Co. Ltd* [2010] ECR I-6055, para 60.

[107] ibid para 78.

[108] Case C-131/12 *Google Spain SL και Google Inc v Agencia Española de Protección de Datos (AEPD) and Mario Costeja González* [2014] ECLI:EU:C:2014:317.

[109] See also *PNR*, *Volker* and *Digital Rights Ireland* cases, discussed below.

[110] I Iglezakis, 'The Right to Be Forgotten in the Google Spain Case (case C-131/12): A Clear Victory for Data Protection or an Obstacle for the Internet?' (2014), www.papers.ssrn.com/sol3/papers.cfm?abstract_id=2472323; R Post, 'Data Privacy and Dignitary Privacy: Google Spain, the Right to Be Forgotten, and the Construction of the Public Sphere' (2018) 67 *Duke Law Journal* 981.

the meantime forwarded M Gonzalez's request to Google Inc., declined to remove or rectify the relevant information, he, subsequently, addressed his complaint to the Spanish DPA. The latter rejected the request as far as the newspaper was concerned; nevertheless, it ordered Google Spain to delist the aforementioned information from its search results.

In this factual context, the Court was expected to pronounce on the material scope[111] of the Directive and particularly on whether the activity of internet search engines, namely indexing automatically, storing temporarily and finally making available information published on different websites to internet users according to a particular order of preference,[112] falls within the notion of 'processing personal data' according to Article 2(b) of the Directive. The Court found the latter applicable to search engines operators like Google as it considered them controllers of the processing.[113] In response to Google's allegations that no personal data processing relating to its search engine took place in Spain and that its processing was exclusively carried out by Google Inc., the Court, examining the territorial scope of the said legislation, adopted an extraterritorial interpretation. In sum, the activities of the subsidiary (ie, Google Spain) are 'inextricably linked' to those of the search engine operator such as the activities of the Google headquarters in the United States in view of the fact that these activities allow Google Inc to be economically viable.[114]

Finally, the Court was asked about the extent of the responsibility of the search engines operators and therefore, the applicability in the present case of Articles 12(b) and 14(1)(a) of the DPD establishing the right to erasure, rectification or blocking of the processing of personal data. According to the CJEU's assertion, these provisions should be interpreted as granting the data subject the right to have a search engine delist from its search results links (related to his name) to websites published by third parties. However, the Court evinced that this right must be balanced with the legitimate interests of internet searchers with regard to the relevant provisions of the Charter, namely Articles 7 and 8 of the Charter.

The almost absolute priority given to data protection rights over the interests of internet users or the economic interests of the search engines operators was later justified by the judges of the Luxembourg Court as they underlined the dangers of the digital age, stating that

> Given the ease with which information published on a website can be replicated on other sites and the fact that the persons responsible for its publication are not always

[111] Regarding the material scope of the Directive's application see also S Kulk and F Zuiderveen Borgesius, '*Google Spain v. González*: Did the Court Forget about Freedom of Expression?' (2014) 5 *European Journal of Risk Regulation* 389; C Kuner, 'The Court of Justice of the EU Judgment on Data Protection and Internet Search Engines' (2014) LSE Legal Studies Working Papers 3/2015, 7, www.papers.ssrn.com/sol3/papers.cfm?abstract_id=2496060.

[112] *Google Spain SL* (n 108) paras 20–21.

[113] ibid para 33.

[114] ibid paras 55–56.

> subject to European Union legislation, effective and complete protection of data users could not be achieved if the latter had to obtain first or in parallel the erasure of the information relating to them from the publishers of websites.[115]

Even though it is clear that, especially after the attribution of full legal effect to the Charter, the CJEU sought to ensure a higher level of protection for the EU citizens with regard to the data protection law opting for a broader interpretation of the relevant legislation, this ruling caught many by surprise. In *Google Spain*, for the first time, the CJEU explicitly recognised the right of an individual to have personal data suppressed from the list of search results made available by an internet search engine and based on a search made on the individual's name. Nevertheless, the Court's judgment dealt with only one aspect[116] of the right to be forgotten as enshrined for the first time in Article 17 GDPR, since it only focused on its application to Internet search engines and thus, it seems inaccurate to misinterpret the decision as concluding to a holistic, comprehensive recognition of the right to be forgotten.[117] Christofer Kuner added that

> A careful reading shows that the right affirmed by the Court is that of obliging the operators of Internet search engines to suppress links to web pages from the list of search results made on the basis of a person's name (see para. 100), not a right to have data itself deleted from the Internet.[118]

In addition to this critique, the judgment is deemed to have severely neglected freedom of expression, particularly in the aftermath of several cases that required a fair balance between the relevant competing rights. Indeed, the Court contented itself with a brief reference to the need of reconciliation between the right of a person to have information related to him erased with the right of the Internet users and the economic interests of the providers without even an explicit reference to the freedom of expression under Article 11 EUCFR[119] or under Article 10 ECHR. Clearly prioritising the right to data protection over the freedom of expression of multiple parties, the Luxembourg Court seemed to ignore not only its prior case law but also the Strasbourg Court's approach in similar cases, according to which 'as a matter of principle these rights deserve equal respect'.[120] Nevertheless, the CJEU examined all the issues raised by the referring court from the data protection perspective. In fact, the CJEU avoided referring to

[115] ibid para 84.

[116] This actually constitutes one of the limitations of the judgment. Judging from the notion of Internet search engines, the Court left the question open for websites with large-scale search function, such as social networks, Internet archives, news databases, which are also used by millions of individuals.

[117] Iglezakis, 'The Right to Be Forgotten (n 110) 12.

[118] Kuner, 'The Court of Justice of the EU Judgment on Data Protection and Internet Search Engines' (n 111) 7.

[119] The provision of Article 11 CFR reads as follows: '1. Everyone has the right to freedom of expression. This right shall include freedom to hold opinions and to receive and impart information and ideas without interference by public authority and regardless of frontiers. 2. The freedom and pluralism of the media shall be respected.'

[120] *Von Hannover* (n 95) para 106.

the specific criteria[121] laid down in the jurisprudence of its Strasbourg counterpart when weighing Article 8 and Article 10 which particularly includes the right to receive and impart information. It is more than clear that the suppression of search results may amount to an interference with the freedom of expression[122] of the original publishers of information and the public's right to find information of general interest on the web.

In sum, the key judgment in *Google Spain* perfectly mirrors the readiness of the CJEU to enhance data protection legal standards[123] while implementing the Lisbon framework particularly in the light of the new EU General Data Protection Regulation[124] in 2012.[125] However, its implications raised questions, as the Court seemed reluctant to shed light on several issues with regard to the disproportionately broad scope of the Directive's application and the exercise of balancing of the individuals' fundamental rights. Hence, as Kuner correctly deduced, 'the judgment provides a strong affirmation of online data protection rights, but fails to indicate a way forward for their effective implementation and realization, the development of which will likely be a struggle for data controllers, DPAs, and courts'.[126]

[121] After acknowledging the need for reconciliation of the conflicting rights, the CJEU mentions, in para 81 of *Google Spain* (n 110), as an aspect which needs to be taken into account, 'the role played by the data subject in public life'. This reference is a clear influence from the Strasbourg Court's position on similar cases since the ECtHR examines, inter alia, how well-known the person concerned is. See also *Axel Springer AG* (n 92) paras 89–95.

[122] JVJ van Hoboken, *Search Engine Freedom. On the Implications of the Right to Freedom of Expression for the Legal Governance of Web Search Engines* (Alphen aan den Rijn, Kluwer Law International, 2012) 351.

[123] While the GDPR is now in force, the Luxembourg Court drew inspiration from *Google Spain* and went further to enhance the protection offered since it expanded the concept of controller in case of joint controllers as was the case of Facebook fan pages in Case C-210/16 *Unabhängiges Landeszentrum für Datenschutz Schleswig-Holstein v Wirtschaftsakademie Schleswig-Holstein GmbH* [2018] ECLI:EU:C:2018:388. Recently, it also applied the EU data protection legislation to the data collected by Jehovah's witnesses while making door-to-door visits. The Court recalled the well-established broadness of the definition of personal data enshrined in the Directive and held that the manner in which the said data was structured by Jehovah's witnesses amounted to a 'filing system' in the sense of the Directive. Case C- 25/17 *Tietosuojavaltuutettu v Jehovan todistajat* [2018] ECLI:EU:C:2018:551. See also the judgment of the CJEU in *Nowak* in which it ruled that exam scripts also fall under the scope of application of the Data Protection Directive and the GDPR. Hence, some limitations to the access to this type of data can be implemented. In a case in which the core issue was the camera surveillance of academic lectures in a university, the Strasbourg Court saw the case also through the lens of academic freedom as an aspect of freedom of expression. Case C-434/16 *Peter Nowak v Data Protection Commissioner* [2017] ECLI:EU:C:2017:994. See especially L Woods, 'Facebook Fan Pages and EU Data Protection Law: The Implications of Unabhängiges Landeszentrum für Datenschutz Schleswig-Holstein v. Wirtschaftsakademie Schleswig-Holstein GmbH' (*EU Law Analysis*, 3 July 2018), www.eulawanalysis.blogspot.com/2018/07/facebook-fan-pages-and-eu-data.html; S Peers, 'Is Data Protection Coming Home? The CJEU on Data Protection Law and Jehovah's Witnesses – and Political Canvassing?' (*EU Law Analysis*, 11 July 2018), www.eulawanalysis.blogspot.com/2018/07/is-data-protection-coming-home-cjeu-on.html.

[124] The EU General Data Protection Regulation explicitly enshrines the 'right to be forgotten' in Article 17.

[125] This tendency of the CJEU is equally illustrated in several recent judgments and especially in *Digital Rights Ireland* which will be discussed in the following chapter.

[126] Kuner, 'The Court of Justice of the EU Judgment on Data Protection and Internet Search Engines' (n 111) 21.

B. The Right to Private and Family Life in Migration and Asylum Cases

Similarly to the CJEU's approach regarding data protection, the enormous migration flows reaching European shores forced the body to desist from prioritising internal market values, and to engage with another new area, also needing to be regulated by EU law.

As far as EU legislation is concerned, a person seeking asylum or protection from expulsion is subjected to diverse treatment according to his/her nationality or citizenship, and this provokes, consequently, a hierarchical classification of rights between different people living within the EU. Therefore, there is a hierarchy of legal residents, with the Union citizens at the apex and third country nationals (hereinafter TCNs)[127] with no connection to the EU at the bottom of the ladder.[128] EU citizens and their family members, including TCNs, enjoy, thereby, a privileged position, as they are protected by EU citizenship/free movement legislation and thus, are very rarely subjected to expulsion or refusal of entry. Regarding EU citizens and the wide scope of the right of free movement they enjoy, they may be subjected to some derogations to this principle,[129] as these are enshrined in Article 45(3) TFEU and in the Free Movement Directive.[130] According to the abovementioned legal framework, EU citizens can be expelled or refused entry on the grounds of public policy, public security and public health.

The Luxembourg Court reaffirmed the position of the EU institutions and refused to restrict the mobility of the Union's citizens within EU borders (through the measure of expulsion or deportation) unless justified, and stated that they have the benefit of an equivalent legal status to the Member State's nationals. These derogations are only related to the personal conduct of the individual concerned. Previous criminal convictions are not in themselves grounds for expulsion. In *Adoui and Cornuaille*[131] the CJEU ruled that Member States exercising a non-discrimination test, may not order an expulsion from their territory or a refusal of entry to a national of another Member State, or refuse entry by reason of criminal

[127] Third country nationals (TCNs) are basically transnational migrants, whose legal status differs from EU citizens and determines their conditions of entry or residence.

[128] S Morano-Foadi and S Andreadakis, 'The Convergence of the European Legal System in the Treatment of Third Country Nationals in Europe: The ECJ and ECtHR Jurisprudence' (2011) 22 *EJIL* 1071, 1076.

[129] Despite the broad scope of the right of free movement, there are some exceptions to this principle. These are laid out in Article 45(3) TFEU and in Article 27 of the Free Movement Directive 2004/38 which provides specific circumstances in which EU citizens can be expelled from or refused entry to another Member State and refers to grounds of public policy, public security, or public health, but these grounds cannot be invoked to serve economic ends. See Consolidated Version of the Treaty on the Functioning of the European
Union [2012] OJ C 326/47

[130] Directive 2004/38/EC of the Council and European Parliament on the right of citizens of the Union and their family members to move and reside freely within the territory of the Member States (Free Movement Directive) [2004] OJ L158/77.

[131] Joined Cases 115 and 116/81 *Adoui and Cornuaille v Belgium* [1982] ECR 1665.

conduct which 'when attributable to their own nationals, does not give rise to genuine and effective or repressive measures intended to combat such conduct'.[132] In 2003, the Court extended the guarantees concerning deportation. Thus, the CJEU held in *Oulane* that 'detention and deportation based solely on the failure of the person concerned to comply with legal formalities concerning the monitoring of aliens impair the very substance of the right of residence directly conferred by Community law and are manifestly disproportionate to the seriousness of the infringement.'[133]

The CJEU also had the opportunity in the *Orfanopoulos and Oliveri* case[134] as well as in the *Tsakouridis* ruling, to clarify the sense of *imperative grounds of public security*. It specified the requirements of a lawful expulsion which are listed in Articles 27 and 28 of the Citizenship Directive.[135] The CJEU held that an expulsion order must not be based solely on a previous criminal conviction, as such a measure is not compatible with EU law, and it ruled that 'the concept of public policy presupposes the existence in addition to the perturbation of the social order involving any infringement of the law of a genuine and sufficiently serious threat to the requirements of public policy affecting one of the fundamental interests of society'.[136]

Confronted with vast migration flows, the EU regime also faced the necessity to protect particularly the fundamental rights of TCNs, whose protection against expulsion appears more complex and is carried out on a lower level of protection.[137] Within this legal context, the Directive on Third Country Nationals[138] who are Long-Term Residents was adopted by the Council, including guarantees for a secure residence right and free movement for either economic or other purposes across the EU for (most) TCNs, who have completed five years' lawful residence in a Member State's territory.

However, the migration jurisprudence revolves mostly around family reunification cases as the phenomenon of TCNs who are family members of EU citizens invoking the EU legislation as well as Article 8 of the ECHR, is more and

[132] ibid para 52.

[133] Case C-215/03 *Salah Oulane v Minister voor Vreemdelingenzaken en Integratie* [2005] ECR I-1215, para 40; see also Case 157/79 *Regina v Stanislaus Pieck* [1980] ECR 2171, paras 18–19; Case C-265/88 *Messner* [1989] ECR 4209, para 14; Case C-459/99 *Mouvement contre le racisme, l'antisémitisme et la xénophobie ASBL (MRAX) v Belgian State* [2002] ECR I-6591, para 78.

[134] Joined Cases C-428 and C-493/01 *Georgios Orfanopoulos and Others and Raffaele Oliveri v Land Baden-Württemberg* [2004] ECR I-5257. See also Case C-145/09 *Land Baden-Württemberg v Panagiotis Tsakouridis* [2010] I-11979.

[135] Directive 2004/38/EC of the European Parliament and of the Council of 29 April 2004 on the right of citizens of the Union and their family members to move and reside freely within the territory of the Member States (EU Citizenship Directive) [2004] OJ L158/77.

[136] *Orfanopoulos* (n 134), paras 66–67.

[137] Nevertheless, at this point, we have to distinguish between third-country nationals who are family members of EU citizens, Turkish nationals who are covered by the EEC Turkey Association Agreement-Decision 1/80 of the Association Council, and other third-country nationals.

[138] Council Directive 2003/109/EC concerning the status of third-country nationals who are long-term residents [2004] OJ L16/44.

more frequent.[139] It is in this particular field that a significant convergence with the Strasbourg Court occurred.[140] Notably, for some scholars, the Strasbourg Court's case law[141] is mainly integrated in the Directive on the protection of family reunification.[142] Hence, the *Baumbast* ruling[143] in 2002 constituted the leading case in the area of free movement as it paved a new route of social solidarity within the EU. Mr Baumbast, a German citizen who, after having pursued an economic activity in the United Kingdom, was hired by German companies outside the EU. The UK authorities refused to renew Mr Baumbast's residence permit, as he no longer qualified as a migrant worker in the United Kingdom and did not satisfy the conditions for a general right of residence, though his family lived in the United Kingdom and his children went to school there. The issue at stake *in casu* was whether persons living in a Member State as family members of an EU migrant worker continue to enjoy the protection offered by EU law when he or she no longer constitutes a migrant worker. The Luxembourg Court held that the Treaty does not require that EU citizens should necessarily have a professional or trade activity in order to enjoy the right of free movement. Consequently, simply as a Member State national, Mr Baumbast was allowed to invoke the right to reside in the country's territory, emphasising its direct effect. In this case, the children of an EU worker were allowed to exercise the right to residence in the UK in order to complete their education even after their father ceased to work there. Hence, the Court adopted clearly the approach of AG Geelhoed, who saw the entire case in the light of the Article 8 ECHR in order to protect the right to family life of these children.[144]

The same latitude in the interpretation of similar provisions is observed in the *Ruiz Zambrano* case[145] in which the CJEU seized the opportunity to contribute

[139] See especially P De Bruycker and S Labayle, 'The Influence of ECJ and ECtHR Case Law on Asylum and Immigration' (Study of the Policy Department C: Citizens' Rights and Constitutional Affairs, European Parliament, 2012), www.europarl.europa.eu/RegData/etudes/etudes/join/2012/462438/IPOL-LIBE_ET%282012%29462438%28SUM01%29_EN.pdf.

[140] The first CJEU case with reference to Article 8 ECHR was Case 36/75 *Rutili v Ministre de l'intérieur* [1975] ECR 1219.

[141] Reluctant to admit the severe impact of the CJEU's case law on its own jurisprudence, the ECtHR cited for the first time a decision of the Luxembourg Court in 2005.

[142] Morano-Foadi and Andreadakis, 'The Convergence of the European Legal System' (n 128) 1083.

[143] Case C-413/99 *Baumbast and R v Secretary of State for the Home Department* [2002] ECR I-7091.

[144] The CJEU confirmed this appraisal in Case C-480/08 *Maria Teixeira v London Borough of Lambeth and Secretary of State for the Home Department* [2010] ECR I-1107 and in Case C-200/02 *Kunqian Catherine Zhu and Man Lavette Chen v Secretary of State for the Home Department* [2004] ECR I-9925. See also the recent case in which the CJEU dived into the notion of 'direct descendants' in the sense of the EU Citizenship Directive and the CFR. The case concerned the child-guardian relationship under the *kafala* system (a form of guardianship in Algeria) and whether this falls within the scope of family life. The Court responded in the affirmative and relied on the similar pronouncements of the Strasbourg Court in *Chbihi Loudoudi and Others v Belgium* and *Harroudj v France*. Case C-129/18 *SM v Entry Clearance Officer, UK Visa Section* [2019] ECLI:EU:C:2019:248, para 66; *Harroudj v France*, Merits, App no 43631/09 (ECtHR, 4 October 2012); *Chbihi Loudoudi and Others v Belgium*, Merits, App no 52265/10 (ECtHR, 16 December 2014).

[145] Case C-34/09 *Gerardo Ruiz Zambrano v Office national de l'emploi* [2011] ECR I-1177. See also Case C-202/13 *McCarthy v Secretary of State for the Home Department* [2014] ECLI:EU:C:2014:2450;

to the development of the EU citizenship concept. More specifically, it assumed that EU citizenship law not only precluded Belgian authorities from refusing Mr Ruiz Zambrano, a TCN, the right of residence and a work permit, but also from depriving his minor children, EU citizens and totally dependent on their parents, of the right to stay within the EU territory.

In the same vein, the *Carpenter* case[146] was one of the cases that rendered the CJEU's approach most evident, and presented a really concrete fundamental rights-based doctrine. Mrs Carpenter, a national of the Philippines, applied for a permit to stay in the United Kingdom as a spouse of a British national, but her application was rejected and a deportation order was issued. Yet, the Luxembourg Court, after having examined whether the declared breach met the requirements of Article 8 as illuminated by Strasbourg case law (accordance with the law, necessary in a democratic society), within the context of the provision of services by Mr Carpenter who was running a business in United Kingdom, held that EU law recognises the right to family life in Article 8 ECHR and that the deportation of Mrs Carpenter did not constitute a fair balance since it would definitely cause a separation of the applicant's family. More precisely, the Court pointed out that the deportation would amount to

> an interference with the exercise by Mr Carpenter of his right to respect for his family life within the meaning of Article 8 … which is among the fundamental rights which, according to the Court's settled case-law, restated by the Preamble to the Single European Act and by Article 6(2) EU, are protected in Community law.[147]

Put differently, drawing from the ECtHR's interpretation, the measure was declared disproportionate in its aim and for that reason, void.

Therefore, in the realm of the direct application of certain rights of the ECHR, such as the right to private and family life, the CJEU seems to have been profoundly influenced by the margin of appreciation doctrine introduced by the ECtHR, leaving more and more discretion to the Member States to balance the EU law provisions with the fundamental rights at risk.[148]

Having said all the above, it becomes apparent that Article 8 ECHR along with its enlarged scope of application embracing different notions of private or family life, offered a field of law apt to encourage not only the judicial dialogue between the Luxembourg Court and its Strasbourg peer; it also inspired the

Case C-256/09 *Murat Dereci and Others v Bundesministerium für Inneres* [2011] ECR I-11339; T Richards, '*Zambrano, McCarthy* and *Dereci*: Reading the Leaves of EU Citizenship Jurisprudence' (2012) 17 *Judicial Review* 272. See also Case C-221/17 *M.G. Tjebbes and Others v Minister van Buitenlandse Zaken* [2019] ECLI:EU:C:2019:189.

[146] Case C-60/00 *Mary Carpenter v Secretary of State for the Home Department* [2002] ECR I-6279. A similar position was adopted by the Luxembourg Court in Case C-459/99 *Mouvement contre le racisme, l'antisémitisme et la xénophobie ASBL (MRAX) v Belgian State* [2002] ECR I-6591.

[147] ibid, para 41.

[148] See, eg Case C-101/01 *Bodil Lindqvist* [2003] ECR I-12971 and Joined Cases C-465/00, C-138/01 and C-139/01 *Rechnungshof v Österreichischer Rundfunk and Others and Christa Neukomm and Joseph Lauermann v Österreichischer Rundfunk* [2003] ECR I-4989.

intrusion of the Court into areas, partially regulated by EU law, in which the proper observance of fundamental rights was formerly not easily accomplished.

II. Articles 6 and 13 ECHR within the EU System: Interpretation of the Procedural Principles

The paramount role that both the right to a fair trial, enshrined in Article 6 ECHR, and the right to an effective remedy, under Article 13 ECHR, play within the ECHR system is dual: besides the fundamental human rights prescribed in the said articles, they also guarantee the enforcement of the other provisions of the Convention and thus, the embodiment of the rule of law formed by the ECHR.[149]

The different aims and objectives of the two European legal jurisdictions originally provided little room for interplay regarding the protection of the individuals' legal position. However, the CJEU slowly started to examine thoroughly the allegations of the parties concerning procedural guarantees, as ensured by the ECHR and the rich ECtHR jurisprudence even when adjudicating cases covered mostly by EU law. The citation of the ECHR's provisions related to procedural guarantees under Articles 6 and 13 has recently changed its form; though, post-Lisbon, the rights to an effective remedy and to a fair trial evolved from general principles of EU law, through the interpretation of the CJEU in the light of the ECHR, to fundamental rights codified in Articles 47 and 48 of the EU Charter.

Focusing more on the Charter's corresponding safeguards, we should not lose sight of the remarkable influence of the ECHR on the language of Article 47 EUCFR,[150] the first paragraph of which guarantees the right to an effective remedy before a court formulated similarly to Article 13 ECHR, while the second paragraph covers similar ground to Article 6(1) ECHR.[151] The last paragraph concerning the right to legal aid has its echo in the well-established case law of the Strasbourg Court, even though it is not *expressis verbis* laid down in the ECHR. The ECtHR jurisprudence needs to be taken into account to determine the content and scope of the Charter's provisions according to the wording of Article 52(3) CFR. Additionally, the presumption of innocence and right of defence, as enshrined in Article 48 CFR, correspond to the rights laid down in Article 6(2)(3) and have the same meaning and scope as the ECHR rights.[152] Moreover, while Article 6 ECHR is engaged with the determination of civil rights and criminal charges, Article 47 CFR covers not only rights and freedoms

[149] See the Preamble to the Convention.
[150] Explanations related to the Charter of Fundamental Rights [2007] OJ C303/17.
[151] ibid Explanation on Article 47 EUCFR.
[152] ibid Explanation on Article 48 EUCFR.

guaranteed by the Charter but also rights emanating from the entire EU legal order (the secondary law included).[153] It should also be highlighted that the procedural rules stemming from these provisions cover not only individuals but also Member States when challenging decisions of the EU bodies before the CJEU. In these terms, the protection offered by the Charter is considered to be more extensive[154] than the one guaranteed by the Convention.

In this multi-level context, it would be helpful to examine the protection offered by the Luxembourg Court in a twofold manner: first, the core procedural safeguards such as the fairness of the hearing and the elements which actually render a remedy effective for the litigants, and secondly, the minimum standards for defence rights which play the central role of fundamental tools in the hands of both individuals and, in some cases, of the EU system as a whole.

A. The Core Elements of Fair Trial and Effective Remedy: The Protection of Legal Persons

Starting from the *Johnston* case[155] in which it was noted that the principles of effective judicial control as laid down in the ECHR 'must be taken into consideration in Community law',[156] the CJEU reiterated this approach[157] applying more and more, in the years that followed, these procedural safeguards outside the scope of their traditional field of application, as this was initially formulated by the ECtHR's case law.

The latter, applying the right to a fair trial not only to civil proceedings but most importantly to 'criminal charges', had clarified the extent of this concept in the leading *Engel* case[158] where it shaped three criteria in view of determining whether the criminal limb of Article 6 ECHR is applicable. According to the ECtHR's position these criteria are the classification of the offence in domestic law, the nature of the offence and the severity of the penalty.[159] Therefore, offences

[153] L Cariolou, 'Article 47' in EU Network of Independent Experts on Fundamental Rights, 'Commentary of the Charter of Fundamental Rights of the European Union' (July 2006) 359, 360, www.sites.uclouvain.be/cridho/documents/Download.Rep/NetworkCommentaryFinal.pdf.

[154] See also regarding the sources and the field of application of the right to a fair trial, M Perakis, *The judicial protection of fundamental rights in the European Union* [in Greek], Studies of European Law (Athens, Nomiki Vivliothiki, 2015) 317–18.

[155] Case 222/84 *Marguerite Johnston v Chief Constable of the Royal Ulster Constabulary* [1986] ECR 1651.

[156] ibid para 18.

[157] Case 222/86 *Union nationale des entraîneurs et Cadres techniques professionnels du football (Unectef) v Georges Heylens and Others* [1987] ECR 4097; Case C-97/91 *Oleificio Borelli SpA v Commission of the European Communities* [1992] ECR I-6313. See also G Florou and K Margaritis, 'Article 47: Right to an effective remedy and to a fair trial' in VG Tzemos (ed), *The Charter of fundamental rights of the EU* [in Greek] (Athens, Nomiki Vivliothiki, 2015) 523–34.

[158] *Engel and Others v the Netherlands*, Merits, Series A no 22 (1976).

[159] WA Schabas, *The European Convention on Human Rights: A Commentary*, Oxford Commentaries on International Law (Oxford, Oxford University Press, 2015) 277–79.

not traditionally classified as criminal with respect to their special nature or the severity of the penalty imposed on the offender might fall within the scope of application of Article 6. This soft approach permitted the Strasbourg Court to gradually broaden the criminal head to cases not strictly related to criminal law, for example to administrative or competition cases.[160]

Surprisingly, the CJEU, since its early cases, found the procedural safeguards of the ECHR applicable to EU competition law. Although these safeguards were first established to guarantee the fairness of the hearing when natural persons were accused of committing a crime and threatened with imprisonment, they were progressively invoked by entities alleging violation of their rights in the context of investigations under competition law. More precisely, as regards the privilege against self-incrimination of undertakings, the two European jurisdictions interlocked – concluding, however, on divergent interpretations. Notwithstanding the fact that the right to remain silent and the protection against self-incrimination are not laid down openly in Article 6 ECHR, the Strasbourg Court has declared them as part of its actual substance.[161]

In 1989, the Luxembourg Court delivered the famous *Orkem* judgment[162] which concerned an undertaking that challenged a request for information made by the Commission. According to the allegations of the Orkem company, the questions asked breached 'the general principle that no one may be compelled to give evidence against himself'.[163] Although not explicitly guaranteed by the wording of Article 6 ECHR, the privilege against self-incrimination is, nonetheless, generally accepted as flowing from the right to a fair trial.

Yet, the CJEU, after pointing out that the right to remain silent – and the right not to incriminate oneself – is not incorporated in the aforementioned Regulation, concluded that

> as far as Article 6 of the European Convention is concerned, although it may be relied upon by an undertaking subject to an investigation relating to competition law, it must be observed that neither the wording of that article nor the decisions of the European Court of Human Right indicate that it upholds the right not to give evidence against oneself.[164]

Nevertheless, the Court underlined the significance of fundamental rights of defence conferred to natural and legal persons, elucidating that the Commission's powers of investigation are not unlimited.[165] Shortly after the *Orkem* case, the Strasbourg Court filled the gap of its case law, also previously cited by the CJEU, and ruled that the privilege against self-incrimination forms a part of the notion

[160] *Jussila v Finland* [GC], Merits, ECHR 2006-XIV 1, para 43. See also *Société Stenuit v France*, Merits, Series A no 232-A (1992).
[161] *Saunders v the United Kingdom*, Merits, ECHR 1996-VI, para 68.
[162] Case 374/87 *Orkem v Commission* [1989] ECR 3283.
[163] ibid para 18.
[164] ibid para 30.
[165] ibid para 32.

of a fair procedure under Article 6 ECHR.[166] In the *Funke* ruling,[167] the ECtHR followed a different path and initiated a divergent jurisprudential approach in this field, since it held that the imposition of fines by the French customs authorities on an individual on the grounds of his refusal to produce potentially incriminating statements concerning financial transactions amounted to a breach of Article 6(1) ECHR.[168] In particular, the ECtHR concluded that the special character of customs law which was invoked by the French government 'cannot justify such an infringement of the right of anyone *charged with a criminal offence*, within the autonomous meaning of this expression in Article 6, to remain silent and not to contribute to incriminating himself.'[169]

Although the *Funke* case concerned an individual and not a legal person, the ECtHR clearly abandoned the *Orkem* principles laid down by the CJEU: it seemed to interpret Article 6 as allowing an undertaking in the context of an investigation not only to decline to openly provide information which could have been potentially incriminating, but also any documentary evidence. With this far-fetched approach,[170] the ECtHR not only acknowledged that the right not to self-incriminate is embodied in the scope of Article 6, but also interpreted broadly the latter and the right to remain silent, leaving the door open to apply these safeguards to any type of evidence.[171] Nonetheless, for some scholars, judging from the absence of a comprehensive reasoning justifying the application of these principles to this specific factual basis, the Court appeared unprepared to take such a position on the matter.[172]

Following the inconsistency that the *Funke* judgment initiated with the CJEU case law, the ECtHR reiterated its stance in the *Murray*[173] and *Saunders*[174] rulings, restraining, though, the right to remain silent and the privilege against self-incrimination on the grounds of implied exceptions provided with regard to their application.

In addition, a few months later, in *Saunders*, the Court seemed to come into line with the CJEU case law[175] and in essence, highlighted the respect for the

[166] B Vesterdorf, 'Legal Professional Privilege and the Privilege against Self-Incrimination in EC law: Recent Developments and Current Issues' (2004) 28 *Fordham International Law Journal* 1179, 1192.

[167] *Funke v France* Series, Merits, A no 256-A (1993).

[168] See also S Frommel, 'The European Court of Human Rights and the Right of the Accused to Remain Silent: Can it Be Invoked to Taxpayers?' (1994) *Int'l Bus LJ* 671.

[169] *Funke* (n 167) para 40.

[170] Vesterdorf (n 166) p.1182.

[171] N Croquet, 'The Right of Silence and not to Self-Incriminate under the European Convention on Human Rights: To Which Extent are they Qualified' (2008) 4 *Cambridge Student Law Review* 214.

[172] For a critique of the judgment see also SH Naismith, 'Current Topic: Self-Incrimination Fairness or Freedom' 3 (1997) *European Human Rights Law Review* 229.

[173] *John Murray v the United Kingdom* [GC], Merits, ECHR 1996-I, para 47.

[174] *Saunders* (n 161). The Strasbourg Court also confirmed the broader protection offered to the applicants (in comparison with the protection offered by the CJEU) in *Heaney and McGuiness v Ireland*, Merits, ECHR 2000-XII 419 and *JB v Switzerland*, Merits, ECHR 2001-III 435.

[175] See especially A Ashworth, 'Self-incrimination in European Human Rights Law – A Pregnant Pragmatism?' (2008) 30 *Cardozo Law Review* 751.

will of an accused person to remain silent. The added value of the judgment is, thus, the criterion of '"independence" of evidence collecting from the accused's will' that the Court introduced, since it relied on the mode of production of the evidence at stake rather than its nature and limited this right to situations requiring the accused's active co-operation.[176] In general though, the Strasbourg Court confirmed subsequently[177] the broader protection offered to the applicants in comparison with the protection offered by the CJEU, in *Heany and McGuiness*[178] and in *JB*.[179]

More recently and in the wake of the jurisprudential developments of the ECtHR regarding the extent of application of the privilege of self-incrimination, the CJEU revisited this issue always in the context of competition cases.[180] The Luxembourg Court dealt with these cases in light of the considerable evolution in the ECtHR's relevant case law, as stated in the famous *PVC II*[181] case. According to the Court's appraisal these developments must be taken into account by the Community judicature when interpreting fundamental rights.[182] Notwithstanding its prior position, the Court concluded that 'both the *Orkem* judgment and the recent case-law of the European Court of Human Rights require, first, the exercise of coercion against the suspect in order to obtain information from him and, second, establishment of the existence of an actual interference with the right which they define.'[183]

The *SGL Carbon*[184] case also reaffirmed the general trend followed by the CJEU without losing sight of the Strasbourg Court's jurisprudence. This ruling was delivered following an appeal by the Commission concerning inter alia the production of documents during a Commission investigation. The Court reiterated its reference to the developments in the ECtHR's case law and, subsequently, established its dissimilar interpretation with regard to the protection against self-incrimination, arguing that 'the undertaking concerned must therefore, if the Commission requests it, provide the Commission with documents which relate to

[176] *Saunders* (n 161) para 69; Croquet (n 171) 224.

[177] In *Jalloh v Germany*, the Grand Chamber ruled that the privilege against self-incrimination may be outweighed due to the severity of 'the public interest in the investigation and punishment'. Hence, surprisingly enough, the ECtHR seemed to adopt a type of proportionality test that is not consistent with such a hardcore fundamental right as the right to a fair trial under Article 6. *Jalloh v Germany* [GC], Merits, ECHR 2006-IX 281.

[178] *Heaney and McGuiness v Ireland* (n 174).

[179] *JB v Switzerland* (n 174).

[180] L Scheeck, 'Solving Europe's Binary Human Rights Puzzle; The Interaction between Supranational Courts as a Parameter of European Governance' (2005) *Sciences Politiques Centre d'Etudes et des Recherches Internationales Questions de Recherche* no 15, www.sciencespo.fr/ceri/sites/sciencespo.fr.ceri/files/qdr15.pdf.

[181] Joined Cases C-238/99 P, C-244/99 P, C-245/99 P, C-247/99 P, C-250/99 P, C-251/99 P, C-252/99 P, C-254/99 *Limburgse Vinyl Maatschappij (LVM) and Others v Commission* [2002] ECR I-8375.

[182] ibid paras 274–77.

[183] ibid para 275.

[184] Case C-301/04 P *Commission of the European Communities v SGL Carbon AG* [2006] ECR I-5915.

the subject-matter of the investigation, even if those documents could be used by the Commission in order to establish the existence of an infringement.'[185]

Despite the persistent divergence of the Court from its Strasbourg peer, the evolution of the EU competition framework[186] played a critical role in the formulation of new procedural rules applicable to all EU citizens, which have finally been codified as individual fundamental rights in the Charter.[187] However, as Nehl correctly put it,

> the Union court's approach could prove problematic in the light of Article 51(1) of the Charter in so far as, when enforcing Articles 101 and 102 TFEU, national authorities and courts would be obliged to apply the 'lower' standard of protection under the Union concept of protection against self-incrimination notwithstanding the fact that their national laws provide for a 'higher' standard in line with that under Article 6(1) of the ECHR.[188]

However, this potential conflict will be further discussed below in light of the famous *Melloni* ruling which manifestly raised similar issues.

At any rate, it should be noted at this point that, despite the distinguished yet key position that the Convention enjoys within the Union's legal order remaining the most useful criterion for the interpretation of the Charter, the explicit references to the Convention are gradually diminishing in the post-Charter judicial practice of the CJEU. Indicatively, in the *Otis* case[189] where the Court dealt with questions of effective judicial protection, it seized the opportunity to clarify that it should, henceforth, refer solely to Article 47, since the latter secures in EU law the protection afforded by Article 6(1) of the ECHR. Furthermore, AG Cruz Villalon opined in *Samba Diouf*[190] that 'the right to effective judicial protection, as expressed in Article 47 of the CFREU, has, through being recognised as part of European Union law by virtue of Article 47, acquired a separate identity and substance under that article which are not the mere sum of the provisions of Articles 6 and 13 of the ECHR.'[191]

[185] ibid para 44.

[186] Council Regulation 1/2003 is the current legal framework of competition law which enhanced the Commission's powers of investigation in competition cases and granted additional procedural guarantees to the undertakings involved. Council Regulation (EC) No 1/2003 on the implementation of the rules on competition laid down in Articles 81 and 82 of the Treaty [2003] OJ L1/1.

[187] S Galera, 'The Right to a Fair Trial in the EU: Lights and Shadows' (2013) 87 *Revista de Derecho Politico* 49, 70.

[188] HP Nehl, 'The Principle of (Limited) Protection Against Self-incrimination' in S Peers, T Hervey, J Kenner, A Ward (eds), *The EU Charter of Fundamental Rights, A Commentary* (Hart Publishing, 2014) 1295.

[189] Case C-191/11 *Europese Gemeenschap v Otis NV and Others* ECLI:EU:C:2012:684, para 47. See also Case C-386/10 P *Chalkor AE Epexergasias Metallon v European Commission* [2011] ECR I-13085, para 51.

[190] Case C-69/10 *Brahim Samba Diouf v Ministre du Travail, de l'Emploi et de l'Immigration* [2011] ECR I-7151.

[191] ibid Opinion of AG Cruz Villalon, para 39.

On the other hand, the ECtHR drew inspiration from the Charter even before the latter was attributed legally binding force, indicating its willingness to bring new air to the ECHR-EU judicial interconnection within the post-Lisbon system. In the context of the application of the pure core of the fair trial principles, the Charter's influence in the ECHR legal order was made clear in the *Vilho Eskelinen and Others v Finland*[192] and *Micallef v Malta*[193] cases. Firstly, in the light of Article 47 EUCFR, the ECtHR extended the applicability of Article 6 ECHR to almost every civil servants dispute. Except for the careful analysis of the CJEU jurisprudence that the ECtHR used in its reasoning, the Court, remarkably enough, relied also upon the Explanations relating to the Charter, stating that 'they are a valuable tool of interpretation intended to clarify the provisions of the Charter'[194] and underlined that the Charter constitutes a codification of the existing case law of the Luxembourg Court.[195] In *Micallef*, the Court reversed its jurisprudential approach with regard to the non-applicability of Article 6 ECHR to interim measures stating the wider scope of application of the equivalent provisions of the EU Charter and, in parallel, taking into consideration that

> In *Bernard Denilauler v. SNC Couchet Frères* (ECJ, Case C 125/79, 21 May 1980) the European Court of Justice … held that provisional measures given *ex parte* without hearing the defendant could not be recognised according to its case-law. This implies that such safeguards should apply also outside the context of final decisions.[196]

Hence, despite the formal link to the Convention enshrined in the Charter and the substantive analysis of the Strasbourg Court's *corpus* of cases that this legal instrument suggests, the CJEU actually tends to prefer lately an autonomous interpretation of the Charter even when these core procedural guarantees, powerfully defended by both Courts, are under discussion. According to Callawert, 'the problem is not that the CJEU disregards the Convention and its case law, but that it no longer deems it necessary to explain its reasoning to the matter, thus leaving it to the litigants to guess its substance'.[197] It is also noteworthy that following these cases, the Strasbourg Court confirmed the strong influence of the Charter, albeit not binding at the time.[198]

Another meeting point of the two jurisdictions pertains to the interpretation of the core elements of Article 6 ECHR, and most importantly, the notion of access to a court. In the more recent *Dhabi*[199] and *Schipani*[200] cases, the ECtHR treated the issue of whether the failure of the Italian Constitutional Court to address a

[192] *Vilho Eskelinen and Others v Finland* [GC], Merits, ECHR 2007-II 1.
[193] *Micallef v Malta* [GC], Merits, ECHR 2009-V 289.
[194] *Vilho Eskelinen* (n 192) para 30.
[195] ibid.
[196] *Micallef* (n 193) para 32.
[197] J Callawaert, *The accession of the European Union to the European Convention on Human Rights* (Strasbourg, Council of Europe Publications, 2014) 40.
[198] *Demir and Baykara v Turkey* [GC], Merits, ECHR 2008-V 333, para 80.
[199] *Dhahbi v Italy*, Merits, App no 17120/09 (ECtHR, 8 April 2014).
[200] *Schipani and Others v Italy*, Merits, App no 38369/09 (ECtHR, 21 July 2015).

preliminary ruling to the CJEU could result in a violation of Article 6 ECHR. In both its pronouncements, the ECtHR stated that the unjustified refusal by a national court of last instance to make a reference to the Luxembourg Court pursuant to Article 267 TFEU, providing no justification, amounted to a breach of the right to a fair trial.

Nevertheless,

> the developments in Strasbourg might prove that such way forward might not be a bad idea at all. Otherwise the Court of Justice might find itself having to reinterpret Article 267 in light of article 6 ECHR, pushed by the increasing pressure of the Strasbourg case-law in cases like *Dhahbi*, *Schipani* and others to come.[201]

This recent evolution in the ECtHR's case law should also be documented in the context of the open discussion on the EU's accession to the ECHR. The *Dhahbi* ruling was delivered in 2014, only a few months before the sonorous rejection of the DAA, and the *Schipani* judgment was delivered in the aftermath of the latter. Therefore, the pronouncement of the ECtHR on a matter extremely close to the heart of the functioning of the CJEU with the view of reinforcing, though, the duty of the national courts to address a request for preliminary rulings could be revealed as a sign of appreciation and *rapprochement* of the EU legal order, despite the failure of reconciliation of the special features of the two legal systems.

Yet, now that the accession project is currently renegotiated, the CJEU approach of the Strasbourg loans – via Article 52(3) Charter – is far more appreciative than its prior position. In the recent *Consob* case,[202] regarding proceedings in relation to the lawfulness of penalties imposed for offences of insider dealing and failure to co-operate in the context of an investigation conducted by the Italian National Companies and Stock Exchange Commission (Consob), the Court relied heavily on Strasbourg's interpretation of the right to remain silent pursuant to Article 6 ECHR. By doing so, it managed to enhance protection offered pursuant to Articles 47 and 48 of the EU Charter,[203] deciding that these rights need to be recognised in administrative proceedings that may lead to the imposition of administrative sanctions of a criminal nature or in other administrative proceedings where the evidence produced may be used against that person in criminal proceedings. The ECHR is, therefore, still considered the main source of inspiration for the Luxembourg Court when the latter attempts to inform the contours of its core human rights standards.

That is also the case when it comes to the protection of the presence at trial guarantees, as analysed in the following pages.

[201] D Sarmiento, 'Schipani v Italy: When Does the ECHR Require National Courts to Refer Questions to the CJEU?' (*EU Law Analysis*, 7 September 2015), www.eulawanalysis.blogspot.gr/2015/09/schipani-v-italy-when-does-echr-require.html.

[202] Case C-481/19 *DB v Commissione Nazionale per le Società e la Borsa (Consob)*, ECLI:EU:C:2021:84 (2 February 2021).

[203] ibid paras 36–43.

B. Fair Trial Minimum Guarantees: Presence at the Trial

In the new Charter era, the CJEU used the Strasbourg Court's jurisprudence to venture into uncharted waters with special regard to minimum standards pertaining to the rights of defence which operate as new tools for the enforcement and the vindication of the core requirements of fair trial and the principle of effectiveness. These tools, some of which are at the disposal of EU citizens and some of the EU institutions, rendered the Luxembourg Court apt to go beyond the protection standards of its counterpart in the field of procedural guarantees, as illustrated in cases touching upon the issues of legal aid and the European Arrest Warrant (EAW) scheme.

Not only the 'presence at trial' requirement but also the right to be represented by a lawyer, both became objects of a whole new network of secondary law provisions introduced by the EU legislator, namely the Roadmap Directives.[204] This Roadmap aimed to articulate the minimum defence rights, as also provided by Article 6(3) ECHR, and is intended to serve as an instrument apt to render the core of the fair trial, in its pure sense, real and effective. In the field of EU co-operation in criminal justice, and, most precisely, in the field of the EAW, which reflects the EU mechanism that is most closely linked to the procedural requirement not to be tried *in absentia*, the CJEU found the opportunity to revisit the interrelationship between the EU legal system with that of the ECHR.

The EAW Framework Decision seemed to ignore the possibility of a violation of procedural guarantees within the surrender mechanism, first in the *Radu* case.[205] *In casu*, CJEU was asked about the compatibility of the EAW with the right to be heard before a court under the Charter and the ECHR, and concluded that the EAW does not require the requested person to be heard before it is issued. Given that the EU legislation was aiming to rationalise and speed up the surrender procedures of persons convicted or suspected of having breached criminal law, the Luxembourg Court strongly defended the EAW framework on the basis of the principle of mutual recognition and the presumption of confidence between Member States.[206] At this point, we should emphasise that the Court seemed to obviate the web of fundamental issues raised by the referring court and by the Opinion of Advocate General Sharpston.[207] The latter seemed to

[204] The so-called Roadmap Directives are: Directive 2010/64/EU of the European Parliament and of the Council on the right to interpretation and translation in criminal proceedings [2010] OJ L280/1; Directive 2012/13/EU of the European Parliament and of the Council on the right to information in criminal proceedings [2012] OJ L142/1; Directive 2013/48/EU of the European Parliament and of the Council on the right of access to a lawyer in criminal proceedings and in European arrest warrant proceedings, and on the right to have a third party informed upon deprivation of liberty and to communicate with third persons and with consular authorities while deprived of liberty [2013] OJ L294/1.

[205] Case C-396/11 *Ciprian Vasile Radu* [2013] ECLI:EU:C:2013:39.

[206] ibid para 33.

[207] *Ciprian Vasile Radu* (n 205) Opinion of AG Sharpston.

have accepted that the problem of defence rights within the surrender procedure remains – even after its recent reform – a weak point, and thus addressed the questions posed, arguing that the fundamental rights dimension should not be sidestepped within the execution of an EAW.[208] Therefore, the Advocate General reached the conclusion that when applying the EAW Framework Decision, the judicial authority of a Member State can oppose such an execution solely based on 'exceptional circumstances' when the surrender of the person involved would amount to an infringement of his defence rights as laid down in the Charter and the ECHR, particularly when the infringement could destroy the overall fairness of the process.

Although the Court had a golden opportunity to pronounce on a matter which traditionally has raised great controversy and divergent interpretations at the Member State level, it opted for a narrower procedural reasoning, prohibiting Member States from denying the execution of an EAW on defence rights grounds. It, thus, left national authorities without useful answers and clarifications on the matter.[209] Consequently, the Court's pronouncement in *Radu* proved that when questions are posed in a way that could impugn the validity or that could leave room for the progressive destabilisation of the mere function of the EAW scheme, the CJEU would defend it as if the whole architecture of mutual trust and co-operation was at risk.[210]

Remaining loyal to the literal application of the EAW procedural rules in the famous *Melloni* case,[211] the Court also revisited the debatable CFR-ECHR interplay. Looking closely at the main facts of the case, Mr Melloni, an Italian businessman prosecuted for bankruptcy fraud, tried to escape conviction by hiding in Spain[212] and as a result, he was sentenced *in absentia* to 10 years' imprisonment. In 2004, the Italian authorities issued an EAW aiming to execute the sentence. After his arrest by the Spanish police, Mr Melloni opposed his extradition to Italy, claiming that in the event of his surrender taking place, it would be impossible to appeal against the sentence imposed in his absence. At first instance, the Spanish Court rejected Mr Melloni's arguments and held that his rights of defence had been respected.

However, Mr Melloni subsequently applied to the Spanish Constitutional Court on the grounds of Article 24(2) of the Spanish Constitution, which establishes the right to a fair trial. According to its well-established jurisprudence,

[208] ibid paras 41, 69–70.

[209] As regards the possible roots of the Court's reserved ruling see A Davies, 'Radu: A case of failed dialogue' (Eutopia Law Blog, 5 February 2013), https://eutopialaw.com/2013/02/05/radu-a-case-of-failed-dialogue/.

[210] L Marin, 'Effective and Legitimate? Learning from the Lessons of 10 Years of Practice with the European Arrest Warrant' (2014) 5 *New Journal of European Criminal Law* 327, 337.

[211] *Stefano Melloni* (n 35).

[212] Despite the fact that he was well aware of the time and place of the trial in Italy, Mr Melloni opted to be represented by his lawyers instead of attending personally the entire criminal process until the case was brought before the Italian Supreme Court.

this right under the Spanish Constitution requires that, in the event of a person's conviction in his absence, extradition based on the execution of the sentence must be conditional on the right to appeal so that the rights of defence is sufficiently guaranteed, even if he had been effectively represented by a lawyer at the trial. On the other hand, according to Article 4a(1)(b) of the Framework Decision on the EAW 2002/584/JHA as amended by Framework Decision 2009/299/JHA,

> the executing judicial authority may also refuse to execute the European arrest warrant issued for the purpose of executing a custodial sentence or a detention order if the person did not appear in person at the trial resulting in the decision, unless the European arrest warrant states that the person, in accordance with further procedural requirements defined in the national law of the issuing Member State: being aware of the scheduled trial, had given a mandate to a legal counsellor, who was either appointed by the person concerned or by the State, to defend him or her at the trial, and was indeed defended by that counsellor at the trial.[213]

Due to the obvious contradiction between its own jurisprudence and the EAW framework, the Spanish Constitutional Court decided to refer to the CJEU for a preliminary ruling. The Luxembourg Court, in its landmark ruling, held that

> Article 4a(1) of Framework Decision 2002/584 must be interpreted as precluding the executing judicial authorities, in the circumstances specified in that provision, from making the execution of a European arrest warrant issued for the purposes of executing a sentence conditional upon the conviction rendered *in absentia* being open to review in the issuing Member State.[214]

As for the compatibility of the Framework Decision with Articles 47 and 48 of the Charter, the Court stated that although the right of the accused to attend personally at his trial constitutes a crucial component of the concept of fair trial, that right is not absolute. In fact, the accused is free to waive that right, albeit in an unequivocal manner.[215]

Having mentioned the correspondence of the Charter's procedural safeguards to Article 6(1) and (3) ECHR, the CJEU expressly referred to the Strasbourg Court's judgments delivered under similar circumstances[216] and concluded that in the case at hand, Mr Melloni had waived his right to be present at his trial and consequently was not entitled to invoke the benefit of retrial, having been informed of the details of his trial and represented by counsel according to the conditions established by Article 4(a)1 of Framework Decision. Hence, the right to an effective judicial remedy and the rights of the defence, as enshrined to the Charter, had been respected in the context of the application of the relevant EU legislation.

[213] Council Framework Decision 2009/299/JHA (n 38).
[214] ibid para 46.
[215] ibid para 49.
[216] *Medenica v Switzerland*, Merits, ECHR 2001-VI 105, paras 56–59; *Sejdovic v Italy*, Merits, App no 56581/00 (ECtHR, 10 November 2004), paras 84, 86, 98; *Haralampiev v Bulgaria*, Merits, App no 29648/03 (ECtHR, 24 April 2012), para 32–33.

Nonetheless, the CJEU partly referred to the Strasbourg Court's case law according to which, even in a case where a person was adequately notified and without adequate reason chose to be tried *in absentia*, that person should not be deprived of the right to be represented by a lawyer.[217] However, as the ECtHR held in *FCB v Italy*,[218] despite the fact that the accused had been represented by a lawyer, Article 6 ECHR had been breached since 'it does not appear that Mr F.C.B., whether expressly or at least in an unequivocal manner, intended to waive his right to appear at the trial and defend himself.'[219] Thus, the surrender of a person under the EAW who, being informed of the trial and represented by a lawyer, was convicted *in absentia* without the possibility to obtain a retrial could, in exceptional cases, amount to an infringement of the ECHR.

Most importantly, the Court of Justice, while answering the final question of the Spanish Constitutional Court, focused on whether Article 53 EUCFR should be interpreted as offering a general authorisation to the Member States to apply higher standards of protection of fundamental rights than those provided by the Charter. Given that such an interpretation would seriously undermine the well-established principles of primacy and effectiveness of EU law, the Court blatantly restricted the reach of Article 53. For the Court, the provision does not allow Member States 'to make the surrender of a person convicted *in absentia* conditional upon the conviction being open to review in the issuing Member State, in order to avoid an adverse effect on the right to a fair trial and the rights of the defence guaranteed by its constitution.'[220]

In other words, the Court found itself in the paradoxical situation in which a national supreme court is prohibited from offering a higher level of fundamental rights protection, in stark contradiction to EU primary law, to preserve the supremacy and uniformity of Union law. It goes without saying that the interpretation of Article 53 EUCFR made by the Spanish Constitutional Court is prima facie in accordance with the spirit of the provision overly extending the human rights protection offered to EU citizens. For Lavranos,

> the perverse result of this approach is that the ECJ effectively allows Member States to adopt Union law measures – which may potentially be in violation of their own constitutions but which are in line with the Charter of Fundamental Rights – without the national (constitutional) courts being able to do anything against it.[221]

It remains unclear, though, how these two contradictory approaches can be reconciled in the context of the highest possible level of fundamental rights

[217] *Pelladoah v the Netherlands*, Merits, Series A no 297-B (1994); *Lala v the Netherlands*, Merits, Series A no 297-A (1994).

[218] *FCB v Italy*, Merits, Series A no 208-B (1991).

[219] ibid para 33.

[220] *Stefano Melloni* (n 35) para 64.

[221] N Lavranos, 'The ECJ's Judgments Melloni and Åkerberg Fransson: Une ménage à trois difficulté' (2013) 4 *European Law Reporter* 133, 140.

protection promoted not only by Article 53 EUCFR but also by the entire post-Lisbon scheme.

From the EU perspective, the approach of the CJEU is understandable, especially at a time of enormous discussion and controversy concerning the Charter-ECHR relationship in the light of the EU's accession to the ECHR, since the Court preferred to promote the Charter to the top of the ladder of legally binding instruments. Looking through the mutual trust lens, seen as the *raison d'être* of the Union, the Court appears to use the Charter and the EAW framework as the ultimate normative tools to ensure the mutual trust principle among Member States. That is the reason why the latter was considered by the Luxembourg Court to be one of the key points and the major concerns expressed in Opinion 2/13 on the draft accession agreement of the EU to the ECHR. Indeed, only a few months later, the Court stressed that

> in so far as the ECHR would, in requiring the EU and the Member States to be considered Contracting Parties not only in their relations with Contracting Parties which are not Member States of the EU but also in their relations with each other, including where such relations are governed by EU law, require a Member State to check that another Member State has observed fundamental rights, even though EU law imposes an obligation of mutual trust between those Member States, accession is liable to upset the underlying balance of the EU and undermine the autonomy of EU law.[222]

Thus, it is common ground that the CJEU sought to avoid giving national jurisdictions, in case of the accession taking place, new ammunition and new argumentative grounds to revisit the heating debate that the Court had hoped to have left behind in *Melloni*.[223]

Such grounds for unbalancing the sensitive EU–Member States equilibrium could also be provided through the equivalent provision of Article 53 ECHR,[224] which sets the interpretative limits of the Convention in terms of the scope of domestic fundamental rights. According to the CJEU's wording in Opinion 2/13,[225] whereas seemingly establishing a similar approach to that sensitive matter, the two articles may create a conflict in theory. As construed by the Strasbourg Court, Article 53 does not dictate a uniform standard, since the Convention constitutes a minimum level guarantee. Nevertheless, the need for enforced harmonisation in several fields of EU law requires a coherent understanding of fundamental rights protection to safeguard the primacy and uniformity of the Union's legal order. The main concern of the EU legislator here is that, post-accession, this conflicting level of fundamental rights protection may result in revisiting the *Melloni*-type situation, since higher standards of protection prescribed by national legislation

[222] Opinion 2/13 (n 32) para 194.

[223] C Krenn, 'Autonomy and Effectiveness as Common Concerns: A Path to ECHR Accession After Opinion 2/13' (2015) 16 *German Law Journal* 147, 158.

[224] Article 53 ECHR holds that 'Nothing in this Convention shall be construed as limiting or derogating from any of the human rights and fundamental freedoms which may be ensured under the laws of any High Contracting Party or under any other agreement to which it is a party.'

[225] Opinion 2/13 (n 32) para 189.

may be applicable even in a field completely regulated by EU law, while not addressing a preliminary referral to the CJEU.[226] Nonetheless, if we ask ourselves whether there is an actual menace to the uniformity and primacy of EU law under the aforementioned circumstances, we should note that, undoubtedly – and in reality – the Strasbourg Court is traditionally engaged with enforcement of the Convention, and not of higher national standards of protection. Thus, this conflict is more virtual than a real one and, in these terms, this wide perception of conflict cannot be construed as the point of departure every time that the compatibility with the EU Treaties of international agreements that the EU intends to conclude, is being questioned. This approach of the Court might prove extremely restrictive as regards the participation of the Union in international law-making since there will always be similar conflicts.[227]

Overall, while analogous questions were asked in *Åkerberg Fransson*[228] – which will be discussed further below – the position of the CJEU in the famous *Melloni* case for Xavier Groussot and Ingrid Olsson is aptly summarised as follows:

> on the one hand, it reflects the pluralist nature of EU law by recognising the cumulative application of several layers of fundamental rights binding Member States and mandates the ECJ to engage in a dialogue with the national constitutional courts. On the other hand, it strongly protects the level of protection of the Charter and the effectiveness and uniformity of EU law.[229]

It is, however, indicative that, following the CJEU's ruling in *Melloni*, the Spanish Constitutional Court adopted a rather defensive approach, pointing out that it used the jurisprudence of the CJEU and the ECtHR only as hermeneutical tools. Therefore, the Spanish Constitutional Court accepted the reversal of its appraisal on the matter, but appeared unwilling to accept this as a 'defeat', portraying the result as the outcome of its own autonomous reasoning.[230]

The Luxembourg Court unquestionably opened a new chapter in the book of judicial dialogue with domestic constitutional courts with applying the EAW scheme, in the joint cases *Aranyosi and Căldăraru*.[231] Unlike *Melloni*, these cases

[226] Or, even worse, turning to the Strasbourg Court for an advisory opinion under Protocol 16.

[227] P Eeckhout, 'The European Convention on Human Rights and Fundamental Freedoms as an Integral Part of EU Law–Some Reflections on Status and Effect' in I Govaere, E Lannon, P van Elsuwege and S Adam (eds), *The European Union in the World: Essays in Honour of Marc Maresceau* (Leiden, Brill, 2013) 13.

[228] C-617/10 *Åklagaren v Hans Åkerberg Fransson* [2013] ECLI:EU:C:2013:105.

[229] X Groussot and I Olsson, 'Clarifying or Diluting the Application of the EU Charter of Fundamental Rights? – The Judgments in Åkerberg and Melloni' (2013) 2 *Lund Student EU Law Review* 7, 35.

[230] A Torres Pérez, '*Melloni* in Three Acts: From Dialogue to Monologue' (2014) 10 *European Constitutional Law Review* 308, 321.

[231] Joined Cases C-404/15 and C-659/15 *Pál Aranyosi και Robert Căldăraru* [2016] ECLI:EU:C:2016:198. See also Case C-237/15 *Minister for Justice and Equality v Francis Lanigan* [2015] ECLI:EU:C:2015:474. In line with the *Aranyosi and Căldăraru* case, the CJEU delivered in October 2019 its *Dorobantu* judgment concerning detention conditions and the execution of EAW in which it reaffirmed that in the EU legal order the ECHR, as interpreted by the Strasbourg Court, applies directly. Case C-128/18 *Dumitru-Tudor Dorobantu v Generalstaatsanwaltschaft Hamburg* [2019] ECLI:EU:C:2019:857, para 7.

touched upon the absolute prohibition of torture, inhuman or degrading treatment under Article 3 ECHR in view of the inadequate detention conditions in the requesting state and the grounds on which the examination of such conditions must take place. This judgment, which was the first EAW judgment delivered after Opinion 2/13, appears as a turning point in the relevant CJEU jurisprudence. In brief, the Court held that an EAW should not be enforced if the individual runs the risk of been subjected to a treatment incompatible with Article 3 ECHR and the corresponding right of Article 4 CFR. A reconciliation, therefore, of fundamental rights and *mutual recognition* principle in the light of the Strasbourg Court's detention standards appeared preferable for the Court. Arguably, this judgment signalled the departure of the judges of the Court from the conception of mutual trust as blind trust. When it comes to the secondary legislation concerning the EAW, its execution lies upon a more fundamental rights-oriented interpretation of this principle.[232] Yet, whether this openness will, as time goes by, the consistent approach of the Court – also when procedural safeguards are in question – remains to be seen.

Besides, the recent debate inflated by the new Polish legislation which interferes with the judicial independence in the country and which inevitably led to the European Commission's proposal for activation of Article 7 TEU[233] imposed severe strains on the domestic and European rule of law,[234] and by extension, on the sustainability of the mutual recognition principle. Indeed, the European Commission has referred Poland to the Court of Justice, challenging the said legislation in September 2018.[235] The Court pronounced on the matter in October 2018 with an order to grant interim measures. Poland was therefore ordered to immediately suspend application of the provisions of national legislation relating to the lowering of the retirement age for Supreme Court judges.[236]

[232] K Bovend'Eerdt, 'The Joined Cases Aranyosi and Căldăraru: A New Limit to the Mutual Trust Presumption in the Area of Freedom, Security, and Justice?' (2016) 32 *Utrecht Journal of International and European Law* 112; S Prechal, 'Mutual Trust Before the Court of Justice of the European Union' (2017) 2 *European Papers* 75; K Lenaerts, 'La vie apres l' avis: Exploring the Principle of Mutual (yet not blind) Trust' (2017) 54 *CML Rev* 805, 839; S Peers, 'Human Rights and the European Arrest Warrant: Has the ECJ turned from poacher to gamekeeper?' (*EU Law Analysis*, 12 November 2016), www.eulawanalysis.blogspot.com/2016/11/human-rights-and-european-arrest.html. On recent developments see J Cortes-Martin, 'The Long Road to Strasbourg: The Apparent Controversy Surrounding the Principle of Mutual Trust' (2018) 11 *Review of European Administrative Law* 5; J Graat, 'Human Rights v the European Arrest Warrant? The Legality of Surrender Detention after 90 Days' (*EU Law Analysis*, 18 October 2018), www.eulawanalysis.blogspot.com/2018/10/human-rights-v-european-arrest-warrant.html?fbclid=IwAR3_eAxF3nZBR4ea93PK7mTiUsb7adwTLFpsAfDOfDOdBtHZQNRObAUt4nE.

[233] This procedure was first triggered by the European Commission publishing on 20 December 2017 its reasoned proposal in accordance with Article 7(1) of the Treaty on European Union regarding the rule of law in Poland.

[234] L Pech and K Lane Scheppele, 'Illiberalism Within: Rule of Law Backsliding in the EU' (2017) 19 *Cambridge Yearbook of European Legal Studies* 3.

[235] European Commission, 'Rule of Law: European Commission refers Poland to the European Court of Justice to Protect the Independence of the Polish Supreme Court' (Press Release, 24 September 2018), www.europa.eu/rapid/press-release_IP-18-5830_en.htm.

[236] Case C-619/18 R *Commission v Poland* [2019] ECLI:EU:C:2019:615, Order of the Vice President. Case C-619/18 *European Commission v Republic of Poland* [2019] ECLI:EU:C:2019:531.

The anticipated decision of the CJEU pertaining to the so-called 'reform' of the Polish judicial system was delivered on 24 June 2019.The Court concluded that it was actually within its competence to rule on the 'judicial reform' since the latter jeopardises the independence of the judiciary and by extension effective legal protection as ensured by EU law.[237]

However, the Court had already faced the legal repercussions emerging from the EU 'rule of law crisis' with regard to the solid enforcement of EU criminal law. Thus, the potential suspension of an EAW, issued by the Polish authorities, was placed at the centre of a heated legal discussion concerning the future of mutual trust in the *LM* case.[238] The Irish Supreme Court specifically asked the CJEU whether the executing state should take the *Aranyosi* road and in case of 'cogent evidence that conditions in the issuing Member State are incompatible with the fundamental right to a fair trial because the system of justice itself in the issuing Member State is no longer operating under the rule of law'. It was also called upon to determine whether it should 'make any further assessment, specific and precise, as to the exposure of the individual concerned to the risk of unfair trial'.[239]

Indeed, the Court replied in the affirmative should the existing conditions in the issuing state not comply with the fair trial standards, albeit in a rather narrow manner. It accepted that the *Aranyosi* test is applicable when the right to fair trial is at stake. It was, therefore, safer for the Court to build on the *Associação Sindical dos Juízes Portugueses*[240] case law and emphasise the importance of the independence of justice in order that fair trial and effective judicial protection may be ensured.[241] Drawing an analogy from the *Aranyosi* judgment, both a systemic and an individual assessment were deemed necessary. In the context of the latter, the Luxembourg Court appeared to have entrusted a certain dialogue between the executing and the issuing states of the EAW.[242] If all fail, the mutual trust can be waived and the execution of the EAW can be suspended.[243]

This emphasis on the individual test has particularly brought a remarkable storm of criticism, as the Court missed the opportunity to see this case through the prism of the recent rule of law crisis in Poland. Having highlighted

[237] Case C-619/18 *European Commission v Republic of Poland* [2019] ECLI:EU:C:2019:531. For a thorough analysis see L Pech and S Platon, 'The Beginning of the End for Poland's So-Called "Judicial Reforms"? Some Thoughts on the ECJ ruling in Commission v Poland (Independence of the Supreme Court case)' (*EU Law Analysis*, 30 June 2019), www.eulawanalysis.blogspot.com/2019/06/the-beginning-of-end-for-polands-so.html.

[238] Case C-216/18 PPU *Minister for Justice and Equality v LM* [2018] ECLI:EU:C:2018:586. See also the more recent Joined Cases C-354/20 PPU and C-412/20 PPU, *Openbaar Ministerie*, ECLI:EU:C:2020:1033. Compare with *Pirozzi* ruling of the Strasbourg Court on EAW. *Pirozzi v Belgium*, Merits, App no 21055/11 (ECtHR, 17 April 2018).

[239] ibid, para 25.

[240] Case C-64/16 *Associação Sindical dos Juízes Portugueses v Tribunal de Contas* [2018] ECLI:EU:C:2018:117.

[241] *LM*(n 238), paras 64–67.

[242] ibid, paras 75–78.

[243] ibid, para 79.

the relevance of the Reasoned Proposal by the European Commission, the Court opted against having a word on the on-going political upheaval around preservation of the rule of law in the European Union.[244] At the level of the second stage of the individual test, the Court leaves room for a case-by-case examination of the mutual trust while disproportionate burden is reserved to individuals and to the executing judicial body to co-operate with a possibly unreliable counterpart which is actually reviewed for not respecting the fundamental values of the EU and human rights. This position of the CJEU partly mirrors the fears expressed in Opinion 2/13 pertaining to limitations to the principle mutual trust.

During the same time, the ECtHR interestingly concluded, in *Romeo Castaño*,[245] that the refusal of Belgium to execute an EAW, invoking the risk of the convicted person being subjected to ill-treatment if extradited to Spain – which was not duly reasoned or based on an individualised review of the case – amounted to a violation of the procedural positive obligation under Article 2 ECHR to co-operate in an investigation with the issuing state. In line with the *Aranyosi* standards and its own earlier case law, the Strasbourg Court took the opportunity to evolve its extradition jurisprudence when an EAW is involved, finding, for the first time, a state accountable for not extraditing the accused or convicted person on human rights grounds. Besides the absolute protection of Article 3 ECHR, the Court also vindicated the utmost importance of the procedural duty of cooperation in the investigation between the issuing and the executing authorities of an EAW which touches upon the principle of mutual co-operation, the cornerstone of the entire EAW scheme.

What is particularly noteworthy here is also the concurring opinion of Judge Spano (now President), also joined by Judge Pavli. They both underlined the so-called *souci de symmetrie* between the ECHR and the EU legal order and the perennial need for solutions to be meticulously elaborated, apt to preserve the nature and integrity of the former without destabilising the delicate institutional balance and the fundamental elements of the latter. In this spirit, the ECtHR delivered a landmark ruling in *Bivolaru and Moldovan v France*[246] on the EAW scheme. With respect to its own equivalent protection doctrine, the Court felt that it should inform its contours and applicable standards affirming that there is still room for the Strasbourg Court's external review of the actions of its State Parties, albeit operating by virtue of an EU mutual recognition scheme.[247]

[244] See, eg P Bard and W van Ballegooij, 'Judicial Independence as a Precondition for Mutual Trust? The CJEU in *Minister for Justice and Equality v LM*' (2018) 9 *New Journal of European Criminal Law* 353; A Frackowiak-Adamsca, 'Mutual trust and independence of the judiciary after the CJEU judgment in LM – new era or business as usual?' (*EU Law Analysis*, 15 August 2018), www.eulawanalysis.blogspot.com/2018/08/mutual-trust-and-independence-of.html.

[245] *Romeo Castaño v Belgium*, Merits, App no 8351/17 (ECtHR, 9 July 2019); M Zamboni, 'Romeo Castaño v Belgium and the Duty to Cooperate under the ECHR' (*EJIL Talk!*, 19 August 2019), www.ejiltalk.org/romeo-castano-v-belgium-and-the-duty-to-cooperate-under-the-echr/.

[246] *Bivolaru and Moldovan v France* (Merits) App nos 40324/16 and 12623/17 (ECtHR, 25 March 2021).

[247] For a more detailed account, see Chapter 2, section IIIA.

Arguably, the CJEU found itself in the middle of a substantial crisis touching upon the EU core values with both legal and political implications, confronted with the task to find the fragile balance between proper function of mutual co-operation and loyalty to its constitutional role to offer precise guidance to national judiciaries. At any rate, the protection of fair trial guarantees within the EU has not only mirrored the ECHR standards in the field but also observed the evolution of the interrelationship between the two Courts. Although they both see the EAW scheme from a differrent angle, there is sound evidence to support that the – recently achieved – more coherent interpretation of the relevant rules in hindsight reinvigorated legal certainty on criminal justice matters, let alone the mere accession concept.

III. The *Ne bis in Idem* Principle in the CJEU Jurisprudence: New Challenges in the Post-Lisbon Era

In essence, the *ne bis in idem* principle establishes a prohibition against being tried or punished twice for the same offence. Its source in EU law is found in both Article 4 of Protocol No 7 ECHR and the constitutions of Member States. Recognised explicitly by the Luxembourg Court as a general principle of EU law, it has also been incorporated into some international agreements concluded by Member States, eg the Convention on the Protection of the European Communities' Financial Interests[248] and the Convention on the Fight against Corruption,[249] as well as in the Convention Implementing the Schengen Agreement (CISA).[250] Following the entry into force of the Treaty of Lisbon, the *ne bis in idem* principle was also incorporated in Article 50 EUCFR. Although it was originally applicable mainly in criminal cases, it is now applied in various legal areas exceeding the scope of the three above-mentioned Conventions.

However, the scope of application of the prohibition of multiple trials for the same offence as developed in the EU legal system is significantly different from that of the ECHR, which constituted its central and absolute source. That said, it remains motivating to dive into the Strasbourg and Luxembourg Courts' jurisprudence and to examine their attempts to build a solid and coherent approach reconciling the different *ne bis in idem* standards and taking into account multiple legal traditions in criminal law developed by the European states.

[248] Convention drawn up on the basis of Article K.3 of the Treaty on European Union, on the protection of the European Communities' financial interests [1995] OJ C316/49.

[249] Convention drawn up on the basis of Article K.3(2)(c) of the Treaty on European Union on the fight against corruption involving officials of the European Communities or officials of Member States of the European Union [1997] OJ C195/2.

[250] The Schengen acquis – Convention Implementing the Schengen Agreement of 14 June 1985 between the Governments of the States of the Benelux Economic Union, the Federal Republic of Germany and the French Republic on the gradual abolition of checks at their common borders (CISA) [2000] OJ L239/19.

In order for Article 4 of Protocol No 7[251] to be applicable, there must be two sets of proceedings of criminal character. The first procedings should be completed, but also a final conviction is required. However, it suffices that the second proceedings have begun in order to establish a breach of the above-mentioned provision.

Despite the fundamental character of the *ne bis in idem* principle as enshrined in Article 4 of Protocol No 7, the Protocol has not yet been ratified by all Contracting Parties.[252] For numerous scholars,[253] this is partially outweighed by the fact that, as human rights laid down in the Convention are deemed to be among the general principles of EU law according to the CJEU's case law, the EU Member States which have not ratified the Protocol are *de facto* bound by its provisions and thus, the sphere of influence of Article 4 Protocol No 7 ECHR also extends to their legal orders, at least when implementing EU rules. In clear contradiction to the equivalent provision of the Charter, Article 4 is only engaged in the national *ne bis in idem* and not the international or transnational *ne bis in idem*, as it only applies within the domestic legal orders of the states which have ratified the said Protocol and are bound by its provisions. The reticence of some Contracting Parties to ratify Protocol No 7 is actually based on the different approaches of the Contracting Parties to the essence of the right not to be tried twice for the same offence.

At first, observing carefully the concept of *ne bis in idem* as interpreted by the Strasbourg Court, it flows from the wording of Article 4 of Protocol No 7 that the provision has limited the principle to domestic cases and, hence, cases in which individuals are prosecuted for trans-border crimes fall out of its scope of application, as it states that no one should be tried or punished twice 'under the jurisdiction of the same State'. Since Article 4 of Protocol No 7 ECHR traditionally concerns criminal offences, the ECtHR applied the *Engel* criteria[254] (the classification of the offence in domestic law, the nature of the offence, and the severity of the penalty that is at risk), similarly to the Court's interpretation of Article 6 ECHR, so as to ascertain whether the *ne bis in idem* principle is applicable *rationae materiae*. As a result, it progressively developed a rather flexible approach extending the concept of *idem* and *bis*. For the ECtHR, in order for Article 4 of Protocol No 7 to be applicable, the judicial proceeding should be of criminal

[251] Article 4 of Protocol No 7 reads as follows: 'No one shall be liable to be tried or punished again in criminal proceedings under the jurisdiction of the same State for an offence for which he has already been finally acquitted or convicted in accordance with the law and penal procedure of that State'.

[252] Belgium, Germany, the Netherlands, Spain and Turkey have signed but not ratified the Protocol. The United Kingdom has not signed it.

[253] WB van Bockel, 'The Ne Bis In Idem Principle in EU Law: a Conceptual and Jurisprudential Analysis' (Doctoral Thesis, Leiden University 2009), 17, www.openaccess.leidenuniv.nl/bitstream/handle/1887/13844/000-diss-VanBockel-26-05-2009.pdf?sequence=1; C Lundeholm, 'The Principle of Ne Bis In Idem: Human Rights and the Enforcement of European Union Competition Law' (Masters Thesis, Lund University 2011), www.lunduniversity.lu.se/lup/publication/2343939.

[254] See n 163 (needs verification).

character and should definitely result in an irrevocable decision, meaning that no ordinary remedies are available under national legislation and hence, the first decision has acquired the force of *res judicata*.[255]

Yet, the cases brought before the ECtHR touched not only upon purely criminal matters but also the simultaneous pending of criminal and administrative proceedings, having, though, a criminal character in most cases, under the national legal traditions. One way or another, the key point within the ECtHR's case law is definitely its position on the element of *idem* as the majority of the cases presented before the Strasbourg Court focuses on this particular aspect of the *ne bis in idem* concept.

Within this ambit, while the Court in the *Gradinger v Austria* case[256] disregarded the legal classification under national law and concluded there was an infringement of Article 4 Protocol No 7 due to the fact that both administrative and criminal sanctions were applied on account of the same factual act, in *Oliveira v Switzerland*,[257] the ECtHR partially overturned its prior position. Notwithstanding the fact that the Court confirmed that the same act, by violating several norms, might result in two proceedings and two relative sanctions, the Strasbourg Court, in order to justify its precedents, held that the *ne bis in idem* principle prohibits double criminal proceedings for the same offence.[258] However, in *Fischer v Austria*[259] the Court opted to reconcile those two contradictory approaches on the matter, relying on the 'same action' element. Nevertheless, in the successive judgment *Göktan v France*,[260] the Court mainly took into account the legal *idem*, concluding that the prohibitive proceedings should be defined on the basis of the *Engel* criteria.

The looming legal uncertainty prompted the Strasbourg Court to harmonise its earlier jurisprudence, shifting to the position of other supranational jurisdictions such as the Inter-American Court of Human Rights and the CJEU, verifying their judicial dialogue once again. Therefore, in 2009, in its landmark *Zolotukhin v Russia* ruling,[261] the ECtHR adopted a broader interpretation of *idem* pursuant to the principle of effectiveness of the Convention rights.[262] The Court defined in detail the notion of 'same offence', stating that 'accordingly, the Court takes the view that Article 4 of Protocol No. 7 must be understood as prohibiting the prosecution or trial of a second "offence" in so far as it arises from identical facts or facts

[255] CoE, Explanatory Report to the Protocol no 7 to the Convention for the Protection of Human Rights and Fundamental Freedoms, para 22.

[256] *Gradinger v Austria*, Merits, Series A no 328-C (1995).

[257] *Oliveira v Switzerland*, Merits, ECHR 1998-V.

[258] ibid para 26.

[259] *Josef Fischer v Austria*, Merits, App no 33382/96 (ECtHR, 17 January 2002).

[260] *Göktan v France*, Merits, ECHR 2002-V 107.

[261] *Sergey Zolotukhin v Russia* [GC], Merits, ECHR 2009-I 291.

[262] D Pyrgakis, 'Article 50: Right not to be tried or punished twice in criminal proceedings for the same criminal offence' in VG Tzemos (ed), *The Charter of fundamental rights of the EU* [in Greek] (Athens, Nomiki Vivliothiki, 2015) 574.

which are substantially the same'. It further elucidated that '[t]he Court's inquiry should therefore focus on those facts which constitute a set of concrete factual circumstances involving the same defendant and inextricably linked together in time and space, the existence of which must be demonstrated in order to secure a conviction or institute criminal proceedings'.[263] Nevertheless, this cutting-edge view of the *idem factuum* as defined by the Strasbourg Court was not followed by several national supreme and constitutional courts, such as the Swedish Supreme Administrative Court and the Austrian Constitutional Court, on the grounds of the specific features of each legal system.[264]

Within the CoE, numerous efforts have been made in recent decades to inaugurate a regional-international *ne bis in idem* principle with regard to mutual legal co-operation framework, especially in extradition cases. As John Vervaele underlines, 'in this cooperation framework the ne bis in idem principle only applies inter partes, which means that it can be or must be applied between the Contracting States in case of a concrete request. It is not considered to be an individual right erga omnes.'[265] Thus, the *ne bis in idem* principle was enshrined in Article 9 of the milestone multilateral Extradition Convention of the Council of Europe of 13 December 1957[266] which applied the principle not only to final judgments, acquiring the force of *res judicata*, but also to final decisions of a procedural nature. The Extradition Convention reads the *ne bis in idem* in an intergovernmental context between the requesting and requested Contracting Party. Nonetheless, in a series of legislative instruments intended to establish mutual co-operation within the CoE framework as regards criminal matters, the prohibition of double jeopardy is totally absent.[267] Whereas the latter is included as a mandatory ground for refusal in several conventions, namely those engaged in the International Validity of Criminal Judgments[268] and the Transfer of Proceedings in Criminal Matters,[269] those texts received a rather low ratification rate and numerous exceptions to the particular provisions containing the *ne bis in idem* principle. That said, the legislative efforts of the CoE mechanisms and the jurisprudential attempts of the Strasbourg Court to establish common standards in the field of the *ne bis in idem* application proved to be a rather puzzling balancing task as a coherent position was accomplished only in the field of extradition cases.

[263] *Zolotukhin* (n 261) paras 82–84.

[264] See especially C Grabenwarter, *European Convention on Human Rights Commentary* (Munich, CB Beck, Hart Publishing, Nomos Helbing Lichtenhahn Verlag, 2014) 439.

[265] J Vervaele, 'Ne Bis In Idem: Towards a Transnational Constitutional Principle in the EU?' (2013) 9(4) *Utrecht Law Review* 211, 215.

[266] European Convention on Extradition (Paris, 13 December 1957).

[267] For instance in the 1959 Council of Europe Convention on Mutual Assistance in Criminal Matters as well as in the Additional Protocol of 1978 or that of 2001.

[268] European Convention on the International Validity of Criminal Judgments (The Hague, 28 May 1970).

[269] European Convention on the Transfer of Proceedings in Criminal Matters (Strasbourg, 15 May 1972).

Despite this fragmented protection of the right not to be tried twice for the same offence, the Strasbourg Court was definitely inspired to align its case law with regard to the application of the *ne bis in idem* principle to the CJEU's case law[270] pursuant to Article 54[271] of the Convention Implementing the Schengen Agreement (CISA).[272] More precisely, in *Van Esbroeck*[273] the CJEU interpreted this provision in the light of the free movement principle in the context of European integration and held that 'the only relevant criterion for the purposes of the application of Article 54 of the CISA is identity of the material acts, understood as the existence of a set of facts which are inextricably linked'.[274] Hence, the Court ruled out,[275] in this case, the legal classification of the action under scrutiny, as the criterion which determines the application of the *ne bis in idem* principle is the factual identity. In the context of the Schengen *acquis*, even though the Contracting Parties recognised the possibility of a severe increase of cross-border crime particularly in a borderless area, it would have been incompatible with the aim of freedom of movement of EU citizens to be subjected to double prosecution for the same offence. As a result, Member States established a legal provision laying down a multilateral treaty-based *ne bis in idem* norm, intending also to harmonise the differentiated national legal schemes in this field and to enhance the mutual trust among Member States.[276]

This tendency of the Luxembourg Court to broadly apply this principle became obvious in the *Gözütok and Brügge* case.[277] The CJEU focused on the very essence of the principle having proper effect and appeared to set aside procedural matters, often linked to its applicability.[278] The way to the enhancement of mutual recognition passes also through the application of the *ne bis in idem* in the field of the EAW Framework Decision. Articles 3 and 4 of the Framework Decision determined precisely the grounds for mandatory non-execution of the EAW and the grounds for optional non-execution of the EAW when it comes to double

[270] See especially H Mock, 'Ne bis in idem: Strasbourg tranche en faveur de l'identité des faits' (2009) 79 *Revue trimestrielle des droits de l' homme* 867, 878.

[271] Article 54 CISA provides that: 'A person whose trial has been finally disposed of in one Contracting Party may not be prosecuted in another Contracting Party for the same acts provided that, if a penalty has been imposed, it has been enforced, is actually in the process of being enforced or can no longer be enforced under the laws of the sentencing Contracting Party'.

[272] Convention implementing the Schengen Agreement of 14 June 1985 between the Governments of the States of the Benelux Economic Union, the Federal Republic of Germany and the French Republic on the gradual abolition of checks at their common borders (CISA) [2000] OJ L239/19.

[273] Case C-436/04 *Van Esbroeck* [2006] ECR I-2333.

[274] ibid para 36.

[275] Case C-469/03 *Criminal proceedings against Filomeno Mario Miraglia* [2005] ECR I-2009; Case C-150/05 *Van Straaten v the Netherlands and Italy* [2006] ECR I-9327; Case C-288/05 *Criminal proceedings against Jürgen Kretzinger* [2007] ECR I-6441.

[276] C van den Wyngaert and G Stessens, 'The International *Non Bis In Idem* Principle: Resolving Some of the Unanswered Questions' (1999) 48 *ICLQ* 779, 787.

[277] Joined Cases C-187/01 and C-385/01 *Hüseyin Gözütok and Klaus Brügge* [2003] ECR I-1345.

[278] J Vervaele, 'The Transnational *Ne Bis In Idem* Principle in the EU: Mutual Recognition and Equivalent Protection of Human Rights' (2005) 1 *Utrecht Law Review* 100, 113.

prosecution within the EU. In particular, the Luxembourg Court clarified its position in the context of Article 3 of the EAW Framework Decision in *Mantello*,[279] pointing out that this provision as well as Article 54 CISA should be interpreted in the same way.

Initially, Advocate General Bot underlined that the obligation to implement EU law goes hand-in-hand with respect for fundamental rights as guaranteed by the ECHR.[280] Subsequently, the Court followed the conclusions of the Advocate General and held that whether there is a final judgment for the purposes of Article 3(2) of the Framework Decision is determined by national law of the Member State. In the Court's words,

> a decision which, under the law of the Member State which instituted criminal proceedings against a person, does not definitively bar further prosecution at national level in respect of certain acts cannot, in principle, constitute a procedural obstacle to the possible opening or continuation of criminal proceedings in respect of the same acts against that person in one of the Member States of the European Union.[281]

Therefore, the autonomous transnational *ne bis in idem* concept, as formulated by the nuanced interpretation of the provisions in the area of freedom, security and justice, was made in the light of the mutual trust principle and found also its place among the fundamental rights incorporated in the Charter. While Article 50 CFR[282] is actually lacking an enforcement clause, in clear contrast with the provision of CISA, the fundamental nature of this principle is also confirmed by its appearance in a wide range of different forms and EU legal contexts providing sometimes conflicting interpretations.

In the aftermath of the Lisbon Treaty, the codification of the right not to be tried or punished twice for the same act in the Charter aimed to also unify the application of this concept within the EU legal order. However, the most striking example of its application is the controversial *Åkerberg Fransson* judgment[283] of the Luxembourg Court which posed questions pertaining to the mere notion of the principle under Article 50 CFR, let alone the controversy about the ECHR–Charter interaction.

In casu, Mr Åkerberg Fransson, a Swedish fisherman, initially subjected to financial penalties (tax surcharges) in the context of administrative proceedings, was also prosecuted for tax fraud, facing a criminal sanction. He appealed to the civil court submitting that, in essence, the *ne bis in idem* principle, read in the light of the ECHR provisions and the Strasbourg Court's case law, along with Articles 50 and 52(3) CFR, would preclude the Swedish court system from

[279] Case C-261/09 *Gaetano Mantello* [2010] ECR I-11477.
[280] ibid Opinion of Advocate General Bot, para 87.
[281] ibid paras 46–47.
[282] Under Article 50 CFR, 'No one shall be liable to be tried or punished again in criminal proceedings for an offence for which he or she has already been finally acquitted or convicted within the Union in accordance with the law.'
[283] *Åkerberg Fransson* (n 228).

permitting double proceedings as this would amount to double punishment for the same conduct. The Luxembourg Court, in contrast with the approach of Advocate General Cruz Villalón, declined to examine the relationship between the *ne bis in idem* in the system of the ECHR and that of the EU, and turned its attention to the scope of application of the Charter. Particularly, the CJEU recalled 'that the Charter's field of application so far as concerns action of the Member States is defined in Article 51(1) thereof, according to which the provisions of the Charter are addressed to the Member States only when they are implementing European Union law.'[284]

As for the substantive question, the Court provided little guidance to the Member States. Despite the fact that it reaffirmed implicitly the application of the *Engel* criteria and that a tax offence may be of a criminal nature, it left the matter open to the national courts to determine whether the *ne bis in idem* is applicable.[285] The CJEU also made clear that sanctions for the evasion of VAT, as in the present case, fall within the implementation of EU law and should respect EU fundamental rights. However, as discussed earlier, in order for the Charter's provision to be fully applicable the contested national legislation should fall within the scope of EU law. Advocate General Kokott and Sobotta correctly pointed out the broadness of the Court's pronouncement, giving examples that would create extensive ambiguity. They further stressed that '[i]f the Court meant to say that all such situations completely fall within the ambit of EU Fundamental Rights law, there would remain very little room for the operation of the Fundamental Rights laws of Member States. Additionally, EU control of Member State action would appear to be significantly extended.'[286] Advocate General Kokott and Sobotta, subsequently, concluded that the actual meaning of the Court's approach was that, in order to trigger the Charter's protection, the situations under scrutiny should be regulated or governed, and not only touched upon, in general, by the EU legislation.

The *Åkerberg Fransson* case also gave rise to interesting and complex issues regarding the interpretation of Article 52(3) CFR. In this context, the Court held that as long as accession to the ECHR has not yet been accomplished, the Convention should not formally be deemed as forming part of EU law and, as a result,

> European Union law does not govern the relations between the ECHR and the legal systems of the Member States, nor does it determine the conclusions to be drawn by a national court in the event of conflict between the rights guaranteed by that convention and a rule of national law.[287]

[284] ibid, para 17.

[285] Ibid, para 36.

[286] J Kokott and C Sobotta, 'Protection of Fundamental Rights in the European Union: On the Relationship between EU Fundamental Rights, the European Convention and National Standards of Protection' (2015) 34 *Yearbook of European Law* 60, 71.

[287] *Åkerberg Fransson* (n 228) at para 45.

Surprisingly enough, the Luxembourg Court concluded that

> European Union law precludes a judicial practice which makes the obligation for a national court to disapply any provision contrary to a fundamental right guaranteed by the Charter conditional upon that infringement being clear from the text of the Charter or the case-law relating to it, since it withholds from the national court the power to assess fully, with, as the case may be, the cooperation of the Court of Justice, whether that provision is compatible with the Charter.[288]

Whereas the Advocate General paid particular attention to the 'homogeneity clause' which is also reaffirmed by the provision of Article 52(3), the Court opted for a rather minimalistic approach of this Article and therefore, an autonomous interpretation of the *ne bis in idem* principle in EU system.[289]

Overall, the Court finds EU fundamental rights system applicable if there is a connection between the national legislation and EU law. However, given the gradual and never-ending expansion of the Union law to new fields of law, it would be impossible in a few years to identify an area of national law untouched by the EU system and thus, totally regulated by the national legislation of the Member States. As a result, due to this significant expansion of the scope of application of the EU Charter, the CJEU might be given the opportunity to use the latter as a tool for controlling and gradually harmonising the multiple standards of fundamental rights protection within the EU. In these terms, the Court of Justice probably seeks to gradually render the EU Charter the exclusive referring text, while shaping a more coherent level of EU human rights protection, giving Article 51 EUCFR the key role, instead of using the general principles and the ECHR, as was the case until recently. This tendency of the Court, expressed only a few months before its Opinion 2/13 on the accession was delivered, inevitably raised complicated issues regarding the relationship and legal hierarchy between the Charter as primary EU law and the ECHR.[290]

In *Åkerberg Fransson*, the Court felt that, at first, it should preserve the autonomous perception of the *ne bis in idem* concept along with its transnational effect, under the EU Charter. Thus, the *ne bis in idem* provision of Article 50 EUCFR, applied in a setting of national enforcement of EU law, protects from all – both administrative and criminal – punitive sanctions in line with the *Engel* criteria. But most importantly, in this landmark case of the Court, which was, interestingly enough, delivered on the same day as the *Melloni* judgment, the CJEU appeared willing to minimise the ECHR's role, signalling the supremacy of the Charter as an interpretative tool within the Union's architecture. The Court excluded the conversation around the ECHR, possibly with the aim of avoiding the thorny issue of compatibility of EU standards with the Convention, particularly in an era marked

[288] ibid para 47.
[289] Kokott and Sobotta (n 286).
[290] Lavranos (n 221) 139.

by severe ambiguity regarding the future coexistence of the two legal instruments. On the other hand, this expansionist approach of the CJEU, which actively enlarged the scope of application of the Charter, seemingly suggests a brand new beginning for EU human rights law.[291] However, the risk of the ECHR being overshadowed or sidestepped – at least from the national courts' perspective – is even more present in the light of the Opinion 2/13, which confirmed the *Melloni* and *Åkerberg Fransson* principles.

However, the more recent jurisprudence fleshed out by the ECtHR and the CJEU has tested the waters of the inter-judicial dialogue between the two adjudicative bodies as regards the duplication of criminal and administrative procedures for the same action. Indeed, the controversial case *A and B v Norway*[292] delivered by the Strasbourg Court added a new criterion, introducing an exception to the *ne bis in idem* principle. In brief, the scope of the prohibition appears to be interpreted as indissolubly connected with the temporal and substantial relation between the two procedures.[293] The finding of the Court signals a remarkable departure from its previous *Zolothukin* and *Engel* jurisprudence and a step back from the extensive protection offered thereby. The narrowness but also the vagueness of the new criterion introduced by the Grand Chamber was questioned by Judge Pinto De Albuquerque in his extended dissenting Opinion as he criticised the transformation of the initial *ratio* of the provision from an individual guarantee to an enforcement tool of tax authorities.[294] Interestingly, the dissenter Judge also underlined the risks that this conclusion of the majority could bring to the destabilisation of the looming coherence that the ECtHR and the CJEU are striving to achieve, as derives from the *Åkerberg Fransson* case law. For the Judge, 'the progressive and mutual collaboration between the two European courts will evidently once again be deeply disturbed, Strasbourg going the wrong way and Luxembourg going the right way.'[295]

Right or wrong, the CJEU indeed has taken a different road, while fulfilling its moral obligation to consistently reply to analogous questions with regard to the corresponding right of Article 50 CFR and its interrelationship with the threshold of Article 7 Protocol No 4 ECHR. Therefore, in three similar cases involving parallel proceedings of criminal and administrative nature against VAT in the *Menci* case,[296]

[291] See also S Douglas-Scott, 'The Relationship between the EU and the ECHR Five Years on from the Treaty of Lisbon' in S de Vries, U Bernitz and S Weatherill (eds), *The EU Charter of Fundamental Rights as a Binding Instrument: Five Years Old and Growing*, Studies of the Oxford Institute of European and Comparative Law (Oxford, Hart Publishing, 2015) 40–41.

[292] *A and B v Norway* [GC], Merits, App nos 24130/11 and 29758/11 (ECtHR, 15 November 2016). See also *Jóhannesson and Others v Iceland*, Merits, App no 22007/11 (ECtHR, 18 May 2017); *Jussila* (n 160) para 43.

[293] *A and B v Norway* (n 292) para 130.

[294] *A and B v Norway* (n 292) dissenting Opinion of Judge Pinto de Albuquerque, para 79.

[295] ibid para 80.

[296] Case C-524/15 *Menci* [2018] ECLI:EU:C:2018:197.

in *Garlsson et al.*[297] and in *Di Puma*,[298] all delivered on the same day, the CJEU took the opportunity to reshape the controversial interpretation of the *ne bis in idem* principle. Indicative of the presence of the ECHR and its respective interpretation by the Strasbourg Court within the EU legal order, Advocate General Sánchez-Bordona's Opinions had already highlighted all the negative repercussions of the *A and B v Norway* and analysed the reasons why the Court should not abandon its *Åkerberg Fransson* legacy following the Strasbourg Court in this new unsafe path.[299]

In the wake of the opinions of the Advocate General, the Court pronounced on the matter on 20 March 2018 and delivered all three judgments.[300] In essence, the Court refrained from remaining close to the *Engel* approach and went on to genuinely rebuild its jurisprudence in this regard, acknowledging that some restrictions to the *ne bis in idem* prohibition are indeed allowed. Neither the road of the Advocate General nor that of the Strasbourg Court is entirely taken: the Court felt that in order to ascertain whether the double prosecution of both administrative and criminal character amounted to a breach of Article 50 of the Charter it should opt for a necessity assessment, strictly applied. In the Court's view, three requirements need to be met for the impugned legislation to reach the Charter's threshold successfully. For this reason, this legislation should: a) pursue an objective of general interest which justifies such a duplication of proceedings and penalties, b) contain rules ensuring coordination which limits to what is *strictly necessary* the additional disadvantage which results from a duplication of proceedings for the persons concerned, and c) provide for rules making it possible to ensure that the severity of all of the penalties imposed is limited to what is strictly necessary in relation to the seriousness of the offence concerned.[301]

[297] Case C- 537/16 *Garlsson Real Estate SA and Others v Commissione Nazionale per le Società e la Borsa (Consob)* [2018] ECLI:EU:C:2018:193.

[298] Joined Cases C-596/16 and C-597/16 *Enzo Di Puma v Commissione Nazionale per le Società e la Borsa (Consob) and Commissione Nazionale per le Società e la Borsa (Consob) v Antonio Zecca* [2018] ECLI:EU:C:2018:192.

[299] *Menci* (n 296) Opinion of AG M Campos Sánchez-Bordona, para 55; *Garlsson Real Estate SA* (n 297) Opinion of AG M Campos Sánchez-Bordona, para 77; see, eg M Simonato, 'Two Instruments but a Difficult Relationship? Some Upcoming Decisions of the CJEU on the Ne Bis In Idem' (*European Law Blog*, 15 November 2017), www.europeanlawblog.eu/2017/11/15/two-instruments-but-a-difficult-relationship-some-upcoming-decisions-of-the-cjeu-on-the-ne-bis-in-idem/; L Maulet, 'Le principe ne bis in idem, objet d'un «dialogue» contrasté entre la Cour de justice de l'Union européenne et la Cour européenne des droits de l'homme' (2017) 109 *Revue trimestrielle des droits de l' homme* 107; L Milano, 'Le principe *non bis in idem* devant la Cour de Luxembourg, vers un abaissement de la protection accordée au principe' (2019) 117 *Revue trimestrielle des droits de l'homme* 161.

[300] For most insightful comments on the three decisions of the Court see G Lo Schiavo, 'The Principle of Ne Bis In Idem and the Application of Criminal Sanctions: of Scope and Restrictions ECJ 20 March 2018, Case C-524/15, *Luca Menci* ECJ 20 March 2018, Case C-537/16, *Garlsson Real Estate SA and Others v Commissione Nazionale per le Società e la Borsa (Consob)* ECJ 20 March 2018, Joined Cases C-596/16 and C-597/16, *Enzo Di Puma v Consob and Consob v Antonio Zecca*' (2018) 14 *European Constitutional Law Review* 644.

[301] *Garlsson Real Estate SA* (n 297) Opinion of AG M Campos Sánchez-Bordona, para 63.

Certainly the Court has always in mind the Strasbourg Court's findings and underscored that its criteria are also compatible with the ECtHR's standing in the recent *A and B v Norway* case.[302] In the *Garlsson* case, the Court took a further step to elucidate what is deemed as an excessive burden that goes beyond the necessity test and held relatively that

> In those circumstances, it seems that the act of bringing proceedings for an administrative fine of a criminal nature under Article 187b of the TUF exceeds what is strictly necessary in order to achieve the objective referred to in paragraph 46 of the present judgment, in so far as the final criminal conviction is, given the harm caused to the company by the offence committed, such as to punish that offence in an effective, proportionate and dissuasive manner, which it is for the referring court to determine.'[303]

Overall, the *corpus* of cases decided by the two bodies suggests that there is an on-going struggle to establish coherent standards;[304] however, each of them approaches the issue differently. The Strasbourg Court opened the door of permissible derogations from the *ne bis in idem* concept and the CJEU, later on, passed through that door and turned the other way. In other words, the ECtHR's rationale was anchored to the requirement of the parallel criminal and administrative proceedings shaping a uniform set of legal actions, while the CJEU examined the *bis* condition through the lens of proportionality.

The underlying aim of the CJEU to promote openness pertaining to the existence of binary proceedings on the same offence might be connected to the initial mandate of the EU to safeguard the sound preservation of EU economic interests – this flows explicitly from the press release published on the occasion of the issuance of the three decisions.[305] At any rate, the correct assessment is left to Member States. The discretionary powers for this balancing task probably lie with national authorities, since the preliminary rulings do not involve questions close to the validity or the core of EU legislation.[306] Be that as it may, the CJEU managed to cautiously frame this context and provide Member States with useful guidance in this respect for future disputes.

Hence, the proportionality-centred approach of the CJEU which sets reasonable and legitimate limits to the *ne bis in idem* prohibition appears to be more in line with the intimate interplay between the concept and legal certainty in both international and domestic settings.

[302] ibid para 62.

[303] *Garlsson Real Estate SA* (n 297) paras 59, 61.

[304] J Baron and E Poelman, 'The Principle of Ne Bis in Idem: On the Ropes, but Definitely Not Defeated' (2018) 46 *Intertax* 805, 809.

[305] B Peeters, 'The Ne Bis In Idem Rule: Do the EUCJ and the ECtHR Follow the Same Track?' (2018) 4 *European Community Tax Review* 182, 185. See also the recent EU framework on the market abuse. Directive 2014/65/EU of the European Parliament and of the Council on markets in financial instruments and amending Directive 2002/92/EC and Directive 2011/61/EU [2014] OJ L173/349, Recital 23.

[306] M Luchtman, 'The ECJ's Recent Case Law on *Ne Bis In Idem*: Implications for Law Enforcement in a Shared Legal Order' (2018) 55 *CML Rev* 1717, 1748.

To date, the ECtHR seems to distance itself from the consolidation of legal guarantees setting the limits for the legitimate restriction to the *ne bis in idem* principle in line with its *Zolothukin* and *Engel* case law, which constituted milestones of its work for over a decade and whose echoes to Luxembourg resulted in the reconstruction of the latter's jurisprudence correspondingly. The Strasbourg Court's case law inevitably remains the first and foremost point of departure for its Luxembourg peer, as illustrated both explicitly with its reference to the *A and B v Norway* and implicitly with the preservation of the *Fransson* reasoning and the adoption of the *Engel* criteria.[307] In the three recent judgments, delivered in the era when accession still appeared a Gordian knot, the Court of Luxembourg selected an autonomous perception of the application of the said principle, writing a whole new page in the book of the inter-judicial dialogue between the two Courts.[308]

The autonomous *ne bis in idem* concept with specific regard to its transnational nature had already been explored in the *Spasic* judgment,[309] in which mutual trust, the cornerstone of the EU, seems to be doubted in the field of the area of freedom, security and justice.[310] Adopting a more security-oriented approach, the CJEU seemed to reconsider the notion of mutual recognition.[311] Unlike Advocate General Jaaskinsen, who underlined the necessity of an interpretation of the EU *ne bis in idem* concept in the light of the corresponding provisions of the ECHR,[312] the CJEU declined the possibility to scrutinise the key element of this case, the enforcement condition of CISA, in this context and mostly ignored the hesitations of the Advocate General who stated that the CISA *ne bis in idem* concept should be absolutely compatible with the level of extended protection offered by Article 50 CFR, always understood in accordance with the ECHR's non-derogable standards. He also held that Article 54 CISA definitely introduces a limitation to the application of *ne bis in idem* as interpreted under the Charter's wording, which puts into jeopardy its transnational character, especially in the field of the EU mutual trust system. Nevertheless, the Court automatically applied the Explanations of the Charter[313] and moved in the entirely opposite direction, declaring that the enforcement condition comes hand-in-hand with the right as enshrined in the EU Charter.[314]

[307] Lo Schiavo, 'The Principle of Ne Bis In Idem' (n 300).

[308] See especially M Vetzo, 'The Past, Present and Future of the Ne Bis In Idem Dialogue between the Court of Justice of the European Union and the European Court of Human Rights: The Cases of Menci, Garlsson and Di Puma' (2018) 11(2) *Review of European Administrative Law* 55.

[309] Case C-129/14 PPU *Zoran Spasic* [2014] ECLI:EU:C:2014:586.

[310] See A Marletta, 'The CJEU and the Spasic Case: Recasting Mutual Trust in the Area of Freedom, Security and Justice?' (*European Law Blog*, 8 January 2015), www.europeanlawblog.eu/?p=2655.

[311] *Zoran Spacic* (n 309), para 69.

[312] *Zoran Spacic* (n 309), Opinion of AG Jaaskinsen.

[313] Explanations related to the Charter of Fundamental Rights (n 150) paras 55–57.

[314] For a thorough analysis see J Vervaele, 'Schengen and Charter-Related *Ne Bis In Idem* Protection in the Area of Freedom, Security and Justice: *M* and *Zoran Spasic*' (2015) 52 *CML Rev* 1339, 1354–55.

However, this surprising appraisal of the Luxembourg Court was partially offset by two rulings, which both dealt with the notion of the final judgment when interpreting the autonomous EU *ne bis in idem* provision. More precisely, in the *M* case,[315] the Court held that the sole fact that a case could be reopened, if new evidence emerges, does not necessarily mean that the decision should be considered as final pursuant to Article 54 CISA. It also stated that the CISA standard on the matter must be interpreted in the light of Article 50 of the EU Charter, since both these provisions share the same meaning and scope as Article 4 of Protocol No 7 ECHR. In order to conclude with the more lenient approach of the notion of *final decision*, the Court explicitly based its reasoning to the cornerstone *Zolotukhin* judgment of the Strasbourg Court.[316]

Once again, in its *Kossowski* judgment,[317] delivered in June 2016, the question revolved around whether an unapplied order of the Polish Prosecutor, issued without examining the case on the merits, constituted a *final* judgment for the German judicial authorities, apt to trigger the application of the prohibition of double prosecution. The reasoning of the CJEU in the case at hand, appears more convincing as the Court, in accordance with its prior case law and Advocate General Bot's Opinion,[318] ruled that since the Polish authorities did not hear any witness in order to shed light on the victim's conflicting statements, as a result, they did not really examine the merits of the case. On these grounds, the Court rejected the *final* nature of the Polish prosecutor's decision. All that said, the CJEU seemed ready to revisit the EU concept of the final character of a decision, which was until recently totally based on the mutual recognition and mutual trust framework. However, this road could prove quite unsafe, particularly in the Area of Freedom, Security and Justice in which the mutual recognition standards provided an area where the suspects or convicted persons enjoyed a cross-border and thereby more protective version of the *ne bis in idem* principle.

Post-Lisbon, both judicial mechanisms strive to identify the proper balance between them, prioritising the more effective observance of fundamental rights in Europe. The differentiated understanding of *ne bis in idem* within EU law having a transnational character stood out again before the ECtHR which was recently invited to review its alleged breach under the Convention. Having already pronounced on this familiar case brought against France some years ago,[319] the applicant this time alleged that its previous conviction in Germany should have prevented its retrial in France. This decision on admissibility of the ECtHR is of merit since it crystallises the extremely cautious and respective standing of the

[315] Case C-398/12 *Criminal proceedings against M* [2014] ECLI:EU:C:2014:1057.

[316] ibid para 39.

[317] Case C-484/14 *Piotr Kossowski* [2016] ECLI:EU:C:2016:483.

[318] M Simonato, 'Ne Bis In Idem in the EU: Two Important Questions for the CJEU (Opinion of the AG in C-486/14 KUSSOWSKI)' (*European Law Blog*, 12 January 2016), www.europeanlawblog.eu/?p=3071.

[319] *Krombach v France*, Merits, ECHR 2001-II 1.

Court of Strasbourg towards its Luxembourg peer. In the *Krombach* decision on admissibility, the Court held that the fact of France and Germany being EU Members, and the transnational concept of the *ne bis in idem* principle within the EU legal order, do not affect the application of the corresponding provision of the ECtHR.[320]

The Court went further to declare that it does not have competence to apply rules contained in EU law or to pronounce on an alleged violation of those rules, except where a violation of an EU rule incidentally also violates a Conventional right. It is, hence, up to the Member States and in particular the national judiciary to interpret and apply national law in line with the provisions of EU law, and the Strasbourg Court is not in a position to rule on a potential violation of EU law. The role of the Court is limited to determining whether the effects of their decisions are compatible with the Convention. The Court found that it was not for the latter in this case to rule on whether the applicant's prosecution in France and his subsequent conviction violated the Union's law. On these grounds, the application was declared inadmissible.[321] The Strasbourg Court, here, refused to decide on the admissibility of a case under EU rules. But most importantly, it manifested the distinct applicable standards when it comes to *ne bis in idem* and made that distinction signalling its unwillingness to enter the sovereign territory of EU law from the 'back door'. Delivered almost five years after the milestone Opinion 2/13 that marked a turning point in its jurisprudence, the Strasbourg Court still feels that it should approach timidly such sensitive matters touching upon the allocation of competences between the two mechanisms.[322]

IV. Conclusion

The aim of this chapter was to shed some light to the specific terms of the direct application of the ECHR by the judicial mechanism of the EU, the Court of Justice. Besides the unquestionable influence of the Convention's principles on the formulation of EU human rights law, the judicial interplay between the Strasbourg and the Luxembourg Courts provided the latter with useful responses in legal fields in which the effective protection of fundamental rights was not a given, notably in a setting where common market and economic integration played the key roles. Therefore, despite the discrepancies observed, the CJEU, on the basis of the Convention's rules, developed and gradually improved the human rights dimension of its growing jurisprudence particularly with regard to the protection of private life, the procedural requirements of fair trial and, last but not least, the

[320] *Dieter Krombach v France* (dec), App no 67521/14 (ECtHR, 20 February 2018), para 38.

[321] ibid para 39.

[322] B van Bockel, '*Krombach* Returns to Strasbourg' (*ECHR Blog*, 16 May 2018), www.echrblog.blogspot.com/2018/05/guest-blog-commentary-on-ne-bis-in-idem.html.

ne bis in idem principle. Post-Lisbon, despite the enhanced scepticism around the complexity of the dual fundamental rights protection within the European legal space, the ECtHR remains the benchmark of EU human rights law, and with the requirement of accession which is now engraved in the Treaties, the Court of Luxembourg always pays meticulous attention to the relevant pronouncements of the ECtHR. Even though the road to Strasbourg proves to be remarkably long, and inconsistencies in terms of interpretation and standards of protection still stand out, the Luxembourg Court strives to foster 'peaceful' coexistence of the Charter with the Convention and their respective monitoring bodies in the hope of success of the perpetual accession project.

2

The Application of the ECHR as a Restriction Mechanism of EU Law

Besides the direct application of ECHR by the EU system, the fundamental rights' echo was also used by the Luxembourg judicature as a restriction mechanism in relation to the interpretation of the Union's rules, even in the most traditional fields of EU law.

More precisely, when the direct application of the ECHR provisions had dominantly become the *conditio sine qua non* parameter in cases in which the CJEU touched upon the fundamental rights dimension of EU legislation, in recent decades the Court has taken the further step of applying these provisions in order to determine whether several aspects of EU law are compatible with the fundamental rights doctrine, as already developed by the Luxembourg Court, in the sense of general principles of EU law. The adoption of the EU Charter brought new light into this area, since it gave the judges of the CJEU more effective control of the EU legislator with regard to human rights. In this chapter, I will embark on an analysis of the fields of EU law in which the ECHR had such an effect, starting from the limitations posed to the core principles of internal market (section I). This will be followed by an examination of the analogous implications of the Strasbourg Court's response to the EU data protection regime (section II), the practice of EU institutions (section III), and EU migration policies under the Dublin legislation (section IV).

I. The ECHR as a Ground for Derogation from the Internal Market Freedoms of the EU

A. The Equilibrium between Fundamental Rights and EU Fundamental Freedoms

The attempt of the Luxembourg Court to reconcile the fundamental freedoms of the EU internal market with the fundamental rights already incorporated in the EU system is the most striking example of the restricting effect of the ECHR with regard to the EU legal order. In the *ERT* case, the Luxembourg Court had famously declared that when Member States derogate from the exercise of the freedom to provide services, they must provide a justification compatible with – and interpreted in light of – the general principles of law and, in particular, the fundamental rights giving specific attention to the interpretation under the ECHR.[1]

In the wake of the *ERT* litigation,[2] the CJEU subsequently found itself in the challenging position of balancing the fundamental rights as embodied in the ECHR, which constituted the crucial material source of human rights in the EU until the adoption of the CFR, with the economic freedoms of the integrated common market.

The famous *Schmidberger* judgment[3] is a *locus classicus* in this field. Schmidberger, a German haulage company based in southern Germany, used to transport goods to Italy via Austria. More precisely, it used the Brenner Pass, to cross from Austria to Italy. Due to a demonstration on the Brenner motorway, organised by an environmental group, the Transitforum Austria Tirol, with authorisation by the Austrian authorities, Schmidberger's lorries were kept stationary and consequently, considerably delayed for four days. Schmidberger brought proceedings against Austria on the grounds that the Austrian authorities had failed to effectively guarantee free movement of goods in accordance with the EC Treaty, claimed damages in respect of the aforementioned grounds and sought compensation since the company's vehicles were prevented from operating on their normal route to Italy, in contravention of the EU free movement rules. The Austrian courts rejected the company's allegations,[4] since the latter had been fully aware in advance of the time and the location of the demonstration to be held on the Brenner motorway, and should have predicted its damaging effects or should have chosen an alternative transit route to Italy. The preliminary ruling concerned whether free movement of goods actually requires a state to keep open major motorways used for those purposes. In the context of the enforced judicial dialogue between the two European jurisdictions, the Austrian Court was, arguably, encouraged to ask the Court whether that requirement takes precedence over the protection of fundamental rights such as the freedom of assembly, as guaranteed by the Austrian Constitution and Article 11 ECHR.

The CJEU replied that not banning a demonstration by individuals on a transport route prima facie constituted a restriction to the free movement of goods. Yet, as for the Austrian authorities' motivation to permit the demonstration on

[1] Case C-260/89 *Elliniki Radiophonia Tileorassi AE (ERT) v Dimotiki Etairia Pliroforissis and Siotirios Kouvelas* [1991] ECR I-2925, paras 41–5.

[2] See also JJ Barcelló III, 'ECJ Review of Member State Measures for Compliance with Fundamental Rights' in JC Masclet, H Ruiz Fabri, C Boutayeb and S Rodrigues (eds), *L'Union européenne: union de droit, union des droits: mélanges em l'honneur du Professeur Philippe Manin* (Paris, Pedone, 2010).

[3] Case C-112/00 *Eugen Schmidberger Internationale Transporte und Planzüge v Republic of Austria* [2003] ECR I-5659.

[4] For further analysis see A Layard, 'Free Movement and Roadblocks: The Right to Protest in the Single Market: Case C-12/00 Schmidberger Internationale Transporte and Planzüge v Austria [2003] ECR I-5659' (2004) 6 *Environmental Law Review* 190, 190–95.

grounds of fundamental rights protection as laid down in its constitution and the ECHR, the CJEU stated, after referring to its *ERT* doctrine on fundamental rights, that 'since both the Community and its Member States are required to respect fundamental rights, the protection of those rights is a legitimate interest which, in principle, justifies a restriction of the obligations imposed by Community law, even under a fundamental freedom guaranteed by the Treaty such as the free movement of goods'.[5]

Confirming that common market freedoms are subjected to certain restrictions, the Luxembourg Court sought to achieve an equilibrium between the freedom of expression under Article 10 ECHR along with the freedom of assembly under Article 11 ECHR, and the EU freedom of movement. To that aim, it adopted a Strasbourg-centred examination of the Austrian authorities' position using an interpretational parallel of the two rights which do not constitute absolute rights and are, thereby, subjected to limitations. On this basis, taking into account the wide margin of appreciation that the state enjoys, the CJEU applied a Strasbourg-type proportionality test and thus, concluded that 'the national authorities were reasonably entitled, having regard to the wide discretion which must be accorded to them in the matter, to consider that the legitimate aim of that demonstration could not be achieved in the present case by measures less restrictive of intra-Community trade.'[6]

For numerous scholars,[7] in the present case, the CJEU 'put the ECHR on top of EU's normative hierarchy'[8] and, seemingly, that is true. Under increasing pressure to take human rights seriously, the CJEU clearly favoured the protection of fundamental rights over the economic freedom at stake. Indeed, the Court applied the proportionality test and examined the exceptions of Articles 10 and 11 paragraph 2, following the path of the Strasbourg Court, whenever conflicting rights/interests need to be weighted. A closer look at this milestone ruling, however, might give us another insight of the judges' delicate approach to the matter and the objectives they sought to serve. Notwithstanding the constant struggle of both the Strasbourg and the Luxembourg Courts to find the most suitable test as regards the degree of discretion afforded to states, the CJEU made only a slight reference to the equivalent test of the ECtHR. In fact, it pointed out that permissible derogations should definitely be 'in accordance with the law, motivated by legitimate aims, necessary in a democratic society and proportionate to the aim pursued'.[9]

[5] *Eugen Schmidberger Internationale Transporte* (n 3) para 74.

[6] ibid para 93.

[7] See especially L Scheeck, 'Diplomatic Intrusions, Dialogues, and Fragile Equilibria: The European Court as a Constitutional Actor of the European Union' in J Christoffersen and M Madsen (eds), *The European Court of Human Rights between Law and Politics* (Oxford, Oxford University Press, 2011).

[8] ibid 174.

[9] See especially C Brown, 'Case C-112/00, *Eugen Schmidberger, Internationale Transporte und Planzüge v. Austria*' (2003) 40 *CML Rev* 1499.

The ECtHR has applied such a test in similar cases, though highlighting in every case the wide discretion that the national authorities enjoy in this field. Besides, while applying Article 11 ECHR, the Strasbourg Court gave particular emphasis to the states' positive obligations to protect similar demonstrations from violent acts aiming to restrict or prevent their exercise and thus, secure the peaceful enjoyment of the right to assembly.[10] From this point of view, it is clear that both positive and negative actions of a Member State are relevant as a matter of protection of Article 11 ECHR. However, in contrast with the ECtHR's overall approach, the CJEU's tendency to look only at the state's intention to authorise the demonstration, rather than also take into account the aim or the purpose of the demonstrators, appears potentially insufficient when examining whether state liability under EU law existed. Additionally, the margin of appreciation granted to the national authorities when the freedom of assembly is at stake, stands closely linked to the nature of the demonstration held. Accordingly, the Strasbourg Court has ruled inter alia that political speech is given enhanced protection under the ECHR in comparison with commercial or artistic speech, and hence, a violation of the former requires stronger and more solid justification.[11]

Despite the fact that *Schmidberger* is one of the rulings in which the ECHR and the human rights embodied therein constituted the guiding principles for delimiting EU internal market freedoms, the approach of the Court of Justice created a certain ambiguity.[12] More precisely, the mere fact that the CJEU considers the protection of fundamental rights a legitimate interest which, in principle, constitutes a justification for the restriction of the obligations imposed by EU law,[13] leaves the matter open as regards the Court's rationale for this. It thus remains debatable whether the protection of fundamental rights is a mandatory requirement for the Court, or a derogation, exceptionally accepted, from the EU common market values. This is a question of who bears the burden of proof. While in the ECHR system, the state, as a proponent of economic interests, needs to justify a restriction on human rights, according to the Luxembourg Court, those who invoke the fundamental rights protection need to justify their actions and establish that the derogation from the freedom of movement is justified in the name of fundamental rights.[14]

[10] See, eg *Plattform "Ärzte für das Leben" v Austria*, Merits, Series A no 139 (1988); *Ouranio Toxo and Others v Greece*, Merits, ECHR 2005-X 245.

[11] See, eg *Castells v Spain*, Merits, Series A no 236 (1992); *Oberschlick v Austria (no 1)*, Merits, Series A no 204 (1991); *Lingens v Austria*, Merits, Series A no 103 (1986); *Markt Intern Verlag GmbH and Klaus Beermann v Germany*, Merits, Series A no 165 (1989); *Müller and Others v Switzerland*, Merits, Series A no 133 (1988).

[12] T Perišin, 'Interaction of Fundamental (Human) Rights and Fundamental (Market) Freedoms in the EU' (2006) 2 *Croatian Yearbook of European Law and Policy* 69, 89–90.

[13] *Eugen Schmidberger Internationale Transporte* (n 3) para 74.

[14] S de Vries, 'Balancing Fundamental Rights with Economic Freedoms According to the European Court of Justice' (2013) 9 *Utrecht Law Review* 169, 187.

Hence, although the Luxembourg Court appeared, with a heavy heart, to give precedence to the freedom of assembly and the freedom of expression over the exercise of the free movement of goods,[15] *Schmidberger* was the first of a series of cases that offered the CJEU the opportunity to dive into new fields posing fresh challenges for the EU system. Thus, the need for harmonisation as regards national standards,[16] the necessary ingredient of the economic integration in the EU common market, pushed the CJEU to use the ECHR and the Strasbourg Court's reasoning – even only ostensibly – as a vehicle to strike a happy medium when EU economic freedoms clash with human rights.

The Court of Justice soon revisited similar dilemmas in *Omega*.[17] Omega was a German undertaking operating a facility called 'Laserdrome' in Germany, where laser games were played. Among these games, players also had access to a murder simulation game with modern laser weapons, during which they were encouraged to shoot at sensory tags placed on the jackets of other players. The German police issued an order prohibiting these games, on the grounds that they constituted a danger to public order since the acts of simulated homicide and the trivialisation of violence thereby engendered were contrary to fundamental values prevailing in public opinion. The company claimed inter alia that the police order was contrary to EU law and specifically the free movement of services, as these games were imported from the United Kingdom, as Omega was contractually connected with Pulsar, a British company.

The Luxembourg Court held that the free movement of services had clearly been restricted, but the restriction could be justified.[18] According to the Court, the exploitation of laser games involving simulated murders clearly violated human dignity, a fundamental value enshrined in the German constitution. In its judgment, the CJEU aligned its approach with the Advocate General's approach on the matter[19] and emphasised also that human dignity constitutes a general principle of the Union's law, irrespective of the self-standing nature of this principle under German law.[20] In its attempt to ascertain whether the restriction of the free movement of services was proportional in light of the protection of human dignity, the Court of Justice clarified that 'the need for, and proportionality of, the provisions adopted are not excluded merely because one Member State has

[15] In relation to the reluctance to scale fundamental rights and fundamental freedoms in a hierarchical order, see also C Kombos, 'Fundamental Rights and Fundamental Freedoms: A Symbiosis on the Basis of Subsidiarity' (2006) 12 *European Public Law* 433, 449.

[16] See Scheeck, 'Diplomatic Intrusions, Dialogues, and Fragile Equilibria' (n 7) 174.

[17] Case C-36/02 *Omega Spielhallen und Automatenaufstellungs-GmbH v Oberbürgermeisterin des Bundesstadt Bonn* [2004] ECR I-9609.

[18] For a thorough analysis of the Court's judgment see the case note of T Ackermann, 'Case C-36/02, *Omega Spielhallen und Automatenaufstellungs-GmbH v. Oberbiirgermeisterin der Bundesstadt Bonn*' (2005) 42 *CML Rev* 1107.

[19] See, eg *Omega Spielhallen* (n 17), Opinion of Advocate General Stix-Hackl, paras 81–92. The Strasbourg Court has ruled that respect for human dignity is the very essence of the Convention. See especially *Pretty v United Kingdom*, Merits, ECHR 2002-III 155, para 64.

[20] *Omega Spielhallen* (n 17) para 34.

chosen a system of protection different from that adopted by another State'.[21] Put differently, there is no need for a common conception of the principle of human dignity in all Member States when it comes to the level of protection offered by EU law.

In this spirit, the Court concluded to a fundamental rights-compliant position according to which 'the contested order did not go beyond what is necessary in order to attain the objective pursued by the competent national authorities'.[22] As Sybe de Vries pointed out 'the particular nature of this case is that the Court first defined a typically *German* concept of human dignity as a general principle of *EU* law, and then, while applying the proportionality test, it demonstrated a predominantly Member State-friendly approach.'[23]

However, the Court was criticised for having applied the proportionality test softly,[24] limiting its review of the German order on laser games to the first element, namely the suitability of giving Member States large discretion *vis-à-vis* the protection of the economic interest of free movement. This is probably justified by the fact that the CJEU found itself in the uncomfortable position of ruling on a matter that not only concerns the conflict between fundamental freedoms and fundamental rights in the EU but also lies at the heart of the sensitive area of constitutional pluralism. Thus, the CJEU opted for a state-centric position since it focused particularly on the German constitutional particularity of human dignity, consequently denying the application of a common legal concept of human dignity in the Member States.[25] Interestingly enough, the Court, using the fundamental rights reasoning of the Advocate General, who thoroughly explored the status of human dignity,[26] combining and linking human dignity with the public policy rule, which is mostly used to restrict rather than protect human rights even under the ECHR, in order to justify derogation from the exercise of freedom of services within the EU internal market.

Closely resembling the *Omega* case, *Sayn-Wittgenstein*[27] is another CJEU case in which the Court drew inspiration from the ECHR and its Strasbourg counterpart when balancing fundamental rights with internal market freedoms. The litigant, Ms Ilonka Sayn-Wittgenstein, an Austrian citizen residing in Germany after her adoption by Mr Lothar Fürst von Sayn-Wittgenstein, a German citizen, obtained a new surname with the title of nobility in the form 'Fürstin von Sayn-Wittgenstein' ('Princess of Sayn-Wittgenstein'). Despite the fact that upon

[21] ibid para 38.
[22] ibid para 39.
[23] de Vries, 'Balancing Fundamental Rights' (n 14) 179.
[24] ibid.
[25] D Augenstein, 'Engaging the Fundamentals: on the Autonomous Substance of EU Fundamental Rights Law' (2013) 14 *German Law Journal* 1917, 1933–34.
[26] The Advocate General also referred to the provision of human dignity embodied in the EU Charter in Article 1 which reads as follows: 'Human dignity is inviolable. It must be respected and protected.' It is also worth mentioning that the Court made no reference to this provision.
[27] Case C-208/09 *Ilonka Sayn-Wittgenstein v Landeshauptmann von Wien* [2010] ECR I-13693.

her adoption she was registered in Austria with her new name, subsequently, the civil registrar of Vienna decided to erase the title of nobility from the litigant's birth certificate and to correct the previous registration to 'Sayn-Wittgenstein'. Having used the name continuously for 15 years, she challenged this decision before the Austrian courts as the aforementioned decision obliged her to use different names in two Member States and to prove her identity every time she crossed the borders. She also alleged that the Austrian authorities' decision breached her right to a name as a particular aspect of the protection of family life. The national court asked the CJEU whether non-recognition of the name, granted to her as a result of her adoption, amounted to an infringement of the freedom of movement[28] pursuant to Article 21 TFEU.

At first, the CJEU admitted that the refusal of Austrian authorities to recognise the noble elements of the litigant's surname posed a serious inconvenience[29] and a limitation on her right to protection of private life under Article 7 of the Charter of Fundamental Rights of the European Union (EUCFR) and Article 8 ECHR and her freedom of movement. Focusing on the reconciliation of the latter with Austria's constitutional abolition of nobility and the constitutional principle of equality of Austrian citizens, the CJEU interpreted this fundamental right, also enshrined in Article 20 CFR,[30] in the light of the public policy concept, using the example of the *Omega* case.[31] The Court reaffirmed once again its option for a stricter application of the concept of public policy when used as a justification for the derogation from a fundamental freedom, 'only if there is a genuine and sufficiently serious threat to a fundamental interest of society'.[32] Having repeated the wide margin of appreciation of national authorities and the EU's respect for Member States' national identities[33] – in the sense of the particular constitutional values as also provided by Article 4(2) TEU – the Court concluded that the refusal of the Austrian state to permit the acquisition or the use of titles of nobility by its nationals, with the aim of protecting the principle of equal treatment, was not disproportionate.[34] The Luxembourg Court referred, this time, to the element of national identity in the general context of the sensitive constitutional pluralism that the Court attempted to safeguard. According to Sybe de Vries, 'the ECJ on the one hand embraces the idea that Member States have considerable leeway in protecting their national constitutional space and identity, yet on the other that

[28] See especially LFM Besselink, 'Case C-208/09, *Ilonka Sayn-Wittgenstein v. Landeshauptmann von Wien*, Judgment of the Court (Second Chamber) of 22 December 2010' (2012) 49 *CML Rev* 671.

[29] See especially Case C-353/06 *Stefan Grunkin and Dorothee Regina Paul* [2008] ECR I-7639.

[30] Art 20 EUCFR reads as follows: 'Everyone is equal before the law.'

[31] *Ilonka Sayn-Wittgenstein* (n 27) para 83. See also K Lenaerts, 'EU Values and Constitutional Pluralism: The EU System of Fundamental Rights Protection' (2014) 34 *Polish Yearbook of International Law* 135, 155–57.

[32] *Ilonka Sayn-Wittgenstein* (n 27) para 86.

[33] See especially A von Bogdandy and SW Schill, 'Overcoming Absolute Primacy: Respect for National Identity under the Lisbon Treaty' (2011) 48 *CML Rev* 1417.

[34] *Ilonka Sayn-Wittgenstein* (n 27) para 95.

national identity is subject to a balancing approach where tensions arise with the economic freedoms.'[35]

The search for the ideal balance between fundamental rights and common market values in the sense of fundamental freedoms in the EU system was continued in the *Dynamic Medien* case.[36] Similar prevalence to fundamental rights was given over the free movement of goods in a dispute which revolved around the importation of Japanese cartoons to Germany. Their sale was prohibited due to the fact that the cartoons had not been examined and classified by the German competent authority, and consequently did not bear an age-limit label corresponding to such a classification. The referring Court asked whether this prohibition was in compliance with the free movement of goods and, in such a case, whether it could be justified. In this respect, the CJEU favoured the protection of the rights of the child on the basis of various international instruments which, according to the Court's appraisal, should be taken into serious consideration when applying the general principles of EU law.[37]

The Court inter alia referred particularly to the Union's specific provision of Article 24 CFR incorporating the rights of children in the EU law. Assessing the proportionality of the impugned measure, taken pursuant to German legislation with the aim of protecting children's well-being against information and materials injurious to them, limitations to the free movement of goods are acceptable when they correspond to the aim pursued and are, thereby, proportionate. The Court reiterated the wide discretion that Member States enjoy in this field due to the different levels of protection of the national rules with regard to children's interests.[38] Notably, the proportionality test[39] applied in *Dynamic Medien* is also seen from the procedural angle,[40] as the Luxembourg Court specifically added that the authorisation procedure which usually results in the measure at issue should be a readily accessible one which can be completed within a reasonable period of time, together with the condition that a refusal should also be easily challenged before a tribunal.[41]

Apart from the decision's added value in relation to the nature of the test exercised by the national authorities, the CJEU, with its explicit reference to the Charter, verified that this instrument may play the crucial role since it can render a fundamental right as a mandatory ground for justification of a restriction on free movement. Additionally, the protection of fundamental rights is not absolute

[35] de Vries, 'Balancing Fundamental Rights' (n 14) 189.

[36] Case C-244/06 *Dynamic Medien Vertriebs GmbH v Avides Media AG* [2008] ECR I-505.

[37] ibid paras 39–40.

[38] ibid para 49.

[39] See especially A Garde, 'The Best Interests of the Child and EU Consumer Law and Policy: a Major Gap between Theory and Practice?' in J Devenney and M Kenny (eds), *European Consumer Protection: Theory and Practice* (Cambridge, Cambridge University Press, 2012) 177–79.

[40] S Prechal, 'Free Movement and Procedural Requirements: Proportionality Reconsidered' (2008) 35 *Legal Issues of Economic Integration* 201, 204.

[41] *Dynamic Medien* (n 36) para 50.

either. Their enjoyment may be restricted when weighted with the internal market freedoms of the EU, as previously analysed with regard to the Luxembourg Court's case law on the matter. The jurisprudential values of the Court's balancing approach are actually illustrated in Article 52(1) of the Charter as well as in Article 52(3) and Article 4(2) TEU which entail that the Court must always take into account the provisions of the ECHR and the Strasbourg Court's case law, besides the national constitutional limits. However, as Sybe de Vries correctly put it, 'although the Charter reinforces the fundamentality and universality of EU fundamental rights, which should steer the orientation and interpretation of free movement rules in this field, the exact added value in conflicts between fundamental rights and the internal market freedoms remains unclear.'[42]

The above-mentioned cases are indicative of the influence of the ECHR that permitted the CJEU to transform fundamental rights and non-commercial interests into self-standing restrictions to cross-border trade protected on the basis of the fundamental freedoms in the EU common market.[43] Nevertheless, the position of the Court is not consistent throughout its judicial production: it is struggling[44] – just like the ECtHR – to conclude to the most suitable test and to further delimit the margin of appreciation of the Member States in this field.

B. The Particularity of Social Rights: Inconsistent Approaches

This struggle for the fairest reconciliation of competing rights and freedoms is even more evident when it comes to the interpretation of social rights clashing with the economic freedoms of the EU. Although the CJEU saw the questions related to collective action in the context of the inspiration already drawn from the ECHR system, its approach seems differentiated in the social rights field. In fact, this inconsistency clearly derives from the CJEU's position in the benchmark *Viking*[45] and *Laval*[46] cases, where the Court was called upon to assess the nature of

[42] S de Vries, 'The EU Single Market as "Normative Corridor" for the Protection of Fundamental Rights: The Example of Data Protection' in S de Vries, U Bernitz and S Weatherill (eds), *The EU Charter of Fundamental Rights as a Binding Instrument: Five Years Old and Growing*, Studies of the Oxford Institute of European and Comparative Law (Oxford, Hart Publishing, 2015) 241.

[43] For an overall analysis see also S Weatherill, 'From Economic Rights to Fundamental Rights' in S de Vries, U Bernitz and S Weatherill (eds), *The Protection of Fundamental Rights in the EU after the Lisbon Treaty*, Studies of the Oxford Institute of European and Comparative Law (Oxford, Hart Publishing, 2013) 11.

[44] S Curzon, 'Internal Market Derogation in Light of the Newly Binding Character of the EU Charter of Fundamental Rights' in G Di Federico (ed), *The EU Charter of Fundamental Rights: From Declaration to Binding Instrument*, Ius Gentium: Comparative Perspectives on Law and Justice 8 (Dordrecht, Springer, 2011) 152.

[45] Case C-438/05 *International Transport Workers' Federation v Viking Line* [2007] ECR I-10779.

[46] Case C-341/05 *Laval un Partneri Ltd v Svenska Byggnadsarbetareförbundet* [2007] ECR I-11767.

the right to strike in EU law and to weigh it up with the exercise of the economic freedom to provide services.

In *Viking*, a Finnish firm owning a ferry named *Rosella* sought to reflag the vessel and re-register it in Estonia because of the higher wages applicable according to the collective bargaining agreement under Finnish labour legislation, with the Finnish Seamen's Union. On the basis of the 'flag of convenience' policy, the International Transport Workers' Federation asked its affiliates to boycott the vessel and to take solidarity industrial action. Following this, and the threat of strike action by the Finnish Seamen's Union, the firm invoked the EU freedom of services and freedom of establishment provisions, seeking an injunction before the English High Court.

After affirming the applicability of economic freedoms also to trade unions,[47] the Court further held that collective bargaining and collective action were inseparably linked, and, hence, collective action also fell outside the scope of the freedom of establishment under Article 43 TEU.[48] In this regard, the CJEU emphasised that 'the right to take collective action, including the right to strike, must therefore be recognised as a fundamental right which forms an integral part of the general principles of Community law the observance of which the Court ensures.'[49] Nevertheless, the exercise of this right is not without certain limitations. The Court, interestingly, recalled the fact that the right to take collective action is also guaranteed by Article 28 CFR.

As for the justification, the Court, having already emphasised the fundamental character of the said right, taking into account the international law instruments ensuring the right to strike, namely the relevant provisions of the European Social Charter and of ILO Convention No 87 on Freedom of Association and the Right to Organise, underlined 'that the right to take collective action for the protection of workers is a legitimate interest which, in principle, justifies a restriction of one of the fundamental freedoms guaranteed by the Treaty.'[50] Subsequently, the CJEU declared the social purpose of the Union[51] and the need for reconciliation of the latter with the economic freedoms protected by EU law. The Court left to the national authorities great scope to apply the justification test[52] and it further referred to the Strasbourg Court's case law, to determine the appropriateness of the trade union's action.[53] Nevertheless, it abstained from giving much guidance to the national courts and was content to highlight, in clear contradiction to its prior *Schmidberger* approach, the aim of the collective action, focusing on whether it

[47] *International Transport Workers' Federation* (n 45) paras 36–7.
[48] Article 43 TEU, Consolidated Version of the of the Treaty on European Union [2008] OJ C115/13.
[49] *International Transport Workers' Federation* (n 45) para 44.
[50] ibid para 77.
[51] ibid para 79.
[52] ibid paras 85,87.
[53] ibid para 86.

indeed served the protection of workers. In this light, in order to establish a potential justification, the Court required there to be at issue a serious threat to jobs or conditions of employment.[54]

At this point, it seems preferable to look closer at the factual basis of the *Laval* ruling, which bears close resemblance to the former. In this case, the crucial question revolved around the right to strike in view of the problem of social dumping[55] and the interpretation of the Posted Workers Directive (hereinafter PWD).[56] Laval was a Latvian company, which operated in Sweden where it was engaged in a school renovation and, for that purpose, it sent workers to Sweden who earned significantly lower wages in comparison with their Swedish colleagues. Under these circumstances, the trade union started negotiations with the company with the ultimate objective of applying the existing collective agreement to the posted workers and thus, allowing the trade union to demand minimum wages on their behalf. In the aftermath of the negotiations' failure and the blockade of Laval's building sites, Laval addressed the Swedish Labour Court to challenge the collective action in the name of the free movement of services and to seek compensation for the losses it had suffered.

In response to the questions raised by the Swedish court, the Luxembourg Court followed mostly its reasoning in *Viking*. In doing so, it reiterated the fundamental character of the right to strike, stating at the same time that 'it must therefore be examined whether the fact that a Member State's trade unions may take collective action in the circumstances described above constitutes a restriction on the freedom to provide services, and, if so, whether it can be justified.'[57] Examining the conditions which form a context permitting a limitation to economic freedoms reaffirmed that such a limitation 'is warranted only if it pursues a legitimate objective compatible with the Treaty and is justified by overriding reasons of public interest'[58] In this regard, the Court of Justice acknowledged that 'the right to take collective action for the protection of the workers from social dumping may indeed constitute such an overriding reason of public interest'.[59]

[54] ibid para 81.

[55] See especially C Barnard, 'Social Dumping or Dumping Socialism?' (2008) 67 *Cambridge Law Journal* 262. For a general overview of the notion of social dumping see J Buelens and M Rigaux, *From Social Competition to Social Dumping*, Social Europe Series 35 (Cambridge, Intersentia, 2016).

[56] Directive 96/71/EC of the European Parliament and of the Council concerning the posting of workers in the framework of the provision of services (Posted Workers Directive – PWD) [1997] OJ L18/1. In March 2016, the European Commission published a proposal amending the Posted Workers Directive: European Commission, 'Proposal for a Directive of the European Parliament and of the Council amending Directive 96/71/EC of the European Parliament and of the Council of 16 December 1996 concerning the posting of workers in the framework of the provision of services' COM (2016) 128 final. The proposal was adopted on 28 June 2018. Directive (EU) 2018/957 of the European Parliament and of the Council amending Directive 96/71/EC concerning the posting of workers in the framework of the provision of services [2018] OJ L173/16.

[57] *Laval un Partneri Ltd* (n 46) para 96.

[58] ibid para 101.

[59] ibid para 103.

With regard to the PWD,[60] although not applicable in the present case due to the lack horizontal effect of the Directive, the Court included the latter in its proportionality test. Nevertheless, since, according to the Court's appraisal, the aim of the collective action was to require the company to observe the collective agreement for the building sector so as to adopt working conditions going beyond the minimum protection provided by the PWD,[61] the Court came to the conclusion that the obstacle which that collective action created cannot be justified on the basis of a fundamental rights reasoning.[62]

The Court surprisingly ruled that such collective actions cannot be justified in cases in which pay negotiations form part of a national legislative context lacking sufficient precision and accessibility 'that they do not render it impossible or excessively difficult in practice for such an undertaking to determine the obligations with which it is required to comply as regards minimum pay'.[63] Overall, the Court of Justice concluded that there was no justification for the aforementioned restriction.[64] Last but not least, in a social policy case before the Luxembourg Court, *Alemo-Herron*,[65] the Court once again declined to prioritise social rights over economic interests protected under EU law. More precisely, the Court interpreted the (economic) freedom to conduct a business, enshrined in Article 16 EUCFR, so as to rule that so-called dynamic clauses of collective agreements were not enforceable against the transferee in the event of the transfer of an undertaking, despite the fact that the Transfer of Undertakings Directive[66] also allows Member States to enact legislation promoting collective agreements which are more favourable to employees.[67] In line with *Viking* and *Laval*, even when the Charter came into play, the Court was content to follow a rather narrow interpretation of the legislation at stake, sidestepping, thus, the Charter's effect in this field.

The *Viking* and *Laval* cases, greatly debated in academia, signified a *revirement* in the case law of the Luxembourg Court with regard to the balancing exercise between fundamental freedoms and rights, raising multiple questions in multiple levels.

Firstly, in these cases, the right to strike and the right to take collective action were treated differently by the Court, in comparison with the other fundamental

[60] In essence, the Posted Workers Directive (PWD) 96/71 required host states to apply 'a nucleus of mandatory rules for minimum protection' in the areas listed in Art 3(1)(a)–(g) PWD.

[61] See relatively Case C-346/06 *Dirk Rüffert v Land Niedersachsen* [2008] ECR I-1989; Case C-319/06 *Commission of the European Communities v Grand Duchy of Luxemburg* [2008] ECR I-4323.

[62] *Laval un Partneri Ltd* (n 46) para 108.

[63] ibid para 110.

[64] ibid paras 116–20.

[65] Case C-426/11 *Mark Alemo-Herron and Others v Parkwood Leisure Ltd* [2013] ECLI:EU:C:2013:521.

[66] Council Directive 2001/23/EC on the approximation of the laws of the Member States relating to the safeguarding of employees' rights in the event of transfers of undertakings, businesses or parts of undertakings or businesses [2001] OJ L82/16.

[67] Art 8 of the Directive reads as follows: 'This Directive shall not affect the right of Member States to apply or introduce laws, regulations or administrative provisions which are more favourable to employees or to promote or permit collective agreements or agreements between social partners more favourable to employees.'

rights when clashing with the EU economic freedoms. The mere fact that the right to strike cannot be seen by the CJEU as a self-standing ground for justification of a potential restriction of a common market freedom, but only in the wider goal of worker protection, seems problematic, especially in the light of the previous jurisprudence of the Court. In this respect, the social rights at issue must also be assessed under the proportionality test in order to determine whether any less restrictive measures are available. The enjoyment of the right to collective action appears, therefore, as a last resort, and this approach seems also detrimental for the fundamental character of this social right.[68]

When examining the Court's methodology, particularly on the question of the proportionality test, we can easily deduce that the Court did not look at the collective action as a fundamental right that was in direct conflict with a common market freedom, but rather focused on the aim pursued during the exercise of this right, namely the protection of workers, which, in the Court's view, is one of the overriding reasons of public interest recognised by the Court. It is thus not surprising that when it comes to the objectives that need to be reconciled, the Court refers to the market freedoms on the one hand and to social policy objectives on the other. Therefore, 'the *fundamentality* of the right at issue is lost out of sight and the balancing is essentially undertaken between the free movement provision and an "overriding reason of public interest" – a narrow exception to the free movement rule which thus has to be interpreted strictly.'[69] In other words, in contrast with the way the Court dealt with the right to assembly and freedom of expression (*Schmidberger*) or human dignity (*Omega*), in *Viking* and *Laval* the Luxembourg Court opted for a defensive recognition of social rights. For the CJEU, when trade unions are being found to be in breach of EU free movement provisions for taking collective action, it is up to them to defend themselves and justify this breach under extremely strict terms.[70] Stephen Weatherill correctly revealed another element of this U-turn approach of the Court in relation to the strict application of the social rights in these cases, observing that

> it follows also from the Court application of the justification test that only action aimed at protecting the jobs of union members is recognized as capable of being justified under EU law. The Court appears to have excluded the possibility of more long-term strategic action taken by unions insofar as it impedes cross border economic activity. This constitutes a dramatic incursion into the scope of collective labour rights as they have been developed – and fought for – over time.[71]

[68] C Barnard, *The Substantive Law of the EU: the Four Freedoms* (Oxford, Oxford University Press, 2010) 259.

[69] V Kosta, *Fundamental Rights in EU Internal Market Legislation*, Modern Studies in European Law 58 (Oxford, Bloomsbury, 2015) 221–22.

[70] ACL Davies, 'One Step Forward, Two Steps Back? The *Viking* and *Laval* Cases in the ECJ' (2008) 37 *Industrial Law Journal* 126, 139.

[71] S Weatherill, 'Protecting Internal Market from the Charter' in S de Vries, U Bernitz and S Weatherill (eds), *The EU Charter of Fundamental Rights as a Binding Instrument: Five Years Old and Growing*, Studies of the Oxford Institute of European and Comparative Law (Oxford, Hart Publishing, 2015) 224.

For several scholars a potential explanation of this overly criticised approach of the Court of Justice could rely on the personal movement rights of EU citizens, which were under scrutiny in these cases, bearing in mind that trade unions could easily touch upon social protectionism, leading to retaliatory measures and eventually to fragmentation. In other words, measures were at issue, albeit socially legitimate, which potentially cloaked protectionism and hence jeopardised the fundamental value of protectionism.[72] At the same time, the Luxembourg Court might have been motivated by the fact that trade unions are not regulated by public law and as a result, they should not enjoy equally wide discretion as Member States. In *Laval* the CJEU held that trade unions, 'not being bodies governed by public law … cannot avail themselves of that provision by citing grounds of public policy in order to maintain that collective action such as that at issue in the main proceedings complies with Community law.'[73]

Justified or not, the CJEU's perception of social rights reflected in *Viking* and *Laval* diverges from the Strasbourg Court's judicial practice which was also marked, during the same period, by a *revirement juriprudentiel*, in 2008. Until then, the Strasbourg Court had repeatedly refused[74] to consider the right to collective bargaining and the right to enter into collective agreements as an inherent element of Article 11 ECHR.[75] Arguably, one may argue that this could be explained by the fact that, within the system of the Council of Europe, a clear distinction[76] was made between the civil and political rights enshrined in the ECHR and social and economic rights embodied in the European Social Charter (ESC).[77]

Among other rights, the ESC explicitly provides the right to bargain collectively (Article 6 ESC/RESC) which, unlike its previous interpretation, constituted the legal source for this new approach of the ECtHR, clearly revealed in the benchmark ruling *Demir and Baykara v Turkey*[78] and confirmed in *Enerji Yapi-Yol Sen v Turkey*.[79] In these cases, the Strasbourg Court interpreted

[72] de Vries, 'Balancing Fundamental Rights' (n 14) 189.

[73] *Laval un Partneri Ltd* (n 46) para 84.

[74] The ECtHR delimited the scope of application of Art 11 ECtHR due to the existence of the relative provision of the ECR of Art 6 and thus, denied applying the former in cases where the right to take collective action was at stake. See, eg *Swedish Engine Drivers' Union v Sweden*, Merits, Series A no 20 (1976), para 39; *Schmidt and Dahlström v Sweden*, Merits, Series A no 21 (1976), para 34; *UNISON v the United Kingdom* (dec) ECHR 2002-I 491; *Wilson, National Union of Journalists and Others v the United Kingdom*, Merits, ECHR 2002-V 49, para 44.

[75] See ECtHR, Guide on Article 11 of the European Convention on Human Rights-Freedom of Assembly and Association, 30 April 2022, 43.

[76] As regards the classical perception of civil political rights and social economic rights, see I Koch, *Human Rights as Indivisible Rights: The Protection of Social-Economic Demands under the European Convention on Human Rights*, International Studies in Human Rights 101 (Leiden, Martinus Nijhoff Publishers, 2009) 5–9.

[77] The European Social Charter (ESC) was adopted in 1961 and its revised version was adopted in 1996 and entered into force in 1999. The ESC was accompanied by a light supervisory "regime", the European Committee on Social Rights, an expert body entitled to supervise compliance with the (ESC) which was also brought back to life after the revision of the text of the Charter. It is noticeable that the jurisprudence of the Committee reveals great interaction with EU law especially after the entry into force of the EUCFR. European Social Charter (revised) (Strasbourg, 3 May 1996).

[78] *Demir and Baykara v Turkey* [GC], Merits, ECHR 2008-V 333.

[79] *Enerji Yapi-Yol Sen v Turkey*, Merits, App no 68959/01 (ECtHR, 21 April 2009).

Article 11 in the context of its 'living instrument' doctrine and also used international instruments to overturn its prior case law and incorporate the right to bargain collectively within the scope of application of Article 11.[80] The Court, interestingly enough relied to specific international sources – among which we can also find the Article 28 CFR – not only because they contributed to the recognition of the right under the Convention, but also because they constituted crucial elements for the determination of whether a restriction to Article 11 is necessary in a democratic society, and therefore, proportionate.

Arguably, if we examine comparatively the perception of social rights of the two European legal systems it follows that, notwithstanding the influence of the Strasbourg Court on the CJEU, the inconsistency with regard to the general structure of the balancing exercise is more than clear.

Firstly, in methodological terms, as Albertine Veldman successfully put it,

> where the ECtHR is compelled to scrutinize the lawfulness of the particular *restriction* or even a ban on the fundamental right to strike, the ECJ must assess the lawfulness of *resorting* to the fundamental right to strike when it considers the particular strike action to be an infringement of a fundamental economic freedom.[81]

Clearly, for the Strasbourg Court, the starting point is the possible breach of the fundamental right to strike, whereas for the CJEU the starting point is the possible breach of a fundamental common market freedom. Secondly, when the question of proportionality arose, unlike the *Schmidberger* and *Omega* cases[82] and the ECtHR's test, the CJEU opted for a rather strict application of the test requiring a sufficient cause for strike action, and more specifically, 'a serious threat to jobs or employment conditions', as well as the exhaustion of all other means to resolve the dispute.

Last but not least, the incoherence in the application of social rights between the two European judicial fora led also to different potential limitations to social rights afforded by the two systems. For the ECHR system, economic interests do not constitute an acceptable ground justifying a restriction of social rights, since they are not considered to normally amount to a pressing social need under Article 11(2). On the other hand, the exercise of a fundamental social right as such is not an adequate ground for justification; however, taking collective action may potentially fit the EU scheme of limitations on free movement provisions, depending on the circumstances of the case. At any rate, in the EU system, the protection of employers' economic interests of establishment or to provide services in the field of the internal market might rank over fundamental social rights.

[80] *Demir and Baykara* (n 78) para 154.

[81] A Veldman, 'The Protection of the Fundamental Right to Strike within the Context of the European Internal Market: Implications of the Forthcoming Accession of the EU to the ECHR' (2013) 9 *Utrecht Law Review* 104, 113.

[82] The Court here departed from its previous longstanding position according to which great leniency was granted to the Member States in the context of this assessment.

Nevertheless, taking into account the new social objectives embodied in the Treaties[83] and the Charter's provisions (Articles 28 and 29 EUCFR), the increased importance given to these rights becomes apparent in the context of the post-Lisbon framework. Even though the Charter put social rights and economic rights on an equal footing, the primordial question here is what is the added value of the Charter in this respect. Since the Charter is addressed to the Member States when implementing EU law, without extending the field of application of the latter or granting any new or modifying any existing powers, its application in social rights cases seems problematic, given that this is a territory mainly regulated by national legislation with restricted competence of the EU in the field.[84] Since *Demir and Baykara*[85] the ECtHR covers the right to take collective action. Article 28 CFR has to be interpreted as a corresponding right of the ECHR providing – at least – the same level of protection. Given that the Strasbourg Court bases its reasoning on universal and regional instruments[86] for determining the notion and the content of the right, the conclusion could be drawn that the same could be expected within the EU legal system as well.

All that said, the adoption of the Charter does not seem to indicate, as we speak, a new era as regards the hierarchical order between social rights and economic rights/freedoms. The distinction of the Charter's provisions as rights and principles[87] apparently makes this classification more complicated, as some of the social rights of Chapter IV of the Charter under the title 'Solidarity' are generally accepted as *principles*. However, in a recent case of the Luxembourg Court, namely the *AMS* case,[88] the latter faced this dilemma – right or principle – concerning the implementation of a Directive[89] potentially giving horizontal (and direct) effect to Article 27 EUCFR which provides for the worker's right to information and consultation within an undertaking. Notwithstanding the fact that the Court rejected the revolutionary proposal of Advocate General Cruz Villallon,[90] who suggested

[83] See Art 3 TEU.

[84] R O'Gorman, 'The ECHR, the EU and the Weakness of Social Rights Protection at the European Level' (2011) 12 *German Law Journal* 1833, 1857; see also Art 5(2), (3) TFEU. The EU's competence, hence, is neither exclusive nor shared. In the spirit of Art 5 TFEU, the EU exercises a kind of coordination competence to provide arrangements within which EU Member States must coordinate social policies.

[85] KD Ewing and J Hendy, 'The Dramatic Implications of *Demir and Baykara*' (2010) 39 *Industrial Law Journal* 2.

[86] It is worth mentioning that the Court did not consider it necessary that the international texts referred to have been ratified by Turkey. *Demir and Baykara* (n 78) para 78.

[87] Explanations related to the Charter of Fundamental Rights [2007] OJ C303/17, Explanation on Art 52(5).

[88] Case C-176/12 *Association de médiation sociale v Union locale des syndicats CGT and Others* (*AMS*) [2014] ECLI:EU:C:2014:2.

[89] Directive 2002/14/EC of the European Parliament and of the Council establishing a general framework for informing and consulting employees in the European Community [2002] OJ L80/29. This directive could be relied upon in a horizontal dispute between an employee and his employer so as to set aside a national law implementing the directive.

[90] *AMS* (n 88), Opinion of Advocate General Cruz Villalon.

to indeed allow some sort of horizontal direct effect of a Directive implementing a 'principle' in the Charter, this issue remains open for the Court.[91] Advocate General Cruz Villallon's suggestion could actually enhance the legal effectiveness of the social rights within the EU.[92] In cases in which economic fundamental freedoms come into conflict with social rights, the Charter is not likely to upset the traditional context of assessing national measures triggering the free movement legislation in light of the *Viking & Laval* jurisprudence. Whether the accession of the EU to the ECHR, if finally achieved, will reposition this balance, giving to the former a more human rights-friendly dimension as regards the protection of social rights within the Union, is still under discussion.

From this analysis it emerges that, in recent decades, fundamental protection has been at the heart of the Luxembourg Court's jurisprudence. However, the new element is the fact that the CJEU faced the new challenge of reconciling human rights protection with the EU economic fundamental freedoms. Sometimes successfully (*Schmidberger* and *Omega*) and sometimes less successfully (*Viking* and *Laval*), this balancing task, influenced by the scheme that the ECtHR traditionally uses to strike a balance between conflicting rights, gave the CJEU the opportunity to accept, albeit in an inconsistent manner, that fundamental rights may outweigh the internal market freedoms so as to restrict the application of the EU rules. We should not, though, ignore the fact that this asymmetry is deep-rooted in the systemic conditions for an autonomous interpretation of fundamental rights in the name of the *sui generis* character of the Union, whose ultimate foundation is the internal market.[93]

Nevertheless, there is also the opposite reading of this jurisprudential approach of the Court, expressed vividly by the former President of the CJEU, Judge Vassilios Skouris. President Skouris stressed that there is no hierarchy between fundamental rights and fundamental freedoms within EU law. As for the balancing procedure, he explained its point remarking that

> we have to keep in mind that this only occurs when fundamental rights are used as a countercheck to the application of the rights resulting from the four economic freedoms. When a fundamental right is seemingly fully applicable along with a conflicting fundamental freedom then the role of the Court is that of balancing conflicting interests and not that of balancing conflicting principles of law. In addition, the task of the Court becomes even more delicate when fundamental rights are used to interpret and expand the scope of a fundamental freedom.[94]

Whatever approach we adopt, judging from the evolving jurisprudence of the Court in light of the ECtHR's methodology, the development of a new mechanism

[91] *AMS* (n 88) para 45.

[92] A Veldman and S de Vries, 'Regulation and Enforcement of Economic Freedoms and Social Rights: a Thorny Distribution of Sovereignty' in T van den Brink, M Luchtman and M Scholten (eds), *Sovereignty in the Shared Legal Order of the EU* (Cambridge, Intersentia, 2015) 91.

[93] Augenstein, 'Engaging the Fundamentals' (n 25) 1937.

[94] V Skouris, 'Fundamental Rights and Fundamental Freedoms: The Challenge of Striking a Delicate Balance' (2006) 17 *European Business Law Review* 225, 239.

for fundamental rights protection in the EU was revealed not only as a necessary complement to the transformation of the four economic freedoms of the EU Treaty but also as a counterweight to those freedoms, with the aim of establishing their proper position within the EU architecture, even if that requires the subordination of economic freedoms to fundamental rights.

The emerging question, however, is whether the Union will continue to be ruled mainly by an economic concern with fundamental rights in the internal market, or 'whether fundamental rights will succeed in giving voice to a genuine political debate about what is entailed in having a market in common.'[95]

II. The ECHR Standards of Protection: The Impact to EU Data Protection Law and Jurisprudence

Data protection definitely constitutes an area of law where potential conflicts between opposing fundamental rights may emerge, as illustrated by the ECtHR's case law. The EU legislator was also lately confronted with the increasing need to regulate this new area of the Union's legislation. Unavoidably, the CJEU incorporated bit by bit the fundamental rights dimension in its jurisprudence to achieve a fairer and more human rights-oriented application of EU secondary law with regard to data protection. But what happens when fundamental rights do not function as a hermeneutical tool or a complement of the said legislation and run counter to the latter?

Within the context of ongoing technological advances and the cross-border exchange of information, especially via the Internet, the multiple challenges posed to human rights in relation to the protection of personal data could not have been ignored by the EU legal order. Hence, the Court seems to have departed from its initial reserved position, especially after the coming into play of the Charter. One could find the first signs of this effect in the *Volker und Schecke* case,[96] in which the CJEU invalidated some clauses of a regulation for breaching the provisions of the Charter on privacy.[97]

In this case, an agricultural partnership complained against the publication of details of financial aid that it was receiving pursuant to the Regulation No 259/2008, seeking to ensure transparency, particularly as regards the use of Community funds within the context of the Common Agricultural Policy. Hence, the validity of the Regulation was at issue in light of the violation of the respect for private life and the right to personal data protection under Articles 7 and 8 EUCFR

[95] Augenstein, 'Engaging the Fundamentals' (n 25) 1938.

[96] Joined Cases C-92/09 and C-93/09 *Volker und Markus Schecke GbR v Land Hessen* [2010] ECR I-11063.

[97] For a thorough analysis of this case see M Bobek, 'Joined Cases C-92 & 93/09, *Volker und Markus Schecke GbR and Hartmut Eifert*, Judgement of the Court of Justice (Grand Chamber) of 9 November 2010' (2011) 48 *CML Rev* 2005.

respectively. The Court reiterated, at first, that, in this balancing exercise between the objective of transparency and the guarantee of the fundamentality of the protection of privacy, it must take into account the application of the corresponding right under Article 8 ECHR.[98] Referring to the ECtHR's jurisprudence,[99] the CJEU interpreted broadly the notion of 'private life' so as to incorporate also activities in the professional sphere, such as information on income received by natural persons in their business capacity. At first, the Court held that the interference with the rights enshrined in Articles 7 and 8 EUCFR within the implementation of the Regulations at issue was provided for by law. Secondly, it acknowledged that the aim pursued by the aforesaid legislation was to serve the general interest of transparency stated in Articles 1 and 10 TEU and in Article 15 TFEU.[100]

Examining the proportionality of the measure, the CJEU recalled the *Satamedia* case[101] and further highlighted that taxpayers had a right to be kept informed of the use of public funds, but also stressed the necessity of striking a proper balance between the conflicting interests and the necessity of ascertaining whether publication on a website of the names of beneficiaries and the amounts of agricultural aid received did or did not go beyond what was absolutely necessary. In light of Articles 7 and 8 EUCFR, the Court underlined that, since the publication was effected with no distinction with regard, eg, to the duration, frequency, nature, or amount of aid received, the Council and the Commission had not taken into account alternative – and less onerous – methods of publishing information. Therefore, the Court concluded that there is no automatic priority given to the objective of transparency pursued by the EU policies and declared invalid the relevant articles of Regulation No 1290/2005 and Regulation No 259/2008.[102]

As discussed in the previous section, striking the correct balance is not new territory for the EU judges, but now it is under the umbrella of the Charter that this exercise will be constantly carried out. This time, the right balance is sought not only between fundamental rights and EU internal market freedoms, but also between conflicting fundamental rights, both embodied in the EU Charter.[103] Nevertheless, the Court was criticised since, even though it appeared to follow the proportionality test under Article 52(1) EUCFR, it finally followed a two-step proportionality test, avoiding examination of the *stricto sensu* proportionality of the publication at stake as it contented itself with putting the appropriateness and the necessity of the latter under scrutiny. The added value of the case is that the Luxembourg Court emphasised the *strict necessity* requirement when looking at

[98] *Volker und Markus Schecke GbR* (n 96), para 52.

[99] See accordingly the previous chapter with regard to the direct application of Art 8 ECHR by the CJEU in cases where legal persons are involved.

[100] *Volker und Markus Schecke GbR* (n 96), paras 67, 68.

[101] ibid, para 77; see also Case C-73/07 *Tietosuojavaltuutettu v Satakunnan Markkinapörssi Oy and Satamedia Oy* [2008] ECR I-9831(Chapter A, section 1.a).

[102] *Volker und Markus Schecke GbR* (n 96), para 89.

[103] F Fontanelli, 'The European Union's Charter of Fundamental Rights: Two Years Later' (2011) 3 *Perspectives on Federalism* 22.

the potential limitations or derogations in relation to the protection of personal data.[104] It thereby avoided the tough balancing exercise in the context of the narrow proportionality concept. Indeed, the Luxembourg Court transferred the two-paragraph structure of Article 8 ECHR into Article 8 of the Charter, suggesting that Article 8(1) should be read as laying down the right to personal data protection, whereas Article 8(2) and 8(3) would introduce the conditions for any lawful restriction to the right.[105] If that position – neglecting the particular structure of Article 8 EUCFR – is indeed taken consciously by the CJEU, serious questions are raised not only concerning the very existence of Article 52 EUCFR and its relation with the above-mentioned rights, but also with regard to the very essence of the right to data protection.[106] Despite the critique on this newly adopted approach of the Court,[107] the *Volker und Schecke* case constituted a dynamic step in the road that the CJEU has apparently taken towards a much stricter scrutiny of the EU legislation on data protection, leaving a restricted margin of appreciation to the national authorities.[108]

This tendency was manifestly confirmed in the landmark *Digital Rights Ireland* ruling,[109] in which the Luxembourg Court opted to strike down the Data Retention Directive[110] in its entirety. The preliminary reference procedure, initiated by the Irish High Court and by the Austrian Verfassungsgerichtshof, touched upon the legality and thus the validity of the Directive in light of Articles 7 and 8 of the Charter. In the aftermath of terrorist attacks in Europe, the Directive placed an obligation on Internet and telephone service providers of publicly available electronic communications services and public communications networks to retain specific types of data relating to the communications of individuals for the purposes of the 'prevention, detection and investigation of serious crime'. These retained types of data were telecommunications traffic data relating to e-mails, internet access and internet telephony, location data, and data needed to identify a subscriber or registered user. Notwithstanding the fact that the text of an e-mail was not retained, the date, time and identifiers relating to

[104] See, eg A Lind and M Strand, 'A New Proportionality Test for Fundamental Rights?: The Joined Cases C-92/09 and C-93/09 Volker und Markus Schecke GbR (C-92/09) and Hartmut Eifert (C-93/09) v. Land Hessen' (2011) Swedish Institute for European Policy Studies European Policy Analysis 7/2011, 6, www.uu.diva-portal.org/smash/get/diva2:441211/FULLTEXT01.pdf.

[105] G Gonzalez Fuster, 'Fighting for Your Right to What Exactly? The Convoluted Case Law of the EU Court of Justice on Privacy and/or Personal Data Protection' (2014) *2 Birkbeck Law Review* 263, 269.

[106] H Kranenborg, 'Article 8: Protection of Personal Data' in S Peers, T Hervey, J Kenner, A Ward (eds), *The EU Charter of Fundamental Rights: A Commentary* (Oxford, Hart Publishing, 2014) 261.

[107] ibid.

[108] See, eg Case C-291/12 *Michael Schwarz v Stadt Bochum* [2013] ECLI:EU:C:2013:670; Case C-446/12 to C-449/12 *WP Willems and Others v Burgemeester van Nuth and Others* [2015] ECLI:EU:C:2015:238.

[109] Joined Cases C-293/12 and C-594/12 *Digital Rights Ireland Ltd v Minister for Communications, Marine and Natural Resources and Others and Kärntner Landesregierung and Others* [2014] ECLI:EU:C:2014:238.

[110] Directive 2006/24/EC of the European Parliament and of the Council on the retention of data generated or processed in connection with the provision of publicly available electronic communications services or of public communications networks and amending Directive 2002/58/EC (Data Retention Directive) [2006] OJ L105/54.

its sender and recipient had to be retained for a period of at least six months and at most two years.[111]

The Court focused, first and foremost, on the validity of the Directive at stake in light of the rights to privacy, data protection and freedom of expression as embodied in the EU Charter. Having declared the relevance of Articles 7 and 8 with regard to the validity of the Directive and putting aside the examination of Article 11 EUCFR, the CJEU stated that

> those data, taken as a whole, may allow very precise conclusions to be drawn concerning the private lives of the persons whose data has been retained, such as the habits of everyday life, permanent or temporary places of residence, daily or other movements, the activities carried out, the social relationships of those persons and the social environments frequented by them.[112]

Therefore, the Court ruled that the obligations deriving from the Directive to retain data as well as the access to that data by Member States' authorities constituted an interference with the right to privacy, and since the Directive was providing for processing of personal data, it also violated the right to the protection of personal data.

As for the justification of the infringement, the CJEU examined the proportionality of the violation pursuant to Article 52(1) EUCFR and stressed that the essence of the rights at stake was respected. It therefore held that 'the fight against international terrorism in order to maintain international peace and security constitutes an objective of general interest'[113] and that 'data relating to the use of electronic communications are particularly important and therefore a valuable tool in the prevention of offences and the fight against crime, in particular organised crime',[114] concluding that the Directive under scrutiny in the present case fulfilled this purpose.

With regard to the final element of the necessity stage of the proportionality test, the CJEU reiterated that derogations from fundamental rights should only be accepted when strictly necessary, and held that the Directive did not provide clear and precise rules regarding the extent of the interference. The EU legislature did not require a clear and strong connection between the data retained and serious crime or public security.[115] Additionally, the Directive failed to provide either substantive or procedural conditions posing limits to the access and use of the data retained by competent national authorities. Nor did the Directive provide objective criteria on the basis of which the time period of the retention of the data could be determined.[116] Regarding data security, the Directive also lacked clear

[111] See especially O Lynskey, 'The Data Retention Directive Is Incompatible with the Rights to Privacy and Data Protection and Is Invalid in its Entirety: *Digital Rights Ireland*' (2014) 51 *CML Rev* 1789.
[112] *Digital Rights Ireland* (n 109) para 27.
[113] ibid para 42.
[114] ibid para 44.
[115] ibid para 59.
[116] ibid para 64.

safeguards for the protection of the retained data as it refrained from clarifying that the data must be retained within the EU and therefore, within the control of national data protection authorities. On these grounds, the Directive was declared *ab initio* invalid by the Court.

The Court, for the first time, blatantly used the EU Charter as a vehicle to strike down an entire EU Directive and to put severe pressure to EU institutions to modify the legal context of the retention of data, confirming the tremendous significance of privacy and data protection within the EU. But what are the implications of the Court's pronouncement in *Digital Rights Ireland* for the EU legal order?

The first and more practical consequence of this milestone judgment relies on its immediate effect. Since the Court's judgment manifestly declared the data retention scheme incompatible with the EU Charter, all legislative measures adopted by the Member States with the aim of implementing the Data Retention Directive will be open to judicial scrutiny as well. National courts can strike down legislation implementing the Directive with no need of additional preliminary reference to the Luxembourg Court. As Federico Fabbrini noted, 'the effects of the ECJ judgment, therefore, are likely to spill over into the national legal system, ensuring a new advanced standard of protection for privacy and personal data throughout the EU'.[117]

What is also surprising about the reasoning of the CJEU's appraisal is the analysis of the interplay between the 'essence' of the right and the concept of proportionality. It is also noteworthy that the Court clearly makes a distinction between the two: respecting the very essence of a right is not sufficient because even if the latter is respected, the legislation at stake can still be disproportionate. Another significant element of the ruling, as Steve Peers correctly stressed, is 'the development of a doctrine indicating when strict scrutiny of the EU legislature's interference with fundamental rights should apply'.[118] That definitely relates to the ECtHR's jurisprudence, which the Court cited many times in its reasoning.[119] Nevertheless, the application of the Charter by the CJEU gave an opportunity to the Luxembourg Court to raise even more the standards posed by its Strasbourg Court which, as we discussed in the previous chapter, clearly served as a 'springboard' for this evolution of the CJEU's case law in this field as it expanded significantly the application of Article 8 ECHR.[120] However, the Luxembourg Court, unlike its Strasbourg counterpart, has recognised a restricted margin of appreciation

[117] F Fabbrini, 'Human Rights in the Digital Age: The European Court of Justice Ruling in the Data Retention Case and its Lessons for Privacy and Surveillance in the U.S.' (2015) 28 *Harvard Human Rights Journal* 65, 88.

[118] S Peers, 'The Data Retention Judgment: The CJEU Prohibits Mass Surveillance' (*EU Law Analysis*, 8 April 2014), www.eulawanalysis.blogspot.fr/2014/04/the-data-retention-judgment-cjeu.html.

[119] *Digital Rights Ireland* (n 109) paras 35, 47, 54–55.

[120] B Petkova, 'Towards an Internal Hierarchy of Values in the EU Legal Order: Balancing the Freedom of Speech and Data Privacy' (2016) 23 *Maastricht Journal of European and Comparative Law* 421, 431.

to Member States when implementing data protection rules even when national security comes into play.[121]

In a nutshell, this ruling definitely opened the door for a stricter scrutiny exercised by the CJEU, particularly in cases in which digital rights are affected. Despite the granted impact of the ECtHR, the Charter appears to be the game-changer in this area and this is also reaffirmed by another milestone data protection case, the *Facebook* or *Schrems* case,[122] delivered by the CJEU in 2015. *In casu*, the emerging matter of the protection of personal data, available through social networks, was at issue. In light of the Edward Snowden revelations and the controversy on mass surveillance conducted by US intelligence services, Maximillian Schrems, an Austrian national and a Facebook user, addressed a complaint to the Irish DPA, arguing that his transferred personal data were subjected to mass surveillance in the United States. The legal basis of such transfers of personal data was the EU/US 'Safe Harbour' agreement, reached in 2000. This was built upon a Commission decision adopted under the Data Protection Directive which declared the United States an *adequate* destination for personal data as far as American companies were willing to enforce this agreement (by signing up) through a self-certification mechanism guaranteeing compliance with a set of data protection rules equivalent to those incorporated in EU Data Protection legislature.

The Irish data protection authority refused to pronounce on the applicant's complaint, so he subsequently challenged the DPA's decision before the Irish High Court, which clearly expressed doubts that the 'Safe Harbour' legal framework was compatible with EU law. Thus, it addressed a preliminary question to the CJEU asking whether the DPAs of Member States should have the power to oppose data transfers to the United States in similar cases.

The CJEU first ruled that *adequate level of protection*, the term used in the Data Protection Directive, should be interpreted as 'requiring the third country in fact to ensure, by reason of its domestic law or its international commitments, a level of protection of fundamental rights and freedoms that is essentially equivalent to that guaranteed within the EU'.[123] Additionally, the CJEU relied on the independent character of the DPAs in order to reaffirm the ongoing obligation for the European Commission or competent DPA to review any adequacy decision in light of any changes in circumstances having arisen after the decision's adoption.

As for the European Commission, it was content to only examine the adequacy of the Safe Harbour agreement, ignoring 'the bigger picture' of applicable US law[124]

[121] *Digital Rights Ireland* (n 109) para 47. F Fabbrini, 'The EU Charter of Fundamental Rights and the Rights to Data Privacy: the EU Court of Justice as a Human Rights Court' in S de Vries, U Bernitz, and S Weatherill (eds), *The EU Charter of Fundamental Rights as a Binding Instrument: Five Years Old and Growing*, Studies of the Oxford Institute of European and Comparative Law 20 (Oxford, Hart Publishing, 2015) 282.

[122] Case C-362/14 *Maximillian Schrems v Data Protection Commissioner* [2015] ECLI:EU:C:2015:650. See also Case C-498/16 *Maximilian Schrems v Facebook Ireland Limited* [2018] ECLI:EU:C:2018:37.

[123] *Maximillian Schrems v Data Protection Commissioner* (n 122) para 73.

[124] ibid para 43.

and its conformity with relevant international agreements. Hence, the decision under discussion failed to guarantee a sufficient level of data protection in the United States equivalent to that formulated by the EU law requirements laid down by EU data protection law. Regarding DPAs' powers to investigate data transfers which have been made lawful pursuant to a binding European Commission adequacy decision, the Court of Justice confirmed 'that the national supervisory authorities are responsible for monitoring compliance with the EU rules concerning the protection of individuals with regard to the processing of personal data and the legality of the relevant data transfers.'[125]

Therefore, the CJEU underlined that provisions of the Data Protection Directive must be applied in conformity with the fundamental human rights ensured by the EU Charter, and most importantly the rights to private and family life, the protection of personal data, and the right to an effective remedy and to a fair trial. In this regard, despite the fact that the Commission's decisions 'are in principle presumed to be lawful', and as such, they 'cannot eliminate or reduce the powers expressly accorded to the national supervisory authorities by Article 8(3) of the Charter and Article 28 of the directive.'[126] In the context of the limits of mass surveillance declared in its prior *Digital Rights* judgment, the additional element of the absence of effective judicial redress was not compatible with the EU Charter either. According to the Court's reasoning, the restriction of the DPAs' competence to review data transfers in order to determine whether or not the level of data protection in the United States within the context of the Safe Harbour Agreement is adequate, was also considered another legal flaw of the EU Commission's Decision. All that said, the Court of Justice invalidated the entire Decision.

Looking more carefully at the basic aspects of the case, it is more than evident that following the Court's findings in *Google Spain* and *Digital Rights Ireland*, the Court now declares that even when a separate regime for external transfers is under scrutiny, an almost identical level of protection is required in order to be compatible with the EU Charter's provision related to data protection. However, as Steve Peers observed,

> with respect, the Court's interpretation is not convincing, since the word 'adequate' suggests something less than 'essentially equivalent', and the EU Charter does not bind third States. But having said that, the American rules on mass surveillance would violate even a far more generous interpretation of the meaning of the word 'adequate'.[127]

The CJEU's standing not only reveals its belief that, in the post-Lisbon era, an even higher level of data protection is required under the Charter, but also its option for an application of such an enlarged protection as regards data transfers to

[125] ibid para 47.
[126] ibid paras 52–53.
[127] S Peers, 'The Party's Over: EU Data Protection Law after the Schrems Safe Harbour Judgment' (*EU Law Analysis*, 7 October 2015), www.eulawanalysis.blogspot.gr/2015/10/the-partys-over-eu-data-protection-law.html.

third countries, introducing, thus, an extraterritorial effect of the Charter's provisions regarding digital rights.

'By defining the standard that third countries must meet to be declared "adequate" as that of essential equivalence with EU law, the CJEU has set the global data protection bar at a high level.'[128] As a result, many third countries willing to conclude agreements similar to the Safe Harbour Agreement need to revisit their data protection legislation and practice in order to meet the standards set out in *Schrems*.

In this regard, the Court restricted itself to conclude that there had been an unjustifiable violation of the rights on the grounds of the general mass surveillance of the content of communications which affected the 'essence' of the rights at issue. This is indicative of the fact that the Court takes the right to privacy so seriously that it reached the conclusion that extended access to personal data by public authorities, even in the name of national security, affects the 'essence' of the right to private life under Article 7 of the Charter. Thus, no proportionality test or balancing exercise involving other rights and freedoms is required as far as the core of this right is breached.[129]

Although the Charter appears as the ultimate measure of data protection – applied in line with the standards of the Strasbourg Court – the post-Lisbon legal architecture might create ambiguity with regard to the application of the Charter's data protection standards when national security is involved. On the one hand, under Article 4(2) TEU the competence of national security weigh entirely upon Member States, whereas on the other, the Charter sets a significantly high standard for the data protection within the EU in the *Schrems* judgment.[130] Consequently, this divergence cannot be easily resolved since it is not always possible to distinguish situations in which personal data are processed for national security purposes. Personal data are collected and transferred for purposes totally irrelevant to national security reasons, such as commercial purposes, and are subsequently subjected to an assessment by national intelligence agencies.

Notably, the invalidation of the Safe Harbour Agreement, despite its fundamental rights dimension, had considerable political implications and risked causing a severe transatlantic rift with regard to the applicable data protection policy. More than 5,000 American and EU undertakings were using the invalidated agreement as a foundation to legally transfer personal data to US servers.[131] As a result of a two-year negotiation, the new EU-US Privacy Shield, which came to replace the

[128] C Kuner, 'Reality and Illusion in EU Data Transfer Regulation Post *Schrems*' (2017) 18 *German Law Journal* 881, 893.

[129] Nonetheless, it is striking how the Luxembourg Court concluded that there had been a violation of the essence of right to private life under Art 7 EUCFR but not to a violation of the essence of the right to the protection of personal data as enshrined in Art 8 EUCFR.

[130] Kuner, 'Reality and Illusion' (n 128) 897.

[131] S Shackelford, 'Seeking a Safe Harbour in a Widening Sea: Unpacking the EJC's *Schrems* Decision and What it Means for Transatlantic Relations' (2015) Kelley School of Business Research Paper no 15–78, www.papers.ssrn.com/sol3/papers.cfm?abstract_id=2680263.

previous framework, representing a serious attempt to enhance the level of protection of individual digital rights in line with the *Schrems* judgment, was reached in February 2016.[132] Providing a rather detailed and weighty agreement regarding transatlantic exchange of data, the EU-US Privacy Shield imposes 'strong obligations on companies handling data', 'clear safeguards and transparency obligations on US government access', 'effective protection of individual rights', along with an 'annual joint review mechanism'.

Nevertheless, several doubts have already been expressed in academia as regards whether it is possible to have any real guarantees for the right to data protection and to private life without a legislative shift to provide for the 'essentially equivalent' degree of data protection required by the *Schrems* judgment.[133] The European Parliament decided to refer the proposed EU/Canada agreement on passenger name records (PNR) data to the CJEU, on the basis of a unique procedure, questioning its compatibility with the rights to privacy and data protection. That judgment will have enormous implications on the legislative as well as on the political level since the separate EU/USA and EU/Australia treaties on PNR data and the proposed PNR Directive will be, as a result, placed under discussion too. This is not the first time that a PNR judgment was delivered by the Court. In 2004, the CJEU was asked to rule on the original EU/USA treaty. Passenger name records contain information provided by passengers and collected by airlines for commercial purposes: passenger names, dates and itinerary of trip and even hotel bookings, car rentals, train journeys, travel associates, etc. This may permit profiling, under specific circumstances, as it definitely gives a massive insight into personal data and thus, into a passenger's private life.

Surprising as it is nowadays, notwithstanding the fact that the question of privacy was also raised back then, the Luxembourg Court opted for a rather restricted analysis and was content to rule that the EU/USA treaty had an inappropriate legal basis for an anti-terrorist measure, which has taken the form of an international agreement.[134] However, the Opinion of Advocate General Mengozzi[135] reveals the constant effort of the EU judicial system to come up with the correct equilibrium between privacy and national interest, as this question is always on the table in light of the present terrorist danger. He stated that when it comes to proportionality, the measures adopted should be not only less intrusive but also sufficiently effective. In the light of the more recent pronouncement of ECtHR in *Zakharov*, in which the latter required 'reasonable suspicion' to permit an interference with the right to private life, the Advocate General highlighted, nevertheless, that in the balancing process the specificity of PNR data should

[132] The European Commission adopted the EU-US Privacy Shield in July 2016. European Commission, 'European Commission launches EU-U.S. Privacy Shield: Stronger Protection for Transatlantic Data Flows' (Press Release, 12 July 2016), www.europa.eu/rapid/press-release_IP-16-2461_en.htm.

[133] Kuner, 'Reality and Illusion' (n 128); Peers, 'The Party's Over' (n 127).

[134] N Skandamis, F Sigalas and S Stratakis, 'Rival Freedoms in Terms of Security: The Case of Data Protection and the Criterion of Connexity' (2007) Challenge, Liberty and Security Research Paper No 7, 15, www.aei.pitt.edu/7588/1/Cp7.pdf.

[135] Opinion 1/15 [2017] ECLI:EU:C:2017:592, Opinion of Advocate General Mengozzi.

also be taken into consideration. More particularly, these data are designed to be based on profiling methods, even though they are not collected for surveillance purposes. Therefore, the main issue here is that the suspicion is not prior to the collection and processing of PNR data but realised following to the collection and processing of the data.[136] Pursuant to the EU-Canada PNR agreement, as well as the new PNR Directive, air carriers are not obliged to proceed to an analysis of the data by themselves, but may leave the processing to the Canada Border Services Agency or to the new 'Passenger Information Units'. There are no guarantees, thus, that it is from this data processing that suspicions will then emerge and then be further analysed by law enforcement authorities.

The CJEU confirmed the line of reasoning of the Advocate General in its *Opinion 1/15*[137] and held that the impugned agreement prima facie interfered with Articles 7 and 8 of the Charter exercising a lengthy proportionality test to ascertain whether this interference could be permitted in the name of public security. Having examined every part of the draft agreement and the specific aspects of the individual rights of the passengers, the Court considered that the measures enshrined therein do not meet the necessity criterion (*stricto sensu*) providing in practice the Member States with strict guidelines for re-drafting the agreement.[138] At any rate, the legal context of data protection within the EU post-Lisbon architecture, particularly after the adoption of the EU Charter, is totally different. Despite the emerging need of extended anti-terrorist protection in Europe, the mass surveillance jurisprudence of the Luxembourg Court has lately had a 'domino effect',[139] with significantly effective results in the field of data protection, and not only within the EU legal order.

Yet, in stark contradiction to the *Schrems I* judgment, the Court engaged in an in-depth evaluation of the decision under scrutiny while addressing similar questions in *Schrems II*,[140] delivered in July 2020. Within the familiar context of the regulation of transborder data flows, the CJEU affirmed the validity of the standard contractual clauses (SCCs) for cross-border data transfers under Commission Decision 2010/87/EU,[141] but invalidated Commission Decision

[136] M Lassale, 'Opinion 1/15: Advocate General Mengozzi Looking for a New Balance in Data Protection' (*European Law Blog*, 18 October 2016), www.europeanlawblog.eu/?p=3395.

[137] Opinion 1/15 [2017] ECLI:EU:C:2017:592.

[138] See, eg C Kuner, 'Court of Justice International Agreements, Data Protection, and EU Fundamental Rights on the International Stage: Opinion 1/15, *EU-Canada PNR*' (2018) 55 *CML Rev* 857; A Vedaschi and C Graziani, 'PNR Agreements between Fundamental Rights and Natural Security: Opinion 1/15' (*European Law Blog*, 23 January 2018), www.europeanlawblog.eu/2018/01/23/pnr-agreements-between-fundamental-rights-and-national-security-opinion-115/.

[139] S Peers, 'The Domino Effect: How Many EU Treaties Violate the Rights to Privacy and Data Protection?' (*EU Law Analysis*, 25 November 2014), www.eulawanalysis.blogspot.fr/2014/11/the-domino-effect-how-many-eu-treaties.html.

[140] *Maximilian Schrems v Facebook Ireland Limited* (n 122).

[141] The Decision was later amended by Commission Decision 2016/2297. Commission Implementing Decision (EU) 2016/2297 of 16 December 2016 amending Decisions 2001/497/EC and 2010/87/EU on standard contractual clauses for the transfer of personal data to third countries and to processors established in such countries, under Directive 95/46/EC of the European Parliament and of the Council (notified under document C(2016) 8471) OJ [2016] L344/100.

2016/1250, namely the legal basis of the EU-US Privacy Shield that succeeded the controversial Safe Harbour Agreement. The Luxembourg Court's decision thoroughly examined the adequacy of this new decision that aimed to regulate data transfers to third countries in the light of the relevant Charter Provisions (Articles 7, 8, 47 EUCFR). A more flexible, yet stringent, approach was adopted by the Court as it applied a four-fold test of minimum standards in order to eliminate the risk of abuse: (1) the primacy of US law enforcement requirements over those of the Privacy Shield; (2) the lack of necessary limitations and safeguards on the power of the authorities under US law; (3) the lack of an effective remedy in the United States by EU data subjects; and (4) deficiencies of the Privacy Shield Ombudsman mechanism.[142]

Irrespective of the strong political will supporting the coherent regulation of international data transfers, the Court has persistently focused on securing the adequate application of EU data protection standards as reflected in the GDPR and the Charter. For the CJEU, the message to states seeking alliances of data policies with the EU is loud and clear: all personal data transfers to third countries (outside EU territory) should meet the requirements of adequate data privacy standards of protection. Arguably, the rationale behind this robust approach concerning the extraterritorial control of trans-border data flows is largely connected to extraterritorial surveillance.

It thus developed high hopes with regard to the data protection of the EU data subjects. At the same time, it equally raised significant concerns considering the future of such extraterritorial transfers. For some commentators, the Court's line of reasoning suffers from a significant lack of pragmatism[143] or even from a lack of certainty when it comes to its legal grounds.[144] On the other hand, arguments about creeping EU data imperialism[145] are gaining ground across the Atlantic,[146] given the practical implications of the EU-US data alliance or of future adequacy decisions of the EU with third counties. Whether the Court has gone too far remains to be seen.

At this point, we should not neglect the Strasbourg Court's perspective, which is quite revealing of the judicial dialogue between Luxembourg and Strasbourg

[142] *Maximilian Schrems* (n 122), paras 164–202.

[143] C Kuner, 'The Schrems II Judgment of the Court of Justice and the Future of Data Transfer Regulation' (*European Law Blog*, 17 July 2020), www.europeanlawblog.eu/2020/07/17/the-schrems-ii-judgment-of-the-court-of-justice-and-the-future-of-data-transfer-regulation/.

[144] T Christakis, 'After Schrems II: Uncertainties on the Legal Basis for Data Transfers and Constitutional Implications for Europe' (*European Law Blog*, 21 July 2020), www.europeanlawblog.eu/2020/07/21/after-schrems-ii-uncertainties-on-the-legal-basis-for-data-transfers-and-constitutional-implications-for-europe/#para_2_a.

[145] S Baker, 'How Can the U.S. Respond to Schrems II?' (*Lawfare*, 21 July 2020), www.lawfareblog.com/how-can-us-respond-schrems-ii.

[146] P Swire, '"Schrems II" backs the European Legal Regime into a Corner – How Can it Get Out?' (*Privacy Perspectives*, 16 July 2020), www.iapp.org/news/a/schrems-ii-backs-the-european-legal-regime-into-a-corner-how-can-it-get-out/#; J Daskal, 'What Comes Next: The Aftermath of European Court's Blow to Transatlantic Data Transfers' (*Just Security Blog*, 17 July 2020), www.justsecurity.org/71485/what-comes-next-the-aftermath-of-european-courts-blow-to-transatlantic-data-transfers/.

in the data protection field. In two major cases the ECtHR probably felt the need to align its case law with that of the CJEU, particularly after the *Digital Rights Ireland* and *Schrems* doctrine and hence, to enhance the protection offered to individuals in the era of mass surveillance.

At first, in the *Roman Zakharov* case,[147] Russian legislation was at issue, after the applicant challenged the surveillance practices of the Russian intelligence agencies, claiming mass interception of telephone communications in the name of national security. The ECtHR sidestepped the 'victim status' issue that arose, as the Court's task is not normally to review *in abstracto* a Contracting Party's legislation due to the mere existence of the secret surveillance methods elucidating particular conditions which justify this deviation from the general rule of admissibility. Subsequently, the Court, in light of *Digital Rights Ireland*, which was included in the section mentioning the applicable law, moved on to specify minimum safeguards that need to be established in the context of mass surveillance legal frameworks in order for the latter to be in line with Article 8 CFR. National legislation should offer sufficiently clear rules as regards the categories of people likely to have their communications intercepted, the duration of the measures, the procedures for storing, collecting and destroying data, the rules concerning the authorisation and supervision of surveillance, and the notification of surveillance measures related to the availability of effective remedies. Taking a strong position against secret surveillance practices, the ECtHR not only developed its own jurisprudence so as to set new rules with regard to the protection of personal data when interpreting Article 8 ECHR but also has definitely raised questions about the validity of a whole surveillance system.[148]

Additionally and on the same page, the ECtHR delivered its famous *Szabo and Vissy v Hungary*[149] case in which the Court had the opportunity to review the Hungarian secret surveillance system. The Court reiterated its reasoning and applied the criteria laid down in its prior *Zakharov* judgment to determine whether the interference with Article 8 was justified or not. In this judgment, the Strasbourg Court referred *expressis verbis* to the jurisprudential developments of the CJEU and more particularly to the *Digital Rights Ireland* case, as well as to the recently delivered *Schrems* ruling reaffirming its tendency to align its case law with the high standards of protection offered within the EU legal order. The Strasbourg Court followed the traces of the CJEU in *Schrems* in which the safeguards of an entire surveillance regime of a particular state were under scrutiny, weighted against fundamental rights protection.

[147] *Roman Zakharov v Russia* [GC], Merits, ECHR 2015-VIII 205.

[148] See, eg P De Hert and PC Bocos, 'Case of Roman Zakharov v. Russia: The Strasbourg Follow Up to the Luxembourg Court's Schrems Judgment' (*Strasbourg Observers*, 23 December 2015), www.strasbourgobservers.com/2015/12/23/case-of-roman-zakharov-v-russia-the-strasbourg-follow-up-to-the-luxembourg-courts-schrems-judgment/.

[149] *Szabó and Vissy v Hungary*, Merits, App no 37138/14 (ECtHR, 12 January 2016).

Nevertheless, at a time of increased terrorist threats, and anti-terrorist policies that are among the major priorities of most European governments, the strict minimum standards set by both European Courts will be tough for any European mass surveillance legislature to live up to. Despite this pessimistic perception of the current situation, the *Zakharov* and *Szabo and Vissy* cases constitute significant revelations of the evolving position of the Strasbourg Court, which is to be welcomed since the latter used its tools and the Luxembourg Court's rulings as a source of inspiration to elucidate the incompatibility of such mass surveillance measures with the provisions of the ECHR.[150]

Hence, it can be argued that in these cases, as Cole and Vandendriessche observed, 'the European Court of Human Rights has taken the deep pass into the box from the CJEU that had originally profited from an opening pass by the ECtHR and has scored a clear goal with these two judgments'.[151] Thus, despite the *lacunae* in the data protection field in Europe and the numerous questions seeking answers in the mass surveillance era, the interrelationship between the two judicial mechanisms appears to be heading in the right direction for a more effective protection of personal data even in the hardest of times. Although the Charter is now the game-changer as regards the level of EU human rights protection, the power of the ECHR is still 'alive and kicking' within the EU legal order. This is also verified by the recently delivered Opinion of Advocate General Saugmandsgaard Øe in the joined cases of *Watson and Tele2*[152] concerning the new data retention regime in which the Court was asked inter alia whether *Digital Rights Ireland* extended the scope of Article 7 and/or Article 8 of the Charter beyond that of Article 8 of the ECHR, as interpreted by the ECtHR. The Advocate General reaffirmed, in light of the ECtHR, the paramount importance of the level of protection offered by the ECHR, which should be the main regulatory element when the Luxembourg Court interprets the provisions of the Charter which correspond to the Convention. He also took the view that the meaning of the wording 'provided for by law' used in Article 52(1) of the Charter needs to be the same as that ascribed to it in connection with the ECHR, so that the 'ECHR standard' could be attained and legal certainty – through consistent interpretation – could be ensured.[153] This position taken by the Advocate General seems even more thought-provoking after Opinion 2/13 and the freezing of the accession process, since it appears to have released the power and luminosity of the ECHR.[154]

[150] M Cole and A Vandendriessch, 'From *Digital Rights Ireland* and *Schrems* in Luxembourg to *Zakharov* and *Szabó/Vissy* in Strasbourg: What the ECtHR Made of the Deep Pass by the CJEU in the Recent Cases on Mass Surveillance' (2016) 2 *European Data Protection Law Review* 121.

[151] ibid 128.

[152] Joined Cases C-203/15 and C-698/15 *Tele2 Sverige AB v Post- och telestyrelsen and Secretary of State for the Home Department v Tom Watson and Others* [2016] ECLI:EU:C:2016:970, Opinion of AG Saugmandsgaard ØE.

[153] ibid paras 140–43.

[154] M White, 'The New Opinion on Data Retention: Does it Protect the Right to Privacy?' (*EU Law Analysis*, 27 July 2016), www.eulawanalysis.blogspot.fr/2016/07/the-new-opinion-on-data-retention-does.html.

It is in this spirit that we should examine the leading *Big Brother Watch v UK* case.[155] In this long-anticipated judgment, the Court took the chance to reshape the data protection jurisprudence of the latter in more realistic terms, adopting at the same time a remarkably integrating approach towards the applicable standards of EU data protection law. Again having as a starting point the Snowden revelations, 14 NGOs submitted joint applications to the Court challenging the mass interception activities exercised by the UK intelligence services and alleging that they led to an unlawful interference with Article 8 ECHR. The Court ruled that the impugned actions of the UK intelligence services constitute a breach of the Convention; however, it also attempted to rationalise the approach of its case law when it comes to the requisite reconciliation of the protection of data protection with state surveillance practices. The Strasbourg Court emphasised the utility parameter, and recalling the wide margin of appreciation that states enjoy when identifying the most appropriate measures to safeguard national security, the Court stressed that 'bulk interception regimes did not per se fall outside this margin'.[156] Yet it is noteworthy that the Court recalls specific standards set out in its earlier judgments: the nature of offences which may give rise to an interception order; a definition of the categories of people liable to have their communications intercepted; limits on the duration of interception; the procedure to be followed for examining, using and storing the data obtained; the precautions to be taken when communicating the data to other parties and the circumstances in which intercepted data may or must be erased or destroyed.[157]

Throughout its argumentation, the Strasbourg Court could hardly overlook the Luxembourg Court's standards. It, nevertheless, refused to enrich the list of minimum standards, introduced in the *Watson* decision of the Luxembourg Court, with which an interception scheme should comply;[158] namely the need to provide evidence of reasonable suspicion before intercepting communications, the presence of judicial authorisation, and the obligation to notify the individuals subject to interception.[159]

Even though this lengthy judgment in *Big Brother Watch* appears to constitute a departure from the stringent approach of bulk interception policies that both European institutions have adopted in the past, the judgment's added value is also related to the safeguards it sets out.[160] Without losing sight of the CJEU's relevant case law,[161] the Strasbourg Court used as a point of orientation the latter and

[155] *Big Brother Watch and Others v the United Kingdom*, Merits, App nos 58170/13, 62322/14 and 24960/15 (ECtHR, 13 September 2018).

[156] ibid para 314.

[157] ibid para 307.

[158] *Tele2 Sverige AB v Post* (n 152).

[159] ibid para 316.

[160] ibid para 328–47. See also D Murray and P Fussey, 'Bulk Surveillance in the Digital Age: Rethinking the Human Rights Law Approach to Bulk Monitoring of Communications Data' (2019) 52 *Israel Law Review* 31, 55.

[161] *Tele2 Sverige AB v Post* (n 152) para 224–36, 463, 467.

took a further step to say something that Luxembourg perhaps wishes to admit. Strasbourg appears to draw a distinction between mass surveillance and bulk surveillance which is not less intrusive than targeted surveillance to protect from terrorist attacks and to ensure the criminal punishment of the perpetrators.[162] As it flows from the outcome of the *Big Brother Watch* decision, this new perception of surveillance is, as it must be, inextricably linked to specific safeguards and the traditional 'necessity test'. Given the fact that the ruling was later referred to the Grand Chamber, this was not the last word on the Strasbourg Court's understanding of bulk surveillance. In fact, the Grand Chamber delivered its highly anticipated ruling on 25 May 2021[163] along with its sibling judgment, the *Centrum för rättvisa v Sweden*.[164] The Grand Chamber took stock from the Chamber's pronouncements and attempted to elucidate its contemporary approach of bulk interceptions in a rather lengthy and complex judgment which has already raised a chorus of criticism in academia.[165] Far from demonising bulk interception per se, the utility argument has gained significant ground and dictated the judgment of the Court, mostly seen as the starting point of normalisation of bulk interception practices driven by intelligence agencies. Regardless of the uncertain implications of such a judgment as we speak, the recent judgment of the Court does not definitely add to the data protection 'toolkit' that the ECtHR judicial practice has hitherto created, nor to the CJEU's approach.[166] Nevertheless, the latter in its La Quadrature du Net and Others[167] ruling appeared to revisit its *Tele 2* legacy when it comes to national security purposes. The judgment gives the green light to Member States to allow law enforcement authorities access to general and indiscriminate retained data to for the purpose of fighting serious crime. Of course, the proportionality requirement always applies.

[162] E Celeste, 'The Court of Justice and the Ban on Bulk Data Retention: Expansive Potential and Future Scenarios' (2019) 15 *European Constitutional Law Review* 134, 155, 157. For an analysis of the judgment see also M Milanović, 'ECtHR Judgment in Big Brother Watch v. UK' (*EJIL:Talk!*, 17 September 2018), www.ejiltalk.org/ecthr-judgment-in-big-brother-watch-v-uk/; J Vermeulen, 'Big Brother May Continue Watching You' (*Strasbourg Observers*, 12 October 2018), www.strasbourgobservers.com/2018/10/12/big-brother-may-continue-watching-you/#_ftn4.

[163] *Big Brother Watch and Others v the United Kingdom* [GC], Merits, App nos 58170/13, 62322/14 and 24960/15 (ECtHR, 25 May 2021).

[164] *Centrum för rättvisa v Sweden* [GC], Merits, App no 35252/08 (ECtHR, 25 May 2021).

[165] See especially M Milanović, 'The Grand Normalization of Mass Surveillance: ECtHR Grand Chamber Judgments in Big Brother Watch and Centrum för rättvisa' (*EJIL:Talk!*, 26 May 2021), www.ejiltalk.org/the-grand-normalization-of-mass-surveillance-ecthr-grand-chamber-judgments-in-big-brother-watch-and-centrum-for-rattvisa/; E Watt, 'Much Ado About Mass Surveillance: the ECtHR Grand Chamber "Opens the Gates of an Electronic 'Big Brother' in Europe" in Big Brother Watch v UK' (*Strasbourg Observers*, 28 June 2021), www.strasbourgobservers.com/category/cases/big-brother-watch-and-others-v-uk/.

[166] Case C-623/17 *Privacy International* [2020] ECLI:EU:C:2020:790.

[167] Joined Cases C-511/18, C-512/18 and C-520/18 *La Quadrature du Net and Others* [2020] ECLI:EU:C:2020:791. See on these cases J Sajfert, 'Bulk Data Interception/Retention Judgments of the CJEU – A Victory and a Defeat for Privacy' (*European Law Blog*, 26 October 2020), www.europeanlawblog.eu/2020/10/26/bulk-data-interception-retention-judgments-of-the-cjeu-a-victory-and-a-defeat-for-privacy/.

All that said, the existing dialogue between the two legal systems will, hopefully, allow them to overcome the nascent inconsistencies in their relevant case law[168] so as to delimit the grey area of the contours of the right to privacy and the right to data protection not only with regard to their substance and their interrelation as established by the Charter but also in relation to the proper interpretation of Article 8 ECHR. It also remains to be seen whether the Court of Justice will align with the more pragmatic standing on interception methods apparent in recent jurisprudential trends of the ECtHR.

Despite the criticism initially raised against the CJEU for not taking fundamental rights seriously enough and its reluctance in producing bold judgments in this area of law, post-Lisbon, its case law on Articles 7 and 8 of the Charter reveals its tendency to be a frontrunner in data protection law, particularly in the digital age. Yet, this task is certainly not a walk in the park. In fact, the CJEU's position on the matter needs to be further clarified, especially when the Court is actively interacting with its Strasbourg peer.

III. The ECHR as an Impediment to Fundamental Rights Violations Exercised by EU Institutions: The Example of UN Sanctions

The issue of a stricter review of the actions of the EU institutions from the human rights angle was brought to light by the CJEU on the occasion of another sensitive area influenced by the enhanced anti-terrorism policies, namely the application of the UN sanctions within the EU legal space. This review, required by the Court, raised the debate about the discrepancies on human rights protection between the two judicial fora and significantly encouraged the CJEU to revisit their relationship confronting new challenges in rather difficult times.

A. The *Bosphorus* Case Formulating the Interrelationship of the Two Judicial Systems

The *Bosphorus* saga[169] was one of the leading cases illustrating the initial approach of both the CJEU and the ECtHR when dealing with the delicate issue of the application of UN sanctions. The *Bosphorus* case concerned an application brought by a Turkish airline company, Bosphorus Airways. In 1993, an aircraft, leased by the

[168] See especially Gonzalez Fuster, 'Fighting for Your Right to What Exactly?' (n 105).

[169] For an analytical review of the lengthy litigation of the *Bosphorus* case before the CJEU and the ECtHR see S Douglas-Scott, '*Bosphorus Hava Yollari Turizm Ve Ticaret Anonim Sirketi v. Ireland*' (2006) 43 *CML Rev* 243.

company from Yugoslav Airlines (JAT), was impounded by the Irish authorities during its presence in Ireland according to Article 8 of the Council Regulation (EEC) No 990/93 of 26 April 1993 concerning trade between the European Economic Community and the Federal Republic of Yugoslavia (Serbia and Montenegro) implementing at Community level sanctions imposed by the UN on the Federal Republic of Yugoslavia, Serbia and Montenegro. The company challenged the aircraft's seizure, invoking a violation of its right to property pursuant to Article 1 Protocol No 1 ECHR. The Irish Supreme Court made a preliminary reference to the CJEU asking whether the Council's Regulation and the UN sanctions incorporated therein were applicable in the present case.

The CJEU, in its judgment delivered in 1996,[170] responded to this question in the affirmative, elucidating that there is no reason under the relevant Security Council Resolution and Article 8 of the EU Council Regulation justifying a distinction between the owner of the aircraft and the person/undertaking having the controlling interest of the aircraft. Reaffirming the significance of fundamental rights in the EU legal order, the Court held, in the context of the proportionality test applied, that the measure imposed on the company was proportionate to the aim pursued by the sanctions.[171]

Later on, the Bosphorus company lodged an application before the ECtHR alleging that its aircraft's seizure amounted to an infringement of its property rights as enshrined in Article 1 Protocol No 1 of the ECHR. In its judgment,[172] the Strasbourg Court took into serious consideration the CJEU's judgment. Examining the legal basis of the interference with Article 1 Protocol No 1 ECHR, the Court held rather quickly that

> the impugned interference was not the result of an exercise of discretion by the Irish authorities, either under Community or Irish law, but rather amounted to compliance by the Irish State with its legal obligations flowing from Community law and, in particular, Article 8 of Regulation (EEC) no. 990/93.[173]

As for Bosphorus's right to property in the light of Ireland's obligations as arising by the EU Council's contested regulation, the ECtHR proceeded to consider the applicant's claim under Article 1 Protocol No 1 ECHR. Thus, the Court stated that the sanctions regime resulted in a 'control of use', rather than a 'deprivation' of property. As regards justification for the seizure, the ECtHR opted to see the action of the Irish Government in the light of its responsibilities under EU law. The Strasbourg Court found that Ireland had no discretion to act, according to its legal obligations flowing from EU law, since the contested legislation implementing

[170] Case C-84/95 *Bosphorus v Minister for Transport, Energy and Communications and others* [1996] ECR I-3953.

[171] ibid para 21.

[172] *Bosphorus Hava Yollari Turizm ve Ticaret Anonim Şirketi v Ireland* [GC], Merits, ECHR 2005-VI 107.

[173] ibid para 148.

the UN sanctions against the Federal Republic of Yugoslavia (FRY) was *generally applicable* and *binding in its entirety*, highlighting also its – by nature – direct application in the domestic legal order. Therefore, the Court emphasised that the general interest pursued by the impugned action was in conformity with the Irish state's obligations under the Union's law. After recalling that the interpretation of the Convention is made in light of relevant international law principles,[174] such as the *pacta sunt servanda* rule, and the increasing weight that the Court gives to international co-operation and the proper functioning of international (and supranational) organisations (as is the case of the European Union),[175] the Court emphasised that there must be a proportionate relationship between the means selected by the authorities and the aim pursued. Hence, a fair balance is required between the demands of the general interests of society and the interests of the individual company concerned, and the state's *marge de manoeuvre* is wide.

Most importantly, in this ruling the Court took the opportunity to outline with detail its *equivalent protection* doctrine[176] and re-examine its interplay with the EU. After reaffirming that the Convention does not prohibit its Contracting Parties from transferring sovereign powers to international organisations in the name of international co-operation, the Court reiterated that

> State action taken in compliance with such legal obligations is justified as long as the relevant organisation is considered to protect fundamental rights, as regards both the substantive guarantees offered and the mechanisms controlling their observance, in a manner which can be considered at least equivalent to that for which the Convention provides.[177]

In this regard, the Court assessed whether it could be presumed that Irish authorities acted in compliance with ECHR requirements in fulfilling such obligations.[178] For that purpose, the Court paid particular attention to human rights protection within the EU legal framework. Given the numerous and repeated references by the CJEU to the ECHR, the adoption of the Charter of the

[174] Art 31(3)(c) of the Vienna Convention on the Law of Treaties (VCLT) which is generally conceived as the main weapon of international law against fragmentation was also invoked by the ECtHR in its ruling: ibid para 150; Vienna Convention on the Law of Treaties (adopted 23 May 1969, entered into force 27 January 1980) 1155 UNTS 116. For a horizontal analysis of the principle of systemic integration as incorporated in the text of Art 31(3)(c) VCLT see P Merkouris, *Article 31(3)(c) VCLT and the Principle of Systemic Integration: Normative Shadows in Plato's Cave*, Queen Mary Studies in International Law 17 (Leiden, Brill Nijhoff, 2015).

[175] *Bosphorus* (n 172) para 150.

[176] This famous doctrine of the Court was introduced in the ECHR legal order in *M & Co v Federal Republic of Germany* and *Matthews* judgments. *M & Co v Federal Republic of Germany* (dec) (1990) 64 DR 138; *Matthews v the United Kingdom* [GC], Merits, ECHR 1999-I 251.

[177] *Bosphorus* (n 172) para 155.

[178] DÞ Björgvinsson, 'The Role of the European Court of Human Rights in the Changing European Human Rights Architecture' in OM Arnardóttir and A Buyse (eds), *Shifting Centres of Gravity in Human Rights Protection: Rethinking Relations between the ECtHR, EU, and National Legal Orders*, Routledge Research in Human Rights Law (Oxford, Routledge, 2016) 34–35.

fundamental rights of the EU, as well as the enforcement mechanism offered by the EU legislation, the Strasbourg Court came to the conclusion that

> In such circumstances, the Court finds that the protection of fundamental rights by Community law can be considered to be, and to have been at the relevant time, 'equivalent' (within the meaning of paragraph 155 above) to that of the Convention system. Consequently, the presumption arises that Ireland did not depart from the requirements of the Convention when it implemented legal obligations flowing from its membership of the European Community.[179]

Nevertheless, according to the Court's appraisal, such a pronouncement of equivalence should always be open to review in the light of any relevant developments in the field of fundamental rights' protection. Hence, the presumption of equivalent protection is rebutted: 'in the circumstances of a particular case, it is considered that the protection of the Convention's rights was manifestly deficient'.[180] At any rate, the Strasbourg Court found that that was not the case under the present circumstances and, thus, Bosphorus's right to property under Article 1 Protocol No 1 ECHR had not been breached.

In an echo of the *Solange* doctrine[181] which paved the way for the establishment of the national-EU hierarchy, the *Bosphorus* case sought to discover the regional (ECHR)-EU balance, with enormous implications in this field. As one of the most important cases that offered a true paradigm of overlapping jurisdiction, the *Bosphorus* saga before the Luxembourg and the Strasbourg Courts allowed us to draw useful conclusions with regard to the interaction between the two judicial mechanisms.

First off, the Court's jurisdiction in the *Bosphorus* case is of paramount importance, particularly as an element of the judgment contributes to the tension between the two European judicial mechanisms. Remarkably, the Court, in order to confirm its jurisdiction in the case under Article 1 of the ECHR, opted for a delicate approach focusing, at first, on the territorial scope of application of the Convention and then, to the concrete national implementation of the EU rule, rather than directly scrutinising the legality of the EU Regulation. Therefore, it overlooked not only the EU obligations but also the responsibility of the Security Council.[182]

[179] *Bosphorus* (n 172) para 165.

[180] ibid para 166.

[181] The doctrine was fleshed out by the German Federal Constitutional Court (Bundesverfassungsgericht), which enunciated the concept of constitutional pluralism in the EU and re-established the relationship between the national courts and EU law. See BVerfGE 37, 271 2 BvL 52/71 Solange I-Beschluß [1974]; BVerfGE 73, 339 2 BvR 197/83 Solange II-decision [1986]. See also C Antpöhler, J Dickschen, S Hentrei, M Kottmann, M Smrkolj and A von Bogdandy, 'Reverse Solange – Protecting the Essence of Fundamental Rights against EU Member States' (2012) 49 *CML Rev* 489; O De Schutter, 'The Two Lives of Bosphorus: Redefining the Relationships between the European Court of Human Rights and the Parties to the Convention' (2013) 4 *Journal européen des droits de l'homme* 584.

[182] K Kuhnert, 'Bosphorus – Double standards in European Human Rights Protection?' (2006) 2 *Utrecht Law Review* 177, 184.

Secondly, the fact that the ECtHR did not decline jurisdiction to deliver its ruling in a case already discussed before the CJEU, raised a number of vexed issues at the time. As Sionaidh Douglas-Scott correctly pointed out in relation to the overlapping jurisdiction of the two Courts '[i]f one adds the jurisdiction of national courts and their role in hearing human rights cases, one might say that Europe currently has a rich, fertile, or perhaps even an excessive, focus on human rights.'[183]

On the contrary, the ruling of the Strasbourg Court responded to the problems that arose during this lengthy litigation of the *Bosphorus* saga, which lasted more than 10 years, providing, though, some problematic issues as well. The privileged position that the Strasbourg Court reserved for the EU legal order, since it clarified that the 'equivalent protection' presumption, developing also the 'manifestly deficient' concept, meant that this presumption can be rebutted only in exceptionally severe violations of fundamental rights. Despite the fact that the Court's approach should be seen in the general context of the political and institutional tension caused in the light of the failure of the EU Constitution's adoption, which explicitly provided for the EU accession to the ECHR,[184] it is more than evident that the Court introduces a significantly high threshold leaving the door open for low standards of fundamental rights protection which appear to be acceptable by the ECtHR.

Even though the Court underlined that this is a case-by-case review, the manner that it selected to exercise this *in abstracto* review in *Bosphorus*, by examining the EU legal system as a whole without evaluating the specific status of property rights' protection within the EU legal system, appeared rather alarming even for some of the Judges of the Court,[185] who, in their concurring opinion, also gave particular emphasis to the danger of developing double standards of protection under the ECHR. They particularly highlighted that the *Bosphorus* judgment seems to have made a distinction with regard to the level of protection between the Contracting Parties which are EU Member States and those which are not, leaving the former outside the stringent scrutiny usually applied by the Court.[186]

Overall, it goes without saying that *Bosphorus* was innovative, expressing a priori the ECtHR's trust in the EU standards as it acknowledged that the level of protection guaranteed by the EU is equivalent to what the ECHR offers itself. The Court perhaps felt that it had to respond to the main concern articulated by the European Commission, during its intervention in the case, stressing that the accession would be seriously jeopardised if the ECtHR declared jurisdiction to place ordinary EU

[183] S Douglas-Scott, 'A Tale of Two Courts: Luxembourg, Strasbourg and the Growing European Human Rights *Acquis*' (2006) 43 *CML Rev* 629, 630.

[184] Kuhnert 'Bosphorus' (n 182) 188.

[185] *Bosphorus* (n 172) Joint Concurring Opinion of Judges Rozakis, Tulkens, Traja, Botoucharova, Zagrebelesky and Garlicki on the *Bosphorus* case, para 4.

[186] ibid; C Costello, 'The *Bosphorus* Ruling of the European Court of Human Rights: Fundamental Rights and Blurred Boundaries in Europe' (2006) 6 *Human Rights Law Review* 87, 106–7.

acts under scrutiny.[187] Nevertheless, the way that the ECtHR chose to do so – sidestepping the EU obligation to implement Security Council economic measures lying under the national act – leads us to the conclusion that, in practice, the *Bosphorus* judgment left plenty of room for the ECtHR to scrutinise the actions of EU institutions, regardless of accession. This conclusion was subsequently reaffirmed by the evolution of the *equivalent protection* doctrine, more specifically in the Dublin cases, where the latter did not impede the Court's will to reconsider emerging issues and to exercise a greater control over EU law.

Although the equivalent protection doctrine was introduced and developed during a time when accession was highly desirable, and signalled enhanced trust and co-operation between the two European legal systems, the question of whether this doctrine will be deprived of its substance after accession inevitably arises.[188] The pronouncement of the ECtHR in *Avotiņš v Latvia*[189] signals, however, that the Court is not yet ready to leave behind the equivalent protection presumption. The Strasbourg Court not only applied its relevant doctrine, but also it did so for the first time in a case concerning obligations of mutual recognition under EU law. This is even more noteworthy due to the concerns expressed by the CJEU in its Opinion 2/13 according to which the EU accession to the ECHR indicates a significant threat to the mutual trust principle and as a result, the underlying balance of the EU and the autonomy of EU law would be imperilled.[190] M Avotiņš alleged that the Latvian Supreme Court had violated his right to a fair hearing under Article 6 ECHR, while acting in the context of enforcement of a Cypriot judgment pursuant to the Brussels I Regulation,[191] which was, according to his view defective due to the fact that it had been delivered in breach of his rights of defence.

As regards the applicability of the *Bosphorus* presumption, the Court reiterated that, besides its jurisprudence that repeatedly found the substantive protection of human rights equivalent, within the EU legal architecture, this is also confirmed by Article 52(3) providing the consistent interpretation with ECHR of the corresponding rights. Subsequently, the Court also stressed that the 'absence of any margin of manoeuvre' on the part of the Latvian authorities while implementing the particular EU law obligation, as well as the 'deployment of the full potential of the supervisory mechanism' provided by EU law, was also fulfilled.[192]

The Strasbourg Court, after having underlined the fact that the Brussels I Regulation relies upon the principle of mutual trust, and therefore, the paramount

[187] *Bosphorus* (n 172) para 122.

[188] See especially O De Schutter, 'Bosphorus Post-Accession: Redefining the Relationships between the European Court of Human Rights and the Parties to the Convention' in V Kosta, N Skoutaris and V Tzevelekos (eds), *The EU Accession to the ECHR*, Modern Studies in European Law 48 (Oxford, Bloomsbury, 2014) 178.

[189] *Avotiņš v Latvia* [GC], Merits, App no 17502/07 (ECtHR, 23 May 2016).

[190] Opinion 2/13 [2014] ECLI:EU:C:2014:2454, para 194.

[191] Council Regulation (EC) No 44/2001 on jurisdiction and the recognition and enforcement of judgments in civil and commercial matters [2001] OJ L12/1.

[192] *Avotiņš* (n 189) paras 105–6.

importance of this principle in EU law (paragraph 113), examined the specific elements of the case and concluded not only that the equivalent protection doctrine is applicable in the case at hand, but also it cannot be rebutted, as fundamental rights protection cannot be considered manifestly deficient.[193] Nevertheless, the Court seemed unconvinced as regards automatic application of the EU mutual recognition mechanism by the domestic courts when the simultaneous application of the *Bosphorus* presumption and the weight that this twofold national obligation brings to the effective protection of fundamental rights in Europe come into play.[194]

More recently, the ECtHR increasingly is asked to rule upon human rights claims related to the enforcement of EU law. In March 2021 the ECtHR delivered a seminal judgment on the EAW scheme on two applications concerning the purpose of the service of prison sentences in Romania. In *Bivolaru and Moldovan v France*,[195] the Court affirmed that there is still room for the Strasbourg Court's external review of the actions of its State Parties, albeit operating by virtue of an EU mutual recognition mechanism. In line with the *Avotiņš* argumentation, the Court applied the famous equivalent protection presumption to scrutinise whether the execution of the EAW by the French authorities exposed the applicants to inhumane detention conditions in Romanian prisons, incompatible with the absolute protection of the Convention.

Whereas the Court for the first time rebutted the presumption concluding a violation of Article 3 ECHR, it did so cautiously, paying meticulous attention to the mutual trust principle underpinning the entire EAW scheme. Examining whether the executing state has any discretionary powers, it emphasised that any such power is limited to the assessment of the facts, and has to be exercised 'within the framework strictly delineated by the case-law of the CJEU'.[196] Despite their different methodological paths, the ECtHR highlighted the convergence between the two Courts pertaining to the individual examination requirement.[197] Yet, for the Court, the mutual trust rationale does not preclude the Court from reviewing whether its mechanical application is compatible with Article 3 ECHR. As the accession project is back on the negotiating table, the Strasbourg Court

[193] ibid paras 113–27.

[194] See, eg S Johansen, 'EU law and the ECHR: the Bosphorus Presumption is Still Alive and Kicking: the Case of Avotiņš v. Latvia' (*EU Law Analysis*, 24 May 2016), www.eulawanalysis.blogspot.fr/2016/05/eu-law-and-echr-bosphorus-presumption.html; JS Bergé, 'Avotiņš ou le calme qui couve la tempêt' (*Réseau Universitaire Européen*, 26 May 2016), www.gdr-elsj.eu/2016/05/26/cooperation-judiciaire-civile/avotins-ou-le-calme-qui-couve-la-tempete/.

[195] *Bivolaru and Moldovan v France* (Merits) App nos 40324/16 and 12623/17 (ECtHR, 25 March 2021).

[196] Johan Callewart, 'Manifest deficiency in the execution of a European arrest warrant – judgment of the European Court of Human Rights in the case of Bivolaru and Moldovan v. France' (*Prof Dr iur Johan Callewaert* Blog 2021), https://johan-callewaert.eu/manifest-deficiency-in-the-execution-of-a-european-arrest-warrant-judgment-of-the-european-court-of-human-rights-in-the-case-of-bivolaru-and-moldovan-v-france/.

[197] *Bivolaru* (n 195) para 114.

felt that it should manifest its trust in the EU system by reapplying its landmark equivalent protection doctrine and inform its contours confirming, however, that mutual recognition should, nevertheless, not be applied in an automatic and mechanical way, to the detriment of ECHR protection.[198] Hence, at a time when mutual trust is being discussed, both institutions seem to emphasise judicial interaction with their peers and at the same time, defend their respective *acquis* accordingly.[199]

Needless to say that, post-accession, the Strasbourg system will be tempted to reassess its pronouncements in the *Bosphorus* litigation. This might not occur overnight; however, the Court might be motivated to take slow steps away from its prior position so as to better define the standards of human rights protection in the implementation of EU law by the national jurisdictions. After all, it flows from the aforementioned line of jurisprudence that the states' acts and omissions fall definitely within the scope of application of the Convention's provisions irrespective of the origin of the relevant legislation.

B. The Decisive Step: The *Kadi* Saga

It was not until 2008 that the CJEU 'rocked the boat', providing, for most commentators, its most important ruling in decades in the ground-breaking *Kadi* case pertaining, this time, to the targeted economic sanctions of the Security Council against individuals. During this long period starting after 9/11, both states and the entire international community introduced a wide range of measures of all types to tackle the alarming situation. However, the counter-terrorism strategies appeared to disregard human rights voices. In this context, the Security Council also took immediate action as it declared the phenomenon of international terrorism a threat to international peace and security, and imposed an extensive and mandatory counter-terrorism agenda upon states through Resolution 1373(2001)[200] pursuant to the provisions enshrined in Chapter VII of the UN Charter.

Besides, through the Security Council, the United Nations resorted to economic sanctions against individuals who were known or suspected terrorists. Therefore, the redaction of the so-called terrorist lists containing individuals and entities amounted most of the time to the freezing of assets or financial transactions of the listed individual or entity, or even to the prevention of any international travel by an individual who is also a presumed terrorist. The *ratio*

[198] *Bivolaru* (n 195) paras 100-1.

[199] See 12th Meeting of the CDDH Ad hoc negotiation group ('47+1') on the accession of the European Union to the European Convention on Human Rights, https://rm.coe.int/cddh-47-1-2021-r12-en/1680a4e547.

[200] UNSC, 'Res 1373 on threats to international peace and security caused by terrorist acts' 28 September 2001 UN Doc S/RES/1373.

of such UN sanctions was based on their preventive effect with regard to the financing of terrorism. These sanctions were, thus, intended to function as disincentives to the persons involved, so that they would abstain from taking part in terrorist acts.[201]

The UN sanctions regime was, undoubtedly, characterised by significant shortcomings which gave rise to much human rights-based criticism.[202] The aforementioned scheme of terrorist listing was also brought into the spotlight of the EU legal order as it became part of EU legislation, and was challenged in the EU judicial fora in the famous *Kadi* litigation which – as discussed below – not only delimited the external relations of the EU with international organisations and more specifically, with the United Nations, but also initiated a new field of interaction with the Strasbourg Court.

The *Kadi* case case is among the best-known cases in academia, so we will briefly summarise the basic facts. Yassin Abdullah Kadi was a presumed supporter of Usama Bin Laden and Al-Qaeda and was, thus, listed by the Sanctions Committee, resulting in a freezing of his assets. Following this, the EU transposed this UN sanction by Council Regulation 467/2001[203] and Commission Regulation 2062/2001[204] which ordered Mr Kadi's listing and the freezing of his funds. He contested the EU measures before the General Court of the EU, claiming a breach of his right to property under Article 1 Protocol No 1 ECHR, and a lack of effective judicial remedy.

At first instance,[205] the General Court had a rather defensive approach towards the Security Council as it refused to examine the lawfulness of the EU regulation because, given that the legislation was adopted so as to give effect to the Security

[201] The Security Council Resolution 1267 sanctions regime was initially used to give effect to these economic measures. The SC sanctions' scheme originally concerned Taliban leaders in Afghanistan, but was subsequently expanded through Security Council Resolution 1390 in order to include a global list of persons associated with Al-Qaeda or the Taliban. As the relevant Security Council Resolutions (1988 and 1989) have been adopted under Chapter VII of the UN Charter, they laid down binding legal obligations for all Member States and are said to enjoy primacy in respect of other international obligations of the same states, pursuant to Art 103 of the UN Charter.

[202] See, eg A Reinisch, 'Should Judges Second-Guess the UN Security Council?' (2009) 6 *International Organizations Law Review* 257; A Grossman, 'A Critical Assessment of the 1267 Sanctions Committee' (*E-International Relations*, 3 March 2012), www.e-ir.info/2012/03/03/a-critical-assessment-of-the-1267-sanctions-committee/; A Tzanakopoulos, 'Kadi Showdown: Substantive Review of (UN) Sanctions by the ECJ' (*EJIL:Talk Blog!*, 19 July 2013), www.ejiltalk.org/kadi-showdown/.

[203] Council Regulation (EC) No 467/2001 prohibiting the export of certain goods and services to Afghanistan, strengthening the flight ban and extending the freezing of funds and other financial resources in respect of the Taliban of Afghanistan, and repealing Regulation (EC) No 337/2000 [2001] OJ L67/1.

[204] Commission Regulation (EC) No 2062/2001 amending, for the third time, Council Regulation (EC) No 467/2001 prohibiting the export of certain goods and services to Afghanistan, strengthening the flight ban and extending the freeze of funds and other financial resources in respect of the Taliban of Afghanistan and repealing Regulation (EC) No 337/2000 [2001] OJ L277/25.

[205] Case T-315/01 *Kadi v Council and Commission* [2005] ECR II-3649 and Case T-306/01 *Yusuf and Al Barakaat International Foundation v Council and Commission* [2005] ECR II-3533.

Council Resolutions and hence, to comply with international obligations, no margin of appreciation was left to the EU institutions. According to the Court's appraisal, this would result in a direct review of the economic sanctions imposed by Security Council which enjoyed immunity from judicial review. Nevertheless and rather paradoxically, the General Court accepted the challenge of reviewing the regulation under scrutiny only through the lens of a potential violation of *jus cogens* norms of international law, that is to say that it took a totally new and dangerous path incorporating, in its reasoning, a question unfamiliar with regard to the body of EU rules. Assessing, therefore, whether the Security Council had respected *jus cogens* norms[206] in the field of fundamental and non-derogable rights, it held that there was no such breach. Subsequently, Kadi appealed the General Court's ruling before the CJEU.

As Giuseppe Martinico correctly observed '[t]he *Kadi* saga responds to a double logic: on the one hand, it develops from a strong perception of EU law autonomy, while on the other hand it reflects the idea of the existence of a mature system in terms of fundamental rights protection.'[207] This was clearly reflected when the Luxembourg Court handed down its long-anticipated decision in 2008, the so-called *Kadi I* decision[208] which loudly overturned the first-instance decision of the General Court. The CJEU was in line with Advocate General Maduro's Opinion[209] who expressed severe criticism regarding the latter and urged the Court to pronounce on the lawfulness of the regulations at issue ensuring the effective protection of fundamental rights within the EU.[210]

In its judgment on appeal, the CJEU reviewed the lawfulness of the EU regulation transposing the resolution. Its central argument was that the protection of fundamental rights forms part of the very foundations of the Union legal order. Accordingly, all Union measures must be compatible with fundamental rights. The Court reasoned that this does not amount to a review of the lawfulness of the Security Council measures. The review of lawfulness would apply only to the Union act that gives effect to the international agreement at issue and not to the latter as such. Having established that, the review for compliance with fundamental rights was a relatively simple task. The claimant had not been informed of the grounds for his inclusion in the list of individuals and entities subjected to the sanctions. Therefore, he had not been able to seek judicial review of these grounds, and consequently his right to be heard as well as his right to effective judicial review and the right to property had been infringed.

[206] Ibid (*Kadi*), para 226.

[207] G Martinico, 'The Autonomy of EU law: A Joint Celebration of *Kadi I* and *Kadi II* and *Van Gend en Loos*' in M Avbelj, F Fontanelli and G Martinico (eds), *Kadi on Trial: A Multifaceted Analysis of the Kadi Trial*, Routledge Research in EU Law (Oxford, Routledge, 2014) 162.

[208] Joined Cases C-402/05 P & C-415/05 P *Kadi & Al Barakaat International Foundation v Council and Commission* [2008] ECR I-6351.

[209] ibid Opinion of AG Maduro.

[210] ibid Opinion of AG Maduro, para 53.

The CJEU rejected the General Court's reasoning,[211] accepting the challenge of scrutinising the EU action despite the fact that the latter was decided in the context of the implementation of the Security Council sanctions. It then opted for moving the spotlight from the previous question which troubled the General Court concerning whether to exercise external judicial review to a more nuanced and delicate one of how to proceed in doing so. After searching for the proper legal basis for the enforcement of these measures, the Luxembourg Court highlighted that

> the obligations imposed by an international agreement cannot have the effect of prejudicing the constitutional principles of the EC Treaty, which include the principle that all Community acts must respect fundamental rights, that respect constituting a condition of their lawfulness which it is for the Court to review in the framework of the complete system of legal remedies established by the Treaty.[212]

Having established that, the Court drew the line between the international agreement and the EU measure that aims to implement the former, elucidating that scrutinising the lawfulness of the Security Council Resolutions is not among the responsibilities of the EU judicature.[213] While underlining the EU's respect for international law in the exercise of its powers, in order to justify why the control of the contested sanctions was also not excluded from its competence, the Court relied on the autonomous character of the EU[214] in relation to the international legal order. The CJEU recalled that the former is among the three constitutional values of the EU, namely the rule of law, the autonomy of the EU legal order and – last but not least – respect for fundamental rights, and then it attempted to examine whether these principles could be reconciled with international agreements. Despite the binding character of the UN resolutions, the Court emphasised that the UN Charter left great leeway to the Members of the UN to choose among the various possible models regarding the transposition of those resolutions into their domestic legal orders.

Therefore, under the international legal order, no judicial review of the internal lawfulness of the contested regulation was excluded by virtue of the fact that it gave effect to a Security Council resolution adopted under Chapter VII UN Charter. Such an immunity for EU measures, like the contested in the present case, lacks legal basis in the EU Treaty.[215] Even in this part of its argumentation,

[211] See eg M Tzanou, 'Case-note on Joined Cases C-402/05 P & C-415/05 P *Yassin Abdullah Kadi & Al Barakaat International Foundation v. Council of the European Union & Commission of the European Communities*' (2009) 10 *German Law Journal* 123; RE Papadopoulou, '"Smart sanctions" and EC Law: Unrolling the "Ariadne's thread": The ECJ Judgment of 3 September 2008 in Kadi and Al Barakaat' [in Greek] (2009) *Efarmoges Dimosiou Dikaiou I* 21.

[212] *Kadi & Al Barakaat* (n 208) para 285.

[213] ibid para 288.

[214] The autonomous nature of the EU legal order was famously announced in the *Van Gend en Loos* case in 1963. Case 26/62 *Van Gend & Loos v Nederlandse Administratie der Belastingen* [1963] ECR 1.

[215] *Kadi & Al Barakaat* (n 208) paras 290–300.

the Luxembourg Court drew an analogy from the control of the Security Council decisions as exercised by the Strasbourg Court's case law and more specifically, the *Behrami and Saramati* position[216] of the ECtHR which also grappled with similar questions of debatable UN actions.

Interestingly, in the joined case *Behrami and Saramati* the Court of Strasbourg denied jurisdiction *rationae personae* since the applicants, and more specifically the Behramis, complained about the death and severe injury of two children in Kosovo caused by the explosion of undetonated cluster bombs dropped by NATO, while Mr Saramati contested his extra-judicial detention by the Kosovo Force (KFOR) which constituted the security force established in Kosovo by UNSC Resolution 1244(1999). Having exercised a widely criticised 'ultimate authority and control test',[217] the Court of Justice held in its debatable reasoning of the admissibility decision that the UN actions were completely attributable to the UN and thus, declared the applications inadmissible. For this reason, this case was clearly used in favour of the CJEU's findings in the case at hand as it was clearly distinguished from the facts of the *Kadi*.[218]

Having drawn this distinction, the Court was allowed to conclude that

> the review by the Court of the validity of any Community measure in the light of fundamental rights must be considered to be the expression, in a community based on the rule of law, of a constitutional guarantee stemming from the EC Treaty as an autonomous legal system which is not to be prejudiced by an international agreement.[219]

Unsatisfied by the mere existence of the re-examination procedure before the Security Council Committee and given the particular significance of fundamental rights forming an integral part of the general principles of Community law, the Court concluded that the EU courts had to ensure the – in principle – full review of the lawfulness of all actions carried out by EU organs in the light of this sensitive area of law.[220]

That said, the Luxembourg Court went on to examine whether the freezing of Mr Kadi's and Al Barakaat's funds constituted an unjustified breach of Mr Kadi's right to property in light of Article 1 Protocol No 1 ECHR. Although the contested restrictions of property rights stemming from the restrictive measures imposed by the EU regulations could, in principle, be justified, the Court once again used the proportionality test of the Strasbourg Court, coming to the conclusion that the regulation in question was adopted without furnishing any guarantee enabling

[216] *Behrami and Behrami v France* and *Saramati v France, Germany and Norway* [GC] (dec) App nos 71412/01 and 78166/01 (ECtHR, 2 May 2007).

[217] See, eg M Milanović and T Papić, 'As Bad as it Gets: The European Court of Human Rights's *Behrami and Saramati* Decision and General International Law' (2009) 58 *ICLQ* 267.

[218] *Kadi & Al Barakaat* (n 208) paras 314–15.

[219] ibid para 316.

[220] ibid para 326. See also the argumentation of the Court in paras 321–25 in which it further explained the reasons for the abovementioned distinction. See, eg Papadopoulou, '"Smart sanctions" and EC Law' (n 211) 51.

Mr Kadi to put his case to the competent authorities. However, given that the latter constitutes also a procedural guarantee inherent in the substance of Article 1 Protocol No 1 ECHR as illustrated by the ECtHR's case law, a comprehensive view of the procedures under scrutiny as regards the general application and continuation of the freezing measures affecting him, was, therefore, considered necessary in order to ensure respect for the appellant's right to property.[221] Taking all the above into consideration, the Court annulled the Council regulation inasmuch as it froze Mr Kadi's and Al Barakaat's funds.

It flows from a thorough overview of the case that the CJEU clearly followed a Strasbourg-type reasoning to approach the fundamental rights complaints of Mr Kadi and Al Barakaat. Nonetheless, it was unexpected that, although it clearly took into account the highly debatable position of the ECtHR in *Behrami and Saramati* and emphasised the pivotal difference between the two approaches, the CJEU passed by this slip in the Strasbourg Court's case law without providing a more detailed and in-depth argument. Taking this road, it appeared to have preferred to avoid any discrepancy with the ECtHR *vis-à-vis* the competence of reviewing UN actions.[222]

Despite the obvious reluctance of raising a differentiated voice, the Court seemed nevertheless not to have missed the opportunity to influence indirectly the ECtHR case law. The mere fact that the Court took the step to order the annulment of an EU regulation penalising the actions of the Council solely on human-rights grounds signals that it is always tempted to verge into new territories such as the EU-international law limits, especially when sensitive questions pertaining to national security and counter-terrorism measures are on the table.

Kadi I openly inspired the ECtHR to distance itself from its 'forgiving' approach towards the UN and the Security Council measures and fuelled the cross-fertilisation between the two institutions. In its prior case law the Strasbourg Court, initially, denied its competence on this matter without keeping the safety net of a 'Solange caveat',[223] and it was inevitably criticised for embracing a remarkably low degree of protection *vis-à-vis* the UN sanctions for so prestigious an international human rights court.[224] Following the *Kadi* litigation, it certainly leveraged the Luxembourg Court's bold position in this field and reached its landmark GC judgment in *Nada v Switzerland*.[225]

[221] *Kadi & Al Barakaat* (n 208) para 368.

[222] See especially KS Ziegler, 'Strengthening the Rule of Law, but Fragmenting International Law: The *Kadi* Decision of the ECJ from the Perspective of Human Rights' (2009) 9 *Human Rights Law Review* 288, 299.

[223] J Kokott and C Sobotta, 'The Kadi Case – Constitutional Core Values and International Law: Finding the Balance?' (2012) 23 *EJIL* 1015, 1018.

[224] In its *Behrami and Saramati* case, the Court based its admissibility decision on a rather narrow and restrictive interpretation of the main objective of the UN, that of maintaining peace and international security, as 'imperative', implying, therefore, that since the operations authorised by Security Council resolutions are designed to serve the aforesaid purpose, they cannot in any way be put under scrutiny by the ECtHR.

[225] *Nada v Switzerland* [GC], Merits, ECHR 2012-V 115.

In casu, the Court was confronted with the issue of the legality of measures taken to enforce targeted sanctions stemming from the UNSC. Therefore, by relying explicitly on the *Kadi I* decision of the CJEU, the ECtHR concluded to violations of the applicants' rights in a similar context. The applicant was an Egyptian-Italian national residing in a small Italian exclave surrounded by Swiss territory, who was listed under Resolution 1267 of the UN sanctions regime, and was, therefore, subjected to an enter and transit ban as well as a freezing of his assets. Having exhausted every possibility of judicial recourse after the rejection of his human rights allegations by the Swiss Federal Court, the applicant sought ultimate review of his case before the Strasbourg Court, claiming, in particular, that the addition of his name to the blacklist, which resulted in his travel ban, had infringed his right to liberty pursuant to Article 5 ECHR, his right to respect for private and family life under Article 8 ECHR, and his right to an effective remedy under Article 13 ECHR. He additionally complained that the aforementioned restrictions were tantamount to ill-treatment and were, thus, falling under the scope of Article 3 ECHR as well as under the scope of Article 9 ECHR since the applicant alleged to have been deprived of his freedom to manifest his religion or beliefs.

The ECtHR took a different approach in this case,[226] and concluded, in substance to a violation of Mr Nada's right to private and family life under Article 8 ECHR. It did so since the Swiss authorities, remarkably enough, failed to inform the Security Council's Sanctions Committee for a long period of four years regarding the discontinuation of the domestic investigations against Mr Nada and the lack of reasonable suspicion concerning his involvement in terrorist activities.[227] In addition, the Court took into serious consideration facts that were neglected by the Swiss authorities, namely 'the unique geographical situation of Campione d'Italia, the considerable duration of the measures imposed or the applicant's nationality, age and health'.[228] Nevertheless, it left it unclear whether the UN Charter did or did not prevail over the Convention and whether Switzerland was allowed to directly disobey the Security Council. The Court avoided the issue by concentrating on violations committed just outside the sanctions regime.[229]

As regards the breach of the right to an effective remedy as enshrined in Article 13 ECHR, the Court appeared even more critical of the Swiss Federal Court, which had declined to scrutinise any of the UN sanctions by virtue of Swiss human rights law. In this respect, the Court followed *expressis verbis* the

[226] See, eg S Guggisberg, 'The Nada Case in front of the ECtHR: a New Milestone in the European Debate on Security Council Targeted Sanctions and Human Rights Obligations' (2012) 8 *Croatian Yearbook of European Law and Policy* 411; M Milanović, 'European Court Decides Nada v. Switzerland' (*EJIL:Talk!*, 14 September 2012), www.ejiltalk.org/european-court-decides-nada-v-switzerland/.

[227] *Nada* (n 225) para 188.

[228] ibid para 195.

[229] ibid para 197. See also K Istrefi, 'The Application of Article 103 of the United Nations Charter in the European Courts: The Quest for Regime Compatibility on Fundamental Rights' (2012) 5(2) *European Journal of Legal Studies* 81.

Kadi I judgment of the Luxembourg Court in stressing that UN law did not prevent judicial review of the domestic implementation of sanctions.[230] By analogy, the ECtHR adopted the same position in relation to the review of the national implementation of the targeted sanctions and the conformity of the latter (implementation) with the Convention. Thus, the Court implied that national authorities should ensure the application of the Convention's provisions even if this could possibly amount to a non-compliance with the Security Council Resolutions adopted under the UN Charter. This conclusion gave the opportunity to the Court to rule in favour of the applicant and conclude to a violation of Article 13 ECHR.

However, it should be highlighted that it follows from the ECtHR's appraisal that the latter put itself in the shoes of the national jurisdiction in order to circumvent a potential direct ECHR-UN conflict in the light of Article 103 UN.[231] In fact, the Court considered that the requirement for the judicial control exercised by the domestic courts is not removed by the mere fact that contested measures are giving effect to UN sanctions, removing, though, the tension from the ECHR-UN to the national-UN level.

Notwithstanding the aforementioned problematic point of the Court's argumentation, looking at the *Nada* judgment as a whole we should not disregard its more progressive stance in comparison with its former one, as depicted in *Behrami and Saramati* and even in *Al-Jedda*[232] in the aim of ensuring a more effective human rights protection when it comes to targeted sanctions. This jurisprudential evolution of the ECtHR could be properly understood in the context of the whole accession process which was already in progress when the *Nada* case was under judicial review before the Court. Additionally, the echo of the *Kadi* case law apparently played a significant role. In the whole context of the – at this time – looming accession, combined with the anxiety of each Court to preserve its jurisprudential *acquis*, the Strasbourg Court, in order to avoid being side-lined by the Luxembourg Court in this field, was all the more motivated not to fall behind the standards established by the EU Courts.[233]

Actually, emphasising particularly the positive obligations not fulfilled by the Swiss authorities,[234] the Strasbourg Court appeared to offer in this case a more extended protection than the one offered by the CJEU in the *Kadi* jurisprudence so as to take over the role of vanguard from the CJEU in this area.

[230] *Nada* (n 225), para 212

[231] Milanović, 'European Court Decides Nada' (n 226).

[232] In *Al-Jedda*, the ECtHR expressed for the first time a clear reluctance to accommodate the SC's intention to limit international human rights standards disproportionately through its binding resolutions. The case concerned the issue of whether the internment without trial of a British/Iraqi national by British forces in Iraq in 2004 violated Art 5(1) of the Convention. *Al-Jedda v the United Kingdom* [GC], Merits, ECHR 2011-IV 305, paras 101–2.

[233] F Fabrinni and J Larik, 'Global Counter-Terrorism Sanctions and European Due Process Rules: the Dialogue between the CJEU and the ECtHR' in M Avbelj, F Fontanelli and G Martinico (eds), *Kadi on Trial: A Multifaceted Analysis of the Kadi Trial*, Routledge Research in EU Law (Oxford, Routledge, 2014) 149–50.

[234] *Nada* (n 225) para 196.

This willingness of the ECtHR to scrutinise the substantial and procedural guarantees offered by the Security Council regime to individuals subjected to counter-terrorism measures was also confirmed in the *Al-Dulimi v Switzerland* judgment.[235] In light of the *Kadi* saga, the ECtHR dealt, once again, with the implementation of the UNSC Resolution 1483 by the Swiss authorities.[236] The Court, examining a potential infringement of Article 6 ECHR found it necessary to engage in a direct assessment of the guarantees afforded by the UN system, comparing them with those secured by the Convention. In doing so, the Strasbourg Court applied its long-established 'equivalent protection' test and concluded that the UN framework does not meet the standards of such a (equivalent) protection. Remarkably, the Grand Chamber[237] departed partially from its previous approach and opted for a more balanced approach, stating that there were no conflicting obligations on the respondent state, as the contested resolution's wording left the door for domestic judicial review wide open. The core conclusion of the Grant Chamber can be summarised as follows: as long as a real normative conflict between clashing obligations in a hierarchical order does not exist, the equivalent protection test does not apply and the state is expected to proceed with the judicial review of the UNSC and the latter's action could be also scrutinised by the ECtHR for their conformity with the ECHR.[238]

Yet, the *Kadi* dispute was not concluded until the pronouncement of the Luxembourg Court in its *Kadi II* judgment in 2013, in which it famously ruled out the appeals against the decision of the General Court of 30 September 2010, insisting on the annulment of the Commission regulation re-listing Mr Kadi. The CJEU reaffirmed the judicial dialogue between the two Courts, openly citing the decision of the Strasbourg Court in *Nada* only once to uphold its argument that, notwithstanding the improvements in the UN sanctions machinery for listing and delisting suspected terrorists, the Security Council still did not ensure effective judicial recourse for 'blacklisted' people.

At this point, it is noteworthy that one of the most significant practical implications of the *Kadi* trial is reform of the UN sanctions regime. In particular, the Security Council introduced, in 2008, the narrative summary which is normally

[235] *Al-Dulimi & Montana Management Inc v Switzerland*, Merits, App no 5809/08 (ECtHR, 26 November 2013).

[236] See, eg A Peters, 'Targeted Sanctions after Affaire Al-Dulimi et Montana Management Inc. c. Suisse: Is There a Way Out of the Catch-22 for UN Members?' (*EJIL:Talk!*, 4 December 2013), www.ejiltalk.org/targeted-sanctions-after-affaire-al-dulimi-et-montana-management-inc-c-suisse-is-there-a-way-out-of-the-catch-22-for-un-members/.

[237] *Al-Dulimi & Montana Management Inc v Switzerland* [GC], Merits, App no 5809/08 (ECtHR, 21 June 2016).

[238] See, eg M Milanović, 'Grand Chamber Judgment in Al-Dulimi v. Switzerland' (*EJIL:Talk!*, 23 June 2016), www.ejiltalk.org/grand-chamber-judgment-in-al-dulimi-v-switzerland/; and ibid *Al-Dulimi* [GC], Concurring Opinion of Judge Sicilianos, para 7; see also V Tzevelekos, 'The *Al-Dulimi* Case before the Grand Chamber of the European Court of Human Rights: Business as Usual? Test of Equivalent Protection, (Constitutional) Hierarchy and Systemic Integration' (2017) 38 *Questions of International Law* 5.

published for every listing, giving in short the main grounds for each inclusion in the list. However, the most significant development in this field is the establishment of the office of an independent Ombudsperson whose main task is to process the requests of individuals or entities to be deleted from the list by collecting data, by communicating with petitioners, and drafting reports to the Sanctions Committee. In case of refusal, the Ombudsperson informs the petitioner of the reasons of this decision, if they are not confidential. At first, it was within the competences of the Sanctions Committee to decide on a possible delisting after the proposal of the Ombudsperson. Nevertheless, as the latter depends on the Committee's unanimous decision, it is obvious that any individual state could easily block such a removal from the list, despite the potentially favourable position of the Ombudsperson.

Although the second *Kadi* case was decided in the context of the abovementioned developments of the UN sanctions, the CJEU was not convinced of the sufficiency of the said advancements.[239] Subsequently, the CJEU highlighted that it is among the tasks of the Court to guarantee that sanctions decisions are 'taken on a sufficiently solid factual basis' and that, '[t]o that end, it is for the Courts of the [EU], in order to carry out that examination, to request the competent EU authority, when necessary, to produce information or evidence, confidential or not, relevant to such an examination.'[240] After having reiterated that the confidentiality of that information or evidence is not an acceptable ground for *objection*,[241] the Court focused on the duty of the EU institutions to exercise an in-depth scrutiny of the targeted sanctions imposed by the UN Security Council. In this regard, the Court referred to the standards laid down in the *Nada* judgment of the ECtHR, confirming that it is on the same page with its counterpart on this matter.[242]

As the *Kadi II* ruling of the Grand Chamber of the Court was handed down only a few months after the *Nada* case, it appears that the CJEU was not willing to backtrack[243] from its prior approach in *Kadi I* whose echo inspired the Strasbourg Court in the *Nada* case law. In short, it held that the actions of the European Commission and EU states cannot be afforded immunity[244] from EU jurisdiction on the sole ground that they were simply implementing binding Security Council's resolutions, as the United Nations failed to provide an appropriate forum for judicial redress within the framework of the targeted sanctions having their origins in Chapter VII of the UN Charter.

[239] Joined Cases C-584/10 P, C-593/10 P and C-595/10 P *European Commission and Others v Yassin Abdullah Kadi* [2013] ECLI:EU:C:2013:518, para 66.

[240] ibid para 119–20.

[241] ibid para 125.

[242] ibid para 133.

[243] See for a different reading of the *Kadi II* judgment N Lavranos and M Vatsov, '*Kadi II*: Backtracking from *Kadi I*?' in M Avbelj, F Fontanelli and G Martinico (eds), *Kadi on Trial: A Multifaceted Analysis of the Kadi Trial*, Routledge Research in EU Law (Oxford, Routledge, 2014).

[244] See, eg B Rashkow, 'Immunity of the United Nations: Practice and Challenges' (2014) 10 *International Organizations Law Review* 332.

In doing so, the Court, using also the Charter as the ultimate human rights tool, managed to cultivate a stringent standard of a thorough EU control over the evidentiary basis of the said sanctions taken in the implementation of Security Council binding decisions of the Security Council and directly affecting individuals who may have *locus standi* before the EU Courts. Arguably, even from different perspectives,[245] both the *Kadi* and the *Nada and Al-Dulimi* case law pointed out that the two European jurisdictions adopted a coherent and rather critical approach towards the insufficient protection of core human rights in the context of the UN system with regard to Security Council sanctions. For Erika de Wet, 'the approach of the CJEU carries with it the risk of the devaluation of international human rights law, as well as of legal uncertainty. Its benchmarks for judicial protections are based purely on EU law and leave unanswered the question whether and to what extent the UNSC has to act in accordance with international human rights standards.'[246]

If we look more carefully at the *Kadi II* judgment as a judgment of tremendous constitutional value, notably in the light of the Opinion 2/13 which manifestly prioritised the concept of the EU autonomy, it can be deduced that even though the CJEU maintains its judicial dialogue with international courts – as is the case of its interaction with Strasbourg – the limits with the international organisations are in sight and the judicial dialogue with international Courts are to be made with great persistence in its own terms.

The whole autonomy architecture of the EU as construed by the Luxembourg Court is clearly linked to the *Solange I*-type argument adopted by the General Court[247] and the refusal to move on to a *Solange II*-type argument, in other words a *Bosphorus*-type argument as the Strasbourg Court did in many cases while revisiting the ECHR-EU relationship. Despite the significant practical repercussions[248] of this position of the EU Courts *vis-à-vis* international law, the latter also contains a great *antiphasis* if we take into consideration the relative objections of the CJEU in Opinion 2/13.

Consequently, the CJEU, undeniably influenced by the ECtHR way of working and vice versa, proceeded to an – arguably – external judicial review of the Security Council sanctions in the name of a more effective protection of fundamental rights; however, it strongly objected to the potential exercise of a similar judicial review of EU actions by the Strasbourg Court.

It is utterly evident that this adoption of double standards of protection and the divergent approach of the external review concept not only

[245] E de Wet, 'From Kadi to Nada: Judicial Techniques Favouring Human Rights over United Nations Security Council Sanctions' (2013) 12 *Chinese Journal of International Law* 787, 801–2.

[246] ibid 799.

[247] Case T-85/09 *Yassin Abdullah Kadi v European Commission* [2010] ECR II-5177.

[248] A Tzanakopoulos, 'The Solange Argument as a Justification for Disobeying the Security Council in the Kadi Judgments' in M Avbelj, F Fontanelli and G Martinico (eds), *Kadi on Trial: A Multifaceted Analysis of the Kadi Trial*, Routledge Research in EU Law (Oxford, Routledge, 2014) 134.

strengthens the legal uncertainty which already derived from the *Kadi* litigation,[249] but also raises serious doubts concerning the motivation of the Court's judicial pronouncements.

The main question seeking an answer in the near future is whether the level of fundamental rights protection varies as a by-product of the main EU aims related to the autonomy of EU law and of the CJEU or, for as long as the accession is not in sight, this option will continue to tip the balance in favour of human rights protection.

IV. The Restriction of the EU Asylum Rules in the Light of the ECtHR's Case Law: The Dublin Cases

As already observed, the two legal systems created a spontaneous dialogue between them with regard to the sensitive field of migration/asylum cases as well. Taking into consideration that the European human rights legacy has been traditionally built on the Convention and its application by the ECtHR, the EU's gradual evolution from a common European market to an area of freedom, security and justice, the CJEU gradually rendered the protection of human rights within the Union an absolute priority. Additionally, the entry into force of the Charter following the Lisbon Treaty has definitely encouraged a closer nexus between Strasbourg and the EU legal system in the human rights context[250] and offered to the EU organs and the Luxembourg Court the opportunity to enhance the fundamental rights' dimension of the EU legislature, particularly when it comes to the heated question of migration and asylum.

Given that asylum policy is a relatively new EU competence, the increasing law-making activity of the EU legal order and the CJEU case law with regard to asylum issues has engaged the two institutions in a dialectic model, in the sense of a mutual attempt to avoid divergent interpretations of their respective legal instruments. Thus, as the field of asylum is definitely an illuminative example of such interaction, this one was even more intense as far as the Dublin Regulation is concerned.

Despite the ECtHR's lack of competence to monitor Member States' actions in the EU policy on asylum, the Court could not avoid dealing with the *lacunae* of the EU legislation concerning the Dublin System as more and more applicants invoked the provisions of the Convention in order to attack national authorities' actions in

[249] P Eeckhout, 'Opinion 2/13 on EU Accession to the ECHR and Judicial Dialogue – Autonomy or Autarky?' (2015) Jean Monnet Working Paper Series 01/15, 6, www.jeanmonnetprogram.org/wp-content/uploads/2015/04/JMWP-01-Eeckhout1.pdf.

[250] See, eg M Mouzourakis, 'The Dublin-Strasbourg-Luxembourg Triangle: Getting the European Courts Dialogue on the Suspension of Dublin Regulation Transfers Right' (*Rights in Exile*, 1 March 2014), www.rightsinexile.tumblr.com/post/78228286353/the-dublin-strasbourg-luxembourg-triangle-getting.

the context of the Dublin II Regulation,[251] designed to spread the asylum burden within the borders of the EU. In this context, the CJEU felt it should be inspired by its Strasbourg counterpart to move towards a more human rights-oriented interpretation of the Dublin rules introducing the need of several reforms of the framework.

First and foremost, the Dublin rules initially appeared in the form of the Dublin Convention,[252] signed in 1990. In 2003, this Convention was replaced by the Dublin II Regulation. That Regulation was later replaced by the Dublin III Regulation in 2013, applicable to all asylum applications made after 1 January 2014.

Under the Dublin Regulation, only one Member State is responsible for examining an asylum application. The aim pursued is to avoid asylum-seekers from being sent from one country to another, and to deter multiple asylum claims. Therefore, the Member State designated as responsible for the asylum application must take charge of the applicant and process the application. If a Member State to which an asylum application is lodged deems that another Member State is responsible, it can call on the latter to examine this application. The Dublin system's logic is based on *mutual trust* between EU Member States and on the presumption that, under the same standards of protection, they are all considered safe for the asylum-seekers. However, the practice clearly illustrated severe deficiencies of this system, as returning an applicant to an EU country under the Dublin legal framework would cause an infringement of his/her human rights. This led to the suspension of the Regulation and its replacement by a less strict legislation, subsequent to an intervention from the domestic legal institutions.

A. ECtHR – CJEU Bras de Fer: Paving the Way for the Dublin Reform

The Strasbourg Court first paved this route to suspension by developing a dynamic case law relevant to Dublin cases mainly with its leading decision in *M.S.S. v Belgium and Greece*[253] in 2011. The applicant was an Afghan asylum-seeker who entered the EU via Greece and, following this, moved to Belgium, where he applied for asylum. Implementing the Dublin II Regulation, the Belgian authorities asked the Greek authorities to take responsibility for the asylum application. Subsequent to his transfer back to Greece, the individual was placed in an overcrowded detention centre with appalling sanitary and hygiene conditions. The applicant denounced

[251] Council Regulation (EC) No 343/2003 establishing the criteria and mechanisms for determining the Member State responsible for examining an asylum application lodged in one of the Member States by a third-country national (Dublin II Regulation) [2003] OJ L50/1.

[252] See, eg S Peers, *EU Justice and Home Affairs Law* (Oxford, Oxford University Press, 2006) 318.

[253] *M.S.S. v Belgium and Greece* [GC], Merits, ECHR 2011-I 121.

his detention conditions and alleged that he had no effective remedy in Greek law in order to support his claims in the context of the deficient asylum processing. Additionally, he complained that Belgian authorities had exposed him knowingly to the risks arising from the *lacunae* in the asylum procedure in Greece to which asylum-seekers were subjected, and invoked the provisions of both Articles 3 and 13 of the Convention.

In this light, the Court declared that both Greek and Belgian authorities breached the ECHR and particularly stated that the sovereignty clause in the Dublin Regulation precludes the application of a *Bosphorus*-type presumption[254] given that Member States are not bound to transfer an asylum-seeker to another country.[255] The Strasbourg Court held that the mere existence of domestic legislation and accession to international human rights instruments are not in themselves sufficient to guarantee adequate protection from ill-treatment pursuant to the ECHR standards.[256] Having said this, it further clarified that the Belgian authorities bore the duty to thoroughly examine whether the Greek asylum system operates in practice in a manner compatible with the ECHR level of protection. In the Court's words 'had they done this, they would have seen that the risks the applicant faced were real and individual enough to fall within the scope of Article 3'.[257] Instead, in this judgment the ECtHR reiterated its well-established case law regarding expulsions and its Article 13 jurisprudence on suspensive effect.[258] Indeed, the Strasbourg Court took the opportunity to intensely question the problematic *safe country concept* providing a solid and complete reasoning. As a result, more and more Member States halted Dublin returns to Greece due to the systemic deficiencies of the national asylum procedure declared by the Court.

A few months later, the Luxembourg Court had the opportunity to re-examine its dialectic relationship with the ECtHR, in *NS*,[259] under similar circumstances. Even though, at first, the CJEU seemed to follow the recent *M.S.S.* reasoning, it did not avoid the discrepancies in its attempt to interpret the said judgment of the Strasbourg Court. As the judgment concerned again an Afghan asylum-seeker at risk of a Dublin transfer to Greece, the Luxembourg Court endorsed the conclusions of the ECtHR on the grounds of the poor detention conditions, the

[254] L Vosyliute, 'The ECtHR and the ECJ Overlapping Jurisdictions on Common EU Asylum Policy Issues: What Matters?' (*Academia*, March 2011), www.academia.edu/2706355/ECtHR_and_ECJ_Overlapping_Jurisdiction_on_Common_EU_Asylum_Policy_Issues_What_Matters.

[255] *M.S.S.* (n 253) para 338.

[256] ibid para 353.

[257] ibid para 359.

[258] See especially C Costello, 'Courting Access to Asylum in Europe: Recent Supranational Jurisprudence Explored' (2012) 12 *Human Rights Law Review* 287, 324.

[259] Joined Cases C-411/10 and C-493/10 *NS v Secretary of State for the Home Department and ME and Others v Refugee Applications Commissioner and Minister for Justice, Equality and Law Reform* [2011] ECR I-13905.

ineffective asylum processing and, most importantly, on the refutability of safe country presumption. Particularly, the Court held that

> the Member States, including the national courts, may not transfer an asylum seeker to the 'Member State responsible' within the meaning of Regulation No 343/2003 where they cannot be unaware that systemic deficiencies in the asylum procedure and in the reception conditions of asylum seekers in that Member State amount to substantial grounds for believing that the asylum seeker would face a real risk of being subjected to inhuman or degrading treatment within the meaning of Article 4 of the Charter.[260]

Concerning the real risk of being subject to inhuman or degrading treatment within the meaning of Article 4 CFR, the Court diverged from the opinion of Advocate General Tristenjak who considered any breach of human rights as a sufficient ground to preclude a Dublin return. The Court did not declare the slightest infringement of fundamental right to be sufficient in order to prevent the transfer of an asylum-seeker to the Member State primarily responsible. By contrast, the transfers operated under Dublin II Regulation should be suspended within the strict boundaries of violations of the Article 4 of the Charter concluding to inhuman or degrading treatment. For Costello,

> there are many legally innovative paths not taken. The AG reads the right to asylum in terms of non-refoulement, avoiding its transformative potential as an individual right to be granted asylum (in contrast to the orthodox right to seek asylum). The judgment is strikingly economical, in that the CJEU traces a path already worn by Strasbourg.[261]

This decision, hence, seems disloyal to its aim to mirror the scope and meaning of the applicants' human rights under Article 52(3) of the Charter which formally institutionalised the dialogue between the two legal orders. In *NS* the preliminary ruling revolved also around the matter of *systemic deficiencies* in the asylum procedure and in the reception conditions of asylum seekers. The Court clearly chose a paradox route to respond to that question of the domestic Court. Although, it explicitly invoked the Strasbourg Court's criterion of the *M.S.S.* test and reckoned that the reception and detention conditions in Greece constituted systemic deficiencies within that sense, subsequently, seemed to confuse requisite conditions to amount to a violation of the Article 4 of the Charter as it held that:

> the Member States, including the national courts, may not transfer an asylum seeker to 'the Member State responsible' within the meaning of Regulation No 343/2003 where they cannot be unaware that systemic deficiencies in the asylum procedure and reception conditions for asylum seekers in that Member State amount to substantial grounds for believing that the asylum seeker would face a real risk of being subjected to inhuman and degrading treatment within the meaning of Article 4 of the Charter.[262]

[260] ibid para 94.
[261] Costello 'Courting Access to Asylum' (n 258) 333.
[262] *NS* (n 259) para 94.

As is shown above, the systemic deficiencies constitute a *conditio sine qua non* for the ECtHR in order to prevent a Dublin transfer to a country, whereas according to the Luxembourg Court's appraisal it is a necessary condition but, in no case, a sufficient one. Highly criticised by scholars, the *NS* ruling was seen as a sign of introspectiveness due to the fact that its narrow interpretation is definitely not in line with the ECtHR's interpretation of the prohibition of inhuman and degrading treatment.

This divergent approach regarding returns to a declared 'unsafe' country under the Dublin II Regulation was reaffirmed in two recent cases of the CJEU. In *Puid*[263] the Court reiterated its finding in the *NS* judgment considering the *systemic deficiencies* of the asylum proceeding in question, a necessary condition to oppose Dublin transfer to Greece. It left, however, great discretion to the Member State to determine the existence of those deficiencies and their gravity.[264] Interestingly enough, in the most recent *Abdullahi* case,[265] the Luxembourg Court revisited this issue without, though, moving from its previous narrow position in the aforementioned case law regarding the systemic flaws concept, as it held in paragraph 60 of this judgment that 'the only way in which the applicant for asylum can call into question the choice of that criterion is by pleading systemic deficiencies in the asylum procedure'.[266] However, in practice, the systemic flaws criterion can be proved problematic despite the fact that the number of incidents caused by a flaw may matter for the assessment of a Dublin removal obstacle, as traditionally the corollaries of a flaw will often, but not always, increase the probability that the situation of the applicant will be affected. Nevertheless, the case in which the individual risks to be affected by an occasional incident that amounts to a deficiency of the whole asylum system.[267]

B. Last Breath for Dublin?

The famous ruling of the Strasbourg Court in the *Tarakhel* case,[268] concerning the Italian reception conditions of asylum-seekers, only a few months after the *Sharifi* judgment,[269] was the decision considered by numerous scholars as the one which probably put the final 'nail in the coffin' of the problematic Dublin system. This case revolved around the refusal of the Swiss authorities to give asylum to an Afghan couple and their six children and their decision to transfer them back

[263] Case C-4/11 *Bundesrepublik Deutschland v Kaveh Puid* [2013] ECLI:EU:C:2013:740.
[264] ibid para 31.
[265] Case C-394/12 *Shamso Abdullahi v Bundesasylamt* [2013] ECLI:EU:C:2013:813.
[266] ibid para 60.
[267] See especially A Lübbe, '"Systemic Flaws" and Dublin Transfers: Incompatible Tests before the CJEU and the ECtHR?' (2015) 27 *International Journal of Refugee Law* 135.
[268] *Tarakhel v Switzerland* [GC], Merits, ECHR 2004-VI 159.
[269] *Sharifi and Others v Italy and Greece*, Merits, App no 16643/09 (ECtHR, 21 October 2014).

to Italy. Particularly, the applicants invoked Article 3 ECHR on the grounds that if they were returned to Italy in the absence of individual guarantees concerning their care, they would be subjected to inhuman and degrading treatment due to the existence of systemic deficiencies of the Italian asylum procedure. They also invoked Article 8 and the right to an effective remedy under Article 13 ECHR.

The ECtHR relied upon the *M.S.S.* judgment and its prior case law in order to build its appraisal. Therefore, the ECtHR made a special reference to the CJEU's systemic deficiencies test established in the *NS* judgment, ignoring, however, the more recent *Abdullahi* ruling of the Luxembourg Court. In this context, it stated that these tests had to be applied in the light of the applicant's individual situation in conjunction with the overall situation prevailing in the receiving state.

The applicants in this case particularly focused their complaints on the slowness of identification procedures, the lack of enough places for asylum-seekers and, most importantly, the reception conditions within the available facilities in Italy. Examining the individual situation of the applicants during, the Court denied to equate this case with the *M.S.S.* case as it was not the Italian asylum system under scrutiny but the living conditions in the reception centre where the Tarakhel family was accommodated.[270] It also refused to generally ban the Dublin transfers. However, we can observe an attempt on the Court's part to define differently the term of 'systemic deficiency' of an asylum proceeding. The Court in *Tarakhel* seems to conclude the existence of systemic deficiencies of an asylum system not only when this system is declared totally deteriorated, but also in case of a particular aspect of the asylum procedure regularly malfunctioning, as was the case for the reception conditions of asylum-seekers in Italy.

Another case of the Strasbourg Court should be read in conjunction with the Court's findings in *M.S.S.* and *Tarakhel*. In *AME v The Netherlands*[271] a Somali national fled Somalia due to his refusal to join a terrorist organisation. After a short period in Italy where he applied for asylum and received subsidiary protection, he travelled to the Netherlands and filed a second application, which was later rejected as Italian authorities were determined responsible for processing his asylum application, pursuant to the Dublin rules. The applicant feared that his transfer to Italy would result in his removal to Somalia on account of the lack of judicial guarantees and effective remedies in Italy, and he invoked not only Article 3 ECHR but also Articles 5, 6 and 13 ECHR. In response to the applicant's allegations, the Court focused on his own statements to the Italian authorities that he was an adult, and his deliberate attempt to mislead the authorities. The Court subsequently noted that the facts of the case are in no way identical to the conditions of *Tarakhel* case, as 'the applicant is an able young man with no dependants'. It also reiterated in its reasoning that the reception arrangements in Italy were not comparable to those of Greece as described in its key ruling *M.S.S.*, and that the

[270] *Tarakhel* (n 268) para 120.
[271] *AME v The Netherlands* (dec), App no 51428/10 (ECtHR, 13 January 2015).

applicant had not proved a sufficiently real and imminent risk enough to reach the threshold of Article 3 ECHR.

Therefore, in *AME*, the ECtHR confirmed the *lacunae* of the Dublin architecture. It built its appraisal, though, in the light of *Tarakhel* with regard to the issue of 'vulnerability' in Dublin cases, and suggested that 'the applicant is an able young man with no dependants', which was not the case in *Tarakhel* due to the particularly vulnerable age of the children of the family. Unfortunately, at this point the Court seemed reluctant to clarify the urgent matter of the relation or the distinction between different levels of vulnerability, and even different levels of particular vulnerability.[272] This debatable issue remains under discussion, especially following the Partly Dissenting Opinion[273] in *Tarakhel* which criticised the Court's position to reverse the recent case law where the Court held that there was no reason to believe that an asylum-seeker and her two young children would not have received adequate support had they been sent back to Italy under the Dublin Regulation, in *Mohammed Hussein and Others v the Netherlands and Italy.*[274]

Having said all that, the ECtHR's aim is traditionally to ascertain, on a case-by-case basis, whether the individual risk of the applicant had been duly considered without focusing only on the systemic or not flaws[275] of the asylum architecture in question. In contrast, the persistence of the CJEU to the Dublin Regulation's initial objectives and the principle of mutual trust, which was repeatedly affirmed in the case law which followed *Abdullahi*, severely impeded the dialogue with Strasbourg. In fact, the Court seemed to have granted to Article 4 EUCFR a much narrower scope of application than the corresponding prohibition of torture of Article 3 ECHR which constituted for decades the cornerstone of asylum-seekers' protection. The lower threshold afforded by the Luxembourg Court seems to be incompatible with the provision of the EU Charter in Article 52 EUCFR that requires that the level of protection offered by the Charter should be at least the same as that offered by the Convention.[276]

However, having in mind the absolute character of the principle of *non-refoulement*, rooted in Article 3 ECHR, and the extended protection against indirect refoulement, we can assume that the CJEU opts for a rather restricted version of the latter, meaning an intra-EU 'non-refoulement' principle. As a result, insofar as both the Courts admit that mutual trust is not, in practice, blind upholding that

[272] S Nicolosi, 'Another Episode in the Strasbourg Saga on the Dublin System to Determine the State Responsible for Asylum Applications' (*Strasbourg Observers*, 20 February 2015), www.strasbourgobservers.com/2015/02/20/another-episode-in-the-strasbourg-saga-on-the-dublin-system-to-determine-the-state-responsible-for-asylum-applications/#more-2771.

[273] *Tarakhel* (n 268) Partly dissenting opinion by Judges Casadevall, Berro-Lefèvre and Jäderblom.

[274] *Mohammed Hussein and Others v the Netherlands and Italy* (dec), App no 27725/10 (ECtHR, 2 April 2013).

[275] This wording ('systemic flaws' instead of systemic deficiencies) was also incorporated in Art 3 para 2 Dublin III Regulation.

[276] See the opinion expressed by Cathryn Costello in C Costello 'Courting Access to Asylum' (n 258); J Vicini, 'The Dublin Regulation between Strasbourg and Luxembourg: Reshaping *Non-Refoulement* in the Name of Mutual Trust?' (2015) 8(2) *European Journal of Legal Studies* 50, 66.

the presumption is rebuttable and as the *Bosphorus* equivalent protection doctrine is not applicable to Dublin cases, the Member States' actions in compliance with this newly created principle of non-refoulement renders the latter susceptible to ECtHR scrutiny.

In any case, the recast Dublin Regulation (Dublin III),[277] which inaugurated the second phase of the Common European Asylum System (CEAS), came to remedy the aforementioned lacunae. In this aim, it adopted a less strict approach towards the asylum-seekers moving within the EU borders as it set up a much more reasonable timetable regarding the applicants' transfers, including a personal interview establishing, thus, a humanitarian clause. It also codified the previous systemic deficiencies in case law of the Luxembourg Court in accordance with the relative provisions laid down in the Charter (Article 3 Dublin III Regulation) and provided useful clarifications on the rights of asylum-seekers as well as an early warning mechanism. It also extended the protection offered to in the Dublin III Regulation, protection of the family unit in the case of minors being extended to the legal presence of siblings or other relatives[278] in an attempt to align with the Strasbourg Court's standards of protection on the matter.

It is beyond any doubt that this reform of EU asylum instruments attempted to address the malfunctions of the Dublin II Regulation in the field of the human rights protection of asylum-seekers. However, the ongoing refugee crisis which started in 2015 with thousands of people crossing the Mediterranean Sea in rough conditions in order to reach the EU borders –mostly the Greek and Italian ones – in order to seek asylum severely aggravated the situation. Thus, its immediate practical, political and legal repercussions revealed the unsustainability of the Dublin system which was initially designed to provide a fair distribution of responsibilities as far as people seeking international protection are concerned. Nonetheless, given the EU institutions' and national governments' lack of preparation to handle the enormous mixed flows of undocumented migrants, the credibility alone of the Union has lately caused great controversy.[279]

Hence, it is surprising that, in the middle of the ongoing refugee crisis, the Luxembourg Court, in the *Mirza* case[280] concerning the right of Member State to return an asylum-seeker to his country of origin, opted for an alarmingly *laissez-faire* interpretation of Article 3(3) of the Dublin III Regulation, finding that

[277] Regulation (EU) No 604/2013 of the European Parliament and of the Council establishing the criteria and mechanisms for determining the Member State responsible for examining an application for international protection lodged in one of the Member States by a third-country national or stateless person (recast) (Dublin III Regulation) [2013] OJ L180/31.This Regulation became applicable on 1 January 2014.

[278] Art 8 of the Dublin III Regulation.

[279] See M Di Filippo, 'The Refugee Crisis and the Executive: on the Limits of Administrative Discretion in the Common European Asylum System' (2016) International Institute of Humanitarian Law Policy Brief, www.statewatch.org/news/2016/feb/eu-from-dublin-to-athens-reforming-dublin-reg-1-16.pdf.

[280] Case C-695/15 PPU *Shiraz Baig Mirza v Bevándorlási és Állampolgársági Hivatal* [2016] ECLI:EU:C:2016:188.

any Member State may apply the 'safe third country' provision at any point in the process without time limitations even before assessing the Dublin criteria.[281] As a result, asylum-seekers may be in danger of being returned to a third country without due consideration being paid to their individual fundamental rights, including the right to family life. The ECRE[282] observed that '[t]he interplay of this concept in the application of the Dublin system already raises critical protection concerns, given that safe country concepts *per se* are liable to violate international obligations.'[283]

In the meantime, following the huge refugee crisis of historic proportions with which Europe is confronted and the closure of the European states' borders in Western Europe,[284] the EU institutions needed to respond immediately to these ever-growing needs and manage the major influx of migrants, particularly the thousands of Syrians who, following the aggravation of the situation in Syria,[285] have arrived in Europe via the Mediterranean routes.

Under these alarming circumstances, the European institutions and Member States opted to obtain the co-operation of Turkey in order to manage the enormous migration flows. Having included Turkey in a European common list of safe countries of origin, the EU institutions negotiated with Turkey in the context of the joint action plan already being formulated in November 2015, and concluded an EU-Turkey statement[286] apparently aiming to reduce the number of asylum-seekers reaching the EU borders. As expected, this agreement provoked a heated debate due to the political and legal particularities in Turkey, with emphasis on persecution and the human rights standards of protection.[287] Within the CoE system, the Parliamentary Assembly expressed severe concerns with regard to the situation of refugees and migrants under the EU–Turkey Agreement of

[281] Especially when the designation of a country as 'safe' is based on national criteria.

[282] European Council of Refugees and Exiles (ECRE).

[283] ECRE, 'ECRE Comments on the Commission Proposal for a Dublin IV Regulation COM(2016) 270' (October 2016), www.ecre.org/wp-content/uploads/2016/10/ECRE-Comments-Dublin-IV.pdf, 6.

[284] See relatively the *Ilias and Ahmed* judgment of the ECtHR, whereby the Strasbourg Court severely condemned Hungary on the basis of Arts 3, 5 and 13 ECHR for practices which led to the de facto deprivation of the applicants' liberty and forced return to Serbia on the grounds of the 'safe third country' doctrine, emphasising the shortcomings of the asylum proceedings in Serbia. The Court's appraisal sends a rather clear message to both the Hungarian and Serbian authorities, doubting, in this way, the lawfulness of Dublin returns to these countries in line with its *M.S.S.* jurisprudence, particularly, in light of the risk of chain refoulement practices. *Ilias and Ahmed v Hungary*, Merits, App no 47287/15 (ECtHR, 14 March 2017). Compare with the more recent *Ilias and Ahmed v Hungary* [GC], Merits, App no 47287/15 (ECtHR, 21 November 2019).

[285] The civil war in Syria started in 2011 and resulted in the enormous refugee crisis which still affects Europe, despite the subsequent decrease in arrivals of migrants.

[286] European Council, 'EU-Turkey statement, 18 March 2016' (Press Release, 18 March 2016), www.consilium.europa.eu/en/press/press-releases/2016/03/18-eu-turkey-statement/. See on the final statement S Peers, 'The Final EU/Turkey Refugee Deal: a Legal Assessment' (*EU Law Analysis*, 18 March 2016), www.eulawanalysis.blogspot.gr/2016/03/the-final-euturkey-refugee-deal-legal.html.

[287] See, eg K Gogou, 'The EU-Turkey Deal: Europe's Year of Shame' (Amnesty International, 20 March 2017), www.amnesty.org/en/latest/news/2017/03/the-eu-turkey-deal-europes-year-of-shame/.

18 March 2016.[288] Among others, the latter highlighted in its Resolution substantive and operational human rights issues in relation to deficiencies of the Greek asylum system concerning timely registration of asylum applications, detention conditions of asylum-seekers in the hotspots on the Aegean islands and most significantly, returns of Syrian asylum-seekers /refugees to Turkey as 'first country of asylum' or 'safe third country' due to the fact that 'Turkey may not ensure protection that is "sufficient", according to the position of the Office of the United Nations High Commissioner for Refugees (UNHCR), and there have been reports of onward refoulement of Syrians.'

However, under all this aforementioned pressure, the EU Commission published its proposal for a Dublin IV Regulation[289] without, nonetheless, addressing the flagrant weaknesses of this framework. Instead, this recast of the Dublin rules pursued a more effective allocation through repressive measures and penalties aiming to deter the mass influx of irregular migrants despite some corrective initiatives retaining gatekeeper responsibilities to the states of first entry.[290] In a nutshell, the Commission's proposal, setting aside human rights issues, sticks rigorously to the idea or hope that claimants will abstain from choosing the state of their initial destination. By all means, this strategy remains in clear contrast with the principal objectives of the CEAS architecture as laid down in Article 78(1) TFEU.

Against this background, at the same time, the CJEU seemed more willing to extend the right to appeal in the context of the Dublin rules as the *Ghezelbash*[291] and *Karim*[292] rulings (both delivered on 7 June 2016) on the right to challenge the Dublin transfers departing from its restrictive approach confirmed in *Abdullahi*. In the cases at hand, the Luxembourg Court interpreted Article 28(4) Dublin III Regulation[293] in the light of the EU Charter's provisions regarding the right to an effective remedy and ruled that the claimants have the right to appeal against Dublin transfers on the basis of the misapplication of the Regulation's criteria which could amount to potential violations of fundamental rights.

It is also noteworthy that the opposite reading would fall below the standards set out in Article 13 ECHR. According to the Strasbourg Court, in Dublin cases, such a violation could be related to the availability of remedies against eg

[288] CoE Parliamentary Assembly, Resolution 2109(2016) on the situation of refugees and migrants under the EU–Turkey Agreement of 18 March 2016 (20 April 2016).

[289] European Commission, 'Proposal for a Regulation of the European Parliament and of the Council establishing the criteria and mechanisms for determining the Member State responsible for examining an application for international protection lodged in one of the Member States by a third-country national or a stateless person (recast)' (Dublin IV Regulation) COM (2016) 270 final.

[290] See, eg F Maiani, 'The Reform of the Dublin III Regulation' (Study of the Policy Department C: Citizens' Rights and Constitutional Affairs, European Parliament, 2016), www.europarl.europa.eu/RegData/etudes/STUD/2016/571360/IPOL_STU(2016)571360_EN.pdf.

[291] Case C-63/15 *Mehrdad Ghezelbash v Staatssecretaris van Veiligheid en Justitie* [2016] ECLI:EU:C:2016:409.

[292] Case C-155/15 *George Karim v Migrationsverket* [2016] ECLI:EU:C:2016:410.

[293] This article was introduced in the Dublin III Regulation after the *Abdullahi* ruling.

refoulement practices which are likely to expose the asylum-seeker to inhuman or degrading treatment (irrespective of whether or not there are 'systemic flaws' of the asylum proceeding), interfering with family life within the meaning of Article 8 ECHR (irrespective of whether the criteria are respected), or raising an issue under Article 3 or 8 ECHR due to the state of applicants' health. Additionally, as stated in ECRE's comments on the new Dublin IV proposal,

> The proposed restrictions on the sovereignty clause also raise problems of compatibility with the ECHR. Although little-used, the sovereignty clause is a key element of the Dublin system that allows Member States to renounce a transfer if it would breach fundamental rights. The limitations flowing from recital 21 and Art.19(2) DIVP would make this impossible, and would place EU Law on a collision course with the ECHR.[294]

Leaving this critique aside, it is generally accepted that the Dublin legislation has to a great extent incorporated many of the Strasbourg Court's positions in asylum cases, paving the way for its Luxembourg peer to interpret these rules in conformity with the Convention's provisions and lately, with the Charter's provisions as well.

Nevertheless, while the discussion regarding the definitive abolition of the Dublin legislation and its replacement by a more effective and fair allocation system is gaining ground, some new developments on the matter appear to be in the wrong direction. In particular, the order of the General Court, a year after the EU–Turkey statement, shockingly denied jurisdiction to pronounce on the actions brought by three asylum-seekers who challenged this statement.[295]

However, not only the intense dissonance of the two Courts in relation to the Dublin system, but also recent jurisprudential and legislative developments seeking mostly to put an impediment to migration flows rather than dealing with emerging human rights issues raised on the occasion of this ongoing refugee crisis, clearly unbalanced the sole endeavour to alleviate the problems documented in this field.

It was this well-documented dissonance between the two Courts and the blatant lack of coherence pertaining to European standards of protection that the recent judicial activity of the CJEU came to remedy. Under the pressure of the ECtHR enhanced guarantees in asylum cases, the Luxembourg case law has revealed some signs of reconciliation with the degree of protection offered by its sister judicial institution in 2017. Apparently, the Court of Justice felt in the *CK* case[296] that it should retain its willingness to 'sacrifice' mutual trust when absolute fundamental rights are at stake, as also expressed in the *Aranyosi Căldăraru* judgment.[297]

[294] ECRE, 'ECRE Comments on the Commission Proposal for a Dublin IV Regulation (n 283).
[295] Case T-192/16 *NF v European Council* (Order) [2017] ECLI:EU:T:2017:128.
[296] Case C-578/16 PPU *CK and Others v Republika Slovenija* [2017] ECLI:EU:C:2017:127.
[297] Joined Cases C-404/15 and C-659/15 *Pál Aranyosi και Robert Căldăraru* [2016] ECLI:EU:C:2016:198.

In *casu*, the Court was asked by the Slovenian Supreme Court whether the individual's risk of ill-treatment due to his/her deteriorated health could suffice for the suspension of a Dublin transfer on these grounds.

Most importantly, the CJEU reconsidered its position on the connection between the risk of inhuman/degrading treatment and the existence of systemic deficiencies. Having applied for asylum in Slovenia, a couple with a baby brought their case to the Slovenian courts when their claim was rejected, since Croatia was deemed responsible for examining the application under the Dublin legislation. They alleged that the fragile medical condition of the mother who, after giving birth to her child, was suffering from serious depression and periodic suicidal tendencies, was likely to worsen if she left the country.

Pursuant to Article 52(3) CFR, the Court used Article 3 ECHR and the respective enforcement by the ECtHR in its *Paposhvili* jurisprudence as an interpretative tool to read accordingly the corresponding provision of Article 4 CFR.[298] According to this judgment, severe illness can reach the high threshold of Article 3 ECHR in similar conditions. In its words 'the suffering which flows from naturally occurring illness may be covered by Article 3, where it is, or risks being, exacerbated by treatment, whether flowing from conditions of detention, expulsion or other measures, for which the authorities can be held responsible'.[299] Taking a step back from its *NS* findings, the CJEU held that even in the absence of systemic flaws in the receiving Member State, the transfer of an asylum-seeker may take place under the Dublin rules 'only in conditions which exclude the possibility that that transfer might result in a real and proven risk of the person concerned suffering inhuman or degrading treatment, within the meaning of that article'.[300]

Put differently, while in the past the Luxembourg Court had strongly defended the systemic deficiencies test as the only reliable criterion to suspend a Dublin transfer, the *CK* case appears to draw an analogy from *Aranyosi Căldăraru* and incorporate the *Tarakhel* principles of the Strasbourg Court introducing some exceptions[301] from the total domination of the mutual trust among EU Member States. However, these exceptional circumstances occur when a fundamental right of absolute character needs to be prioritised. The overall meaning of the case should not definitely be construed as leaving room for prioritising every human right over mutual trust.[302] Probably the Court has recently acknowledged

[298] *CK and Others* (n 296) para 68.

[299] *Paposhvili v Belgium* [GC], Merits, App no 41738/10 (ECtHR, 13 December 2016), paras 174–75. In the aftermath of the *Paposhvili* judgment, the Luxembourg Court, in *MP*, and enlarged the scope of subsidiary protection encompassing also former victims of torture or inhuman and degrading treatment who, upon return, are intentionally deprived of necessary medical treatment by the authorities in their country of origin in light of Arte 4 of the Charter. Case C-353/16 *MP v Secretary of State for the Home Department* [2018] ECLI:EU:C:2018:276.

[300] *CK and Others* (n 296).

[301] Nevertheless, the Court sought to underline that its overall conclusion is perfectly compatible with its mutual trust concept in para 95.

[302] Case C-163/17 *Abubacarr Jawo v Bundesrepublik Deutschland* [2019] ECLI:EU:C:2019:218, para 98; Joined Cases C-297/17, C-318/17, C-319/17 and C-438/17 *Bashar Ibrahim and Others v Bundesrepublik Deutschland and Taus Magamadov* [2019] ECLI:EU:C:2019:219, para 101.

that the smooth functioning of the mutual trust architecture passes through the effective protection of fundamental rights as the ECtHR has also manifested in *Avotiņš v Latvia*.[303] For President Lenaerts, 'the successful operation of the principle of mutual trust and the effective judicial protection of fundamental rights require the national courts, the ECtHR and the ECJ to engage in a constructive dialogue.'[304] While the Court of Justice avoided explicit reference to the *Tarakhel* influence, it seemed willing to keep its relationship with the Strasbourg Court alive. This being so, if read together with the seminal *Aranyosi* judgment in relation to EAW and EU criminal law, also delivered in the post-Opinion 2/13 era, the *CK* ruling can be perceived as a positive sign apt to ease the tension between the two systems arisen by the said Opinion – at least as regards human rights protection within the Dublin framework.[305]

In the *Jawo* case,[306] the CJEU recalled its *CK* standards,[307] drew inspiration from the ECtHR's case law on Article 3 ECHR, and took the opportunity to define the accepted threshold for suspending the Dublin return of an asylum-seeker to the responsible Member State. It therefore extended the monitoring obligation of the State to guarantee that the rules governing the grant of international protection – not just the Dublin transfer – are respected, in conformity with the Charter.[308] Yet, the Court probably fears that such a line of argumentation would open the door to restrictions of mutual confidence that would destabilise the entire CEAS. Such an understanding explains the CJEU's option to recall the high threshold that the prohibition of ill-treatment entails under the ECHR and to define its outer limits when balanced with mutual trust and applied in the context of the Dublin architecture. To legitimise such an approach, the CJEU referred to *M.S.S.* and the interconnection of the two systems via Article 52(3) CFR, stressing that 'the deficiencies … must attain a particularly high level of severity, which depends on all the circumstances of the case'. The Court further clarified that

> That particularly high level of severity is attained where the indifference of the authorities of a Member State would result in a person wholly dependent on State support finding himself, irrespective of his wishes and personal choices, in a situation of extreme material poverty that does not allow him to meet his most basic needs, such as, inter

[303] *Avotiņš* (n 189).
[304] K Lenaerts, 'La vie apres l' avis: Exploring the Principle of Mutual (yet not blind) Trust' (2017) 54 *CML Rev* 805, 838.
[305] E Gill-Pedro and X Groussot, 'The Duty of Mutual Trust in EU Law and the Duty to Secure Human Rights: Can the EU's Accession to the ECHR Ease the Tension?' (2017) 35 *Nordic Journal of Human Rights* 258; Š Imamovic and E Muir, 'The Dublin III System: More Derogations to the Duty to Transfer Individual Asylum Seekers?' (2017) 2(2) *European Papers* 719; C Rizcallah, 'The Dublin System: the ECJ Squares the Circle between Mutual Trust and Human Rights Protection' (*EU Law Analysis*, 20 February 2017), www.eulawanalysis.blogspot.com/2017/02/the-dublin-system-ecj-squares-circle.html.
[306] Case C-163/17 *Abubacarr Jawo v Bundesrepublik Deutschland*, ECLI:EU:C:2019:218, para 98.
[307] ibid paras 77–78.
[308] ibid paras 88–90.

> alia, food, personal hygiene and a place to live, and that undermines his physical or mental health or puts him in a state of degradation incompatible with human dignity.[309]

Therefore, when it comes to living conditions of asylum-seekers, only situations that might entail extreme material poverty might trigger the protection of Article 4 CFR.

Jawo is, hence, indicative of the ongoing struggle of the CJEU to strike a balance between the effective protection of the most vulnerable claimants with the EU common principles. Although at first sight, the CJEU seems to expand the 'mutual, not blind' exception of the usual test which is applicable because of the expected degrading living conditions that the transferee might face, it appears to take a step back from its *CK* protective take. Its narrow perception of the absolute protection of Article 4 CFR is restricted to a 'real and proven' risk of facing extreme conditions of utmost vulnerability. While mutual trust is high in the agenda of EU-CoE negotiations on the accession, the CJEU feels that it should defend the utmost importance of the presumption for the functioning of the dysfunctional CEAS despite the ever-expanding reasons suggesting otherwise. It also creates some ambiguity as to whether the EU indeed offers a level of equivalent protection within the meaning of Article 52(3).[310]

In a nutshell, in the face of uncontrolled migration flows, the EU judicature alarmingly prioritised the protection of the allocation mechanism at any cost in a coercion-oriented direction[311] instead of guaranteeing the fundamental rights of the most vulnerable in this time of crisis. In fact, the hypocritical standing of EU institutions, which initially declared Turkey a safe third country on the basis of a political exchange,[312] and only a year after the EU-Turkey deal adopted a Pontius Pilate approach, washing their hands while reviewing the latter, revealed that the Union's system had a rather faulty and unprepared reaction to the current situation. For the CJEU, rethinking its understanding of mutual trust under exceptionally pressing conditions for human dignity and thus reshaping its human rights standards was lately revealed as a new road that should be probably taken.

In light of all the above, the Dublin system seems to be stagnated, unable to remedy all the malfunctions of the past. The responses of the EU institutions, as the proposal for the Dublin's reform flagrantly illustrated, failed to address the thorny spots of this scheme that arose in the recent past and might arise again in case of new migratory challenges. The political upheaval around the sustainability

[309] ibid paras 91–92.

[310] See Andrea Galea, 'The *Jawo* case: the limits of the principle of mutual trust', European Law Blog (2019), https://europeanlawblog.eu/2019/05/13/the-jawo-case-the-limits-of-the-principle-of-mutual-trust/; Anagnostaras, G, 'The Common European Asylum System: Balancing Mutual Trust Against Fundamental Rights Protection' (2020) 21 *German Law Journal* 1180.

[311] See relatively M den Heijer, J Rijpma and T Spijkerboer, 'Coercion, Prohibition, and Great Expectations: The Continuing Failure of the Common European Asylum System' (2016) 53 *Common Market Law Review* 607.

[312] For relieving the uneven burden at the external borders of the EU in the context of this co-operation, Turkey was incentivised with visa liberalisation and re-energising the accession process to the EU.

and the future of the Dublin system has inevitably locked up the entire machinery and the 'dirty job' was actually done through the EU's temporary arrangements that aimed to serve as a bridge to the proposed Dublin IV Regulation.[313] Since its publication, the latter remained just a proposal and the European Commission came, in September 2020, with an holistic, yet enormous, legislative package, namely the New Pact on Migration and Asylum,[314] which is currently negotiated within the EU institutions. The package is composed of a number of Commission Recommendations and Regulations, some of which will replace existing legal framework with the aim to build a robust system of migration management, also apt to predict and respond to potential crises. Communicated as a 'fresh start', the New Pact has already created ambiguity as for the innovative response that it promises. Only indicatively, solidarity (ie the return sponsorship concept), when it comes to relocation, is voluntary and raises human rights compliance concerns, the proposed Screening Regulation creates *de nouveau* additional pressure at the European borders and, arguably, does not sit comfortably with the anticipated fair allocation system. Last but not least, the Regulation that seeks to recast the Dublin system maintains the rule of the country of first entry when determining the responsible Member States for the examination of asylum application.

Seemingly, the envisaged provisions are definitely taking stock from the EU's previous controversial legislative steps adopting an ensemble of new rules that, on the one hand, need to restore the 'wounded' mutual trust with respect to EU human rights law and on the other hand, attempt to appease the concerns of the Eastern EU Member States. Apparently the EU, which possibly strives to see that people on the move might also be part of the solution, still needs the human rights guidance of its Strasbourg counterpart to bear this additional burden, so that the dialogue and the balance of powers between the two Courts would be consistently readjusted.

V. Conclusion

In sum, there is no doubt that the EU human rights law was formulated and developed under the shadow of the ECHR. Arguably, the two European judicial fora followed convergent interpretations but sometimes dissimilar approaches due to the distinct legislations on the protection of fundamental rights and their different objectives. Overall, as analytically discussed in this first part of the book, the impact of the Strasbourg system on the EU legal order was realised not only through the direct application of the Convention's provisions in several fields of

[313] European Commission, 'Managing Migration: Commission Calls Time on Asylum Reform Stalling' (Press Release, 4 December 2018), www.europa.eu/rapid/press-release_IP-18-6627_en.htm.

[314] European Commission, Migration and Asylum Package: New Pact on Migration and Asylum documents adopted on 23 September 2020, www.ec.europa.eu/info/publications/migration-and-asylum-package-new-pact-migration-and-asylum-documents-adopted-23-september-2020_en.

EU law, but also by revisiting the EU normative framework in the light of the ECHR and the relevant ECtHR case law. The latter, served as a guiding light not only for the judicial work of the Court of Justice when reviewing human rights-sensitive EU rules but also for EU policymaking. Data protection and migration policies and legislative amendments, for example, were – and still are – developed with due consideration to the ECtHR judicial production. In this light, traditional EU concepts (ie internal market, mutual trust, solidarity) have indeed been reinvented to address novel, more complex challenges and be compatible with the contemporary reading of the Charter and the ECHR, as interactively harnessed by the respective fora.

The latest failed attempt for the EU's accession to the ECHR along with the overshadowed role of the Charter readjusted the judicial dialogue between the Luxembourg and the Strasbourg Court, advanced some controversial issues and, thus, left open a number of key questions. Ever since the release of Opinion 2/13, both jurisdictions have readdressed some of these questions and significant progress has been recently made towards a more comprehensive and consistent human rights enforcement. Thorny as they may be, all relevant issues that lie at the core of the intertwined relationship between the two Courts entail further reflection and are currently on the table of the Negotiation Group that works on the ambitious accession project.

PART II

Exporting the ECHR to the International Legal Order

In an era of phenomenal proliferation of interrelated human rights judicial and quasi-judicial fora, the ECtHR has remarkably set the paradigm of building a self-standing, autonomous interpretation of an international human rights text with the rich endorsement of external sources of law, normative and jurisprudential. As the ultimate gatekeeper of regional human rights protection and the frontrunner in international law-making in these terms, the Strasbourg Court has provided a robust case law whose echo has remarkable implications on the judicial practice of its counterparts both at the regional and the global levels.

3

Regional to Regional: The Impact of the ECtHR Case Law on Human Rights Protection in the Americas

In the realm of international human rights law, the fruitful interaction between the European and the Inter-American human rights systems offers the most luminous example of a meaningful judicial dialogue. The main monitoring mechanism of the latter construed the American Convention on Human Rights (hereinafter ACHR) as a legal instrument that needs to be interpreted with remarkable openness to other legal orders, borrowing, when deemed necessary, valuable tools in order to fight against the strenuous vulnerabilities of this troubled region and to foster the rule of law. While the main focus of the following chapter is on the Inter-American Court of Human Rights (hereinafter IACtHR), some analogies enlightening the manner in which the African Court on Human and Peoples' Rights (hereinafter ACtHPR)[1] imports the ECHR norms are also drawn, as appropriate.

[1] Similarly to the Inter-American system, the African human rights system has borrowed its structure extensively from the European architecture whilst it has also presented its own novelties since its dawn. The cornerstone of the African system is arguably the African Charter on Human and Peoples' Rights (also known as the 'Banjul Charter'), adopted on 27 June 1981 under the auspices of the African Union (former Organisation of African Unity – OAU) and entered into force on 21 October 1986. The African Commission on Human and Peoples' Rights was institutionalised in 1987 and its headquarters are now situated in Banjul, Gambia. The African Commission has echoed the practices and standards of its European sister institution, albeit in a restricted manner. Given the openness of the African system pursuant to Articles 60 and 61 of the Charter that legitimise the use of external legal sources, the Commission has referred spontaneously to the ECtHR and IACtHR case law in cases touching upon the freedom of expression or the *ne bis in idem* principle. It has also used the approaches of these tribunals as interpretative tools for similar approaches of the Charter, or to fill the gaps of the latter. The Protocol to the African Charter on Human and Peoples' Rights on the Establishment of the African Court on Human and Peoples' Rights was adopted in 1998 and the ACtHPR was set up. However, the protocol came into effect in 2005 and the Court came into being in 2006 and a few years of inactivity followed until its first judgment *in merito* was issued in 2009. In 2008, the merger of the ACtHPR and the Court of Justice of the African Union was decided, as laid down in the Protocol on the Statute of the African Court of Justice and Human Rights. Albeit not yet completed, the new mechanism is intended to adjudicate disputes falling within the scope of both human rights law and general international law. African Charter on Human and Peoples' Rights (adopted 27 June 1981, entered into force 21 October 1986) (1982) 21 ILM 58 (Banjul Charter); African Charter on Human and Peoples' Rights Protocol on the Establishment of an African Court on Human and People's Rights (adopted 9 June 1998, entered into force 25 January 2004).

I. Introduction

The Inter-American system was originally founded on the Charter of the Organization of American States[2] in 1948 (hereinafter OAS) containing also – among others – core human rights provisions. At the same time, the American Declaration of the Rights and Duties of Man[3] was adopted and the American Convention on Human Rights[4] (hereinafter ACHR) followed, in 1969, to entrench the protection of individuals from gross human rights violations, common in the Americas. Besides the particularities of this part of the world due to a long tradition of brutal dictatorships, violent repression of political enemies, forced disappearances and terrorism, the OAS played a politically pivotal role. It had also to tackle a certain dislocation within the region, between the United States of America and Canada and the rest, since the system can be easily characterised as a Latin-American one, judging from the rare presence of the northern American states.[5]

It was in the context of OAS that the first supervisory organ of the said normative instruments came into being, namely the Inter-American Commission on Human Rights. However, notwithstanding the institutionalisation of the Inter-American Commission as an autonomous mechanism of the OAS (1959), it was the ACHR that gave true meaning to the Commission's arsenal. The American Convention on Human Rights (or Pact of San José),[6] signed in San José (Costa Rica) in 1969, ever since its adoption has constituted the most solid normative basis for the protection of individuals in the Americas. Closely modelled on the ECHR and inspired to a certain extent by the International Covenant on Civil and Political Rights (ICCPR), the ACHR managed to provide a distinguishable legal instrument with the aim of ensuring human rights standards and remedies for human rights violations.

The American Convention incorporated a long and detailed catalogue of civil and political rights, richer than that of the ECHR, since the American text established more advanced and enlightened guarantees, echoing the particularities of the region. As regards the institutional framework of the entire system, the Inter-American system followed the CoE paradigm which relied on the European

[2] The OAS was created in 1948 with the signing in Bogotá (Colombia) of the Charter of the OAS, which entered into force in 1951 and was later amended by a number of Protocols (the Protocol of Buenos Aires in 1967, the Protocol of Cartagena de Indias signed in 1985, the Protocol of Managua, signed in 1993 and the Protocol of Washington, signed in 1992).

[3] American Declaration of the Rights and Duties of Man, OAS Res XXX adopted by the Ninth International Conference of American States (1948) reprinted in Basic Documents Pertaining to Human Rights in the Inter – American System OEA/Ser L V/II.82 Doc 6 Rev 1 at 17 (1992).

[4] American Convention on Human Rights 'Pact of San José, Costa Rica' (adopted 22 November 1969, entered into force 18 July 1978) 1144 UNTS 123 (ACHR).

[5] D Harris, 'Regional Protection of Human Rights: The Inter-American Achievement' in D Harris and S Livingstone (eds), *The Inter-American System of Human Rights* (Oxford, Clarendon Press, 1998).

[6] The ACHR was signed in 1969, entering into force in July 1978 following the 11th ratification.

Commission and the European Court of Human Rights to guarantee the implementation of the ECHR. By the same token, the American Convention mandates the creation of two supervisory organs entrusted with the legal protection of human rights, namely the Inter-American Commission and the Inter-American Court of Human Rights.[7]

The Commission's role in the promulgation of human rights standards was based not only on the examination of individual petitions but also on on-site visits and drafting thematic reports of its findings with regard to the situation of the OAS Member States.[8] Furthermore, the Commission is also responsible for making specific recommendations to American states so as to promote compliance with international human rights norms, but most importantly, it functions as a filter of the cases brought before the IACtHR. As regards individual complaints filed with the Commission, the latter is the first to examine the petition and, after having found a complaint admissible, seeks for a friendly settlement between the parties. If such a settlement cannot be achieved, the Commission, through a fact-finding procedure, finds – or not – a breach of the Convention's provisions, whereafter it may make recommendations to the respondent state, with which the latter needs to comply within a three-month period. If that is not the case, the Commission may submit the case to the Inter-American Court[9] or the State Party may challenge the Commission's attribution of international responsibility before the Court. By analogy, interstate cases must first be considered by the Commission before they can be referred to the Court.

Hence, the Court adjudicates the human rights obligations set forth in the ACHR and, in the case of a violation, it provides legally binding rulings, ordering the responsible state to make reparations in this respect. Despite the distinct, but complementary, roles that the Commission and the Court serve, the structural and normative complexity of the Inter-American system produced severe inequalities and inconsistencies. Since, during the first decade of its short life, the IACtHR did not exercise its competence to resolve contentious disputes, it restricted itself to only issuing advisory opinions. Given that the Commission operated, for almost 20 years, as an autonomous OAS organ charged with monitoring the overall protection of human rights in the absence of a regional treaty of binding character or a regional tribunal, it initially expressed a certain reluctance to forward individual cases to the Court.[10] As a result, the Court notably,

[7] See on the duality of human rights protection in the ambit of the Inter-American system D Contreras-Garduño, 'The Inter-American System of Human Rights' in A Mihr and M Gibney (eds), *The SAGE Handbook of Human Rights* (Los Angeles, SAGE Publications, 2014).

[8] The Inter-American Commission is headquartered in Washington DC and composed of seven members elected from OAS State Parties. The Commissioners act in their own capacity, not representing – thus – their countries of origin.

[9] The Inter-American Commission can refer an individual case to the Court only if the respondent state has accepted the contentious jurisdiction of the Court. See IACommHR, 'Rules of Procedure of the Inter-American Commission on Human Rights' (13 November 2009), Art 45.

[10] See, eg G Neuman, 'Import, Export, and Regional Consent in the Inter-American Court of Human Rights' (2008) 19 *EJIL* 101, 103.

during this time, contributed to international law, exercising its advisory competence under the American Convention to engage in the interpretation not only of the said Convention but also of other human rights instruments. Thus, the Court was – since its dawn – equipped to rule on truly sensitive issues that incite great controversy in international law, such as the application of the death penalty,[11] reciprocity in human rights treaties[12] or the derogation of procedural guarantees in times of emergency.[13]

The necessity of advisory opinions emerges from doctrinal and interpretative differences pertaining to international treaties and for that reason they may contribute significantly to an international common law.[14] Therefore, this alternative function of the Court played a key role: it offered State Parties the opportunity to engage in the proper application of the ACHR using a non-confrontational practice while resolving human rights disputes and circumventing, thus, the formalism or the sanctions linked to the contentious jurisdiction.[15]

The San José Court, even before delivering its first decision on a contentious dispute, had gradually managed to establish its jurisdiction *vis-à-vis* national authorities and international human rights law.[16] In fact, the extensive advisory competence of the Court and the frequency observed of advisory opinions delivered, paved, to a great extent, the way of its ground-breaking jurisprudence in contentious cases as well.

Notwithstanding the fact that it took almost a decade for the Court to deliver its very first pronouncement on an individual complaint in the landmark *Velásquez Rodríguez v Honduras* case,[17] this judgment set the scene of the Court's intentions. Grappling with systemic enforced disappearances in Honduras, the San José Court manifested its individual-centric approach. In its seminal judgment, it attempted to enlarge the scope of application of the ACHR so as to address successfully the present needs deriving from the specificities of the region, establish an effective contentious regional jurisdiction in the Americas. Under its competence to conduct contentious proceedings, the IACtHR applied, mainly, the American Convention[18] using the interpretative rules of the VCLT, which are

[11] *Restrictions to the Death Penalty*, Advisory Opinion OC-3, Inter-American Court of Human Rights Series A no 3 (8 September 1983).

[12] *Compulsory Membership in an Association Prescribed by Law for the Practice of Journalism*, Advisory Opinion OC-5, Inter-American Court of Human Rights Series A no 5 (13 November 1985).

[13] *Judicial Guarantees in States of Emergency (Arts 27(2), 25 and 8 American Convention on Human Rights)*, Advisory Opinion OC-9, Inter-American Court of Human Rights Series A no 9 (6 October 1987).

[14] See especially J Pasqualucci, *The Practice and Procedure of the Inter-American Court of Human Rights* (Cambridge, Cambridge University Press, 2012) 38.

[15] *Restrictions to the Death Penalty*, Advisory Opinion (n 11) para 43.

[16] T Buergenthal, 'The Advisory Practice of the Inter-American Human Rights Court' (1985) 79 *American Journal of International Law* 1.

[17] *Velásquez Rodríguez v Honduras* (Merits), Inter-American Court of Human Rights Series C no 4 (29 July 1988).

[18] See, eg *The Right to Information on Consular Assistance in the Framework of the Guarantees of the Due Process of Law*, Advisory Opinion OC-16, Inter-American Court of Human Rights Series A no 16 (1 October 1999), paras 112–14.

specified in Article 31(1). Furthermore, the Court's perception of human rights moves away from a traditionalist perception of international human rights law dictating the use of the *pro homine* principle.[19] Under the latter, the dignity of individuals is of utmost importance when interpreting the rights enunciated in international human rights instruments and more specifically, in the ACHR.[20] Text aside, human dignity is judicially guaranteed through the *effet utile* principle of the said Convention.

Unlike the Strasbourg Court, the IACtHR, in its early life, expressed in a rather dynamic manner its intention to greatly incorporate international law norms within its interpretation of the ACHR. As Raphaele Rivier correctly underlined, the stance of both control mechanisms of the ACHR allowed them 'to escape from the limited role assigned to them by Inter-American law.'[21] This approach is indissolubly connected to the IACtHR's three-fold conception of human rights under the auspices of the whole Inter-American framework. At a really early stage, the Court declared that 'the concept of rights and freedoms as well as that of their guarantees cannot be divorced from the system of values and principles that inspire it.'[22] Fundamental rights, their guarantees and the rule of law in the context of representative democracy[23] constitute the three pillars of the system.[24] This idea along with the Court's dialogue with the Strasbourg Court and with international law in general encouraged the former to tackle vigorously the major issues of this troubled region and overcome, up to a point its own difficulties.[25] To date, the American continent still suffers from widespread poverty, rampant human rights violations, generalised illiteracy, not to mention domestic judicial systems reluctant to keep up with the principles of the two Inter-American control mechanisms. Nevertheless, the Inter-American Court in its almost 300 decisions and advisory opinions has initiated significant progress in the overall human rights situation and it has also set 'precedents for the entire *corpus* of international human rights law'[26] at the international level.

[19] See especially D Ribeiro and V de Oliveira Mazzuoli, 'The *Pro Homine* Principle as a Fundamental Aspect of International Human Rights Law' (2016) 3 *Indonesian Journal of International & Comparative Law* 77.

[20] *Vargas Areco v Paraguay* (Merits, Reparations and Costs), Inter-American Court of Human Rights Series C no 155 (26 September 2006), para 85.

[21] R Rivier, 'Responsibility for Violations of Human Rights Obligations: Inter-American Mechanisms' in J Crawford, A Pellet and S Olleson (eds), *The Law of International Responsibility* (Oxford, Oxford University Press, 2010) 741.

[22] *Habeas Corpus in Emergency Situations, (Arts. 27(2), 25(1) and 7(6) American Convention on Human Rights)*, Advisory Opinion OC-8, Inter-American Court of Human Rights Series A no 8 (30 January 1987), para 26.

[23] *The Word 'Laws' in Article 30 of the American Convention on Human Rights*, Advisory Opinion OC-6, Inter-American Court of Human Rights Series A no 6 (9 May 1986), para 32.

[24] See especially S Davidson, *The Inter-American Court of Human Rights* (Brookfield, Dartmouth Publication, 1992) 181ff.

[25] The substantial problems of the Court are the significant lack of funding and low rates of compliance with its judgments, not to mention the blatant absences of Canada and the United States.

[26] D Shelton, 'The Jurisprudence of the Inter-American Court of Human Rights' (1996) 10 *American University International Law Review* 333, 371.

Certainly, the Inter-American judicial mechanism greatly copied the pioneer human rights protection offered by the ECtHR, the case law of which constituted the substantial archetype of the Inter-American system. However, this is not just a mutual interaction in the sense of mutual cross-citation between the two systems, and the Strasbourg Court's jurisprudence is more than a point of reference for the San José Court. Since the main focus of this enquiry is the extension of the ECHR's influence to other regional human rights regimes, we should, first, trace the manner in which the IACtHR integrated the Strasbourg Court's perspective of fundamental rights' legal protection. In this part, we should determine whether and in which fields of law this well-established influence takes the shape of analogy or constitutes the point of departure towards a diversification pertaining to the IACtHR's approach in matters also greatly treated by the ECHR system. Secondly, the present study will aim to shed light on the legal fields in which the IACtHR has attempted to extend the human rights protection in the continent. In this context, this chapter seeks to ascertain whether this severe extension can lead, in some cases, to a true judicial interaction and cross-fertilisation between the two leading regional systems.

II. Importing the ECtHR's Human Rights Norms: Analogous Application or Differentiated Appraisal?

This chapter intends to draw attention to the different cross-citation patterns through which the key standards of the ECHR system are exported to the Inter-American system and the receptive – or unreceptive – approach adopted by the latter. In methodological terms we need to draw, at the outset, a distinction between the doctrinal tools that cover horizontally the corpus of cases delivered by the San José Court (Section A – Horizontal Perspective) and then, specific legal treatment of equivalent human rights norms by the European and the Inter-American Court (Section B – Vertical Perspective).

A. The Horizontal Perspective

i. Positive Obligations under the ACHR: 'Telle Quelle' Approach of the ECtHR Case Law

Given the duality that characterises the nature of human rights law, encompassing not only the corpus of human rights proclaimed in treaties but also the necessary specification of the relative obligations of their holders, the emergence of the positive obligations doctrine marked the law-making of the Strasbourg Court and the true consolidation of Conventional rights. While the ECtHR affirmed, at a very early stage,[27] that the ECHR aims to safeguard 'not rights that are theoretical or illusory but rights that are practical and effective', it suggested that the scope of state obligations is both negative and positive in nature, imposing on a state not only the duty to abstain from interfering with the enjoyment of the right, but also to take all the affirmative steps so that the right at stake could be effectively protected from third parties as well. It is within this *effet utile* that the European Court developed progressively its positive obligation doctrine.

Initially, both negative and positive obligations are intimately connected with the vast concept of international responsibility.[28] However, at the European level, the textual basis of positive obligations of states under the ECHR is, by all means, the first article providing that national authorities shall secure to everyone within their jurisdiction the rights and freedoms enshrined therein. Arguably, the Strasbourg Court began to invoke the positive duties of the states when enforcing core and non-derogable human rights under Articles 2 and 3 of the ECHR containing both substantial and procedural aspects. Nevertheless, the positive obligation doctrine was rapidly expanded so as to cover the right to private life, the right to a fair trial or the freedom of expression, mapping slowly but surely specific obligations of the states in order to guide them to take preventive measures and truly embrace almost every provision of the text.

In its attempt to raise the standards of human rights protection in Latin America, the IACtHR, naturally, espoused the positive obligations to enhance human rights protection in the entire region. The right to life, under Article 4 ACHR, provided the most fruitful domain for the development of the positive obligations doctrine since the vast majority of the disputes brought before the Court revolved around gross human rights violations and severe atrocities in countries struggling to leave behind the nightmare of cruel dictatorships. Hence, the San José Court resorted to the nuanced interpretation of the right to life by the Strasbourg Court, which formulated a broad range of positive obligations of both substantial and procedural nature. Since absolute rights also embody fundamental values protected in all respects against encroachment from every possible actor, they can create legal responsibilities for third parties as well. Read in conjunction with the horizontal effect that the drafters of the ECHR aimed to give to the latter, this principle draws inspiration from the German constitutional tradition and the legal theory of *Drittwirkung*, which was not neglected by the European Court.[29] Such a perception of the third-party effect of the ACHR was also chosed by the IACtHR. For the latter, '[t]his obligation has been developed in legal writings, and

[27] *Airey v Ireland*, Merits, Series A no 32 (1979), para 24.

[28] D Shelton and A Gould, 'Positive and Negative Obligations' in D Shelton (ed), *The Oxford Handbook of International Human Rights Law* (Oxford, Oxford University Press, 2013) 1.

[29] See especially F Sudre, L Milano, H Surrel and B Pastre-Belda, *Droit européen et international des droits de l'homme*, 8th edn (Paris, Presses Universitaires de France, 2006) 244–45.

particularly by the Drittwirkung theory, according to which fundamental rights must be respected by both the public authorities and by individuals with regard to other individuals'.[30]

In any case, given the content of the disputes brought before the IACtHR, for the judges of the San José Court, the state remains the basic bearer of both negative and positive obligations, putting them on an equal footing even since its first contentious case, the seminal *Velásquez Rodríguez*.[31] The IACtHR set the scene of its own positive duties doctrine[32] giving true meaning to Articles 1(1) and 2 ACHR laying down the principle obligations of the States Parties to the ACHR. The drafters of the Convention felt that they should encompass explicitly in the first article not only the negative aspect of these obligations described as the duty to respect the human rights and freedoms but also the positive one, to ensure their true enjoyment by all individuals within the jurisdiction of the states bound by the American Convention.

In this landmark decision, the IACtHR clarified relatively that

> the second obligation of the States Parties is to 'ensure' the free and full exercise of the rights recognized by the Convention to every person subject to its jurisdiction. This obligation implies the duty of States Parties to organize the governmental apparatus and, in general, all the structures through which public power is exercised, so that they are capable of juridically ensuring the free and full enjoyment of human rights. As a consequence of this obligation, the States must prevent, investigate and punish any violation of the rights recognized by the Convention and, moreover, if possible attempt to restore the right violated and provide compensation as warranted for damages resulting from the violation.[33]

Certainly, an exhaustive catalogue of such preventive measures cannot be provided. At any rate, this dimension of positive obligations is identified as the duty of the state to build up a legislative and administrative framework apt to effectively prevent human rights violations. A more specific obligation derived from the development of the Inter-American Court's case law, which is seen as the duty to provide operational prevention measures when particular human rights might be at stake. Hence, the positive obligation of the state is broad enough to involve not only legislators, but all state institutions and those who must protect security, and in particular, its police and armed forces.[34]

[30] *Juridical Condition and Rights of Undocumented Migrants*, Advisory Opinion OC-18, Inter-American Court of Human Rights Series A no 18 (17 September 2003), para 140. See on this doctrine indicatively A Bleckmann, 'General Theory of Obligations under Public International Law' (1995) 38 *German Yearbook of International Law* 26, 28–30.

[31] *Velásquez Rodríguez* (n 17).

[32] L Lavrysen, 'Positive Obligations in the Jurisprudence of the Inter-American Court of Human Rights' (2014) 7 *Inter-American and European Human Rights Journal* 94.

[33] *Velásquez Rodríguez* (n 17) paras 166–67.

[34] *Juan Humberto Sanchez v Honduras* (Preliminary Objections, Merits, Reparations and Costs), Inter-American Court of Human Rights Series C no 99 (7 June 2003), para 110.

It should be further noted that the Court, which does not hesitate to refer to external sources of international law,[35] opted for seeing positive obligations under the prism of due diligence[36] which plays a key role when attributing international responsibility to state organs.[37] Pursuant to the rules of customary international law, the question of positive obligations derives from the lack of due diligence in cases where the contested interference with the right at stake emerged not directly by state agents but mainly by private persons or circumstances due to external factors, such as emergency situations, environmental risks, or – in general – hazardous activities.[38] This technique not only offers to the judges the opportunity to impose action obligations on the domestic authorities; it also acknowledges the Court's competence to monitor their implementation and to name – besides the obligations of prevention – obligations of reparation as well. In doing so, the ECtHR succeeded in giving true horizontal effect to the Convention while revisiting the notion of 'jurisdiction' in the sense of Article 1 ECHR.

With regard to use of the due diligence principle, the ECtHR, even when it is not inferred as such, made clear that it is the background in which serious violations are examined, particularly related to individuals who are in a vulnerable position. In the seminal *Osman v United Kingdom*,[39] in which the Strasbourg Court also looked to its Inter-American counterpart, the Court did not accept 'that the failure to perceive the risk to life in the circumstances known at the time or to take preventive measures to avoid that risk must be tantamount to gross negligence or wilful disregard of the duty to protect life'.[40] More recently, in a case touching the sensitive issue of domestic violence[41] against women, the ECtHR recalled that the Inter-American Court's interpretation of Article 1(1) ACHR passes though the due diligence rule to prevent human rights violations, to investigate and sanction perpetrators or to provide appropriate reparations to their families.

[35] See especially S Pavageau, 'Les obligations positives dans les jurisprudences des Cours européenne et Inter-americaine' (2005) 6 *International Law: Revista Colombiana de Derecho International* 201, 208. See also H Tigroudja, 'L'autonomie du droit applicable par la Cour interaméricaine des droits de l'homme: en marge d'arrêts et avis consultatifs récents' (2002) 49 *Revue trimestrielle des droits de l' homme* 69.

[36] The ECtHR has repeatedly connected positive obligations to the due diligence concept yet avoiding to name it. There are only a few references to due diligence when it comes to the state's positive duties. See V Waisman, 'Human Trafficking: State Obligations to Protect Victims' Rights, the Current Framework and a New Due Diligence Standard' (2010) 33 *Hastings International and Comparative Law Review* 385, 415.

[37] D Shelton and A Gould, 'Positive and Negative Obligations' (n 28) 4–5. See also on this issue B Conforti, 'Reflections on State Responsibility for the Breach of Positive Obligations: The Case-Law of the European Court of Human Rights' (2003) 13 *Italian Yearbook of International Law* 3.

[38] *Velásquez Rodríguez* (n 17) para 172.

[39] *Osman v the United Kingdom*, Merits, ECHR 1998-VIII.

[40] ibid para 116.

[41] *Opuz v Turkey*, Merits, ECHR 2009-III 107, paras 83–84.

On the other side of the Atlantic a similar approach was adopted in the famous *Cotton Field* decision with regard to the violent abuse and murder of three women in Juarez, which revealed the blatant failure of the Mexican government to protect women's rights. In paragraph 258, the IACtHR confirmed its standing with regard to women in need of protection invoking the said rule and specified the nature and objectives of the required positive measures.[42]

Another illustrative point of the Strasbourg Court's approach exported to the Inter-American Court in this field is the acknowledgment that under no circumstances are the state's positive obligations unrestricted. First, the ECtHR had stepped cautiously on this road as it felt in the *Osman* ruling that this type of obligations should be clearly described; otherwise it would be impossible for states not to be found guilty for breaches of the Conventional rights.[43] This brings us back to the distinction between obligations of means and obligations of result. In this respect, the Court has resolved the issue, concluding that the concept of positive obligations endorses solely obligations of means. The former President of the ECtHR, Linos-Alexander Sicilianos recalled that, at any rate, such obligations are obligations of means, not of result. In his words, 'states have an obligation to try to avoid the risk, not a strict obligation to achieve the desired result. They have an obligation to make an effort – a diligent effort – but not necessarily an obligation to succeed in saving human lives.'[44] The prudence of the Court not to impose a disproportionate burden on national authorities when taking the appropriative measures to safeguard the right to life of individuals led the Court to gradually specify the necessary conditions for the attribution of responsibility to the state and, undoubtedly, inspire its Inter-American colleague to espouse analogous position as illustrated in several cases.[45]

[42] *González et al v Mexico* ('*Cotton Field Case*') (Preliminary Objection, Merits, Reparations, and Costs), Inter-American Court of Human Rights Series C no 205 (16 November 2009), para 258.
With regard to generalised violence against women, the Court delivered a landmark decision in 2018 that built upon its earlier findings and offered the opportunity to the court to break new ground to the adjudication of such disputes. Hence, in *López Soto v Venezuela*, the IACtHR added the gendered dimension of the impugned actions of private actors and declared that due diligence is required by the state even in cases of sexual slavery and torture when committed also by non-state actors. By the mere fact of the victim's abduction the authorities of Venezuela should have attentively investigated the case and prosecuted the perpetrator, as abduction is deemed in itself a form of violence against women. There is no need for an established routine of gender-based violence to be existent in order to conclude to the accountability of the state. See *López Soto et al v Venezuela* (Merits, Reparations and Costs), Inter-American Court of Human Rights Series C no 362 (26 September 2018); *Women Victims of Sexual Torture in Atenco v Mexico* (Preliminary Objection, Merits, Reparations and Costs), Inter-American Court of Human Rights Series C no 371 (28 November 2018); D Kravetz, 'Holding States to Account for Gender-Based Violence: The Inter-American Court of Human Rights' decisions in López Soto vs Venezuela and Women Victims of Sexual Torture in Atenco vs Mexico' (*EJIL:Talk!*, 21 January 2019), www.ejiltalk.org/holding-states-to-account-for-gender-based-violence-the-inter-american-court-of-human-rights-decisions-in-lopez-soto-vs-venezuela-and-women-victims-of-sexual-torture-in-atenco-vs-mexico/.

[43] See *Osman* (n 39) para 116.

[44] LA Sicilianos, 'Preventing Violations of the Right to Life: Positive Obligations under Article 2 of the ECHR' (2014) 3 *Cyprus Human Rights Law Review* 117.

[45] *Cotton Field Case* (n 42) para 252.

In *Pueblo Bello Massacre v Colombia*,[46] the Court underlined the non-automatic nature of the mechanism of attribution, adopting the language as well as the argumentation of the ECtHR. It recalled the latter's answer to this balancing challenge and explained that

> the nature *erga omnes* of the treaty-based guarantee obligations of the States does not imply their unlimited responsibility for all acts or deeds of individuals, because its obligations to adopt prevention and protection measures for individuals in their relationships with each other are conditioned by the awareness of a situation of real and imminent danger for a specific individual or group of individuals and to the reasonable possibilities of preventing or avoiding that danger.'[47]

Subsequently, in the *Sawhoyamaxa Indigenous Community v Paraguay*[48] the Court applied the criteria also developed by the ECtHR when it sought to ascertain when the state's omission amounted to a breach of its positive obligation under Article 2 ECHR.[49] In this case, the Court affirmed that the crucial factor that determines whether the state acted in compatibility with the positive obligations arising from the ACHR is, firstly, the knowledge of the situation posing immediate and certain risk to life and secondly, whether or not the response of the states was appropriate in terms of the measures taken to circumvent the risk.[50] Normally, since the use of these basic standards was proliferated by the Strasbourg judges not only in relation to the inalienable right to life but also to the whole *construction prétorienne* of positive obligations, the IACtHR, seemed to embrace the broad conception of these principles when a potential violation of human rights – other than the right to life – occurs.[51]

On these grounds, the IACtHR developed its positive obligations agenda in a manner analogous with that of the ECtHR. This is reflected not only in the tendency of the IACtHR to start steadily imposing positive duties on states to enhance the effective enforcement of the said rights on the basis of the first provisions of the ACHR and the core principles that constituted the normative foundations of the positive obligations doctrine. It is also revealed by the

[46] *Pueblo Bello Massacre v Colombia* (Merits, Reparations and Costs), Inter-American Court of Human Rights Series C no 140 (31 January 2006).
[47] ibid para 123.
[48] *Sawhoyamaxa Indigenous Community v Paraguay* (Merits, Reparations and Costs), Inter-American Court of Human Rights Series C no 146 (29 March 2006).
[49] See, eg *Osman* (n 39) para 11, *Kiliç v Turkey*, Merits, ECHR 2000-III 75, paras 62–63; *Mahmut Kaya v Turkey*, Merits, ECHR 2000-III 149, para 86; *Akkoç v Turkey*, Merits, ECHR 2000-X 389, para 78; *Keenan v the United Kingdom*, Merits, ECHR 2001-III 93, para 90; *Medova v Russia*, Merits, App no 25385/04 (ECtHR, 15 January 2009), para 96; *Fedina v Ukraine*, Merits, App no 17185/02 (ECtHR, 2 September 2010), para 53; *Giuliani and Gaggio v Italy* [GC], Merits, ECHR 2011-II 165, para 246; *Tsechoyev v Russia*, Merits, App no 39358/05 (ECtHR, 15 March 2011), para 136; *Shumkova v Russia*, Merits, App no 9296/06 (ECtHR, 14 February 2012), para 90; *Marro and Others v Italy* (dec), App no 29100/07 (ECtHR, 8 April 2014), para 41.
[50] *Sawhoyamaxa Indigenous Community* (n 48) para 155.
[51] Lavrysen, 'Positive Obligations' (n 32) p 105.

evolution of the concept parallel to the evolution of the Inter-American jurisprudence and the expansion of requirements of substantive and procedural character pertaining to the positive duties of states. The IACtHR, hence, acknowledged the existence of positive obligations in respect of the freedom of expression, the right to effective judicial remedies, right to private life et al.

Encouraged by its European peer, the IACtHR applied this concept of vulnerability – though in a more emphatic manner – to facilitate and legitimise such an expansion. Given the realities of the region, the Court expressed great sensitivity with regard to women, children, people suffering from mental disabilities, indigenous communities and undocumented migrants. In most of the cases in which the Court has declared the existence of a positive obligation, it had earlier confirmed that the applicant was in a vulnerable situation or was a member of one of the above-mentioned vulnerable groups. Therefore, it may be deduced that vulnerability is considered a precondition of most positive obligations. Vulnerability applies as the foundation for an over-arching obligation which can create specific positive obligations for states in every possible respect as depicted by the broadness of the Court's language whenever it invokes the vulnerable status of applicants.[52]

Arguably, this section cannot cover the numerous aspects of the multifaceted influence of the ECtHR's positive obligations tradition on the IACtHR's equivalent doctrine. Suffice it to say that the San José Court followed the guidelines of the Strasbourg Court with regard to the content, legal nature and justification of the positive duties deriving from the American Convention. At the same time, the ECHR was also inspired by the particularities of the application of the IACtHR. In most recent instances, the Strasbourg Court followed the practice introduced by the IACtHR and felt free to use Article 1 ECHR in order to fortify and legitimise the effectiveness of its judgments entailing sometimes harsh positive obligations for the Contracting Parties to the Convention.[53]

Overall, having taken for granted the severe influence of the Strasbourg Court's case law to the formulation of the Inter-American version of the positive obligations, one might say that the positive obligations doctrine under the American Convention has been reaffirmed and even facilitated by the introduction of the aforementioned conventionality control. The successful exercise of the latter presupposes the conformity of national authorities with general positive obligations and in particular, with those of procedural character.[54] At any rate, the ups

[52] See, eg *Ximenes-Lopes v Brazil* (Merits, Reparations and Costs), Inter-American Court of Human Rights Series C no 149 (4 July 2006), para 103; *Perozo et al v Venezuela* (Preliminary Objections, Merits, Reparations, and Costs), Inter-American Court of Human Rights Series C no 195 (28 January 2009), para 118.

[53] See, eg *Assenov and Others v Bulgaria*, Merits, ECHR 1998-VIII, para 102; *MC v Bulgaria*, Merits, ECHR 2003-XII 1, para 311; *Storck v Germany*, Merits, ECHR 2005-V 111, para 102; *Siliadin v France*, Merits, ECHR 2005-VII 289, para 77.

[54] MN Montoya Céspedes, 'The Inter-American Court of Human Rights' Positive Obligation Doctrine: Between Unidirectional Influence and Judicial Dialogue' in Y Haeck, O Ruiz-Chiriboga and C Burbano-Herrera (eds), *The Inter-American Court of Human Rights: Theory and Practice, Present and Future* (Cambridge, Intersentia, 2015) 774.

and downs observed with regard to the manner that the San José Court often opts for incorporating the relevant principles of the ECtHR have fuelled the debate concerning whether we stand before a true and ever-evolving judicial dialogue with its European counterpart in this field. The vagueness that characterises the quality of references has undoubtedly reinforced this ambiguity.[55]

Despite the witnessed irregularities and inconsistencies in the IACtHR's case law, the Court has evolved greatly from its starting point, namely the recognition of positive obligations solely regarding the right to life. It thus managed to cover the realities of the region, which amounted to gross human rights violations and deep-rooted impunity that required the Court's guidelines in order that social or political rights could be effectively ensured. In a manner analogous to its European counterpart, the IACtHR has sought to build a concrete context of positive obligations, as illustrated by its brand-new jurisprudence. In its more recent Advisory Opinion on Environment and Human Rights, released on 7 February 2018, the IACtHR identified for the first time positive-and negative – obligations under international environmental law and human rights law in the transboundary context.[56] This is also indicative of the willingness of the IACtHR to seize the opportunity, whenever is given, to grapple with new issues offering valuable clarifications, now that it has consolidated its jurisprudence in relation to blatant violations of inalienable rights. This being so, the last observed attitude of the Court encourages us to suggest that it seems highly possible that the Court will not be shy to move on delineating the precise boundaries of the state's positive duties in order to even more enhance its persuasiveness in this field of human rights law.

ii. The Principle of Subsidiarity: The MoA Doctrine in the IACtHR Case Law

The ECtHR constitutes the most powerful judicial body in the field of international human rights law and, as previously discussed, it *de facto* influenced other regional human rights Courts with its nuanced case law. It did so through several doctrines which remarkably contributed to the solid consolidation of the Court's jurisdiction and the constant interpretation of the ECHR as a living instrument. Moreover, in the Europe of political stability the debate continues as to whether

[55] ibid 782.

[56] *The Environment and Human Rights (State Obligations in Relation to the Environment in the Context of the Protection and Guarantee of the Rights to Life and to Personal Integrity – Interpretation and Scope of Articles 4(1) and 5(1) of the American Convention on Human Rights)*, Advisory Opinion OC-23/18, Inter-American Court of Human Rights Series, Series A no. 23 (15 November 2017); M Feria-Tinta and S Milnes, 'The Rise of Environmental Law in International Dispute Resolution: Inter-American Court of Human Rights issues Landmark Advisory Opinion on Environment and Human Rights' (*EJIL:Talk!*, 26 February 2018), www.ejiltalk.org/the-rise-of-environmental-law-in-international-dispute-resolution-inter-american-court-of-human-rights-issues-landmark-advisory-opinion-on-environment-and-human-rights/.

international judicial bodies should have the authority to review national legal frameworks dealing with sensitive rights or whether democratically elected governments should have the final word in the process of adoption and implementation of domestic policies.

Hence, it was within this context of the tension between national deference and international supervision that the famous 'margin of appreciation' doctrine (MoA)[57] was introduced by the Strasbourg Court, serving as a significant device in the Court's hands when engaged with this tension or with balancing tasks in sensitive cases related to conflicting rights. Inevitably, the MoA doctrine goes hand-in-hand with the long-established principle of subsidiarity of international fora.[58] 'The doctrine of subsidiarity provides one framework for the allocation of power in global governance. Subsidiarity comes into play as a mechanism that helps address some of the problems that the rise of international authority creates, particularly the increased perception that international authority has a democratic deficit.'[59] Nevertheless, this traditional notion of subsidiarity seems rather problematic when it comes to human rights protection in international law. If international tribunals take a step back so that principles of sovereignty and political self-determination may be sufficiently respected, their hands are tied in addressing human rights violations stemming from domestic actions.

In any case, the margin of appreciation formula[60] derives from the basic perception of the subsidiary function of international human rights tribunals, however, its delicate use by these courts reveals their intention to rather reconcile the aforementioned conflicts.

At the outset, the Strasbourg Court initiated the MoA doctrine that allows a certain margin of manoeuvre in the restriction of human rights. The famous doctrine was first given birth to[61] in the European Commission's case law revolving around the *Cyprus* cases.[62] Article 15 ECHR offered the initial basis for the MoA doctrine in the sense of national derogations from Convention guarantees

[57] See, eg E Brems, 'The Margin of Appreciation Doctrine in the Case-Law of the European Court of Human Rights' (1996) 56 *Heidelberg Journal of International Law* 240; E Benvenisti, 'Margin of Appreciation, Consensus, and Universal Standards' (1999) 31 *New York University Journal of International Law & Politics* 843; K Dzehtsiarou, *European Consensus and the Legitimacy of the Strasbourg Court* (Cambridge, Cambridge University Press, 2015).

[58] In the context of the protection of the core right to a fair trial, the African Court has timidly expressed its willingness to adhere to the position of the European Court as regards the application of the MoA doctrine. See *Mohamed Abubakari v Tanzania* (Merits), African Court Law Report Vol I 599 (3 June 2016), para 173.

[59] J Contesse, 'Contestation and Deference in the Inter-American System of Human Rights' (2016) 79(2) *Law and Contemporary Problems* 123, 125.

[60] HC Yourow, *The Margin of Appreciation Doctrine in the Dynamics of European Human Rights Jurisprudence*, International Studies in Human Rights 28 (Dordrecht, Martinus Nijhoff Publishers, 1996) 13.

[61] Actually, 'the origins of the margin doctrine lie in both classical martial law doctrine and in the jurisprudence of the French *Conseil d'Etat* and other equivalent continental institutions in their modes of review of the legality of administrative action and discretion': ibid 14.

[62] *Greece v the United Kingdom* I, App no 176/56 (Commission Report, 26 September 1958).

in emergency situations. However, the doctrine's ambit has expanded, encompassing almost all ECHR articles but mainly Articles 8–11 containing limitations and requiring a balancing procedure from national authorities so that adequate human rights protection can be guaranteed. These non-absolute rights, the enforcement of which corresponds to specific prohibitions for the states, have also endorsed, through the nuanced jurisprudence of the ECtHR, positive obligations to be implemented by national authorities. Given the nature of those positive duties, states enjoy a certain discretion to implement those rights by adopting different normative schemes. In this regard, there is no single correct pattern of implementation and hence, the Court approaches these rights with careful steps on a case-by-case basis.

This being so, when national authorities are under scrutiny for determining whether they have struck a fair balance between national interests and human rights, they are granted a certain latitude which is not permitted within the scope of application of 'core' human rights.

As clarified by the Strasbourg judges,

> By reason of their direct and continuous contact with the vital forces of their countries, State authorities are in principle in a better position than the international judge to give an opinion on the exact content of these requirements as well as on the 'necessity' of a 'restriction' or 'penalty' intended to meet them.[63]

Since this pronouncement of the Court, as well as its subsequent rulings in *Sunday Times v United Kingdom*[64] and *Marckx v Belgium*[65] the ECtHR developed this formula in order to delve into a wide variety of dissimilar cases while exercising the proportionality test. The Court's attempt is, thus, to ascertain whether a pressing social need dictating the impugned measures exists in order to pronounce on the proportional character of the latter with regard to the legitimate aim pursued. Thus, the threshold of protection afforded to the rights embodied in the Convention progressively constituted the key factor to regulate the extent of national discretion allowed in every case. More specifically, the Court has denied granting a margin of appreciation – or has severely delimited its extent – in cases touching upon the right to life, human dignity in general, or non-derogable rights.[66]

However, when national authorities need to weigh up competing individual rights, their latitude is significantly wider in the scope of the limitation clauses of Articles 8–11 ECHR. The domestic assessment of the relevant facts is reviewed, nevertheless, the Court exercises a less stringent control on the basis of the subsidiary nature of the Court and the respected sovereignty of the Contracting

[63] *Handyside v the United Kingdom*, Merits, Series A no 24 (1976).

[64] *The Sunday Times v United Kingdom (no 1)*, Merits, Series A no 30 (1979).

[65] *Marckx v Belgium*, Merits, Series A no 31 (1979).

[66] See, eg *X v the United Kingdom*, Merits, Series A no 46 (1981); *Leander v Sweden*, Merits, Series A no 116 (1987); *Kokkinakis v Greece*, Merits, Series A no 260-A (1993); *Hirst v the United Kingdom (no 2)* [GC], Merits, ECHR 2005-IX 187; *SH and Others v Austria* [GC], Merits, ECHR 2011-V 295.

parties. In addition, the ECtHR decides on the width of the margin offered on a case-by-case basis, since the political or schematic realities of each state or the characteristics of each individual application must be taken into consideration. The Court also revisits its own decisions leaving wide margin to states when the discretionary standards applied are not wisely met.

As McGoldrick correctly pointed out in this regard, '[t]he MoA is not an instrument of surrender or abdication. Even if the applicable MoA is wide, it is not all-embracing. European supervision is not limited to ascertaining whether the state exercised its discretion reasonably, carefully and in good faith. These elements are necessary but not sufficient.'[67]

In recent decades the Strasbourg Court has used – and still uses – in various manners its seminal doctrine, some of which has raised severe criticism.[68] Judge Rozakis, former judge of the ECtHR, condemned the fact that the Court often opts for an automatic manner of application of the MoA scheme, particularly in cases in which similar clashes of conflicting interests are solved through the Court's well-established case, famously admitting that 'the Court should carefully reconsider the applicability of the concept of the margin of appreciation, avoid the automaticity of reference to it, and duly limit it to cases where a real need for its applicability better serves the interests of justice and the protection of human rights.'[69] In addition, for instance, the empty reference of 'a certain margin of appreciation' without specifying its extent in the conclusion of judgments[70] comes to reinforce this approach.

In any case, the flexibility of such a semi-theoretical and semi-technical structure fuelled the mere jurisprudential evolution of the Court and showed the way of applying state discretion standards to international tribunals[71] and most importantly, to regional human rights courts.

This being so, the IACtHR could not bypass the most famous doctrinal creation of the Strasbourg Court, notwithstanding the specificities of the region dictating a rather nuanced approach in this respect. The corpus of cases of different nature and severe gravity with which the San José Court is confronted as well as the lack of regional consensus in the Americas do not offer fertile ground for international deference. On the contrary, they bespeak a stricter supranational judicial control so that the state's conformity with human rights obligations can be reassured.

[67] D McGoldrick, 'Affording States a Margin of Appreciation: Comparing the European Court of Human Rights and the Inter-American Court of Human Rights' in C Buckley, A Donald, P Leach (eds), *Towards Convergence in International Human Rights Law: Approaches of Regional and International Systems*, Nottingham Studies in Human Rights 5 (Leiden, Brill Nijhoff, 2013) 330.

[68] G Letsas, 'Two Concepts of the Margin of Appreciation' (2006) 26 *Oxford Journal of Legal Studies* 705.

[69] *Egeland and Hanseid v Norway*, Merits, App no 34438/04 (ECtHR, 16 April 2009), Concurring Opinion of Judge Rozakis.

[70] J Kratochvíl, 'The Inflation of the Margin of Appreciation by the European Court of Human Rights' (2011) 29 *Netherlands Quarterly of Human Rights* 324, 340.

[71] Y Shany, 'Toward a General Margin of Appreciation Doctrine in International Law?' (2006) 16 *European Journal of International Law* 907.

Consequently, and similarly to its Strasbourg counterpart, the IACtHR applies the MoA concept, albeit in a different manner. The former has dealt mostly with cases involving arbitrary arrests or detentions, forced disappearances and extra-judicial killings or, in general terms, violations of the right to life, to personal liberty, and to the right to personal integrity. Due to the lack of sufficient democratic credentials of American states, the IACtHR seemed reluctant to apply such a formula to states experiencing military dictatorships, or even fragile democracies with low levels of judicial independence.[72] However, during its first years, it looked into the possibility of granting a *margin of appreciation* to domestic authorities in the context of its advisory powers. Firstly, the Court grappled with this issue in 1984, in its advisory opinion concerning proposed amendments to the constitutional rules regulating naturalisation in Costa Rica.[73] The Court was asked to opine on the Proposed Amendments to the Naturalisation Provisions of the Political Constitution of Costa Rica. The latter state asked, specifically, whether the amendments establishing different naturalisation standards on the basis of the place of birth were incompatible with the right to nationality and the right to equal protection under the American Convention.

The Court, initially, stated that it is among the state's sovereign powers to regulate the legislative framework pertaining to naturalisation. Furthermore, while reaching its conclusion, it made explicit reference to the MoA formula. However, for the judges of the Court, its opinion cannot be considered as a *carte blanche* and it definitely 'should not be viewed as approval of the practice which prevails in some areas to limit to an exaggerated and unjustified degree the political rights of naturalized individuals'.[74] Regardless of the fact that the Court circumvented to openly refer to the origins of the formula, it recognised that the Costa Rican authorities retain – to some extent – the sovereign control over constitutional amendments related to nationality and naturalisation.

In casu, the Court overstepped its reluctance to restrict itself to its subsidiary nature[75] when asked by Costa Rica – one of the most enthusiastic supporters and sources of funding of the Court – and went on to look into the application criteria of naturalisation of Costa Ricans, paying particular attention to the fact that the case touched upon constitutional questions close to the core of sovereign powers of that state. If, however, we look at the bigger picture, this openness of the Court

[72] A Follesdal, 'Exporting the Margin of Appreciation: Lessons for the Inter-American Court of Human Rights' (2017) 15 *International Journal of Constitutional Law* 359, 368–69.

[73] *Proposed Amendments to the Naturalisation Provisions of the Political Constitution of Costa Rica*, Advisory Opinion OC-4, Inter-American Court of Human Rights Series A no 4 (January 1984).

[74] ibid para 60.

[75] J Contesse, 'Subsidiarity in Inter-American Human Rights Law' (2016), www.law.yale.edu/sites/default/files/documents/pdf/SELA15_Contesse_CV_Eng.pdf; the Inter-American Court declared its subsidiary character through the application of the fourth instance formula and the exhaustion of local remedies. See especially B Duhaime, 'Subsidiarity in the Americas: What Room is There for Deference in the Inter-American System?' in L Gruszczynski and W Werner (eds), *Deference in International Courts and Tribunals: Standard of Review and Margin of Appreciation* (Oxford, Oxford University Press, 2014).

in its early years is rooted in the fact that this was the fourth time that the Court delivered its opinion in the context of its consultative mechanism without having, by that time, pronounced on a contentious dispute.[76] Subsequently, the IACtHR struggled to establish its international jurisdiction as a human rights tribunal providing international supervision *vis-à-vis* the democracies of the region. There was little room for deference in this context and more importantly, within the power of the Court to decide contentious disputes. According to the respectful position of the former President of the Court, Antonio Cançado Trindade, '[h]ow could we apply [the margin of appreciation doctrine] in the context of a regional human rights system where many countries' judges are subject to intimidation and pressure? How could we apply it in a region where the judicial function does not distinguish between military jurisdiction and ordinary jurisdiction?'[77] Certainly, Cançado Trindade's thesis is inextricably related to both the universality of the very notion of human rights and the nature of cases brought before the Court. His absolute words are possibly explained by the fact that human rights in the sense of *jus cogens* obligations for the states leave no room for relativism in the application of such standards; and the truth is that a lack credibility of Latin American states supports this idea.

This total prohibition of domestic deference led to a huge debate around the matter, since already new types of disputes are being adjudicated by the Court. Nevertheless, and in spite of the echo of such a perception of the MoA doctrine, the Court revisited its hesitation to grant national discretion in a freedom of expression case in *Herrera Ulloa v Costa Rica*.[78] In this case, the Court treated the conviction of a reporter of a newspaper for criminal defamation stemming from the publication of offences against a Costa Rican diplomat and, for the first time in its contentious career, reviewed the proportionality of the restrictive response of the state, namely the application of criminal defamation legislation. Giving particular attention to the democratisation of the region and more importantly, to the role of the mass media and journalism in relation to freedom of thought and expression, the Court cited relatively the *jurisprudence constante* of the Strasbourg Court[79] in cases where freedom of expression clashes with reputational rights, and acknowledged that '[d]emocratic control exercised by society through public opinion encourages the transparency of State activities and promotes the accountability

[76] P Contreras, 'National Discretion and International Deference in the Restriction of Human Rights: A Comparison between the Jurisprudence of the European and the Inter-American Court of Human Rights' (2012) 11 *Northwestern Journal of International Human Rights* 28.

[77] AA Cançado Trindade, 'Reflexiones sobre el Futuro del Sistema Interamericano de Protección de los Derechos Humanos' in J Méndez and F Cox (eds), *El futuro del sistema interamericano de proteccion a los derechos humanos* (San José, Instituto Interamericano de Derechos Humanos, 1998); AA Cançado Trindade, *El derecho internacional de los derechos humanos en el siglo XXI* (Santiago, Editorial Jurídica de Chile, 2001) 380; Contreras, 'National Discretion and International Deference' (n 76) 62; Follesdal, 'Exporting the Margin of Appreciation' (n 72) 362.

[78] *Herrera-Ulloa v Costa Rica* (Preliminary Objections, Merits, Reparations and Costs), Inter-American Court of Human Rights Series C no 107 (2 July 2004).

[79] ibid para 125.

of public officials in public administration, for which there should be a reduced margin for any restriction on political debates or on debates on matters of public interest.'[80] Finally, the Court found the measure disproportionate since it espoused the 'pressing social need' formula, which did not justify such a restriction of the freedom of the journalistic speech and repeated in its final conclusions that '[w]hile States have a margin of discretion in regulating the exercise of that remedy, they may not establish restrictions or requirements inimical to the very essence of the right to appeal a judgment.'[81]

The Court had already clarified its fears relating to the destabilisation that the use of the MoA doctrine might cause. There is no doubt, therefore, that the thoughtful and limited use of the margin's concept by the San José Court aims, in fact, to reduce national latitude as much as possible in similar cases. Therefore, the overall meaning of this case is that national authorities enjoy some latitude in the selection of the necessary judicial remedies, but they are always subject to international supervision which comes to guarantee that the very essence of the right is being impaired.

The MoA was reinvented in another case adjudicated by the Inter-American Court – once again against Costa Rica. In the *Artavia-Murillo*[82] case, the protection of the right to life was at issue when in vitro fertilisation (IVF) comes into play. The claimants were infertile couples who, after the declaration of in vitro fertilisation as unconstitutional by the Costa Rican judiciary, were denied access to any form of assisted reproductive methods and thus, alleged a violation of their right to private and family life under the American Convention. Costa Rica claimed a margin of appreciation on the basis of the language of Article 4(1)[83] and of the lack of regional consensus on IVF invoking the discretion that the ECtHR allows in such controversial cases.

The IACtHR cited the relevant case law of the European Court of Human Rights on the lack of European consensus as regards the beginning of the life of the foetus.[84] However, it used a number of interpretative tools in its conclusion on the proper reading of Article 4(1), and consensus on the application of IVF by the State Parties was one of them.[85]

[80] ibid para 127.

[81] ibid para 161.

[82] *Artavia-Murillo et al v Costa Rica* (Merits, Reparations and Costs, Preliminary Objections), Inter-American Court of Human Rights Series C no 257 (28 November 2012). See also the similar *Gómez Murillo et al v Costa Rica* (Preliminary Objections, Merits, Reparations and Costs), Inter-American Court of Human Rights Series C no 326 (29 November 2016).

[83] Art 4(1) ACHR provides that '[e]very person has the right to have his life respected. This right shall be protected by law and, *in general*, from the moment of conception. No one shall be arbitrarily deprived of his life.' See G Candia, 'Comparing Diverse Approaches to the Margin of Appreciation: The Case of the European and the Inter-American Court of Human Rights' (2014), www.papers.ssrn.com/sol3/papers.cfm?abstract_id=2406705.

[84] *Artavia-Murillo et al* (n 82), paras 237, 238.

[85] ibid, paras 256, 264; L Lixinski, 'The Consensus Method of Interpretation by the Inter-American Court of Human Rights' (2017) 3 *Canadian Journal of Comparative and Contemporary Law* 65, 79.

Nevertheless, the IACtHR declined to pronounce on the margin's issue, stating that '[t]he Constitutional Chamber based itself on an absolute protection of the embryo that, by failing to weigh up or take into account the other competing rights, involved an arbitrary and excessive interference in private and family life that makes this interference disproportionate. Moreover, the interference had discriminatory effects.'[86]

This part of the judgment was hotly debated in academia and by some of the judges of the Court. According to the dissenting opinion of Judge Vio-Grossi, '[o]ther jurisdictional bodies have already highlighted the difficulty – and even the inappropriateness – of deciding an issue which is within the realm (although not exclusively) of medical science, an issue regarding which there is still no consensus, even in this particular field'.[87] Indeed, as used by the Strasbourg Court, European consensus was not the *conditio sine qua non* for granting a margin of appreciation to states, but mostly, a factor determining the extent of it.[88]

More recently, in the *Atala-Riffo* case, the Court revisited its approach of regional consensus when it comes to deference allowed to national judicial authorities. While adjudicating a sexual orientation case against Chile,[89] it clarified that the lack of consensus cannot lead the latter to abstain from pronouncing on the matter at stake.[90] Interestingly enough, judging from this general holding of the Court, the latter opted to clarify its stance on the interconnection between regional consensus and deference in a case falling out of its 'privileged territory'. This being so, the San José Court appears less hesitant to leave a margin of manoeuvre, even a limited one, in cases that, social disagreement is gaining attention and little consensus can be achieved among Latin-American states. This is also confirmed

[86] ibid para 316.

[87] *Artavia-Murillo* (n 82) Dissenting opinion of Judge Vio-Grossi.

[88] Benvenisti, 'Margin of Appreciation (n 57); K Cavanaugh, 'Policing the Margins: Rights Protection and the European Court of Human Rights' [2006] 4 *European Human Rights Law Review* 422, 423; K Dzehtsiarou, 'European Consensus and the Evolutive Interpretation of the European Convention on Human Rights' (2011) 12 *German Law Journal* 1731, 1740; Follesdal, 'Exporting the Margin of Appreciation' (n 72) 370. See also on the various perspectives of the daunting task of reaching European consensus P Kapotas and V Tzevelekos (eds), *Building Consensus on European Consensus: Judicial Interpretation of Human Rights in Europe and Beyond* (Cambridge, Cambridge University Press 2019).

[89] The IACtHR took the opportunity to pronounce for the first time on LGBTQI rights in the *Atala-Riffo* case in which it condemned Chile for refusing custody of her three daughters to a lesbian judge after her divorce. More recently, in its Advisory Opinion on Gender Identity, Equality, and Non-Discrimination of Same-Sex Couples delivered on 9 January 2018, the Court declared that recognition of name change in conformity with gender identity and patrimonial rights deriving from same-sex marriage are protected by the ACHR which does not permit any discrimination on the basis of sexual discrimination despite the lack of consensus in the region. See accordingly *Atala-Riffo and Daughters v Chile* (Preliminary Objections, Merits, Reparations and Costs), Inter-American Court of Human Rights Series C no 239 (24 February 2012); *State Obligations Concerning Change of Name, Gender Identity, and Rights Derived from a Relationship Between Same-Sex Couples (Interpretation and Scope of Articles 1(1), 3, 7, 11(2), 13, 17, 18 and 24, in relation to Article 1, of the American Convention on Human Rights)*, Advisory Opinion OC-24, Inter-American Court of Human Rights Series A no 24 (24 November 2017). See also the most recent *Vicky Hernández et al v Honduras* (Merits, Reparations and Costs), Inter-American Court of Human Rights Series C no 422 (26 March 2021).

[90] *Atala-Riffo* (n 89) para 92; Candia, 'Comparing Diverse Approaches' (n 83) 18.

by the tendency of the Court, lately, to grant national authorities significant deference when it comes to social rights.[91]

Bearing in mind that the political landscape in the Americas, nowadays, is different from at the very beginning of the Inter-American system, dictating a stringent review of domestic powers in the implementation of their human rights obligations, the question arises whether it is preferable to go for other forms of deference.[92] As we speak, most of the Latin-American states have successfully made the transition to democracy,[93] with independent judicial authorities; therefore the cases brought before the Court are, steadily, moving away from claims of mass atrocity to new types of disputes. This new reality led to the proliferation of academic voices calling for a shift in the IACtHR's position regarding the use of the doctrine since the IACtHR's difficulty to truly embrace its subsidiary character impedes the solid consolidation of the Court's jurisdiction.[94] This tendency of the Court is also emphasised by the recent adoption of the *conventionality control* concept.[95] This newly introduced doctrine of the Court, indicative of its audacity and its judicial activism, puts the latter in the place of a supreme constitutional court since, pursuant to this scheme, state courts must review the compatibility of national legislation not only with national constitutions but also with the ACHR and its respected interpretation by the IACtHR. Despite the fact that this formula may serve as an additional tool in the hands of the Inter-American judge in order to foster the rule of law and democratisation in the Americas, it has already come under great criticism.[96] Combined with the already expressed hesitancy of the Court to resort to the MoA formula, the conventionality control was seen by many scholars as another way to keep for itself the final word on domestic internal affairs concerning human rights issues as it intends to interfere with the domestic sovereign competence to adjudicate local cases.[97]

Within a constitutional environment that not exactly promotes interaction between national and international law, a horizontal and mechanical application

[91] See, eg '*Five Pensioners*' *v Peru* (Merits, Reparations and Costs), Inter-American Court of Human Rights Series C no 98 (28 February 2003). See also on this matter Duhaime, 'Subsidiarity in the Americas' (n 75) 313.

[92] In *Castaneda-Gutman v Mexico* in 2008, the Court, without explicitly referring to the MoA formula, implicitly acknowledged that restricting such political rights within the limits of the American Convention is, in fact, a responsibility of the state. *Castañeda Gutman v Mexico* (Preliminary Objections, Merits, Reparations and Costs), Inter-American Court of Human Rights Series C no 184 (6 August 2008), para 155.

[93] D Rodríguez-Pinzón, 'The Inter-American Human Rights System and Transitional Processes' in A Buyse and M Hamilton (eds), *Transitional Jurisprudence and the ECHR: Justice, Politics and Rights* (Cambridge, Cambridge University Press, 2011) 239, 242–43.

[94] See, eg J Contesse, 'Contestation and Deference' (n 59) 145.

[95] A Dulitzky, 'An Inter-American Constitutional Court? The Invention of the Conventionality Control by the Inter-American Court of Human Rights' (2015) 50 *Texas International Law Journal* 46.

[96] E Malarino, 'Judicial Activism, Punitivism and Supranationalisation: Illiberal and Antidemocratic Tendencies of the Inter-American Court of Human Rights' (2012) 12 *International Criminal Law Review* 665.

[97] O Ruiz-Chiriboga, 'The Conventionality Control: Examples of (Un)Successful Experiences in Latin America' (2010) 3 *Inter-American and European Human Rights Journal* 200.

or decision of non-application of the IACtHR's standards might have the adverse effects as some countries may use it so as to disapply the said standards and denounce the Convention. Taking more into account the constitutional characteristics of each system (eg concentrated or diffuse constitutional review)[98] and the overall human rights situation prevailing in the respondent state while applying the conventionality control or granting deference to the respondent state is more likely to provide fertile ground for the kind of integrative interpretation of the ACHR that the IACtHR seeks to impose.

Without exaggerating the perils associated with the stringent scrutiny that the IACtHR has opted for, we can maintain that the Court struggles to find its own path of fostering the domestic rule of law in the region. It has managed, therefore, to give extremely proactive and comprehensive responses to several topics, particularly related to the causes of the deeply installed impunity and injustice in the continent. However, the political and judicial backlash against the Court and the specific features of the latter's findings by the domestic judiciaries rather point towards a more dialectic pattern adjusted to the particularities of each domestic framework. In recent years, political pressure over the entire Inter-American system has strengthened. Trinidad and Tobago, and Venezuela, have already denounced the American Convention and state discontent was powerfully expressed by Brazil, Peru and Dominican Republic, which posed an additional burden to the Court.[99] However, political hostility and lack of persuasiveness *vis-à-vis* national jurisdictions are not hardships that only the San José Court is facing. On the contrary, the ambiguity that stems from the questionable use of the MoA doctrine by the Strasbourg Court is also considered to result in an abdication by the latter in hotly debatable disputes. The ECtHR has recently responded to the expressed disapproval for its inconsistent and mysterious approach of the margin of appreciation by explicitly incorporating[100] it in Article 1 of the new Protocol No 15 ECHR.

Yet, in the new political environment, the IACtHR may, indeed, benefit from affording greater trust to domestic tribunals to make the correct assessment in order to enhance their legitimacy and, by extension, the legitimacy and credibility of the IACtHR. As Follesdal correctly put it, 'the doctrine may itself serve to promote democratic deliberation and independence of the judiciary, by "nudging" states to perform an independent proportionality test as a necessary condition for enjoying a margin of appreciation.'[101] By the same token, the reconceptualisation

[98] J Contesse, 'The Final Word? Constitutional Dialogue and the Inter-American Court of Human Rights' (2017) 15 *International Journal of Constitutional Law* 414, 424.

[99] X Soley and S Steininger, 'Parting Ways or Lashing Back? Withdrawals, Backlash and the Inter-American Court of Human Rights' (2018) 14 *International Journal of Law in Context* 237; R Uruena, 'Double or Nothing: The Inter-American Court of Human Rights in an Increasingly Adverse Context' (2018) 35 *Wisconsin International Law Journal* 398.

[100] See M Iglesias Vila, 'Subsidiarity, Margin of Appreciation and International Adjudication within a Cooperative Conception of Human Rights' (2017) 15 *International Journal of Constitutional Law* 393.

[101] Follesdal, 'Exporting the Margin of Appreciation' (n 72) 371.

of the conventionality control in the sense of an inter-judicial dialogue between equals, allowing the Court to also count on domestic stakeholders for supporting a new era of human rights adjudication might be actually a win-win solution.[102]

It goes without saying that the IACtHR, as a relatively new international tribunal and taking into account the specificities of the system, needs the support of Latin American states. Thus, embracing a less intimidating stance for a more collaborationist model of human rights enforcement might prove more effective for the implementation of the Convention, encouraging reconnection with domestic judicial authorities.[103]

Ultimately, it appears that it is not only the aforementioned corpus of cases that calls for a change pertaining to the more effective application of the MoA doctrine but it is also the mere nature of the pioneer IACtHR as the ultimate guarantor of human rights in the Americas – which often dares to reinvent itself in order to fulfil its purpose – that points towards a more evolutive and less intrusive use of the MoA doctrine.

iii. The Provisional Measures in the IACtHR Case Law

While times of urgency (eg, coups, terrorist attacks or environmental damage) are more and more common, human rights protection is occasionally endangered under these uncontrollable circumstances instead of being even more fortified. In this context, provisional measures, as a procedural, yet core aspect of the protection mechanism of the IACtHR, constitute a significant part of the loans that the latter has taken from its European peer and thus, deserves our attention.

Pursuant to Article 63(2), the Court, in cases of extreme gravity and urgency, is entitled to issuing provisional measures[104] to combat gross human rights violations, the dreadful scourge of the region. With the aim of preventing irreparable damage, a situation which has proved extremely common in Latin America, the San José Court has used provisional measures as a tool to protect especially the right to life and the right to personal (physical, mental and moral) integrity.

By all means, the issuing of measures of provisional character is not a new mechanism in international law. Almost all international treaties or conventions authorise the bodies reviewing compliance with the relevant instruments to

[102] Benvenisti and Downs highlighted the effects of judicial cooperation for the consolidation of democratic rule of law. E Benvenisti and G Downs, 'Democratizing Courts: How National and International Courts Promote Democracy in an Era of Global Governance' (2013) Global Trust Working Paper no 5/2013, www.papers.ssrn.com/sol3/papers.cfm?abstract_id=2646879.

[103] The non-use or the timid use of the said doctrine was also denounced by the former president of OAS, César Gaviria. C Gaviria, 'Towards a New Vision of the Inter-American Human Rights System' (1996) 4(4) *Journal of Latin American Affairs* 9, 11.

[104] The Inter-American Commission may also order measures of preventive nature, the so-called 'precautionary measures' that should be distinguished from the provisional measures issued by the Court. Pursuant to Art 25(1) of the Rules of Procedure of the IACommHR, the latter may, at the request of a party or on its own initiative, request that a state takes precautionary measures to prevent irreparable harm to individuals.

order provisional measures so that irreparable damage can be circumvented. The International Court of Justice (ICJ) has preceded and shown the way for both the ECtHR and IACtHR. Its legacy includes the heated debate among academics on the binding – or not – nature of its provisional measures, which only recently has come to an end with the ICJ's pronouncements in the seminal *LaGrand* case.[105] The ICJ interpreted widely the term 'decisions' in Article 94(1) UN Charter[106] regulating compliance with the Court's decisions so as to attribute binding force to the provisional measures issued by the Court and remedy the linguistic softness of Article 41 of the Statute of the ICJ on provisional measures[107] which fuelled the controversy around the provision.

Conversely, within the Inter-American system, the matter was made clear from the very beginning since the drafters of the ACHR felt that they should not leave any ambiguity on this and laid down the provision of Article 63(2).[108] Arguably, it is absolutely indicative of the specifics that apply in this part of the world where the ACHR is the only international human rights instrument to provide expressly for judicially enforceable measures of provisional nature.

As former President of the IACtHR Cançado Trindade has noted, provisional measures under the Pact of San José go beyond the judicial formalism around this issue. In his words,

> in fact, such measures besides their essentially preventive character, effectively protect fundamental rights, in so far as they seek to avoid irreparable harm to the human person as subject of the international law of human rights. In the ambit of this latter which is essentially a law of protection of the human being, provisional measures reach effectively their plenitude, being endowed with a character, more than precautionary, truly tutelary.[109]

As for the binding nature of provisional measures, their conventional basis and their inclusion in the 8th Chapter of ACHR under the title 'Jurisdictions and Functions' underlined the intention of the drafters to give undisputed

[105] *LaGrand Case (Germany v United States of America)* (Merits) [2001] ICJ Rep 466, para 109. See, eg JA Frowein, 'Provisional Measures by the International Court of Justice – The LaGrand Case' (2002) 62 *Heidelberg Journal of International Law* 55; J Kammerhofer, 'The Binding Nature of Provisional Measures of the International Court of Justice: The "Settlement" of the Issue in the LaGrand Case' (2003) 16 *Leiden Journal of International Law* 67.

[106] Art 94(1) UN Charter provides: '1. Each Member of the United Nations undertakes to comply with the decision of the International Court of Justice in any case to which it is a party'.

[107] Art 41 of the Statute of the ICJ reads as follows '1. The Court shall have the power to indicate, if it considers that circumstances so require, any provisional measures which ought to be taken to preserve the respective rights of either party. 2. Pending the final decision, notice of the measures suggested shall forthwith be given to the parties and to the Security Council.'

[108] T Buergenthal, 'Interim Measures in the Inter-American Court of Human Rights' in R Bernhardt (ed), *Interim Measures Indicated by International Courts* (Berlin, Springer, 1994) 48–51.

[109] AA Cançado Trindade, 'The Evolution of Provisional Measures of Protection under the Case-Law of the Inter-American Court of Human Rights (1987–2002)' (2003) 24 *Human Rights Law Journal* 162, 163.

binding force.[110] In addition, the drafters of the cornerstone instrument of the IAHRS interestingly opted for the clarity of the phrase 'shall adopt' instead of the traditional but controversial verb 'indicate' that has created so much uncertainty on this issue. Hence, having examined the common requirements of extreme gravity, urgency and irreparable damage under international human rights law, the Court is entitled to pronounce on the matter of ordering provisional measures when a case is pending before the latter or at the request of the Commission for a case which has not yet been brought before the IACtHR. The usual procedure of the former concerns, hence, precautionary measures of non-compulsory character. The Court delivers a decision on the need – or otherwise – to issue provisional measures assessing the situation in the light of the aforementioned criteria. This decision is not subject to appeal.[111]

From the case law perspective, the compulsory effect of the provisional measures ordered by the San José Court has never been doubted by the State Parties that have accepted the contentious jurisdiction of the Court. In the famous case *Hilaire et al v Trinidad and Tobago*[112] in which the Court ordered provisional measures to prevent the death penalty that the applicants were facing, the respondent state did not deny that it had violated the provisional measures previously issued by the Court, suggesting recognition of their mandatory value.

Regardless of the different starting point that distinguished the provisional measures under the ACHR (conventional basis) from the mechanism of interim measures of the Strasbourg system (regulatory basis),[113] the Court followed a similar pattern and managed to render such measures a significantly common and ever-evolving tool for human rights protection in the Americas. In the spirit of the relevant ECtHR case law on interim measures, the Inter-American Court developed, mostly in the 2000s, its jurisprudence so as to cover urgent situations that stem from expulsions, extraditions[114] or freedom of expression cases, which is a common practice for the ECtHR as well.[115] Both the human rights tribunals have

[110] ibid 164; C Burbano Herrera and Y Haeck, 'Letting States off the Hook? The Paradox of the Legal Consequences following State Non-Compliance with Provisional Measures in the Inter-American and European Human Rights Systems' (2010) 28 *Netherlands Quarterly Human Rights* 332, 336.

[111] See, eg Pasqualucci, *The Practice and Procedure* (n 14) 251.

[112] *Hilaire, Constantine and Benjamin et al v Trinidad and Tobago* (Merits, Reparations and Costs), Inter-American Court of Human Rights Series C no 94 (21 June 2002).

[113] The possibility of ordering provisional measures is only enclosed in the Rules of Procedure of the ECtHR in Art 39 of the Rules of Procedure of the Court.

[114] See, eg *Community of San Jose de Apartado v Colombia* (Provisional Measure Order), Inter-American Court of Human Rights Series E no 2 (24 November 2000); *Expelled Dominicans and Haitians v Dominican Republic* (Preliminary Objections, Merits, Reparations, and Costs), Inter-American Court of Human Rights Series C no 282 (28 August 2014).

[115] Factsheet of the ECtHR on Interim Measures published in February 2022, www.echr.coe.int/documents/fs_interim_measures_eng.pdf; L Burgorgue-Larsen, 'Interim Measures in the European Convention System of Protection of Human Rights' (2009) 2 *Inter-American and European Human Rights Journal* 99.

expanded their jurisprudence on urgent measures taking, simultaneously, each other's case law into consideration.[116]

Thus, some traces of cross-fertilisation could be detected pertaining to the issue of the provisional measures' binding force since it constituted a point of interrogation for the Strasbourg Court as well. As previously mentioned, the wording of Article 39 of the Rules of Court leaves room for ambiguity which was also supported by the inconsistencies in the ECtHR jurisprudence. In the *Cruz Varas* case, the Strasbourg Court blatantly abstained from affirming the binding character of the interim measures in a deportation case issued to protect from inhumane and degrading treatment under Article 13. It did so on the basis of the same uncertainty that characterises similar rules of international law.[117] Thus, the Court deduced that the binding nature of the measures under scrutiny cannot be inferred by the right to individual petition to let the states 'decide whether it is expedient to remedy this situation by adopting a new provision notwithstanding the wide practice of good faith compliance'.[118] Some years later, the Court remained faithful to its approach in relation to its own interim measures in the *Conka* case[119] until its spectacular *revirement* on the matter in the *Mamatkulov* judgment.[120]

In casu, the Court felt ready to endorse the *LaGrand* principles as well as the Inter-American Court's position to support its complete opposition to the *Cruz Varas* standing. Relying on the living instrument doctrine and on the preservation of the right to individual petition, the Strasbourg Court managed to build up on its credibility and authority *vis-à-vis* the Contracting Parties as it explicitly declared the mandatory force of the interim measures issued by the Court. In particular, two Uzbek nationals, both arrested by the Turkish authorities, were later extradited to Uzbekistan on the basis of a bilateral convention on extraditions between the two states, despite the decision on interim measures issued by the President of the ECtHR (Article 39 Rules of Procedure) to prevent the extradition of the applicants. Besides the substantial grounds that amounted to violation of Article 3 ECHR due to serious risk of torture or inhuman/degrading treatment in case of extradition to their home country, the non-compliance with the Court's interim measure as well as the lack of contact with their legal representatives resulted in a violation of the ECHR since their extradition severely undermined

[116] In a parallel manner, the analogous question of binding nature of provisional measures has arisen – albeit timidly – in the purview of the African human rights system. See on the matter D Juma, 'Provisional Measures under the African Human Rights System: The African Court's Order against Libya' (2012) 30 *Wisconsin International Law Journal* 344, 366–67.

[117] *Cruz Varas and Others v Sweden*, Merits, Series A no 201 (1991), para 101.

[118] ibid para 102.

[119] *Čonka v Belgium*, Merits, ECHR 2002-I 47.

[120] *Mamatkulov and Abdurasulovic v Turkey*, Merits, App nos 46827/99 and 46951/99 (ECtHR, 6 February 2003). See also *Mamatkulov and Askarov v Turkey* [GC], Merits, ECHR 2005-I 225.

the applicants' right to individual petition.[121] The Court emphasised the vital role that the interim measures played in avoiding irreversible damage being caused that would prevent the Court from properly examining the applicants' claims and, therefore, would hinder them in enjoying, in effect, the ECHR's rights.

Importantly, the Strasbourg Court managed to overcome its traditional hesitations with relation to the use of external legal sources and referred in length not only to the ICJ's standing on the matter but also to its Latin-American peer.[122] In the Court's words,

> In various orders concerning provisional measures, the Inter-American Court of Human Rights has stated that in view of the fundamental objective of the American Convention on Human Rights, namely guaranteeing the effective protection of human rights, 'States Parties [had to] refrain from taking actions that may frustrate the *restitutio in integrum* of the rights of the alleged victims' (see the orders of 25 May and 25 September 1999 in James et al. v. Trinidad and Tobago).'[123] That said, the Grand Chamber concluded that it flows from the examination of the appraisal of all the previously cited jurisdictions that '... whatever the legal system in question, the proper administration of justice requires that no irreparable action be taken while proceedings are pending' (see, mutatis mutandis, *Soering*, cited above, p. 35, § 90).[124]

At this point, we need to remark that one of the benchmarks of the IACtHR case law on provisional measures is the *pacta sunt servanda* rule of international law. As the Court has noted in *James and others v Trinidad and Tobago*, it also applies to the procedural elements of an international obligation, connecting, thus, the issue explicitly with the attribution of international responsibility to the state.[125] Nevertheless, the San José Court appears, to date, reluctant to derive a violation of an individual right from the refusal of a state to comply with binding provisional measures.[126] Paradoxically, the Court abstained from dealing with the disrespectful attitude of states in cases in which provisional measures have been ordered before the Court and examined the case on the merits. It has contented itself to state

[121] H Tigroudja, 'La force obligatoire des mesures provisoires indiquées par la Cour européenne des droits de l'homme: Observations sous l'arrêt Mamatkulov contre Turquie' (2003) 107 *Revue Générale de Droit International Public* 601.

[122] *Mamatkulov and Askarov v Turkey* [GC](n 120) paras 50–53. However, the use of international jurisprudence as an additional yardstick legitimising its reasoning does not seem convincing to some scholars. Tigroudja, 'La force obligatoire' (n 121) 615.

[123] ibid para 116; O De Schutter, 'The Binding Character of the Provisional Measures Adopted by the European Court of Human Rights' (2005) 7 *International Law FORUM du droit international* 16, 21.

[124] ibid para 124.

[125] See *James et al v Trinidad Tobago* (Order for Provisional Measures) (28 February 2005); *Hilaire, Constantine and Benjamin* (n 112) para 38.

[126] *Bámaca Velásquez v Guatemala* (Merits), Inter-American Court of Human Rights Series C no 70 (25 November 2000), paras 65–70. However, the Court, with its order, maintained the provisional measures. *Bámaca Velásquez v Guatemala* (Order for Provisional Measures and Monitoring Compliance with Judgment) (27 January 2009); *Luisiana Ríos and Others v Venezuela* (Preliminary Objections, Merits, Reparations, and Costs), Inter-American Court of Human Rights Series C no 194 (28 January 2009), paras 57–59, 125.

that 'this situation is aggravated because the victim was protected by Provisional Measures ordered by this Tribunal, which expressly indicated that his execution should be stayed pending the resolution of the case by the Inter-American human rights system.'[127] Hence, the state's failure to successfully implement the provisional measures does not amount to a separate violation of the right to petition under the American Convention as is the case of the ECHR system following to the *Mamatkulov* jurisprudence.

A potential justification of the Court's standing could lie on the Commission's competence to request from the Court to adopt such measures. In that sense, it cannot be said that the right to individual petition of the beneficiaries of provisional measures is breached.[128] If the Court, following an order of provisional measures, pronounces on the contested dispute without finding a violation of a substantial right, the potential non-compliance of the state with the order remains totally unpunished. This position seems to soften the figure given to such measures by the San José Court on the basis of conventional guarantees. Thus, the effective protection of individual beneficiaries of provisional measures from irreparable damage under the ACHR appears theoretical and illusory, which is exactly the case that the ECtHR has repeatedly attempted to avoid.[129] More importantly, the IACtHR's position favouring sate's latitude also contradicts with its refusal to leave some leeway to the states in less grave cases as the non-use of the MoA doctrine by the same Court has already revealed.

In any case, as the Strasbourg Court stated, in every judicial system, the proper administration of justice – national or international – implies the possibility of indicating measures with suspensive effect so as all human rights claims can be safely brought before the Court with particular vigilance when there is serious risk of irreparable damage.[130] It remains to be seen, hence, if the Inter-American Court can truly draw from the Strasbourg Court's *revirement*; it has all the necessary tools to do so.

B. The Vertical Perspective

i. Consolidation of Free Speech in the Americas: The Influence of ECtHR

In a region where the consolidation of democratic values is of utmost importance, the jurisprudential evolution of the Strasbourg Court in relation to the

[127] *Bámaca Velásquez v Guatemala* (Merits) para 198.

[128] See especially Pasqualucci, *The Practice and Procedure* (n 14) 293.

[129] Burbano Herrera and Haeck, 'Letting States off the Hook?' (n 110) 356.

[130] On the very essence of provisional measures see especially G Cohen-Jonathan, 'Sur la force obligatoire des mesures provisoires: L'arrêt de la Grande Chambre de la Cour Européenne du 4 février 2005, *Mamatkulov et Askarov contre Turquie*' (2005) 109 *Revue Générale de Droit International Public* 421, 434.

thorny issues of political speech, the role of journalism and prior censorship constituted the cornerstone of the IACtHR case law on this matter. The ACHR embodies freedom of expression in Article 13 in a more descriptive and expansive manner than the ECHR, that explicitly sets the limits of the permitted restrictions within the enjoyment of the said freedom. The latter is thus given particular attention not only under the Inter-American Democratic Charter[131] but it is also embodied in the Declaration of Principles on Freedom of Expression, adopted in 2000.[132]

Most importantly, the duality of the freedom of expression is the aspect that gives this right its crucial role in a democratic regime. This duality is manifested since freedom of expression consists, firstly, of the right to hold an opinion and to share information and ideas 'of all kinds'. Further, the freedom equally guarantees the right to 'receive' such information – and, to 'seek' it, making a uniquely emphatic reference to the right to seek state-held information. Hence, setting forth this collective strand of freedom of expression, the drafters of the ACHR attempted to establish that the right is not only addressed to those purporting to disseminate opinions or information but also to the public audience as a whole who deserves to take note of information affecting the daily life of individuals.

In the light of the robust safeguards that the ECHR and the Strasbourg Court's jurisprudence, the San José Court adopted the dual function of this right even more generously. At first, in the context of the individual dimension, the IACtHR took the opportunity to manifestly declare the fundamental role of journalistic speech in a democratic society in a number of cases just like its European peer.[133] In order to serve such a role, the media should be protected not only as far as the content of the information disseminated is concerned; the means through which such information is channelled is also covered by the protection of the ECHR. Aside the limits of journalistic speech with regard to reputational rights and the right to private life,[134] the decisive role of media within a democratic framework is the one that allows tolerance and broadmindedness pertaining to a certain exaggeration when it comes to transmission of information that might offend, shock or disturb.[135] Journalistic sources are also covered by the scope of the Convention's

[131] OAS, 'Inter-American Democratic Charter' General Assembly Res AG/RES 1 (XXVIII-E/01) (San José, 11 September 2001).

[132] IACommHR 'Declaration of Principles on Freedom of Expression', approved by the Inter-American Commission during its 108th regular period of sessions (October 2–20 2000).

[133] *The Sunday Times v The United Kingdom (no 2)*, Merits, Series A no 217 (1991), para 50; *Goodwin v the United Kingdom*, Merits, ECHR 1996-II, para 39; *Bladet Tromsø and Stensaas v Norway* [GC], Merits, ECHR 1999-III 289.

[134] D Voorhoof, 'Freedom of Expression versus Privacy and the Right to Reputation: How to Preserve Public Interest Journalism' in S Smet and E Brems (eds), *When Human Rights Clash at the European Court of Human Rights Conflict or Harmony*? (Oxford, Oxford University Press, 2017).

[135] *Lingens v Austria*, Merits, Series A no 103 (1986), para 41. In the *Radio France* case the Court reiterates its position on the broad limits of the media. *Radio France and Others v France*, Merits, ECHR 2004-II 83, para 37.

provision so as the press could be freely expressed and proceed to the necessary revelations related to issues of general interest promoting, hence, transparency in public and political life.[136] Thus, under Article 10 ECHR, whose field of application was enlarged over the years, media enjoy a widely exercised freedom of expression. As a result, the ECtHR remains apt to effectively review governmental actions and put pressure on states pertaining to the collective aspect of freedom of expression in the sense of the right to have access to state-held information and to demand disclosure of such information from state organs.

Since, in the Americas, journalists are frequently in a vulnerable position, being intimidated or even persecuted, more and more cases concerning the freedom of the press were brought before the Commission and later on, before the IACtHR.[137] Naturally, the IAHRS saw these cases in the light of the safety net offered by the ECtHR to journalists, taking into account the ever-evolving conditions of the public debate. Both the Commission and the Court have been over-protective towards the unhindered function of the press, issuing precautionary or provisional measures in order to immediately tackle situations in which journalists have been found kidnapped or even murdered.[138] In its landmark *Ivcher Bronstein v Peru* case,[139] the Court reiterated the dual nature of the said right and emphasised the crucial role of independent media within a democratic society[140] As for the role of pluralism, it goes without saying that the standing of the Strasbourg judges in similar cases constituted the principal source of inspiration for the IACtHR.[141]

The added value of the Inter-American system is the explicit prohibition of prior censorship which was deemed necessary by the drafters of the ACHR. If we examine closely the political history of the region, it is not surprising that the leading case on this matter was brought against Chile, a Latin American states where the transition from a brutal authoritarian regime to a well-functioning democracy in the 1990s was, in fact, a rather challenging task. This transition was, unfortunately, combined with the proliferation of judicial censorship of films, books, plays or television programmes on an everyday basis. The *ratio* of such measures was the national doctrine of the Chilean courts according to which the right to honour

[136] *Sanoma Uitgevers BV v The Netherlands* [GC], Merits, App no 38224/03 (ECtHR, 14 September 2010), para 100.

[137] See especially *Compulsory Membership in an Association* (n 12) paras 70–71.

[138] See, eg *Sánchez Cerezo v. Mexico*, (Precautionary Measures 5/15) Inter-American Commission of Human Rights (2015); *'Globovisión' Television Station v Venezuela* (Order of Provisional Measures) (4 September 2004); *Luisiana Ríos et al v Venezuela* (Order of Provisional Measures) (8 September 2004).

[139] *Ivcher Bronstein v Peru* (Merits, Reparations, and Costs), Inter-American Court of Human Rights Series C no 74 (6 February 2001). The Court reiterated its findings and its emphasis on free press in the more recent *Vélez Restrepo and family v Colombia* (Preliminary Objection, Merits, Reparations and Costs), Inter-American Court of Human Rights Series C no 248 (3 September 2012).

[140] *Ivcher Bronstein*, paras 149,150.

[141] See *Perozo* (n 52) para 116 in comparison with the *Handyside* judgment of the ECtHR, *Handyside* (n 63) para 49.

prevails over freedom of expression when those two rights clash.[142] Naturally, the IACtHR took the opportunity to grapple with this issue in the landmark *Olmedo Bustos et al v Chile*,[143] also known as *The Last Temptation of Christ* case. The case[144] concerned the well-known film by Martin Scorsese which was censored on the basis of the Chilean Constitution for the moral protection of children. The Court shed light to the notion of prior censorship prohibition and the limits within which the exceptions under the American Convention are to be applied. In paragraph 70, the Court held that '[i]t is important to mention that Article 13(4) of the Convention establishes an exception to prior censorship, since it allows it in the case of public entertainment, but only in order to regulate access for the moral protection of children and adolescents'.[145]

For the Court, in the general context of the existing system of prior censorship in Chile which allowed the banning of the film, the actual decision in the instant case was not, in principle, rooted on the exception allowed by the Convention but in the 'name of … Jesus Christ' and of 'the Catholic Church'[146] which was dishonoured according to the allegations of the applicants before the national courts of Chile. Further, the Court restrictively applied the exception related to prior censorship whose prohibition is the rule and not the exception. Hence, the morals of childhood could be easily protected by the authorities by taking less restrictive measures than prior censorship – for instance by banning the entrance of children to cinemas where the film was shown. Notably, it took the chance to rule on the attribution of international responsibility to the state arising from decisions of the judicial authorities, since the Chilean government alleged that the violation of freedom of expression in the present case was not attributable to the state on the basis of the non-interference of the executive.[147] According to the Court, the specific position of the actor does not mitigate or affect the determination of the state's responsibility.[148] Following this ground-breaking decision on prior censorship, Chile was forced to proceed to a constitutional reform so as to protect freedom of expression as enshrined in the ACHR.

However, the extreme measure of prior censorship, as it may be, cannot be entirely excluded within the meaning of Article 13(3) ACHR.[149] Any cases, to

[142] L Burgorgue-Larsen and A Úbeda de Torres, 'The Right to the Freedom of Thought and Expression' in L Burgorgue-Larsen and A Úbeda de Torres (eds), *The Inter-American Court of Human Rights: Case Law and Commentary* (Oxford, Oxford University Press, 2011) 549.

[143] *Olmedo Bustos et al v Chile* ('*The Last Temptation of Christ Case*') (Merits, Reparations and Costs), Inter-American Court of Human Rights Series C no 73 (5 February 2001).

[144] J McCormick, ''The Last Temptation of Christ' (Olmedo Bustos et al.) v. Chile' (2016) 38 *Loyola of Los Angeles International and Comparative Law Review* 1189.

[145] *Olmedo Bustos* (n 143) para 70.

[146] ibid para 71.

[147] ibid para 72.

[148] See, eg Pasqualucci, *The Practice and Procedure* (n 14) 183; Rivier, 'Responsibility for Violations' (n 21).

[149] A Úbeda de Torres, 'Freedom of Expression under the European Convention on Human Rights: A Comparison with the Inter-American System of Protection of Human Rights' (2003) 10(2) *Human Rights Brief* 6, 9.

date, in which the Court has pronounced on such a sensitive matter in up-front censorship cases, have not touched the limits of the exceptions on the grounds of national security or public order. It remains thus surprising that the IACtHR saw several cases related to the renewal of a television station's licence[150] or the persecution of journalists through the lens of 'indirect' restrictions pursuant to Article 13(3)[151] bypassing, thus, the potential link of those cases to prior censorship.[152]

From the Strasbourg Court's perspective, no similar loud prohibition of practices constituting prior censorship exists. Therefore, the ECtHR examined the imposition of *prior restraints* to the press in the light of the general provisions of Article 10(2) ECHR pertaining to the legitimate restrictions to the freedom of expression.[153] Initially, the Strasbourg Court dealt with such cases in two similar cases against the UK, namely the *Sunday Times (No. 2)*[154] and *Observer and Guardian.*[155] These cases concerned the general imposition of a permanent injunction restraining the British newspapers from any further domestic publication of extracts from a book telling the story of a former member of the British Security Service, for the protection of national security. The Court held that

> does not in terms prohibit the imposition of prior restraints on publication … the dangers inherent in prior restraints are such that they call for the most careful scrutiny on the part of the Court. This is especially so as far as the press is concerned, for news is a perishable commodity and to delay its publication, even for a short period, may well deprive it of all its value and interest.[156]

Subsequently, the Court has reiterated its standing regarding prior restraints on publications in several cases.[157]

Aside from the individual dimension of freedom of expression, its collective strand constitutes another crucial aspect whose social impact is beyond any doubt. Therefore, the ACHR also provides explicitly for the right and freedom to seek, receive and impart information and ideas of all kinds, and most importantly, of the state-held information not only for the sake of individuals but also for the public

[150] *Granier et al (Radio Caracas Television) v Venezuela* (Preliminary Objections, Merits, Reparations and Costs), Inter-American Court of Human Rights Series C no 293 (22 June 2015).

[151] *Manuel Cepeda Vargas v Colombia* (Preliminary Objections, Merits, Reparations and Costs), Inter-American Court of Human Rights Series C no 213 (26 May 2010); *Vélez Restrepo and family* (n 139).

[152] T Antkowiak and A Gonza, *The American Convention on Human Rights* (Oxford, Oxford University Press, 2017) 245.

[153] See, eg D Voorhoof et al, *Freedom of Expression, Media and Journalists: Case-law of the European Court of Human Rights*, IRIS Themes Vol III (Strasbourg, European Audiovisual Observatory, 2015).

[154] *The Sunday Times (no 2)* (n 133).

[155] *Observer and* Guardian *v the United Kingdom*, Merits, Series A no 216 (1991).

[156] ibid para 60.

[157] See, eg *Association Ekin v France*, Merits, ECHR 2001-VIII 293; *Éditions Plon v France*, Merits, ECHR 2004-IV 39; *Ürper and Others v Turkey*, Merits, App nos 14526/07, 14747/07, 15022/07, 15737/07, 36137/07, 47245/07, 50371/07, 50372/07 and 54637/07 (ECtHR, 20 October 2009); *Mouvement raëlien suisse v Switzerland* [GC], Merits, ECHR 2012-IV 293.

interest. This American perception of freedom of expression is well-described in the famous *Claude Reyes* judgment.[158]

With its ruling, the IACtHR became the first international court to recognise the right to access to public information as a fundamental human right protected by human rights treaties that require states to comply with its positive obligations in this respect. *In casu*, Marcel Claude Reyes, the main claimant asked for information from Chile's Foreign Investments Committee on the Río Cóndor project, a forestry exploitation plan, since the environmental impact of the latter was under discussion. However, he received only a part of the information requested. The Court, with regard to the dimension of free expression, manifested that Article 13 protects not only the right of the individual to receive such information but also the positive obligation of the state to provide it, which thereby gives the opportunity to individuals to come up with solid answers when it comes to the justification of a limitation to this freedom.[159] The Court also took a further step and underlined that '[t]he information should be provided without the need to prove direct interest or personal involvement in order to obtain it, except in cases in which a legitimate restriction is applied.' Hence, the Court offered a broader interpretation than the one given by its Strasbourg peer in this respect. Particular emphasis was also given to the social impact of the right to seek state-held information since, according to the judgment, there is an underlying dual dimension of the right, both individual and social.[160] Within, a democratic society, the Court stated that national authorities 'are governed by the principle of maximum disclosure, which establishes the presumption that all information is accessible, subject to a limited system of exceptions'[161] and concluded in finding a violation of Article 13 ACHR.[162]

Interestingly enough, the IAHRS has also incorporated the principle of *habeas data*,[163] namely the right of individuals to have access to their personal data.[164] It interlinked two fundamental rights that traditionally clash in human

[158] *Claude Reyes et al v Chile* (Merits, Reparations, and Costs), Inter-American Court of Human Rights Series C no 151 (19 September 2006).

[159] ibid para 77.

[160] ibid.

[161] ibid para 92.

[162] See IACommHR Office of the Special Rapporteur for Freedom of Expression 'The Inter-American Legal Framework regarding the Right to Access to Information' OEA/Ser.L/V/II. CIDH/RELE/INF.9/12 (2nd edn, 7 March 2011), www.oas.org/en/iachr/expression/docs/publications/2012%2009%2027%20access%20to%20information%202012%20edits.pdf.

[163] IACommHR, 'Report on Terrorism and Human Rights' OEA/Ser.L/V/II.116 Doc. 5 rev. 1 corr. (22 October 2002), Chapter III, Section E, www.cidh.oas.org/Terrorism/Eng/toc.htm. See also on this matter Burgorgue-Larsen and Úbeda de Torres, 'The Right to the Freedom of Thought and Expression' (n 142) 546. See also IACtHR 'Annual Report of the Office of the Special Rapporteur for Freedom of Expression 2001' OEA/Ser/L/V/II.114 doc. 5 rev. (16 April 2002), Chapter III.

[164] However, the legal basis upon which the right to personal data lies under the ECHR is Art 8 establishing the right to private and family life, as discussed in Pt I. On the different legal basis of this right in the two systems, see IACtHR 'Annual Report of the Office of the Special Rapporteur for Freedom of Expression 2001' ibid para 28.

rights legal practice at both national and international level. For the IACtHR, which does not acknowledge the enjoyment of free expression to legal persons, the right to privacy of the investor in this case – since the confidentiality of business data was the basis of the company's argument – comes second when the right to access government-held information is on the table.[165]

According to well-established international human rights law, freedom of expression, as a non-absolute right, is subject to restrictions when necessary. The peaceful and unobstructed enjoyment of the right to express oneself freely might conflict with the exercise of other fundamental rights, such as the right to have one's honour respected and one's dignity recognised (Article 11 ACHR) and the right to private and family life (Article 17 ACHR). The two main categories of restrictions laid down therein echo, to a great extent, the permitted limitations under the ECHR, and are based first, on the reputational rights of others and secondly, on the protection of national security, public order or public health or morals.[166]

To date, the San José Court has mostly touched upon freedom of expression cases where the said right should be weighed against the reputational rights of individuals or public officials invoking defamation. Most importantly, the Court has approached the matter of limitations with great caution, especially, as far as journalistic speech is concerned, given the significance of the role of the press within a democratic society, as previously discussed. However, in the Court's words in the famous *Kimel* case,[167] 'journalists have the duty to verify reasonably, though not necessarily in an exhaustive manner, the truthfulness of the facts supporting their opinion. Therefore, it is valid to claim equity and diligence in the search for information and the verification of the sources'.[168] The *Kimel* case concerned the conviction of Eduardo Kimel, a historian and a journalist for a publication criticising the actions of the national judiciary during the military dictatorship in

[165] S Karamanian, 'Human Rights Dimensions of Investment Law' in E de Wet and J Vidmar (eds), *Hierarchy in International Law: The Place of Human Rights* (Oxford, Oxford University Press, 2012) 243; S Joseph, 'Trade Law and Investment Law' in D Shelton (ed), *The Oxford Handbook of International Human Rights Law* (Oxford, Oxford University Press, 2013) 854.

[166] Nevertheless, the IACtHR has not yet pronounced on such sensitive issues already brought before the ECtHR, for profoundly historical reasons. Since the drafters of the American Conventions opted for specific conditions under which propaganda or hate speech could provide a legitimate justification for a limitation to free expression, the possibility of a broader interpretation of the aforementioned provision is rather dubious. It should be noted that the ECtHR sometimes saw the hate speech cases under the scope of Art 17 prohibiting the abuse of rights embodied in the Convention since it excluded these cases per se from protection under Art 10(1) and thus, declined to examine whether there is room for a permissible restriction according to the second paragraph of the said provision. See *Jersild v Denmark* [GC], Merits, Series A no 298 (1994). With regard to the interconnection of Art 17 ECHR and Art 10 see D Shelton, 'Balancing Rights and Responsibilities: Human Rights Jurisprudence on Regulating the Content of Speech' in P Wahlgren (ed), *Human Rights: Limitations and Proliferation*, Scandinavian Studies in Law 55 (Stockholm, Stockholm Institute for Scandinavian Law, 2010) 222–25.

[167] *Kimel v Argentina* (Merits, Reparations and Costs), Inter-American Court of Human Rights Series C no 177 (2 May 2008).

[168] ibid para 79.

Argentina. The Inter-American Court felt that it should apply the proportionality test to ascertain whether a restriction to free expression is acceptable in the name of the protection of the reputation and honour of the judges targeted in the book authored by Mr Kimel. After having explained how information pluralism works in a democracy and taking into consideration the equity which must govern the flow of information, the Court concluded that strict proportionality criteria must apply.[169] In doing so, notwithstanding the fact that according to the wording of the decision there is still room for criminal libel laws to be viable under more protective standards,[170] the Court made clear its pedagogic nature and described analytically that a limitation to a provision of the Convention can be compatible if it respects the four above-mentioned conditions. Those four stages of the proportionality test under the ACHR – instead of three under the ECHR – indicate the willingness of the Court to minimise the potential restrictions to the absolutely necessary. It is within the context of this last condition of *stricto sensu* necessity that the principle of proportionality applies[171] according to the reading of the Strasbourg Court, whereas for the IACtHR the necessity of the measure under scrutiny (third condition) is distinct from its proportionality (which constitutes clearly the fourth condition) and has to be reconciled with respect to the aim pursued.

Needless to say, the IACtHR has relied on the case law of its Strasbourg peer in order to build its jurisprudence when it has had to rule upon permissible limitations of the rights under discussion. The Court had, already, reiterated its source of inspiration and indicated the path that it was willing to take in *Herrera-Ulloa*.[172] It thus clarified the content of the necessity imposing the measure and embodied, once again,[173] the concept of pressing social need, holding that

> in its interpretation of Article 10 of the European Convention, the European Court of Human Rights ruled that 'necessary,' while not synonymous with 'indispensable,' implies 'the existence of a 'pressing social need' and that for a restriction to be 'necessary' it is not enough to show that it is 'useful,' 'reasonable' or 'desirable'.[174]

This tendency of the Court was later reaffirmed in several freedom of expression cases. The same course was also taken in *Uson Ramirez*,[175] a case which concerned the right to protect the honour of armed forces, in the classic *Tristan Danoso* case[176]

[169] ibid para 58.

[170] See EA Bertoni, 'The Inter-American Court of Human Rights and the European Court of Human Rights: A Dialogue on Freedom of Expressions Standards' [2009] 3 *European Human Rights Law Review* 332, 344.

[171] See especially T Cottier, R Echandi, R Liechti-McKee, T Payosova and C Sieber, 'The Principle of Proportionality in International Law: Foundations and Variations' (2017) 18 *Journal of World Investment & Trade* 628.

[172] *Herrera-Ulloa* (n 78).

[173] See, eg *Compulsory Membership in an Association* (n 12).

[174] ibid para 122.

[175] *Usón Ramírez v Venezuela* (Preliminary Objections, Merits, Reparations and Costs), Inter-American Court of Human Rights Series C no 207 (20 November 2009), para 49.

[176] *Tristán Danoso v Panamá* (Preliminary Objections, Merits, Reparations and Costs), Inter-American Court of Human Rights Series C no 193 (27 January 2009).

as well as in the famous *Claude Reyes* case, discussed earlier. In the latter case, the Court clarified that the state has the burden of proof to show that it has complied with the established requirements when enforcing restrictions to the freedom of expression and in the instant case, to the state-held information.[177]

Having said all the above, it is more than evident that the IACtHR opted for drawing extensively from the Strasbourg standards when dealing with disputes affecting the freedom of expression in the American States notwithstanding the different emphasis given to several aspects of the interests protected under the ACHR and the ECHR. Given the specificities of the region, the IACtHR considered that the European jurisprudence set a minimum threshold. The Court, acknowledging that the European Convention constitutes its basic source of inspiration, deemed that the wording of Article 13 ACHR has been designed to be more generous than the corresponding provision of the ECHR. Therefore, as Eduardo Andreas Bertoni correctly mentioned 'the interpretation of Art 10 by the European Court may provide a minimum standard for the interpretation of Art 13, but never a ceiling.'[178]

Despite the recent decrease in the number of references by the San José judges to the European level of protection in freedom of expression cases,[179] in reality, European case law is deeply rooted in the Inter-American understanding of free speech and constitutes the lighthouse that crucially contributed to its development. It flows from this analysis that the nascent democratic regimes in Latin America would have plunged into chaos without the European precedent giving (initial) shape to the entitlements of the American Convention. Last but not least, the parallel and pioneer development of the Inter-American case law in this field could not pass unnoticed by the ECtHR, which explicitly referred to the leading *Claude Reyes* ruling of the IACtHR. Thus, the Grand Chamber delivered the *Stoll v Switzerland*[180] judgment enhancing its argumentation which revolved around the 'even greater importance of press freedom in circumstances in which state activities and decisions escape democratic or judicial scrutiny on account of their confidential or secret nature.'[181]

Naturally, while contributing to the democratisation of the continent, the IACtHR largely borrowed from the Strasbourg Court when adjudicating one of the most crucial types of disputes, namely freedom of expression cases. Taking a parallel road, the San José judicature managed to dynamically interpret the ACHR incorporating the ECtHR's criteria of lawful derogations from the freedom of expression and inspiring, thereby, transjudicial communication in this field of law even more.

[177] *Claude Reyes* (n 158) paras 92–93.

[178] See especially Bertoni, 'The Inter-American Court of Human Rights' (n 170) 352.

[179] In the *Danoso*, *Perozo* or *Velez Restrepo y Familiares* cases we can hardly find a reference to the Strasbourg precedent on the matter. *Vélez Restrepo and family* (n 139); *Tristán Danoso* (n 176); *Perozo* (n 52).

[180] *Stoll v Switzerland* [GC], Merits, ECHR 2007-V 267, para 111.

[181] ibid para 110.

ii. The Divergent Legal Treatment of Irregular Migrants: The Rights of Detainees

The particularly vulnerable case of migrants in irregular situations[182] is, universally, at the centre of attention of both governmental authorities and non-governmental institutions. Having in the past repeatedly been affected by large displacement of populations within its territory, Europe was once again confronted with an unprecedented refugee crisis which clearly unbalanced even more the institutional endeavour to alleviate the problems already documented in this field.[183] Despite having breached migration law, irregular migrants remain in a legal limbo for undefined duration, and as a particularly vulnerable group of people should be entitled to enhanced protection under international human rights law. Unauthorised migration has, hitherto, provoked contentious political debates. However, the meagre responses of policy-makers in states and international organisations reveal the important role of international human rights courts in mapping irregular migrants' rights and, specifically, defining their content and scope.

It comes as no surprise that in a land where major internal conflicts have repeatedly uprooted populations, the dominant regional human rights mechanism could not have ignored the most troubled aspect of international migration law. Hence, the Strasbourg Court has significantly developed its case law on irregular migration, rendering it one of the most dynamic facets of its jurisprudence related to the protection of people seeking international protection. In addition, it influenced the decision-making process, not only at the domestic level but at the EU level as well. In its landmark decisions it has shaped its own standards pertaining to the prohibition of inhuman and degrading treatment, the right to asylum and the right to effective remedy when it comes to irregular migrants. However, the ECtHR was subjected to criticism with regard to the inconsistencies of its jurisprudence on the matter[184] and its hesitancy to touch upon some core issues in a field dominantly regulated by domestic powers with the same sensitiveness that it approached other aspects of migration or refugee law. Immigration detention offers an illustrative example of the ECtHR's standing in this regard.

Regardless of its slow start, the IACtHR looked into a wide range of migration cases, from disputes on the nationality/naturalisation agenda to the peremptory norms of equality and non-discrimination. Using the Strasbourg Court's human

[182] See especially E Guild, 'Who is an Irregular Migrant?' in B Bogusz, R Cholewinski, A Cygan and E Szyszczak (eds), *Irregular Migration and Human Rights: Theoretical, European and International Perspectives*, Immigration and Asylum Law and Policy in Europe 7 (Leiden, Brill Nijhoff, 2004).

[183] See I Mann, *Humanity at Sea: Maritime Migration and the Foundations of International Law* (Cambridge, Cambridge University Press, 2016); V Moreno-Lax and E Papastavridis (eds), *'Boat Refugees' and Migrants at Sea: A Comprehensive Approach Integrating Maritime Security with Human Rights*, International Refugee Law Series 7 (Leiden, Brill Nijhoff, 2016).

[184] L Lavrysen, 'Is the Strasbourg Court Tough on Migration?' (*Strasbourg Observers*, 5 December 2012), www.strasbourgobservers.com/2012/12/05/is-the-strasbourg-court-tough-on-migration/.

rights standards on migration, the San José Court attempted to hand down rulings that form its own safeguards, mostly, inspired by the *pro homine* principle that dominates its jurisprudence. The latter is even more understandable with regard to the detention of migrants.

At any rate, the initiation of IACtHR into migration cases was made with a couple of Advisory Opinions which offered the opportunity to the Court to make some important statements. Its first case affecting the rights of migrants was *Advisory Opinion 4/84 on the Proposed Amendment to the Naturalisation Provision of the Constitution of Costa Rica*, discussed earlier[185] on the issue of the Court's position on the margin of appreciation granted to states. Citizenship complaints raising human rights issues, which are still approached timidly by the ECtHR[186] since they are situated in the heart of national sovereign powers, constituted the basis upon which the IACtHR moderately built its migration case law.

From the migrants' rights perspective, notwithstanding the initial borrowing of the margin of appreciation formula from its Strasbourg peer concerning the proposed amendment of the national constitution, the IACtHR seemed to opt for a differentiated position on nationality issues, placing them at the centre of human rights migration law. The first observation of the Court is indicative. For the Court, nationality is inevitably linked to the individual's legal capacity; nevertheless, its contemporary understanding entails the reconciliation of the state's broad powers relatively with the respect of human rights when exercising these powers.[187] Thus, the state enjoys some latitude on these matters; nevertheless, its discretionary powers emanating from national sovereignty are not unlimited. Hence, human rights are not perceived as an exception to the rule of state sovereignty, while human rights come first and state sovereignty follows, since the Inter-American Court commences building its argumentation by affirming the human right to nationality.[188]

Marie-Bénédicte Dembour doubted the looming intention of the San José Court to replicate the discretional approach of the Strasbourg Court in general and maintained instead that

> In this early ruling the Inter-American Court shows itself speaking with a distinct voice of its own. This is a voice which is propitious to a potentially broad interpretation of migrants rights, as a state powers in the field of naturalization are recognized, but are nonetheless viewed as significantly limited by human rights norms.[189]

[185] *Proposed Amendments to the Naturalisation Provisions* (n 73).

[186] On the occasion of the *Ramadan* judgment of the ECtHR, Marie-Bénédicte Dembour brought to light the reluctance of the Strasbourg Court to embrace nationality's human rights facets. MB Dembour, 'Ramadan v. Malta: When will the Strasbourg Court Understand that Nationality is a Core Human Rights Issue?' (Strasbourg Observers, 22 July 2016), www.strasbourgobservers.com/2016/07/22/ramadan-v-malta-when-will-the-strasbourg-court-understand-that-nationality-is-a-core-human-rights-issue/.

[187] *Proposed Amendments to the Naturalisation Provisions* (n 73) para 32.

[188] See also *Ivcher Bronstein* (n 139).

[189] MB Dembour, *When Humans Become Migrants: Study of the European Court of Human Rights with an Inter-American Counterpoint* (Oxford, Oxford University Press, 2015) 131.

And, thus, this broad interpretation of migrants' rights was subsequently reaffirmed by another Advisory Opinion[190] touching specifically more pressing issues that directly affect irregular migrants. In this case, the IACtHR felt that it should elaborate on the vulnerability of undocumented migrant workers.[191] Looking through the lens of 'equality' and 'non-discrimination', recognised by the Court as *jus cogens* norms, the latter declared that undocumented migrants enjoy *equal* labour rights with nationals, irrespective of their status. According to the Court, the right to work offers a protective net of *erga omnes* obligations binding all states and 'in this way, the migratory status of a person can never be a justification for depriving him of the enjoyment and exercise of his human rights, including those related to employment'.[192] However, novel as these pronouncements may seem, they remain quite controversial in academia.[193] In any case, we can see the chasm regarding the legal treatment of similar issues between the San José and the Strasbourg Court. Interestingly, the IACtHR only at the end of its reasoning felt that it should balance the peremptory status of equality and non-discrimination with the long-established duty of the state to regulate its migratory policies.[194]

Subsequently, the aforementioned chasm was clearly illustrated in the celebrated *Vélez Loor v Panama* case,[195] the Inter-American Court's first contentious case on irregular migration, in 2010. In the present case,[196] the claimant, a citizen of Ecuador, was arrested in Panama in 2002, transferred to a detention centre with poor detention facilities, where the Director of the National Migration Office sentenced him to two years of imprisonment for violation of previous deportation orders. The alleged victim revealed that he was not informed of the decision

[190] *Proposed Amendments to the Naturalisation Provisions* (n 73).

[191] ibid paras 111–17.

[192] ibid para 134.

[193] For the so-called 'misuse' of *jus cogens* norms, see A Beduschi, 'The Contribution of the Inter-American Court of Human Rights to the Protection of Irregular Immigrants' Rights: Opportunities and Challenges' (2015) 34(4) *Refugee Survey Quarterly* 45. The overall approach of the concept of *jus cogens* by the Inter-American Court of Human Rights will be analysed in the following chapter.

[194] Dembour, *When Humans Become Migrants* (n 189) 299–300; see also in this respect *Juridical Condition and Rights of Undocumented Migrants* (n 30) para 169. See inter alia the recent judgment of the IACtHR that constitutes the benchmark of labour rights and protection of workers in Brazil, namely the *Workers of the Hacienda Brasil Verde v Brazil* case. The Court examined the generalised practice of recruiting poor workers, mostly Afro descendants, to work under conditions of servitude in plantations. The Court borrowed the definition of 'servitude' given by the Strasbourg Court and based its conclusions on its similar findings in relevant disputes. *Workers of the Hacienda Brasil Verde v Brazil* (Preliminary Objections, Merits, Reparations and Costs), Inter-American Court of Human Rights Series C no 318 (20 October 2016), paras 280, 287–88, 365.

[195] *Vélez Loor v Panama* (Preliminary Objections, Merits, Reparations and Costs), Inter-American Court of Human Rights Series C no 218 (23 November 2010), para 139.

[196] A Mason, 'Interpretation of the American Convention in Latin America: The Impact of the Inter-American Court of Human Rights' Decision in *Velez Loor v. Panama* on Irregular Migrant Rights' (2012) 18 *Law and Business Review of the Americas* 71, 82; G De León, 'Contributions and Challenges for the Inter-American Court of Human Rights for the Protection of Migrants' Rights: The Case of Vélez Loor v. Panama' (2014) 7 *Inter-American and European Human Rights Journal* 39.

or of his right to consular assistance and was neither provided with a counsel nor with the opportunity to challenge the deportation before administrative authorities. After sentencing, he was transferred to another detention centre with blatantly poor facilities. Mr Vélez Loor complained that, during his 10-month detention, was subjected to severe physical and mental abuse and tortures, not to mention that he was deprived from basic judicial guarantees.

On the occasion of the assessment of the particular detainee's situation, the IACtHR opted for mapping the human rights standards of migrants' detention, significantly contributing, thus, to the protection of migrants in the Americas. In a similar way to its appraisal on the Advisory Opinion on migrant workers, the Court focused extensively on the vulnerability of this group that requires special attention, shedding light, as well, on the cultural aspects that often impede the smooth integration of irregular migrants within societies.[197] Moving to the lawfulness of the claimant's arrest and its compatibility with the ACHR, the Court held that the protection offered by this instrument is not limited when it comes to the detention of migrants, in clear contrast to the ECHR's relevant provisions. The Court felt that it should draw a clear distinction from the limitations imposed on the right to liberty by the drafters of the European Convention in view of migrants' unauthorised entry and deportation or extradition.

Thereby, for the Court, the ACHR dictates a more human rights-oriented approach of migration procedures according to which detention is subject to prompt and effective review given the special vulnerability of detainees.[198] Subsequently, the Court crystallised its additional requirements applied so that each detention could be deemed lawful under Article 7(5), namely the independence and impartiality of the judicial body. Finally, the Court clarified that in order for the judicial review to be acceptable, a personal evaluation by the relevant authority of the clarifications that the detainee may eventually provide is required before the issuance of the decision that maintains the deprivation of liberty.[199] After having found a violation of Article 7(5) since the applicant was not informed of the judicial means at his disposal, the Court examined the potential justification of the decision resulting in Mr Loor's detention and the effectiveness of the judicial remedies apt to challenge the disputed order of detention. For the IACtHR, specific time limits[200] and available and accessible remedies (including legal aid)[201] provided by the administrative authorities in charge are considered indispensable for the detention to be compatible with the ACHR.

More importantly, the Court took a further step in order to improve the enforcement of migrants' rights in the Americas since it heavily rejected the

[197] *Vélez Loor* (n 195) para 98.
[198] ibid para 107.
[199] ibid para 109.
[200] ibid para 117.
[201] On the basis of the observations of the Special Rapporteur on the Human Rights of Migrants, the Court underlined the *effet utile* of the remedies to challenge the legality of the detention. Ibid para 129.

penalisation of measures. It further stated that 'it is clear that detaining people for non-compliance with migration laws should never involve punitive purposes. Hence, a custodial measure should only be applied when it is necessary and proportionate in the specific case, to the purposes mentioned supra and only for the shortest period of time.'[202] Thus, the principle of proportionality plays, once again, a major role in the selection of the suitable measure while regulating irregular entry of migrants.

Moreover, the non-punitive character of the measures aiming to control migration should be reflected in the detention conditions in the sense of the separation of convicted criminals in penitentiary centres from persons detained for non-compliance with domestic migration laws. For the Court, different purposes of detention require different detention facilities.[203] All these considered, the Court condemned the Panamanian authorities for violating Mr Loor' s right to personal liberty under Article 7 ACHR, the right to fair trial under Article 8 ACHR and the right to humane treatment under Article 5 ACHR.

This ruling brought emphatically to light the divergence on this matter with the ECtHR, which is much more restricted in acknowledging such an extended protection from detention to irregular migrants. Notably, the Strasbourg Court does not consider the necessity of the detention an indispensable component of compatibility with Article 5(1)(f) ECHR.[204]

On the contrary, necessity is a common requirement for all sub-categories covered by Article 5(1). Interestingly enough, the only exception is the last one pertaining to persons effecting an unauthorised entry into the territory of a Contracting Party or persons against whom action is being taken with a view to a deportation or an extradition. The rule of the prohibition of arbitrariness applies here; however, the level of protection offered by the European system appears severely poorer than the American.

In two landmark cases against the United Kingdom, the ECtHR consolidated its restricted criteria applicable to the detention of migrants. In the *Chalal*[205] case delivered in 1996, the Strasbourg Court famously admitted that

> Article 5 para. 1 (f) (art. 5-1-f) does not demand that the detention of a person against whom action is being taken with a view to deportation be reasonably considered necessary, for example to prevent his committing an offence or fleeing; in this respect Article 5 para. 1 (f) (art. 5-1-f) provides a different level of protection from Article 5 para. 1 (c) (art. 5-1-c). Indeed, all that is required under this provision (art. 5-1-f) is that 'action is being taken with a view to deportation'. It is therefore immaterial, for the purposes of

[202] ibid paras 170–71.
[203] ibid paras 207–8.
[204] Nevertheless, this *lacuna* deriving from the lack of the necessity requirement for the detention of irregular migrants could be covered by national legislation, the legality of which – as previously mentioned – is scrutinised by the Court.
[205] *Chahal v the United Kingdom* [GC], Merits, ECHR 1996-V.

> Article 5 para. 1 (f) (art. 5-1-f), whether the underlying decision to expel can be justified under national or Convention law.[206]

Nevertheless, the Court stressed that deprivation of liberty is not justified for unlimited duration, and only for as long as deportation proceedings are in progress with reference to the principle of due diligence that also applies. Similar pronouncements can also be found to almost every decision of the Court on migrant detention.

As Dembour relatively observed, 'taking into account the absence of a necessity test, a judge would have no reason to find the detention of a person to be deported unlawful under the Convention (as long as there is a real prospect that the deportation is being pursued and will take place).'[207] In the more recent *Saadi v the UK*[208] case the Court clarified with regard to the first limb of Article 5(1)(f) that

> until a State has 'authorised' entry to the country, any entry is 'unauthorised' and the detention of a person who wishes to effect entry and who needs but does not yet have authorisation to do so can be, without any distortion of language, to 'prevent his effecting an unauthorised entry'.[209]

At this point, the Court explained that the opposite interpretation would disproportionately restrict the national powers to control migration flows arriving at their borders.

Given the wording of Article 5 ECHR, the only possible way of finding that the detention had not violated the Convention was to find that it was covered by the first limb of the exception provided in Article 5(1)(f). Hence, the critical issue became the following: had the applicant been detained in order to prevent him from effecting unauthorised entry to the UK? The Court deemed it appropriate to establish the criteria that characterise a non-arbitrary detention. In the Court's words,

> such detention must be carried out in good faith; it must be closely connected to the purpose of preventing unauthorised entry of the person to the country; the place and conditions of detention should be appropriate, bearing in mind that 'the measure is applicable not to those who have committed criminal offences but to aliens who, often fearing for their lives, have fled from their own country' …; and the length of the detention should not exceed that reasonably required for the purpose pursued.[210]

As anticipated, the stance of the Court was greatly criticised, both inside and outside the Court. Judges Rozakis Tulkens, Kovler, Hajiyev, Spielmann denounced

[206] ibid para 112.

[207] Dembour, *When Humans Become Migrants* (n 189) 376. See also G Cornelisse, *Immigration Detention and Human Rights: Rethinking Territorial Sovereignty*, Immigration and Asylum Law and Policy in Europe 19 (The Hague, Martinus Nijhof, 2010).

[208] *Saadi v the United Kingdom* [GC], Merits, ECHR 2008-II 207.

[209] ibid para 65.

[210] ibid para 74.

the majority's approach on the necessity test and famously interrogated whether it is acceptable for the ECtHR to provide a lower level of protection than the one afforded by other organisations.[211] Nevertheless, the Court attempted with its subsequent case law, particularly, when the detention of children is being reviewed,[212] and more obviously following its seminal *M.S.S. v Greece and Belgium*, to reverse its rather reserved stance. In the aforementioned decision, the Court revisited the vulnerability aspect and recognised the inherent vulnerability in the situation of irregular migrants that is also a function of previous experience or trauma.[213] Despite some signs of second thoughts on the application of its *Saadi* standards,[214] the Strasbourg Court does not seem ready to reach the Inter-American ones or to elucidate the legal obligations of domestic authorities when it comes to the deprivation of liberty of migrants which is for the Strasbourg Court outlined, to a great extent, by the will of the states.[215]

Its *Vélez Loor* ruling constitutes the major contribution of the IACtHR to the promotion of migrants' rights in the troubled Latin American region.[216] The judges of the Court used the occasion of such a multifaceted violation of the applicant's rights to meticulously analyse all the requirements emanating from the ACHR and its *pro homine* guarantees pertaining to the most vulnerable migrants, namely irregular migrants.

By contrast, since the ECtHR's tendency with regard to immigration detention is not compatible to the values generally applied to detention cases, namely the presumption of liberty and the existence of specific grounds justifying the measure, Cathryn Costello proposed another path. For her, the ECtHR 'could abandon *Saadi v UK* and commit to a presumption of liberty for migrants. The conditional right of residence of those whose refugee status is being determined could be treated as immunizing them from detention, except in exceptional cases.'[217] In any case, the ECtHR fell short in drawing clearly the line between the state's right to regulate its migration policies and the effective promotion of the rights of irregular migrants in detention.[218]

[211] ibid Joint Dissenting Opinion of Judges Rozakis Tulkens, Kovler, Hajiyev and Spielmann.

[212] *Muskhadzhiyeva and Others v Belgium*, Merits, App no 41442/07 (ECtHR, 19 January 2010), para 55.

[213] See the relevant paragraphs of the seminal *M.S.S.* judgment. *M.S.S. v Belgium and Greece* [GC], Merits, ECHR 2011-I 121, paras 232–33, 259ff.

[214] See on the use of the 'less stringent measures' criterion L Lavrysen, 'Less Stringent Measures and Migration Detention: Overruling Saadi v UK?' (*Strasbourg Observers*, 25 January 2012), www.strasbourgobservers.com/2012/01/25/less-stringent-measures-and-migration-detention-overruling-saadi-v-uk/.

[215] C Costello, 'Immigration Detention: The Grounds beneath our Feet' (2015) 68 *Current Legal Problems* 143.

[216] In the context of the monitoring of the compliance phase of its earlier judgment in *Vélez Loor*, the Court issued a decision of provisional measures to urge Panama to take extra protective measures for detainees amid the COVID 19 pandemic. See *Vélez Loor v Panamá* (Resolution of the President of the Inter-American Court of Human Rights on the Adoption of Urgent Measures) (26 May 2020).

[217] Costello (n 215), p 176.

[218] In its recent case law regarding detention of migrants the Court attempted to rationalise the 'unauthorised entry' requirement. See, eg *Rusu v Austria*, Merits, App no 34082/02 (ECtHR, 2 October

The stark differences between the two regional *fora* on the matter are possibly entrenched in their contrasting judicial *habitus*. Besides the textual divergence, each judicial mechanism has adopted its own way of responding to these questions. The observed continuity, particularly as far as the Strasbourg Court is concerned, seems to be incompatible with its living instrument doctrine. While the detention limits pertaining to asylum seekers are set, when it comes to migrants in an irregular situation, the legal treatment of their detention remains unclear.

All that said, the IACtHR appeared, within the context of its contentious powers, compatible with its prior jurisprudential lines as reflected in its advisory opinions regardless of the high non-compliance rates of its rulings. Therefore, it developed a forward-looking case law aiming to enrich the received human rights protection of irregular migrants with a clear and firm set of obligations upon domestic authorities. While the Strasbourg Court adopted a rather uneasy position towards deprivation of liberty of unauthorised migrants, the IACtHR has proved willing to take further steps and seized the opportunity of the *Vélez Loor* case in order to reach overall conclusions delivering a judgment with general implications and significant impact worldwide.[219]

C. Conclusion

Besides a structural paradigm, the ECHR system offered to its sibling institution the normative clarity as well as a remarkable interpretative toolkit emanating from the Strasbourg Court's judicial practice to combat the entrenched atrocities of the region. Inevitably, human rights adjudication therein passes through the direct invocation of the ECHR provisions and the relevant standards of the Strasbourg Court. At first glance, parallel approaches of common human rights challenges can be easily traced in the work of both judicial mechanisms. The IACtHR felt free, since its dawn, to apply extensively the ECtHR's standards in an analogous manner so as to shape the proper interpretation of the ACHR and to foster the credibility of the organ itself in the troubled legal landscape of the American Convention. The Court was inspired, thus, by the ECtHR's application of Conventional rights in freedom of expression cases and from the Strasbourg Court's doctrinal approach, by and large, to states' positive obligations. Nevertheless, an adjusted approach of the Strasbourg Court's standards has been documented in several legal fields (eg detention of irregular migrants) or in the horizontally applied legal treatment of the IACtHR's corpus of cases (eg the MoA application). Overall, it appears rather difficult to find a judgment of the Inter-American Court without

2008); *SD v Greece*, Merits, App no 53541/07 (ECtHR, 11 June 2009); *RU v Greece*, Merits, App no 2237/08 (ECtHR, 07 June 2011); *Yoh-Ekale Mwanje v Belgium*, Merits, App no 10486/10 (ECtHR, 20 December 2011); *Suso Musa v Malta*, Merits, App no 42337/12 (ECtHR, 23 July 2013).

[219] See Beduschi, 'The Contribution of the Inter-American Court of Human Rights' (n 193).

quoting the relevant case law of the ECtHR. At any rate, the IACtHR borrowed in an extremely creative manner from its counterpart without overlooking the particular features of national judicatures and left, at the same time, enough room for cross-fertilisation with the European Court which also seeks to constantly adapt to new exigencies.

III. The Expansion of Human Rights Protection by the IACtHR: Any Room for Cross-Fertilisation?

Crucially, the IACtHR has not contented itself to step into the road already taken by the ECtHR. Leveraging the experience of the latter, it has paved new roads of human rights adjudication covering also the paucity of international human rights law in challenging fields in need of ground-breaking responses. In the following pages, meticulous attention is paid to the doctrinal appraisals of the Court when developing enhanced human rights protection in the Americas. Indicative of the judicial audacity of the IACtHR, the proliferation of peremptory norms as well as its extensive remedial powers have demonstrated that the Court is willing to move far from the expected and possibly inspire other regional mechanisms to act accordingly.

A. The Proliferation of *Jus Cogens* Norms in the IACtHR Case Law

In the context of the Latin American region, which has largely been plagued by impunity, the IACtHR felt that the strengthening of *jus cogens* norms,[220] in the sense of identification of specific human rights as peremptory norms of international law, could enhance the effects of the ACHR's safeguards within its dynamic jurisprudence.

In general, the concept of *jus cogens*[221] was debated for decades in relation to the work of the International Law Commission (ILC) on the law of treaties, which was, subsequently, accepted almost unanimously and codified in Articles 53 and 64 VCLT. Until its addition to the 'positive law' family and the formal definition embedded in the Vienna Convention, it constituted a fundamental rule

[220] C Rozakis, *The Concept of Jus Cogens in the Law of Treaties* (Amsterdam, North-Holland Publishing Company, 1976) 1–2.

[221] *Jus cogens* is in contradistinction to *Jus Dispositivum*, which contains norms which are not imperative and from which derogations are permissible under specific circumstances. L Hannikainen, *Peremptory Norms (Jus Cogens) in International Law: Historical Development, Criteria, Present Status* (Helsinki, Finnish Lawyers' Publishing Company, 1988) 727; For a comprehensive discussion see A Orakhelashvili, *Peremptory Norms in International Law* (Oxford, Oxford University Press, 2006).

of international customary law.[222] Hence, a peremptory norm of international law can be considered a norm accepted and recognised by the international community of states (as a whole), from which no derogation is permitted. Its modification is, thus, only operated by a subsequent norm of general international law having the same character.

Despite the generalised effort both in academia and judicial practice, the content of *jus cogens* norms and their *modus* of identification have remained ill-defined until now. However, the concept of *jus cogens* has exceeded the limits of the law of treaties and constitutes an illustrative example of the hierarchy of rules[223] as a general principle of international law.[224] To date, the fuzziness that revolves around instances of peremptory norms and the particular problem of who has the judicial power to determine them has not been resolved by the ICJ, which is, by definition, in a better position to provide binding interpretations of international law rules, greatly respected within international community.[225]

When it comes to human rights, most of the human rights treaties have endorsed core and basic guarantees as non-derogable fundamental rights that Member States cannot suspend even in emergency situations, such as the right to life and the prohibition of torture or inhuman and degrading treatment, arbitrary detention and so on. Conversely, can we suggest that such non-derogable human rights obligations should take the shape of *jus cogens* norms? In reply, as Stefan Kadelbach stated relatively that 'if such treaty obligations are recognized also in international customary law, a strong case can be made for them to belong to international jus cogens.'[226] In any case, the identification of a right as non-derogable in an international human rights convention would be one of the most crucial factors to grant the *jus cogens* title to this right, albeit not the only one.

As regards the issue of which judicial organ is capable to pronounce on the existence of a *jus cogens* norm, we can trace a certain decentralisation accruing such a power not only to the ICJ but also to other international judicial bodies,

[222] D Shelton, 'Sherlock Holmes and the Mystery of Jus Cogens' (2015) 46 *Netherlands Yearbook of International Law* 23.

[223] See on the problem of hierarchical order of norms in international law E Roucounas, 'Engagements parallèles et contradictoires' (1987) 206 *Recueil des Cours de l'Académie de Droit International* 13, 56–70.

[224] E Roucounas, *Public International Law* [in Greek] (Athens, Nomiki Vivliothiki, 2015) 162.

[225] The ICJ seemed to refer indirectly to jus cogens through naming core human rights obligations as *erga omnes* obligations contributing to the well-established confusion between *jus cogens* norms and *erga omnes* rules under international law. See *Case Concerning the Barcelona Traction, Light and Power Company, Limited (Belgium v Spain)* (Merits) [1970] ICJ Rep 3, 32–33; *Western Sahara* (Advisory Opinion) [1975] ICJ Rep 12, 68; *Case Concerning East Timor* (*Portugal v Australia*) (Merits) [1995] ICJ Rep 90, 102.

[226] S Kadelbach, 'Jus Cogens, Obligations Erga Omnes and Other Rules: The Identification of Fundamental Norms' in C Tomuschat and JM Thouvenin (eds), *The Fundamental Rules of the International Legal Order: Jus Cogens and Obligations Erga Omnes* (Leiden, Martinus Nijhoff, 2006) 31.

mostly international criminal tribunals[227] and regional human rights courts. Focusing on the latter category, Europe has approached the matter with similar reluctance. The Strasbourg Court, in *Al-Adsani v UK*,[228] in which state immunities in civil proceedings in respect of alleged torture were on the table, refused to put the *jus cogens* character of torture at the centre of its legal reasoning. In the Grand Chamber's words,

> Notwithstanding the special character of the prohibition of torture in international law, the Court is unable to discern in the international instruments, judicial authorities or other materials before it any firm basis for concluding that, as a matter of international law, a State no longer enjoys immunity from civil suit in the courts of another State where acts of torture are alleged.[229]

The Court advanced its position by drawing clear distinction from criminal liability and refused to draw an 'automatic' legal inference from the peremptory character of the prohibition of torture, though fuelling the ambiguity as regards the practical effects of *jus cogens*.

Nevertheless, for some scholars, this ambiguity concerning the exact notion of *jus cogens*, its identification rules as well as its overall role in international law, does not cause serious problems to the evolution of the said concept. It remains contested, though whether this ambiguity impedes their evolution within contemporary international law.[230] If that is not the case, the nuanced jurisprudence of the IACtHR pertaining to *jus cogens* norms could be seen through this exact prism. In particular, the entire IAHRS revealed a willingness to touch upon this conflicting issue from its early cases. In 1993, in the *Aloeboetoe*[231] case, the Court, following to the Commission's decision, manifestly declared that the treaty between a group of indigenous peoples and the Netherlands was *ab initio* null and void, irrespective of its controversial nature empowering this group to capture and sell slaves to the Dutch. Its decision is vindicated by the fact that the latter contradicts *jus cogens superveniens*, and thus, it cannot be brought before an international human rights forum.[232]

[227] *Prosecutor v Anto Furundzija* (Judgment) ICTY-95-17 (10 December 1998).

[228] *Al-Adsani v United Kingdom* [GC], Merits, ECHR 2001-XI 79. See, eg E Bates, 'The Al-Adsani Case, State Immunity and the International Legal Prohibition on Torture' (2003) 3 *Human Rights Law Review* 193.

[229] *Al-Adsani* (n 228) para 61. For the legal treatment of state immunities in connection with *jus cogens* norms before national courts and most particularly, on the *Distomo* case before the Greek Supreme Court, Areios Pagos, see M Gavouneli and I Bantekas, 'Prefecture of Voiotia v. Federal Republic of Germany, Case no 11/2000, Areios Pagos (Hellenic Supreme Court), May 4, 2000' (2001) 95 *AJIL* 198.

[230] P Tavernier, 'L'identification des règles fondamentales un problème résolu?' in C Tomuschat and JM Thouvenin (eds), *The Fundamental Rules of the International Legal Order: Jus Cogens and Obligations Erga Omnes* (Leiden, Martinus Nijhoff, 2006) 20.

[231] *Aloeboetoe et al v Suriname* (Reparations and Costs), Inter-American Court of Human Rights Series C no 15 (10 September 1993), para 57.

[232] ibid paras 56–57. However, Dina Sheldon expressed doubts on the horizontal and rigorous application of the said rule. Shelton, 'Sherlock Holmes' (n 222) 36.

Later on, the same Court revisited *jus cogens* and managed to enlarge the concept at the regional level so as to incorporate the right to equality and non-discrimination, as depicted in the *Advisory Opinion 18/03 on the Juridical Condition and Rights of Undocumented Migrants*[233] pertaining to migrants' rights in the workplace. After having recalled the initially close nexus of *jus cogens* with the law of treaties, it reaffirmed that the concept of peremptory norms has largely developed in the general international legal order. Having said that, the Court followed a reasoning anchored in natural law and more particularly, to the connection of equality with the respect for human dignity that should permeate all domestic states under the ACHR. Due to the horizontal and holistic character of such imperative obligations and according to the Court's appraisal, this rule gives rise not only to the negative obligation of states to refrain from actions that directly or indirectly create situations of *de facto* or *de jure* discrimination. It also creates positive obligations for states that may improve equality standards among their nationals, redressing long-established injustices against particular groups of individuals.[234]

However, the reliance of the Court on natural law[235] in its attempt to establish a newly introduced strand to the timidly used *jus cogens* scheme within the international legal community provoked serious scepticism around the credibility of the concept. This basis of the Court's position on the peremptory nature of the principle of equality is well described in the separate opinion of the former President of the IACtHR, Cançado Trindade. He interestingly linked this origin of *jus cogens* to law's intertemporal aim to fulfil its purpose: law should serve individuals and not states, since the latter emanates from human conscience and not from states' will, which is traditionally at the centre of the making of general international law.[236]

Progressive as this approach may seem, it does not appear entirely convincing to academics. Andrea Bianchi underlined in this regard that given the vagueness that characterises the concept, an excessive characterisation of more and more rules as peremptory risks undermine the mere credibility of *jus cogens*.[237] Dinah Shelton also highlighted in relation to the justification that the Court selected, that notwithstanding the use of numerous international treaties containing provisions on equality, it opted for a higher obligation that seems to emerge more from common sense, that calls for essential human dignity.[238] The Court, at this point, appears to follow the road taken by the Inter-American Commission. While

[233] *Juridical Condition and Rights of Undocumented Migrants* (n 30).

[234] ibid paras 97–100. See also T de AFR Cardoso Squeff and M de Almeida Rosa, 'Jus Cogens: An European Concept?: An Emancipatory Conceptual Review from the Inter-American System of Human Rights' (2018) 15 *Revista de Direito Internacional* 123, 132.

[235] E de Wet, 'Jus Cogens and Obligations Erga Omnes' in D Shelton (ed), *The Oxford Handbook of International Human Rights Law* (Oxford, Oxford University Press, 2013) 544.

[236] *Juridical Condition and Rights of Undocumented Migrants* (n 30) Separate Opinion of Judge Cançado Trindade, para 87.

[237] A Bianchi, 'Human Rights and the Magic of Jus Cogens' (2008) 19 *EJIL* 491, 507.

[238] D Shelton, 'Normative Hierarchy in International Law' (2006) 100 *AJIL* 291, 299, 313.

affirming that the right to life has *jus cogens* status, the Commission stated that the latter 'is derived from a higher order of norms established in ancient times and which cannot be contravened by the laws of man or of nations.'[239]

Arguably, all of these conclusions pinpoint the basic issue that arises: whether the justification that lies on the identification of non-discrimination and equality as *jus cogens* – since they permeate all Conventional rights – could be more consensual, rather than grounded on positive law. The Court invoked a wide variety of instruments, in particular, 19 treaties and 14 soft law texts in order to consolidate the universal approval of the principle of non-discrimination as a peremptory norm of international law. However, there are cases of *de jure* inequalities which cannot, hence, be covered by the absolute and holistic character of *opinio juris* in terms of positive international law.[240]

At any rate, the IACtHR has been quite active in describing almost every grave violation of non-derogable rights as a violation of *jus cogens*. Particularly during the presidency of Antônio Augusto Cançado Trindade, it seems that the Court clearly deemed as self-evident that besides the prohibitions on slavery, which are among the peremptory norms of *jus cogens* nature as decided in *Aloeboetoe*,[241] the absolute prohibition of physical and psychological torture belong also of this category.[242] Likewise, physical punishment of a person suffering from mental disease was treated as a form of inhuman and degrading treatment under the *jus cogens* umbrella[243] as is also the case of crimes against humanity as declared in the *Almonacid-Arellano* case[244] and of relevant violations.

In most of these cases, the separate opinions of the former President Cançado Trindade can be extremely enlightening as regards the legal reasoning of the Court on the matter. In his famous separate opinions, he also included in the realm of peremptory norms the right of access to justice for all violations of rights,[245] as well as the minimum guarantees of international human rights law and international humanitarian law due to their universality,[246] and the disrespect of personal honour and beliefs.[247]

[239] *Victims of the Tugboat '13 de Marzo' v Cuba*, Case 11.436, IACommHR Report no 47/96, OEA/Ser.L/V/II.95, doc. 7 (16 October 1996). Analogous to this is the legal reasoning of the Court of First Instance (at the time) in Case T-315/01 *Kadi v Council and Commission* [2005] ECR II-3649, paras 226–42.

[240] Gerard Neuman takes as an example the unequal treatment of coastal fishermen and open sea-fishermen, as well as that of drug traffickers. Neuman, 'Import, Export' (n 10) 120.

[241] *Aloeboetoe* (n 231).

[242] *Maritza Urrutia v Guatemala* (Merits, Reparations and Costs), Inter-American Court of Human Rights Series C no 103 (27 November 2003), paras 91–92.

[243] *Caesar v Trinidad and Tobago* (Merits, Reparations and Costs), Inter-American Court of Human Rights Series C no 123 (11 March 2005), para 70; *Ximenes-Lopes* (n 52) para 126.

[244] *Almonacid-Arellano et al v Chile* (Preliminary Objections, Merits, Reparations and Costs), Inter-American Court of Human Rights Series C no 154 (26 September 2006), paras 99, 153.

[245] See *Ximenes-Lopes* (n 52) Separate Opinion of Judge Cançado Trindade, paras 19–21.

[246] See *Serrano-Cruz Sisters v El Salvador* (Preliminary Objections), Inter-American Court of Human Rights Series C no 118 (23 November 2004), Separate Opinion of Judge Cançado Trindade, para 40.

[247] See *Plan de Sánchez Massacre v Guatemala* (Merits), Inter-American Court of Human Rights Series C no 105 (29 April 2004), Separate Opinion of Judge Cançado Trindade, para 30.

Articulating both fundamental and derogable human rights obligations as *jus cogens* norms in international human rights law,[248] the Court has proved equally over-expressive pertaining to its feelings for *jus cogens* when a certain category of violations came into play, namely enforced disappearances.[249] This multi-faceted violation under international law was treated in-depth by the body due to the frequency with which claims of gross human rights breaches were brought before the Court. Hence, the IACtHR was given the opportunity to hear a whole new category of cases and develop its criteria and principles by enhancing the level of protection in cases of enforced disappearances through *jus cogens*.

While the Court dealt with this category of crimes even from the very first steps of its compulsory jurisdiction,[250] it explicitly manifested the *jus cogens* nature of the prohibition of enforced disappearances in *Goiburú et al v Paraguay*[251] citing the preamble of the Inter-American Convention on Forced Disappearances of persons[252] and invoking the gravity of the violations and the fundamental character of the rights infringed. The Court, having underlined the continuing and serious nature of the criminal activity, concluded that 'the prohibition of the forced disappearance of persons and the corresponding obligation to investigate and punish those responsible has attained the status of jus cogens.'[253] Furthermore, in the context of the severity and the multi-dimensional status of the prohibition of enforced disappearances, the Court took a further step in this case to declare access to justice a peremptory norm of international law in the name of the fight against impunity.[254]

It can be deduced, thus, that the procedural obligation to investigate and punish perpetrators is intimately linked to the fundamental right of access to justice which was also attributed to *jus cogens* status. Nevertheless, naming also the obligation of effective investigation and punishment as a *jus cogens* norm and equating to the core prohibition of enforced disappearances can even weaken, for some academics, the meaning of this bold pronouncement of the Court. The mere labelling of such an obligation, which has a settled content within the jurisprudence of the Inter-American Court, as a peremptory norm of international law

[248] See, eg Neuman, 'Import, Export' (n 10) 118.

[249] AA Cançado Trindade, 'Enforced Disappearances of Persons as a Violation of Jus Cogens: The Contribution of the Jurisprudence of the Inter-American Court of Human Rights' (2012) 81 *Nordic Journal of International Law* 507.

[250] See the seminal first case of the Inter-American Court, namely *Velásquez Rodríguez* (n 17).

[251] *Goiburú et al v Paraguay* (Merits, Reparations and Costs), Inter-American Court of Human Rights Series C no 153 (22 September 2006).

[252] The Inter-American Convention on Forced Disappearances of Persons was adopted in 1994 under the auspices of the Organisation of American States (OAS) and entered into force in 1996. Inter-American Convention on Forced Disappearance of Persons (adopted 6 September 1994, entered into force 28 March 1996) OASTS 60.

[253] *Goiburú* (n 251) para 84.

[254] ibid para 131.

as a – mostly – theoretical construction gives rise to only opaque practical effects in terms of international legal practice.[255]

However, according to the IACtHR' s legal reasoning, it seems that the one has led to the other and, hence, the expansion of the *jus cogens* concept was gradually understood even more on the occasion of the combat of enforced disappearances. Despite the controversy that this issue has raised, there are still voices that vote for the audacity expressed by the San José Court on this matter. Moreover, the stability and the clarity of the said case law is needed and may offer a potential paradigm to other international judicial bodies. Particularly in the Americas, as far as the generalised practice of enforced disappearances is concerned, *jus cogens* has a preventive role to play against large-scale impunity. Notwithstanding the lack of exact repercussions of such characterisation, the symbolic power of the scheme lies in the understanding that for all members of international community – both states and individuals – this prohibition is absolute and no exception is allowed. Importantly, the same goes for the states as regards the obligation to investigate, judge and punish those responsible for the said crimes.

Yet, it is clear that now the prohibition of enforced disappearance and the corresponding obligation to investigate and punish those responsible are granted the character *jus cogens* norm. Furthermore, on the basis of its universal acceptance, codifying the aforementioned prohibition to domestic criminal law could actually carry serious legal consequences as more litigation could be expected.[256]

Overall, the *jus cogens* case law of the IACtHR serves as an amazing example of judicial activism when it comes to basic human rights guarantees. On the one hand, the wide perspective of the IACtHR was seen as an act of rebellion against the deeply rooted Euro-centralised epistemological legacy pertaining to the overly cautious use of *jus cogens* not only in the realm of general international law but also of international human rights law.[257] On the other hand, sceptics view this visionary – or even abusive – use of peremptory norms by the San José Court as a potential danger for their credibility and rather opt for the restraint of the Strasbourg Court[258] – also adopted by the ICJ – defending mostly their subsidiary role and states' will.[259]

[255] N Kyriakou, 'An Affront to the Conscience of Humanity: Enforced Disappearances in the Case Law of the Inter-American Court of Human Rights (2014) 7 *Inter-American and European Human Rights Journal* 17, 37.

[256] J Sarkin, 'Why the Prohibition of Enforced Disappearance Has Attained Jus Cogens Status in International Law' (2012) 81 *Nordic Journal of International Law* 537, 582.

[257] See de AFR Cardoso Squeff and de Almeida Rosa, 'Jus Cogens' (n 234) 134.

[258] As far as the ECtHR is concerned this is clearly illustrated in its MoA jurisprudence. On the contrary, as largely analysed in a previous chapter, such is not the case for this Court, which leaves extremely restricted latitude to the states.

[259] de Wet, 'Jus Cogens' (n 235) 547.

Sustainable or not in the contemporary legal practice or reality, these explicit common references to *jus cogens* aiming to more effectively enforce human rights obligations in the Americas constitute the benchmarks upon which human rights defenders can rely before diverse international fora,[260] taking, thus, progressively human rights protection one step ahead.

B. The 'Endless Story' of Reparations in the IACtHR Case Law

This broad wording of Article 63(1) ACHR[261] conferring remedial powers to the IACtHR constituted, arguably, the starting point of the famously developed jurisprudence of the San José Court which, indeed, deserved the attention that it received in this regard.

Nonetheless, this is not the case under general international law since the international responsibility of the state towards individuals is indeed a topic missing from the Articles on State responsibility (hereinafter ARSIWA) adopted in 2001 by the UN International Law Commission,[262] mainly focused on the international responsibility for inter-state disputes. ARSIWA constitute the main source of remedial provisions that influenced several judicial bodies when seeking just redress for human rights violations. The ambiguity that covers the term[263] is greatly caused by its extended, yet varied use encompassing both the narrow interpretation, in the sense of monetary damages and the broader referring to a wide variety of remedies available for a breach of an international obligation. Regardless of the meaning given to *reparations*, the aim is always the same: to turn back the clock. In other words, reparations generally aim to place the injured state at the existing situation before the occurrence of the wrongful act, namely the restoration of the *status quo ante*.

From the international law perspective, the notion was famously described in the *Chorzów Factory (Indemnity)* decision delivered by the Permanent Court of International Justice (PCIJ).[264] Specific types of reparation were established in

[260] Dembour, *When Humans Become Migrants* (n 189) 312.

[261] Despite the resemblance with the corresponding ECHR provision (Art 50), the drafting procedure of ACHR reveals the will of the states to confer greater latitude to the Inter-American mechanisms when deciding on reparations. As a matter of procedure, in the absence of an agreement between the IACommHR and the respondent state within the time limits fixed by the judgment *in merito*, the Court, frequently, delivers a separate judgment solely on reparations and costs.

[262] ILC, 'Articles on Responsibility of States for Internationally Wrongful Acts' in 'Report of the International Law Commission on the Work of its 53rd Session' (23 April–1 June and 2 July–10 August 2001) UN Doc. A/56/10.

[263] S Haasdijk, 'The Lack of Uniformity in the Terminology of the International Law of Remedies' (1992) 5 *Leiden Journal of International Law* 245.

[264] *Case Concerning the Factory at Chorzów* (*Germany v Poland*) (Merits) PCIJ Series A no 17, 21, 47; see also the most recent judgment of its successor *LaGrand* (n 105) para 48.

Article 34 ARSIWA. Thus, these forms of reparation contain restitution (*restitutio in integrum*) enshrined in Article 35, compensation in Article 36 and satisfaction in Article 37. While compensation is targeted to remedy material damage, satisfaction seeks to repair mostly moral damage; however, both come into play when, given the restrictions of possibility and proportionality, *restitutio in integrum* is not achievable.[265] In practice, the latter has proved a rather challenging task and for this reason, compensation or satisfaction can actually serve as more appropriate solutions to bring back the *status quo ante*.

From the international human rights law perspective, ARSIWA, the principal instrument of general international law pertaining to state responsibility, did not remain silent when the question of its application to the disputes between individuals was posed. According to the commentary of Article 33(2) ARSIWA, the ILC has cautiously extended the scope of international obligations stating '[t]his Part is without prejudice to any right, arising from the international responsibility of a State, *which may accrue directly to any person* or entity other than a State.'[266]

Yet, state responsibility under human rights treaties entails obligations that require reparations directly addressed to victims, rather than the injured state of which the individual who suffered the violation is a national. The specificity of human rights in terms of state responsibility was mirrored in the Basic principles and Guidelines on the Right to a Remedy and Reparation for Victims of Gross violations of International Human Rights law and serious violations of International Humanitarian law, adopted by the UN GA in 2005 as a result of the work produced by the Sub-Commission for the Promotion and Protection of Human Rights.[267]

It is against this particular background that the ECtHR contented itself to award mainly monetary compensation to the victims of human rights violations. The relevant provision of Article 41 ECHR is indicative of the less rigorous approach of the CoE system on reparations. Apparently, the question of subsidiarity governs the whole reparation mechanism under the Convention. It stems, indeed, from the broadness of the Convention's provision that the Court's competence to grant just satisfaction is subsidiary to remedial measures under national law. In line with the language of the ECHR, the Court restricted itself to

[265] A Buyse, 'Lost and Regained? Restitution as a Remedy for Human Rights Violations in the Context of International Law' (2008) 68 *Heidelberg Journal of International Law* 129, 132. See *Chorzów Factory* (n 264) 48. See ILC, 'Articles on Responsibility of States' (n 262) 239.

[266] D Shelton, *Remedies in International Human Rights Law* (Oxford, Oxford University Press, 2015) 37; see A Buyse, 'Lost and Regained?' (n 265) 134.

[267] UNGA, Basic Principles and Guidelines on the Right to a Remedy and Reparation for Victims of Gross Violations of International Human Rights Law and Serious Violations of International Humanitarian Law (21 March 2006) A/RES/60/147. The Basic Principles lack binding force and serve as general guidelines in the field of reparations. See C Tomuschat, 'Individuals' in J Crawford, A Pellet and S Olleson (eds), *The Law of International Responsibility* (Oxford, Oxford University Press, 2010) 988.

acknowledge that the mere issuing of a decision declaring a human rights violation suffices as reparation to the victim of the violation. Otherwise, the Court orders monetary compensation as just satisfaction in the spirit of Article 41 ECHR.

In *Scozzari and Giunta v Italy*, the Court highlighted the elements and conditions shaping its interpretation of just satisfaction stating with extreme caution that 'the purpose of awarding sums by way of just satisfaction is to provide reparation solely for damage suffered by those concerned to the extent that such events constitute a consequence of the violation that cannot otherwise be remedied.'[268] Until recently, the almost sole perception of just satisfaction was the monetary compensation. Discretionary powers are granted to states to decide on further means of reparation to remedy non-pecuniary or moral damage of the applicants. The Court has refused repeatedly to award satisfaction to the injured party if, in its view, the latter has been engaged in some sort of reprehensible activity, or on the basis of sufficient proof of a causal link between the violation and the damage caused. Actually, on numerous occasions the Court declined to award the sum of compensation claimed by the applicants and rejected requests of remedial approaches other than just satisfaction in the sense of monetary indemnification. In fact, the Court was not convinced to order investigation in cases in which the prohibition of torture or ill-treatment was infringed.[269] In addition, the Court was hesitant to declare that the respondent state which was found responsible for the violation was bound to refrain from corporal punishment of children, to take preventive steps as guarantees of non-repetition in the future[270] or even to respond favourably to family reunification requests made by applicants who have suffered arbitrary expulsions.[271]

Within the boundaries of the ECtHR's subsidiary role, this stance of the Court is, probably, reinforced by the execution mechanism of its judgments functioning under the auspices of the Council of Europe, namely the Committee of Ministers.[272] Therefore, since every rule has its exceptions, the Strasbourg Court has notably declared the utmost importance of the principle of *restitutio in integrum* in the *Papamichalopoulos* case in which it stated that 'it follows that a judgment in which the Court finds a breach imposes on the respondent State a legal obligation to put an end to the breach and make reparation for its consequences in such a way as to restore as far as possible the situation existing before the breach.'[273]

[268] *Scozzari and Giunta v Italy* [GC], Merits, ECHR 2000-VIII 471, para 250.

[269] See especially *Kukayev v Russia*, Merits, App no 29361/02 (ECtHR, 15 November 2007).

[270] *Dudgeon v the United Kingdom*, Merits, Series A no 45 (1981), para 15; *Campbell and Cosans v the United Kingdom*, Merits, Series A no 48 (1982), para 16; *McGoff v Sweden*, Merits, Series A no 83 (1984), para 31; *Gillow v the United Kingdom* (Article 50), Series A no 124-C (1987), para 9.

[271] *Mehemi v France*, Merits, ECHR 1997-VI, 1959.

[272] S Palmer, 'The Committee of Ministers' in S Schmahl and M Breuer (eds), *The Council of Europe: Its Law and Policies* (Oxford, Oxford University Press, 2017). See also the Statute of the Council of Europe (London, 5 May 1949), Chapter IV.

[273] *Papamichalopoulos v Greece* (Art 50), Series A no 330-B (1995), para 34.

Besides the *Scozzari* judgment,[274] the Court started to acknowledge the insufficiency of monetary compensation as a means of full restitution in cases of grave moral damage. For instance, in a case concerning the continuing violation of Article 5 ECHR, since Georgian authorities were continually ignoring orders of release issued by the domestic courts in the *Assanidze v Georgia* case,[275] the Strasbourg Court felt that 'by its very nature, the violation found in the instant case does not leave any real choice as to the measures required to remedy it'[276] and thus, ordered Georgia to release the applicant at the earliest possible date. Hence, slowly but cautiously, the Court took the first steps towards seeing legislative amendments as potential modus of redress.[277]

From this point onwards, the Court felt that slowly but steadily it might consent to some exceptions from its initial restraint. The critical point was, once again, the expansion of the CoE eastwards. Since the 1990s the Court was repeatedly forced to grapple with the pressing issue of enforced disappearances. The complexity of the phenomenon led the Court to follow a more stringent strategy pertaining to the reparative methods. In a significant number of cases against Russia emanating from the continuing Chechen conflict, the Court went on to specify the reparative measures required in obiter dicta.[278]

Furthermore, the more recent pilot-judgment procedure offered the opportunity to the ECtHR to interpret differently Article 41 in conjunction with Article 46 ECHR mapping the executions of its judgments. Institutionalised in 2011 to unburden the Court from its extreme case load, the formula was applied in cases of systemic violations of procedural rights occurred on the basis of dysfunctional domestic judiciaries. The Court's seminal pilot judgment *Maria Atanasiu and others v Romania*[279] offers an illustrative example of the tendency of the Court to indicate specific measures that the respondent states should adopt in order to fulfil the principle of *restitutio in integrum* besides monetary relief.

Combining these recent trends within its jurisprudence, in 2012 the Strasbourg Court, in an enforced disappearance case, appeared willing to bring new air to its case law on reparations, in the light of the present-day conditions in some of the Contracting Parties. More specifically, in *Aslakhanova and others v Russia*,[280]

[274] *Scozzari and Giunta* (n 268) para 249.

[275] *Assanidze v Georgia* [GC], Merits, ECHR 2004-II 221.

[276] ibid para 202.

[277] ibid para 198.

[278] *Bazorkina v Russia*, Merits, App no 69481/01 (ECtHR, 27 July 2006), paras 117–19; see also JP Costa, 'Responsibility for Violations of Human Rights Obligations: European Mechanisms' in J Crawford, A Pellet and S Olleson (eds), *The Law of International Responsibility* (Oxford, Oxford University Press, 2010) 774; see also the dissenting opinion in *Medova* (n 49) Partly Dissenting Opinion of Judge Spielmann.

[279] *Maria Atanasiu and Others v Romania*, Merits, App nos 30767/05 and 33800/06 (ECtHR, 12 October 2010), paras 195–242.

[280] *Aslakhanova and Others v Russia*, Merits, App nos 2944/06, 8300/07, 50184/07, 332/08 and 42509/10 (ECtHR, 18 December 2012), paras 217, 220.

it observed that the lack of effective investigations in disappearances is the outcome of systemic problems for which there is no effective remedy available domestically. The Court's proposal included, indicatively, the establishment 'of a single, sufficiently high-level body in charge of solving disappearances in the region of Northern Caucasus, which would enjoy unrestricted access to all relevant information and could compile and maintain a unified database of all disappearances'.[281] While the Strasbourg Court has surely evolved on the matter through the years, the content under the heads of 'pecuniary damage', 'non-pecuniary damage', 'costs and expenses' or 'default interest' remains more or less the same. Monetary compensation still remains the main remedial practice of the ECtHR.[282]

All that said, the ECtHR's unwillingness to be more welcoming to varied forms of reparations has, arguably, received great academic attention.[283] Actually, the Strasbourg Court appears to be a victim of its own success. It probably adopted its reserved interpretation of its remedial powers due to the fact that the individual was not the absolute focus of the system at its inception.[284] Trapped in a huge backlog of applications, it paved, from the very beginning, its narrow road to the land of reparations with stringent requirements and pure conservatism. In general terms, the Strasbourg Court continues to have a minimalist approach to redress.

This perception of the Court's approach could be one of the roots of the divergence witnessed between the former and the IACtHR. The latter, since its dawn, has captured a wide variety of vitally crucial dimensions of remedies, as identified under international human rights law and general international law. The contribution of the San José Court not only to the universalisation of its enlarged Inter-American notion of reparations[285] but also to the development of peacebuilding processes and conflict management patterns in the region can be examined, at first, in the light of the reconceptualisation of the usual remedial practice followed by international tribunals and secondly, through the lens of the broad measures ordered by the IACtHR.

Pertaining to the San José perception of reparations, the first signs appeared in its first contentious case, the landmark *Vélasquez Rodriguez* case[286] in which

[281] ibid paras 223–37.

[282] See President of the ECtHR, 'Practice Directions on Just Satisfaction Claims' (1 August 2018), www.echr.coe.int/Documents/PD_satisfaction_claims_ENG.pdf.

[283] See, eg Tomuschat, 'Individuals' (n 267) 987.

[284] Shelton, *Remedies in International Human Rights Law* (n 266) 215; DJ Harris, M O'Boyle, EP Bates and CM Buckley, *Harris, O'Boyle and Warbrick: Law of the European Convention on Human Rights*, 2nd edn (Oxford, Oxford University Press, 2015) 33.

[285] K Bonneau, 'La jurisprudence innovante de la Cour Interaméricaine des Droits de l'Homme en matière de droit à réparation des victimes de violations des droits de l'homme' in L Hennebel and H Tigroudja (eds), *Le particularisme interaméricain des droits de l'homme* (Paris, Pedone, 2009) 380.

[286] *Velásquez-Rodríguez v Honduras* (Reparations and Costs), Inter-American Court of Human Rights Series C no 7 (21 July 1989); see in relation to damage awards in the first Honduran cases B Fontana, 'Damage Awards for Human Rights Violations in the European and Inter-American Courts of Human Rights' (1991) 31 *Santa Clara Law Review* 1127.

the Court bravely distanced itself from the rigorous conception of subsidiarity,[287] persistently followed by its Strasbourg counterpart. At the end of the day, the Court awarded only monetary indemnification for the violation of multiple rights; however, given the expansion of its reparation jurisprudence the IACtHR would have opted for even more effective and wide-ranging remedies under the circumstances of the present case.[288] The autonomous character of the obligation of the state to repair, which also derives from Article 1 ACHR, has been declared from the very beginning along with the acceptance that the mere failure of the State Party to provide effective remedies for human rights breaches in itself constitutes a breach of the IACHR's provisions.[289] Thus, it flows from the Court's understanding of reparations that among the obligations of the state is a duty to take all appropriate measures to prevent human rights violations and to use the means at its disposal to carry out a serious investigation of violations committed within its jurisdiction, to identify and punish the perpetrators of the violations and to provide the necessary guarantees of the victim's adequate compensation.[290]

In stark contrast with its European counterpart, the San José Court is not hesitant to interpret Inter-American human rights law in the spectrum of international law of state responsibility both classic and customary[291] or of other regional or universal instruments. Thus, it managed to reinforce and ensure the protection offered within the limits of the Inter-American system, irrespective of the fact that the latter does not contain judicial organs of general competence.[292]

Further, the Court has repeatedly stated that the cornerstone of the Inter-American jurisprudence on reparations, namely the provisions of Article 63(1) ACHR, is governed in its entirety by international law.[293] Therefore, since the obligation to repair must be understood as imposing international legal obligations, derogations are not permitted on the basis of the state's invocations of national provisions.[294]

[287] *Velásquez-Rodríguez* (Reparations and Costs) (n 286) para 30.

[288] D Cassel, 'The Expanding Scope and Impact of Reparations Awarded by the Inter-American Court of Human Rights' in M Bossuyt, P Lemmens, K de Feyter and S Parmentier (eds), *Out of the Ashes: Reparations for Gross Violations of Human Rights* (Cambridge, Intersentia, 2006) 97.

[289] *Judicial Guarantees* (n 13) para 24; *Constitutional Court v Peru* (Merits, Reparations and Costs), Inter-American Court of Human Rights Series C no 71 (31 January 2001), para 89.

[290] *Velásquez Rodríguez* (n 17) para 174.

[291] The Court cited the *Factory at Chorzów* jurisprudence of the ICJ to declare the customary nature of the State's international obligation to repair. See *Velásquez-Rodríguez* (Reparations and Costs) (n 286) para 25; *Aloeboetoe* (n 231) para 43; *El Amparo v Venezuela* (Reparations and Costs), Inter-American Court of Human Rights Series C no 28 (14 September 1996), para 14.

[292] See Rivier, 'Responsibility for Violations' (n 21); see, eg *Juan Humberto* (n 34) para 148; *Almonacid Arellano* (n 244) para 135; *La Cantuta v Peru* (Merits, Reparations and Costs), Inter-American Court of Human Rights Series C no 162 (29 November 2006), para 200; *Manuel Cepeda Vargas* (n 151) para 211.

[293] Entity is understood, here, as containing all aspects that have accorded to international law its special nature and supported its function: its scope, specific characteristics and beneficiaries.

[294] *Velásquez-Rodríguez* (Reparations and Costs) (n 286) para 30.

Within the system, the concept of reparations has evolved over time. This evolution can also be greatly explained by the choices of the Court in terms of procedure. Admittedly, the authorisation of the victims' representation before the Court, the lesser evidentiary burden and burden of proof, the enlargement of the notion of victim status and the control of the execution of its judgments are all manifestations of the strong will of the San José Court to more effectively repair damage caused in favour of the victims.[295] Unlike its European peer, the Inter-American human rights system has not endorsed a supervisory organ of the execution of the Court's judgments, equivalent to the Committee of Ministers.

The main objective of the Inter-American reparations regime is full restitution (*restitution in integrum*) which lies at the core of the sense of reparation.[296] Yet, the Court had already acknowledged that, due to the very nature of the cases adjudicated by the Court touching upon the right to life of the victim (eg cases of enforced disappearances, extrajudicial killings etc) full restitution is out of question. Hence, in the *Aloeboetoe* case, a case in relation with human rights abuses of this type, the Court stressed that restitution can also take alternative forms such as pecuniary compensation.[297] Despite the fact that restitution remains the preferred means of reparation, the Court will opt for another remedial measure if the restoration of the situation existing prior to the violation is impossible, insufficient or inadequate.[298]

Mapping the outer boundaries of restitution, the Court recalled the principle of proportionality on which all reparative measures rely. Hence, in the process of determining the most suitable form of reparation in the aim of *restitutio in integrum*, the Court should take into consideration the specificities of each dispute and each violation inflicted, on a case-by-case basis. Remarkably, the Court seemed to carefully approach the issue and reiterated its *jurisprudence constante* making a synthesis of its early case law and of its recent, more delimited understanding of reparations.[299] Therefore, on the occasion of its landmark *Cotton Field* case, the Court clarified the exact content of the concept of *restitutio in integrum*.[300]

Another element of the Inter-American protection offered in terms of reparation stems from the Court's reference to the 'life plan' *(proyecto de vida)*, introduced in *Loayza Tamayo v Peru*.[301] This case concerned the arbitrary arrest and detention of Professor Maria Elena Loayza Tamayo of the Universidad San Martín de Porres by the Peruvian authorities on suspicion of having engaged in

[295] Bonneau, 'La jurisprudence innovante' (n 285) 354ff.

[296] *Velásquez-Rodríguez* (Reparations and Costs) (n 286) para 25.

[297] *Aloeboetoe* (n 231) para 46, 49–50.

[298] *Gangaram-Panday v Suriname* (Merits, Reparations and Costs), Inter-American Court of Human Rights Series C no 16 (21 January 1994). Rivier, 'Responsibility for Violations' (n 21) 749.

[299] See I Piacentini de Andrade, 'La réparation dans la jurisprudence de la cour interaméricaine des Droits de l'Homme' (Doctoral Thesis, Université Panthéon-Assas 2013) 150.

[300] *Cotton Field Case* (n 42) para 450.

[301] *Loayza-Tamayo v Peru* (Reparations and Costs), Inter-American Court of Human Rights Series C no 42 (27 November 1998), paras 144–54.

terrorist activity. The victim was brought before military 'faceless' courts then again before civilian courts, in violation of the *ne bis in idem* principle. During her four years of imprisonment, Ms Loayza Tamayo was subjected to cruel, inhuman, and degrading treatment. The IACtHR described the so-called life plan of the applicant as 'akin to the concept of personal fulfilment, which in turn is based on the options that an individual may have for leading his life and achieving the goal that he sets for himself.'[302] Understood as the anticipated personal accomplishment of the individual which is both reasonable and attainable in practice, its loss or severe diminution, in a manner that could be irreparable or hardly reparable cannot be ignored by the IACtHR.[303]

Since the victim in the case under scrutiny was kept in captivity for several years, the Court felt that this particular damage should have been taken into serious consideration. Consequently, besides the order for her release,[304] the Court ordered the state to reinstate the victim to her former teaching positions. Even though the Court refrained from awarding monetary damage to Ms Loayza Tamaro, it particularly ordered that her salaried status should be restored at the level that the victim enjoyed at the time of her detention, 'adjusted to its value as of the date of this Judgment'.[305]

When it comes to the specific content of the extraordinary reparations ordered by the IACtHR, these are largely influenced by the particularities of the disputes adjudicated by the Court. The cornerstone *Vélasquez Rodriguez* case,[306] mirroring the basic principle of international law according to which 'every violation of an international obligation which results in harm creates a duty to make adequate reparation', has been fleshed out with a variety of different types of reparations. The main general categories under which all specific measures of relief may fall are restitution, rehabilitation, satisfaction and compensation. In the Inter-American case law, we can also find more theoretical remedial measures such as the naming of the Court's decision *per se* as a form of reparation[307] and more practical ones such as the obligation of the Court to investigate, prosecute and punish[308] and

[302] ibid para 148.

[303] ibid para 150. See also Shelton, *Remedies in International Human Rights Law* (n 266) 350.

[304] See Pasqualucci, *The Practice and Procedure* (n 14) 199, 322. Following the judgment, Peru amended its anti-terrorism legislation.

[305] *Loayza-Tamayo* (n 301) para 113.

[306] *Velásquez-Rodríguez* (Reparations and Costs) (n 286) para 25.

[307] *The Last Temptation of Christ Case* (n 143) para 99. With regard to both pecuniary and non-pecuniary (moral) measures of compensation see *Castillo-Páez v Peru* (Reparations and Costs), Inter-American Court of Human Rights Series C no 43 (27 November 1998), para 84; *Paniagua Morales et al v Guatemala* (Reparations and Costs), Inter-American Court of Human Rights Series C no 76 (25 May 2001), para 105; *Myrna Mack Chang v Guatemala* (Merits, Reparations and Costs), Inter-American Court of Human Rights Series C no 101 (25 November 2003), paras 260, 330.

[308] See *Velásquez-Rodríguez* (Reparations and Costs) (n 286) para 33; *Manuel Cepeda Vargas*(n 151), para 216. The said obligation of the state lasts until the latter has totally fulfilled its obligations. See relatively *Trujillo Oroza v Bolivia* (Reparations and Costs), Inter-American Court of Human Rights Series C no 92 (27 February 2002), para 111.

the guarantees of non-repetition, deterring potential human rights abuses and paving a safer route for the future.

As regards measures targeted to redress the individual's situation, the main objective is the full restitution of the existing situation prior to the occurrence of the violation at hand. Hence, the Court has incorporated, for instance, the release of persons who were wrongfully detained and the reinstatement of their employment in use of the life plan concept. Secondly, the IACtHR has also used rehabilitation when victims were subjected to extreme physical and/or psychological suffering or harm, and may include the provision of appropriate and effective health care with specific provisions on both medical and psychological treatment.[309] The treatment must be adequate, free of charge, personalised, and provided by experts on the particular kind of harm that the victim has endured.

As for satisfaction, this is conceptualised as encompassing non-monetary acts that seek to offer moral relief to the victims. Public acts of the state to acknowledge responsibility,[310] a state's apology covered by the media[311] or the broad publication of the judgment constitute types of reparations that attempt to restore the dignity of victims, rectifying misinformation that may have been disseminated about them. While there are some measures of satisfaction that are solely addressed to individuals, most of the aforementioned remedial strategies of satisfaction offer relief individually but have also a tremendous effect to the society as well.

However, reparations to individuals can also take the form of compensation, namely the most common, traditional and, sometimes, the most effective type of pecuniary remedy under international law. Arguably, the concept of pecuniary damages entails the loss of earnings and benefits of the applicant and any consequential loss having a causal link with the harmful situation to which the victim was entitled.[312]

However, irrespective of the fact that the IACtHR doesn't share the same views on victim status with the Strasbourg Court,[313] it appeared that the former used

[309] *Anzualdo Castro v Peru* (Preliminary Objection, Merits, Reparations and Costs), Inter-American Court of Human Rights Series C no 202 (22 September 2009), para 203; *Chitay Nech et al v Guatemala* (Preliminary Objections, Merits, Reparations, and Costs), Inter-American Court of Human Rights Series C no 212 (25 May 2010), paras 253–56; *The Barrios Family v Venezuela* (Merits, Reparations and Costs), Inter-American Court of Human Rights Series C no 237 (24 November 2011), para 330.

[310] *Gomes Lund et al v Brazil* ('*Guerrilha do Araguaia Case*') (Preliminary Objections, Merits, Reparations, and Costs), Inter-American Court of Human Rights Series C no 219 (24 November 2010), para 277. See, eg *Serrano Cruz Sisters v El Salvador* (Merits, Reparations and Costs), Inter-American Court of Human Rights Series C no 120 (1 March 2005), para 194; *Rosendo Cantú et al v Mexico* (Preliminary Objections, Merits, Reparations and Costs), Inter-American Court of Human Rights Series C no 216 (31 August 2010), para 226.

[311] *Tibi v Ecuador* (Preliminary Objections, Merits, Reparations and Costs), Inter-American Court of Human Rights Series C no 114 (7 September 2004), para 261; *Radilla Pacheco v Mexico* (Preliminary Objections, Merits, Reparations and Costs), Inter-American Court of Human Rights Series C no 209 (23 November 2009), para 350.

[312] *Bámaca-Velásquez v Guatemala* (Reparations and Costs), Inter-American Court of Human Rights Series C no 91 (22 February 2002), para 43; *Vélez Loor* (n 195) para 299.

[313] D Rodríguez Pinzón, 'The "Victim" Requirement, the Fourth Instance Formula and the Notion of "Person" in the Individual Complaint Procedure of the Inter-American Human Rights System'

the ECtHR's criteria in order to enhance its reasoning regarding cases in which family members are considered direct victims of the violation and hence, are entitled to redress. In the *Bámaca-Velásquez v Guatemala* case[314] the Court recalled the findings of the Strasbourg Court in *Kurt* as enriched by its *Timurtas* and *Çakici* jurisprudence against Turkey.[315] Thus, when ascertaining whether the next of kin of a direct victim are also victims, the Court needs to examine

> the closeness of the family relationship, the particular circumstances of the relationship with the victim, the degree to which the family member was a witness of the events related to the disappearance, the way in which the family member was involved in attempts to obtain information about the disappearance of the victim and the State's response to the steps undertaken.[316]

These criteria have contributed to the enlargement of the concept so that family members of direct victims whose right to life or right to humane treatment is infringed can be equally protected.

Besides individual-oriented measures, the Court has ordered also the state responsible for the breach of the ACHR to take measures restoring the well-being of a whole community whose interests are at stake or in general, affecting the whole population of the state. The Inter-American Court, in respect of its thoughtfulness pertaining to the communal traditions in the Americas, has proved extremely attentive of communities, especially the indigenous and tribal ones. In this regard, it has taken community-based measures to offer true relief not only to individuals involved in sub judice cases but also to the community as a whole or to smaller communities whose existence needs to be reassured. Hence, in terms of measures of restitution the return of land, the demarcation and award of title to the ancestral land of indigenous populations was considered the most appropriate strategy in this respect. In most of the cases mentioned in the previous section, the Court, due to the spiritual linkage of indigenous peoples with their traditional lands, ordered the state to return or demarcate and title their land to ensure their ownership.[317] Furthermore, the Court has felt that, in order to achieve the principal

(2001) 7 *International Law Student Association Journal of International & Comparative Law* 369; C Sandoval-Villalba, 'The Concepts of "Injured Party" and "Victim" of Gross Human Rights Violations in the Jurisprudence of the Inter-American Court of Human Rights: A Commentary on their Implications for Reparations' in C Ferstman, M Goetz and A Stephens (eds), *Reparations for Victims of Genocide, War Crimes and Crimes against the Humanity* (Leiden, Brill, 2009).

[314] *Bámaca-Velásquez v Guatemala* (Merits), Inter-American Court of Human Rights Series C no 70 (25 November 2000), paras 162–63.

[315] *Kurt v Turkey*, Merits, ECHR 1998-III, paras 130–34; *Çakici v Turkey* [GC], Merits, ECHR 1999-IV 583, para 98; *Timurtaş v Turkey*, Merits, ECHR 2000-VI 303, para 95.

[316] *Bámaca-Velásquez v Guatemala* (Merits) n 314.

[317] See, eg *Mayagna (Sumo) Awas Tingni Community v Nicaragua* (Merits, Reparations and Costs), Inter-American Court of Human Rights Series C no 79 (31 August 2001), paras 168, 173(4); *Yakye Axa Indigenous Community v Paraguay* (Merits, Reparations and Costs), Inter-American Court of Human Rights Series C no 125 (17 June 2005), para 215; *Saramaka People v Suriname* (Preliminary Objections, Merits, Reparations and Costs), Inter-American Court of Human Rights Series C no 172 (28 November 2007), para 95; *Xákmok Kásek Indigenous Community v Paraguay* (Merits, Reparations and Costs), Inter-American Court of Human Rights Series C no 214 (24 August 2010), para 281.

aim of *restitutio in integrum* in cases where the cultural traditions of a particular group could be in peril, it should order more targeted measures,[318] such as educational measures for the preservation of the indigenous cultures, maintenance and improvement of road systems, the construction of health infrastructure etc.[319]

However, the Court is extremely enthusiastic and inventive when it comes to measures seeking to commemorate the victims and community-based measures of satisfaction.[320] Being symbolic in nature, these measures are addressed to society as a whole. As for the first, a wide variety of such remedial measures, such as building monuments or naming streets or routes[321] and the designation of a day in the memory of victims of human rights violations,[322] are only some of the remedies that the Court has repeatedly ordered states to adopt, to remind people of the crimes committed and thus ensure that similar human rights abuses never again occur.

Moving to the only future-oriented form of reparation, namely the guarantees of non-repetition, the Court has indicated the adoption of some practical measures designed to deter future violations of the same character and extent. Training of police authorities, judges and attorneys taking part in investigation procedures,[323] and lately, the design and implementation of socioeconomic development programmes[324] have served as preventive reparations of this kind. In several instances, the IACtHR ordered the responsible state to reform its legislative framework[325] in order that the latter would be in conformity with the ACHR. Nevertheless, the recent jurisprudential approach of the Court on preventive reparations reveals that, perhaps, the Court feels readier to leave some room to the states, at least when they attempt to enable their internal system to

[318] *Plan de Sánchez Massacre v Guatemala* (Reparations), Inter-American Court of Human Rights Series C no 116 (19 November 2004), para 49(12).

[319] ibid para 125(9).

[320] D Attanasio, 'Extraordinary Reparations, Legitimacy, and the Inter-American Court' (2016) 37 *University of Pennsylvania Journal of International Law* 813, 861–70.

[321] *Case of the 'Street Children' (Villagrán-Morales et al) v Guatemala* (Reparations and Costs), Inter-American Court of Human Rights Series C no 77 (26 May 2001), paras 103, 115(7); *Trujillo Oroza v Bolivia* (n 308) para 141(6) and (4); *Myrna Mack Chang* (n 307) paras 126, 146, 285; *Gómez-Paquiyauri Brothers v Peru* (Merits, Reparations and Costs), Inter-American Court of Human Rights Series C no 110 (8 July 2004); *Contreras et al v El Salvador* (Merits, Reparations and Costs), Inter-American Court of Human Rights Series C no 232 (31 August 2011), para 208.

[322] *Serrano Cruz Sisters v El Salvador* (Merits, Reparations and Costs) (n 310) para 196; *Contreras* (n 321) para 52.

[323] See, eg *Fernández Ortega et al v Mexico* (Preliminary Objections, Merits, Reparations and Costs), Inter-American Court of Human Rights Series C no 215 (30 August 2010), para 260; *Gelman v Uruguay* (Merits and Reparations), Inter-American Court of Human Rights Series C no 221 (24 February 2011), para 278.

[324] *Workers of the Fireworks Factory in Santo Antônio de Jesus and their Families v Brazil* (Preliminary Objections, Merits, Reparations and Costs), Inter-American Court of Human Rights Series C no 407 (15 July 2020).

[325] See, eg *The Last Temptation of Christ Case* (n 143) paras 97–8, 103(4); *Hilaire, Constantine and Benjamin* (n 112) paras 86, 212, 223(8); *Raxcacó-Reyes v Guatemala* (Merits, Reparations and Costs), Inter-American Court of Human Rights Series C no 133 (15 September 2005), para 89.

ensure effective guarantees of non-repetition. In some recent cases concerning Colombia, a country that has struggled to make progress in terms of political stability and democratic legitimacy, the IACtHR seems to be reinventing its role. In *Santo Domingo Massacre*, the Court opted for recognising the steps taken by the Colombian authorities and most importantly, the new reparative mechanism institutionalised to offer true relief to millions of victims following the Colombian armed conflict. Hence, in the cases against Colombia adjudicated by the IACtHR during the last decade, the latter refrained from examining the domestic reparation regime from its own perspective and opted for transferring the entire responsibility for determining compensation measures to Colombia's new administrative justice institutions.[326] Was the Strasbourg Court the source of inspiration for this shift in the stance of the Court? Unfortunately, there is no obvious response to this inquiry. At any rate, this newly introduced standing on reparations will, seemingly, contribute to reinstall the interrelationship between the IACtHR and national judiciaries, which is more likely in Europe given the classic perception of subsidiarity of the Strasbourg Court.

All that said, the apparent divergence between the two judicial fora pertaining to their remedial practices has, seemingly, its roots to their structural differences and to the divergent perception of their role. Functioning in the context of the CoE which has institutionalised a specialised organ monitoring the execution of its judgments, the ECtHR stuck to its *stricto sensu* subsidiary role and saw, from the very beginning, its remedial competence from a distance. Persistent to award monetary compensation to the applicants within the limits of Article 41 ECHR, the ECtHR only recently has reoriented its understanding when it ventured into new territories of systemic violations which required effective adjudication.

Yet, the IACtHR, which has dealt with rampant human rights violations since its creation, has been more invasive of state sovereignty. Unlike the Strasbourg system, the Inter-American one lacked a mechanism of enforcement of its judgments and as a result, came up with a whole new ensemble of diverse reparations apt to cover the lacunae of domestic remedial justice. Article 63 afforded broader powers to the Court in this respect. From the *pro homine* perspective, financial relief that tolerates the wrong and leaves room to the perpetrators to buy off injustice is not in conformity with the Inter-American standards on reparations, particularly when complaints of core, inalienable human rights are under discussion. On the other hand, since the rate of compliance with the remedial orders in the Inter-American system is remarkably lower than in the European system,[327]

[326] See especially *Santo Domingo Massacre v Colombia* (Preliminary Objections, Merits and Reparations), Inter-American Court of Human Rights Series C no 259 (30 November 2012), paras 28, 38, 336–37; *Case of the Afro-Descendant Communities Displaced from the Cacarica River Basin (Operation Genesis) v Colombia* (Preliminary Objections, Merits, Reparations and Costs), Inter-American Court of Human Rights Series C no 270 (20 November 2013), paras 469–76.

[327] D Hawkins and W Jacoby, 'Partial Compliance: A Comparison of the European and Inter-American Courts of Human Rights' (2010) 6 *Journal of International Law and International Relations* 35; AC Fortas, *La surveillance de l'exécution des arrêts et décisions des Cours européenne et interaméricaine des droits de l'homme* (Paris, Pedone, 2015).

deciding merely symbolic measures or combining measures of symbolic nature with remedies entailing hands-on effects can often be difficult to implement. In any case, the Court's specificity in adjudicating the most suitable type of redress encouraged domestic authorities to rethink their political practices, and the Court itself to exercise its wide reparative competence even more enthusiastically as time was passing. Having incorporated the values of international law on state responsibility, the IACtHR has definitely fuelled international reparations for damage affecting private persons, with wide-ranging jurisprudential creations.[328]

Recent developments of the jurisprudence on reparations of both Courts reveal their willingness to depart from their initial positions and hence, they will possibly meet in the middle. The openness of the Strasbourg Court to new reparative patterns on the one hand, and the leeway attributed by the IACtHR to states on the other hand, that have proved their systemic improvements and may guarantee – to some extent –sufficient domestic remedies could reinstall the inter-judicial dialogue between the two mechanisms, to the benefit of the victims.

IV. Conclusion

Discussing the influence of the ECtHR outside Europe, the main topic of this chapter has been the 'exportation' of Strasbourg's human rights norms to the judicial production of the IACtHR. In its attempt to entrench the democratic rule of law and to tackle the atrocities that have traumatised the Americas for decades,[329] the IACtHR relied heavily on the *modus operandi* of the Strasbourg Court. Modelled on the European human rights system, the Inter-American one appears, to date, to be a student who has become the master in several fields of human rights protection. Having the Strasbourg Court as its main source of inspiration, the Court has borrowed extensively from its European sibling when it comes to cross-cutting approaches of well-known doctrines (positive obligations, MoA) but also when it comes to specific types of disputes. However, it has hitherto paved its own way and as it has adjusted Strasbourg's norms of protection to the realities of the continent either following an analogous pattern (eg freedom of expression, positive obligations) or a different path of work (eg the void application of subsidiarity, migration detention).

[328] The Inter-American Court's principles have influenced the 2005 UN Basic Principles and the Updated Set of Principles to Combat Impunity. Basic Principles and Guidelines on the Right to a Remedy and Reparation for Victims of Gross Violations of International Human Rights Law and Serious Violations of International Humanitarian Law (n 267); UN Economic and Social Council, 'Updated Set of Principles for the Protection and Promotion of Human Rights through Action to Combat Impunity' (8 February 2005) E/CN.4/2005/Add.1.

[329] ML Deftou, 'Fostering the Rule of Law in the Americas: Is There any Room for Judicial Dialogue between the IACtHR and National Courts?' (2020) 38 *Nordic Journal of Human Rights* 78.

The Court's conceptual creations related to human dignity (ie, *pro homine* principle) have led it to prove itself as the true trailblazer in regional human rights protection. Besides the well-documented sensitivity that the IACtHR has shown for types of disputes indissolubly related to the specificities of the region (ie, enforced disappearances, the protection of indigenous groups), it is also the generous approach of its powers to order reparations and to identify human rights obligations as peremptory norms that has expanded the protection offered, encouraging analogous reactions across the Atlantic.

There is no doubt that the Inter-American Court is exercising its contentious and advisory powers in a hostile political environment. Following the evolution of the political landscape over the latest decades, the Court appears to be more willing to largely borrow from the normative and jurisprudential experience of the European system in order to also intervene in legal territories that pose new challenges in Latin America. Overall, it goes without saying that both legal systems have been engaged in a multifaceted horizontal judicial dialogue which has brought new air to the human rights protection in the American continent. However, the interplay between the ECtHR and the UN Human Rights Committee, which is to be visited in the pages to come, is in stark distinction with the meaningful judicial interaction that has been established between the ECtHR and the IACtHR.

4

Regional to Global: Exporting the ECtHR's Norms to the Human Rights Committee

I. Introduction

Besides its tremendous regional impact, the ECHR and its understanding as mapped in the ECtHR's case law echoes universally. Traces of this echo can be found as well in the work of the monitoring body of the younger sibling of the ECHR, namely the International Covenant on Civil and Political Rights (hereinafter ICCPR).[1] The practice of the Human Rights Committee (hereinafter HRC, or the Committee), which is entitled to review the implementation of the ICCPR, is prominent among the monitoring bodies of the UN treaties grappling with the enforcement of human rights of all kinds. Pursuant to Article 28 ICCPR, the Committee is composed of 18 independent experts and its mandate is twofold: first, to assess reports from the States Parties on the improvements made to give effect to the provisions of the ICCPR, and second, to elaborate General Comments seeking to clarify the exact notion of human rights embodied in the Covenant and the specific obligations arising from its text. State Parties may also sign the two Optional Protocols of the ICCPR. The first has offered the HRC the powers to receive and examine individual complaints, the so-called communications scheduled during the sessions of the Committee as well as inter-state complaints. Its quasi-judicial mandate amounts to the delivery of the HRC's views,[2] which despite their non-binding nature *vis-à-vis* the State Parties, offers a favourable forum for claimants of human rights abuses and has been fleshed out as a successful machinery for the development of the concept of core human rights on a global scale.

[1] International Covenant on Civil and Political Rights (adopted 16 December 1966, entered into force 23 March 1976) 999 UNTS 171 (ICCPR). On the same day the International Covenant on Economic, Social and Cultural Rights was adopted as well. International Covenant on Economic, Social and Cultural Rights (adopted 16 December 1966, entered into force 3 January 1976) 993 UNTS 3 (ICESCR).

[2] See, eg HRC, 'General Comment no 33: The Obligations of States Parties under the Optional Protocol to the International Covenant on Civil and Political Rights' (5 November 2008) UN Doc CCPR/C/GC/33, paras 11, 13.

Having served as the main source of inspiration of the principal UN quasi-judicial mechanism, the ECtHR was silently incorporated in the argumentation of the HRC as expressed in its views. In stark contrast with the regional human rights tribunals, as previously discussed, the global voice of the Committee abstains persistently to expressly speak the words of the ECtHR despite the fact that both the authors and State Parties routinely invoke the Strasbourg Court's case law in order to enhance their legal reasoning.[3]

Indeed, the refusal of the HRC to explicitly refer to its sources of inspiration probably has its roots in the fact that its membership represents all parts of the world. Thus, the body prefers seeing human rights norms from a universal perspective, not through a restricted geographical lens. The Committee has felt even from its very first pronouncements that this approach may strengthen its weaknesses emanating from the non-binding force of its views. However, this negative stance of the Committee[4] towards regional human rights systems has provoked severe reactions in academia.[5]

The remoteness of the HRC from other systems, as illustrated by the non-use of external sources of law other than the ICCPR and its interpretation[6] by the Committee itself, is not in conformity with the theory of the global system of international tribunals and the intensified *dialogue des juges*, particularly in the realm of international human rights law. Despite the particularity of the HRC, the latter has been largely influenced by the European gatekeeper of human rights protection, silently taking into consideration its jurisprudential trends. Assessing the potential convergences and divergences between the UN and the ECHR system is revealed as the main objective of this part of the research, with particular focus on the HRC's communications in which complainants have largely invoked the Strasbourg Court's standards of protection.

For the needs of this section, attention will, firstly, be drawn to the points of interaction between the two regimes that cover their law production in a horizontal

[3] AH Robertson and JG Merrills, *Human Rights in the World: An Introduction to the Study of the International Protection of Human Rights*, 3rd edn (Manchester, Manchester University Press, 1989) 62–63; AM Slaughter, 'A Typology of Transjudicial Communication' (1994) 29 *University of Richmond Law Review* 99, 106.

[4] The approach of the Committee has been emphatically described in several reports. See HRC, 'Annual Report to the UN General Assembly' (1994) UN Doc A/49/40 vol. 1, para 76. In addition, the antagonistic standing towards the Strasbourg Court is reflected in some of the dissenting opinions of the Committee's members. See for instance, the laconic declaration of Nisuke Ando, according to which "I do not think it proper for the Committee to quote here a judgment of the European Court of Human Rights in footnote 59". See *Francisco Juan Larrañaga v the Philippines* (2004) UN Doc CCPR/C/87/D/1421/2005, Individual Opinion of Committee Member Mr Nisuke Ando, para 2.

[5] For Antoine Buyse, the position of the HRC reveals a certain "jalousie de métier" towards the ECtHR. See A Buyse, 'Tacit Citing – The Scarcity of Judicial Dialogue between the Global and the Regional Human Rights Mechanisms in Freedom of Expression Cases' in T McGonagle and Y Donders (eds), *The United Nations and Freedom of Expression and Information: Critical Perspectives* (Cambridge, Cambridge University Press, 2015) 443–46.

[6] See B Schlütter, 'Aspects of Human Rights Interpretation by the UN Treaty Bodies' in H Keller and G Ulfstein (eds), *UN Human Rights Treaty Bodies: Law and Legitimacy* (Cambridge, Cambridge University Press, 2012).

manner (section II). It is, thus, deemed necessary to elaborate on the choice of the HRC to adjudicate disputes also adjudicated by the Strasbourg Court despite the admissibility limitation of the 'same thing being examined before' (procedural). Additionally, this section will determine to which extent the Committee has imported the MoA doctrine of the ECtHR or has, in general, granted some deference to the State Parties to the Covenant (substantive). This impediment often arises before the Committee, since all of the CoE members are State Parties to the ICCPR.[7] Secondly, the focus will turn again to specific issues that have been assessed within the limits of the two architectures and treated similarly or differently in the light of the parties' allegations before the HRC (section III). Migration issues, the rights of vulnerable groups including women's reproductive rights as well as issues touching upon religious freedom are among fields of law greatly addressed by both the ECtHR and the HRC with interesting, yet conflicting conclusions.

II. The Horizontal Dimension of the Interaction between the HRC and the ECtHR

A. HRC: The 'Same Thing being Already Examined' by the ECtHR

Due to the multiplication of international and regional procedures of judicial review with overlapping jurisdictions, the phenomenon of forum shopping has alarmed not only national jurisdictions but it has also been discussed at the level of international adjudication. Pursuant to Article 5(2)(a) of the Optional Protocol to the ICCPR, 'the Committee shall not consider any communication from an individual unless it has ascertained that: (a) the same matter is not being examined under another procedure of international investigation or settlement'. However, since all State Parties to the ECHR are also bound by the ICCPR, quite a number of the HRC's communications are failed attempts of the authors to receive a favourable outcome from the ECtHR and its capacity to enforce its judgments.

The avoidance of forum shopping lies at the heart of the existence of specific rules governing coexistence with other international human rights legal orders. Hence, the European Convention in Article 52 provides in this respect that

> The High Contracting Parties agree that, except by special agreement, they will not avail themselves of treaties, conventions or declarations in force between them for the purpose of submitting, by way of petition, a dispute arising out of the interpretation or application of this Convention to a means of settlement other than those provided for in this Convention.

[7] Conversely, Anne Marie Slaughter supported the idea of forum shopping: AM Slaughter, 'A Global Community of Courts' (2003) 44 *Harvard International Law Journal* 191, 210.

The coexistence of the two texts brought, nevertheless, some complications since some State Parties to both instruments reacted to their potential review by both the ECtHR and the Committee for the same complaint, supporting the view that the Strasbourg Court's conclusions on a case are final and second re-examination of the same facts would amount to a *de facto* appeal under the UN regime. As a result, they entered reservations to the Optional Protocol[8] excluding individual petition which had already been considered under another system of international adjudication from the purview of the Human Rights Committee. At any rate, the Geneva system has engaged with a remarkable approach of the objections usually raised by State Parties when it comes to a case already been examined by the ECtHR.[9]

In numerous communications in which this objection has arisen, the Committee has not easily abstained from scrutinising the claims brought before it on these grounds. Looking at the basic elements of this restriction, as regards the notion of the 'same matter' the Human Rights Committee has taken the view that this has to be understood as including the *same claim* built upon the *same facts* and strictly concerning the *same individual* who brought it before the ECtHR or someone filing the complaint on his behalf.

The convergence between the two mechanisms is obvious when it comes to the examination of the same claims by different litigants. In a case dealing with the religious freedom of students in a Norwegian school, the Strasbourg Court found the application admissible even though the case had already been decided by the HRC, in *Leirvag and others v Norway*.[10] On the merits, the Court referred largely to the views of the Committee and revisited its traditional standing that prioritises the wide margin of appreciation in cases where freedom of religious expression is concerned.[11] Thus, it concluded to a violation of Article 9 ECHR. However, the slim majority (nine judges) which concluded in favour of the applicants was accompanied by the dissenting minority of eight judges who were strongly opposed to the mere pronouncement of the Court regarding the admissibility of the claim on the grounds of the previously delivered views of the HRC.[12]

[8] HRC, 'General Comment no 24: Issues Relating to Reservations Made upon Ratification or Accession to the Covenant or the Optional Protocols thereto, or in Relation to Declarations under Article 41 of the Covenant' (4 November 1994) UN Doc CCPR/C/21/Rev.1/Add.6. See inter alia on the history on reservations to the Optional Protocol of the Covenant and the General Comment no 24 that the HRC has adopted to tackle the increased number of reservations made by the State Parties M Scheinin, 'Reservations by States under the International Covenant on Civil and Political Rights and its Optional Protocols, and the Practice of the Human Rights Committee' in I Ziemele (ed), *Reservations to Human Rights Treaties and the Vienna Convention Regime: Conflict, Harmony or Reconciliation*, The Raoul Wallenberg Institute Human Rights Library 17 (Leiden, Brill Nijhoff, 2004).

[9] L Heffernan, 'A Comparative View of Individual Petition Procedures under the European Convention on Human Rights and the International Covenant on Civil and Political Rights' (1997) 19 *Human Rights Quarterly* 78, 103–4.

[10] See especially *Leirvåg and Others v Norway* (2004) UN Doc CCPR/C/82/D/1155/2003, paras 10.3–10.4.

[11] *Folgerø and Others v Norway* [GC], Merits, ECHR 2007-III 51, paras 45, 100.

[12] ibid Separate Opinion of Judges Zupančič and Borrego Borrego and Dissenting Opinion of Judges Wildhaber, Lorenzen, Bîrsan, Kovler, Steiner, Borrego, Hajiyev and Jebens.

The dissenting opinions clearly challenged the coexistence of the UN and the ECHR systems and highlighted the risk of conflicting decisions within the ambit of international human rights adjudication, the avoidance of which is exactly the objective of the procedural safeguards.[13] This example is indicative of how matters touching mostly upon procedural aspects can be endorsed 'by the back door' as elements of substantive nature that can significantly affect the said systems accordingly.

Although many provisions of the ICCPR have their equivalent in the ECHR, they may not be interpreted in the same way by the Committee and the ECtHR. Hence, most petitioners relied upon the divergent interpretations given by both instances on corresponding provisions reaching, therefore, different conclusions.

Overall, the HRC has clearly opted for having the last word in cases seeking its examination despite being already brought before the Strasbourg system. It has persistently attempted to define restrictively this limitation set forth by the Optional Protocol interpreting as 'same matter' the same complaint, based on the same facts and events, by the same person, invoking violations of the same substantive rights.[14] Similarly, the notion of 'examination' was approached in an equal manner. The basic rule for the Committee seems to be the following: cases declared inadmissible by the ECtHR on purely procedural grounds are generally declared admissible by the Committee.[15] For instance, where the case was declared inadmissible by the ECtHR because of the non-exhaustion of domestic remedies or because it was submitted after the six-month deadline imposed by Article 35 of the ECHR, the Committee decided that it had not been examined.

In *Cassanovas v France*, the Committee took a further step and treated similarly the invocation of the 'same matter' argument on the basis of the complaint's rejection by the European Commission on the grounds of *rationae materiae*

[13] See, eg L Lixinski, 'Choice of Forum in International Human Rights Adjudication and the Unity/Fragmentation Debate: Is Plurality the Way Ahead?' (2009) 9 *University College Dublin Law Review* 23, 38; S Walker, 'International Human Rights Law: Towards Pluralism or Harmony? The Opportunities and Challenges of Coexistence: The View from the UN Treaty Bodies' in C Buckley, A Donald and P Leach (eds), *Towards Convergence in International Human Rights Law*, Nottingham Studies on Human Rights 5 (Leiden, Brill Nijhoff, 2017) 507–8.

[14] The Committee recalled its perception of the 'same matter' concept in *Franz Wallmann and Rusella Wallmann v Austria* (2004) UN Doc CCPR/C/80/D/1002/2001, para 8.4; *Nikolai Alekseev v the Russian Federation* (2013) UN Doc CCPR/C/109/D/1873/2009; C Phuong, 'Relationship between the European Court of Human Rights and the Human Rights Committee: Has the Same Matter Already Been Examined' (2007) 7 *Human Rights Law Review* 385, 390.

[15] See, eg *O.F. v Norway* (1984) UN Doc CCPR/C/23/D/158/1983, para 5.2; *Dietmar Pauger v Austria* (1999) UN Doc CCPR/C/65/D/716/1996, para 6.4; *Franz and Maria Diesl v Austria* (2004) UN Doc CCPR/C/81/D/1060/2002, para 10.2; *Bertelli Galvez v Spain* (2005) UN Doc CCPR/C/84/D/1389/2005, para 4.3; *Dušan Šoltés v Czech Republic and Slovak Republic* (2005) UN Doc CCPR/C/85/D/1034-1035/2001, para 7.2; *Barbara Wdowiak v Poland* (2006) UN Doc CCPR/C/88/D/1446/2006, para 6.2. See also CEDAW, *X and Y v Georgia* (2015) UN Doc CEDAW/C/61/D/24/2009, paras 6.1–6.7.

jurisdiction of the Court. The European Commission had stated that the ECHR does not cover procedures governing the dismissal from employment of civil servants and the State Party alleged that Article 6 ECHR and Article 14 ICCPR are identical. Nevertheless, the Committee decided that

> since the rights of the European Convention differed in substance and with regard to their implementation procedures from the rights set forth in the Covenant, a matter that had been declared inadmissible *rationae materiae* had not, in the meaning of the reservation, been 'considered' in such a way that the Committee was precluded from examining it.[16]

Progressively, the Committee clarified – and since then, systematically concludes – that even a slight or limited assessment of the factual basis *in merito* carried out by the Strasbourg Court suffices for the Committee to declare the communication inadmissible as it has been in a way examined by the Court.[17] The most illustrative instance as regards the evolutive interaction between the two mechanisms can be traced in the views adopted by the Committee in *Correia de Matos v Portugal.*[18] *In casu*, Mr Correia de Matos, a Portuguese lawyer, complained for being prevented from enjoying his right to defend himself in court without a lawyer pursuant to Article 14(3)(d) of the Covenant since the Portuguese criminal law contained an abstract and statutory prohibition of defending oneself without a lawyer.[19] This was made possible by the fact that Portugal had not formulated a reservation to Article 5(2)(a) of the Optional Protocol.[20] However, the ECtHR had rejected the said application as manifestly ill-founded concluding to a non-violation of Article 6(3)(c) ECHR, given the margin of appreciation afforded to the State Parties to the Convention when it comes to such procedural requirements of a national criminal legal framework.

Conversely, the Committee considered that there had been a violation of the right to defend oneself in person under Article 14(3)(d). The deafening silence of the Committee with regard to the judgment of the Strasbourg Court passes without surprise, however. Indeed, despite recognising a certain degree of deference granted to the Portuguese state on these matters, the HRC explained that Portuguese legislation allowed for no exceptions pertaining to the status of the accused, the seriousness of the charges or the behaviour of the accused.[21]

Regardless of the fact that the said approach has implications on the internal coherence within the Committee's own jurisprudence,[22] some of the HRC's members also highlighted the risks deriving from the divergent jurisprudence of

[16] *Casanovas v France* (1994) UN Doc CCPR/C/51/D/441/1990, para 5.1.
[17] *Chanderballi Mahabir v Austria* (2004) UN Doc CCPR/C/82/D/944/2000, para 8.3.
[18] *Carlos Correia de Matos v Portugal* (2006) UN Doc CCPR/C/86/D/1123/2002.
[19] *Correia de Matos v Portugal* (dec) ECHR 2001-XII 161.
[20] *Carlos Correia de Matos* (n 18) para 6.2.
[21] ibid para 7.5.
[22] See, eg *Walter Kollar v Australia* (2003) UN Doc CCPR/C/78/DR/989/2001.

the two international human rights regimes that can be developed when actually examining 'the same matter', particularly when one keeps ignoring the other's conclusions.[23]

Only a few months earlier, the Grand Chamber re-examined the same case and this latter judgment of 2018 brought to light once again the *problématique* fuelled by the parallel or consecutive review of identical cases by more than one international instances.[24] In line with its previous judgment, the ECtHR has given particular emphasis to Portugal's margin of appreciation and held that the justifications of the government for the requirement to be assisted by counsel had been both relevant and sufficient.[25] Thus, the Grand Chamber found that the criminal proceedings involving the applicant did not amount to an infringement of Article 6 ECHR. In sharp contradistinction to the practice followed by the HRC confirmed in its prior pronouncement on this exact same case, the Strasbourg Court referred to the equivalent provision of the ICCPR and the aforementioned views of the HRC in paragraph 133.[26] Therefore, it implicitly declared that it took into account the relevant rules under the UN system, also applicable in the relations between the parties citing Article 31(3)(c) of the 1969 Vienna Convention on the Law of Treaties. Nonetheless, while the ECHR is not interpreted 'in a vacuum' according to the classic phrasing of the Court, this appears to be here an obiter dictum since the latter elucidated that 'even where the provisions of the Convention and those of the ICCPR are almost identical, the interpretation of the same fundamental right by the HRC and by this Court may not always correspond'.[27]

Bearing in mind how a rather procedural restriction as the one of the 'same matter being already examined' could have extensions of substantive nature, this rather controversial finding of the Court brings us back to the main question around the fragmentation of international human rights adjudication. It appears that the progressive interpretation of Article 14 given by the Committee as regards the same authoritative requirement to be assisted by counsel does not represent for the Grand Chamber an international development providing a higher level of protection with which it should align its jurisprudence.[28] On the basis of these 'international developments under public international law' calling for a narrower margin of appreciation, three of the judges of the ECtHR dissented and observed that this judgment constitutes a rather missed opportunity to signal a remarkable contribution to the harmonisation and coherence in international

[23] ibid Dissenting Opinion of Mr Nisuke Ando, Mr Michael O'Flaherty and Ms Elisabeth Palm, Dissenting Opinion of Sir Nigel Rodley.

[24] *Correia de Matos v Portugal* [GC], Merits, App no 56402/12 (ECtHR, 4 April 2018).

[25] ibid paras 143, 159.

[26] ibid para 133.

[27] ibid para 135.

[28] ibid para 134.

human rights law.[29] In this spirit, as Dorothea Staes allegorically put it, comparing the pluralist normative framework to a jungle, 'the Court should make use of the lianas to connect with other organisms, such as the HRC. Organisms are not isolated but part of a wider ecosystem. Within this system, the law of the jungle forces the organisms to live together in harmony. Harmony does not necessarily imply unity.'[30] As the example of the *Correia de Matos v Portugal* case illustrates, dissimilar interpretation of the same rules of international human right protection can also cause severe hardships to legal certainty. This could also make State Parties opt for the lower level of protection and deter them from developing more human rights-friendly domestic legislation giving them ammunition for not aligning their legal frameworks with the decisions which are not in favour of them due to extended fragmentation.[31]

As neither of the two systems is bound by the decisions of the other, and their conflicting jurisprudence might not constitute a problem in itself, their pronouncements on the matter are indicative of the unwillingness of Geneva and Strasbourg to urge themselves to initiate a meaningful dialogue between them. By the same token, the openness of the HRC to assess matters already being examined by the ECtHR remains a blind spot of their interrelationship.

B. The MoA of the States before the HRC: Acceptance or Opposition?

As previously demonstrated, the margin of appreciation doctrine lies at the centre of the interaction between HRC and ECtHR, as is the case of the relationship of the latter with the IACtHR.[32] The famous doctrine has definitely been tailor-made to the needs of European human rights protection. However, this does not preclude it from being applied to other international human rights instances. This section, therefore, seeks to examine how the Committee has incorporated within its quasi-judicial powers such a dynamic concept which, as a reflection of the principle of subsidiarity, mirrors the interplay between the international judicature and the national authorities.[33]

[29] ibid Joint Dissenting Opinion of Judges Tsotsoria, Motoc and Mits; I Motoc and M Volikas, 'The ECHR and the UN Human Rights Committee: Je t'aime plus, moi non-plus. Some Remarks on the *Correia de Matos v. Portugal* and the Right to Defend Oneself in Person' in E Decaux, I Motoc and P Gillibert (eds), *Justice et droits de l'homme: Mélanges in tribute to Judge Christine Chanet* (Paris, Pedone, 2019).

[30] D Staes, 'Correia de Matos v. Portugal: Fragmented Protection of the Right to Defend Oneself in Person' (*Strasbourg Observers*, 24 May 2018), www.strasbourgobservers.com/2018/05/24/correia-de-matos-v-portugal-fragmented-protection-of-the-right-to-defend-oneself-in-person/.

[31] *Correia de Matos v Portugal* [GC] (n 24) para 70.

[32] See the previous chapter on the subsidiarity in the Americas.

[33] D Spielmann, 'Allowing the Right Margin: The European Court of Human Rights and the National Margin of Appreciation Doctrine: Waiver or Subsidiarity of European Review' (2012) 14 *Cambridge Yearbook of European Legal Studies* 381; E Bjorge, 'Been There, Done That: The Margin of Appreciation and International Law' (2015) 4 *Cambridge Journal of International and Comparative Law* 181, 190.

As an expression of the respect for the diversity of historical developments, national legal traditions, cultural backgrounds and constitutional values coexisting within the Council of Europe's human rights system, the margin of appreciation doctrine has met serious resistance from the HRC. Its rejection by the latter runs through its entire jurisprudence irrespective of the field of law within the limits of which the State Party has invoked its application.[34] Likewise the resistance of the IACtHR, this stricter standing of the Committee *vis-à-vis* the State Parties to the Covenant is largely explained by the significantly greater legal diversity and the democratic deficit observed among State Parties. In its attempt to entrench its legitimacy within the inconsistent and often, unfriendly background, the Committee has deemed it unwise to make extensive use of the MoA doctrine while attempting to harmonise the standards of the ICCPR's among its 172 State Parties. This would severely hinder the elaboration of universally feasible legal standards and common practices, manageable in the sense of being subjected to review by judicial or quasi-judicial bodies.[35] What's more, such a concept does not appear to enhance the already weak legal effects of the non-binding nature of the Committee's decisions and arguably, does not add to the persuasiveness of the body. In a similar vein to the Latin American case, it is unexpected for the HRC to depart from the well-established choice of closely monitoring wide-ranging and – in many instances – politically unstable domestic decision-makers.

Nonetheless, some of the views adopted by the HRC actually echo the well-known jurisprudential construction of the Strasbourg Court. Apart from the right to life (Article 6 ICCPR) and the prohibition of torture, inhuman or degrading treatment (Article 7 ICCPR), understood by the Committee as requiring absolute protection, it can be argued that this phenomenally complete rejection of the HRC has at some point been controverted by MoA-like approaches, in the words of Professor Yuval Shany, Member of the Human Rights Committee.[36] Notwithstanding the fact that the HRC blatantly refused to embrace the margin of appreciation doctrine as such, it can be deemed that it has felt appropriate to instead use comparable terms and thus, to *de facto* allow some deferential moves to the states echoing the tendency of

[34] See, eg H Keller and L Grover, 'General Comments of the Human Rights Committee and their Legitimacy' in H Keller and G Ulfstein (eds), *UN Human Rights Treaty Bodies: Law and Legitimacy* (Cambridge, Cambridge University Press, 2012) 125; S Sheeran, 'Reconceptualizing States of Emergency under International Human Rights Law: Theory, Legal Doctrine, and Politics' (2013) 34 *Michigan Journal of International Law* 491, 539.

[35] S Joseph and M Castan, *The International Covenant on Civil and Political Rights: Cases, Materials, and Commentary*, 3rd edn (Oxford, Oxford University Press, 2013) 625; See also HRC, 'General Comment no 34: Article 19: Freedoms of Opinion and Expression' (12 September 2011) UN Doc CCPR/C/GC/34; Y Shany, 'All Roads Lead to Strasbourg?: Application of the Margin of Appreciation Doctrine by the European Court of Human Rights and the UN Human Rights Committee' (2018) 9 *Journal of International Dispute Settlement* 180, 190.

[36] ibid 191.

the Strasbourg Court,[37] particularly in cases that traditionally fall within the limits of national regulatory policies.

One of the sets of cases that has provided fertile ground for a certain leeway left to the State Parties is shaped by deportation, expulsion or extradition cases.[38] In particular, the traditional reluctance of the Court to grant significant latitude to the national authorities is often yielded when the assessment of facts comes up.[39] This approach bears great resemblance to the 'better position' argumentation which has been one of the structural elements of the MoA concept of the Strasbourg judicature[40] and a 'transnational device'.[41] When it comes to the fact-finding aspects of communications grappling with migration issues, national authorities are in a better position to obtain and assess local knowledge. Otherwise, the Committee, which lacks fact-finding powers, runs the risk of misjudging the mere existence or the significance of facts or domestic administrative procedures.

This possibility arises while assessing the lawfulness of the deportation or extradition decisions as regards the risk of irreparable harm of the person subjected to the order at the country of destination.[42] Indeed, in such cases the Committee felt that national authorities should be entrusted with the exercise of this risk-assessment test invoking the rejection of the 'fourth instance formula'.[43] Recently, the HRC further held that the State Party should be trusted 'unless it is found that the evaluation was clearly arbitrary or amounted to a denial of justice, and that it is generally for organs of States parties to the Covenant to review or evaluate facts and evidence in order to determine whether such a risk exists'.[44]

[37] In the Preface of the Yutaka Arai-Takahashi's book, James Crawford observed that 'the Committee has been "speaking silently" the language of the MoA doctrine', Y Arai-Takahashi, *The Margin of Appreciation Doctrine and the Principle of Proportionality in the Jurisprudence of the ECHR* (Antwerp, Intersentia, 2002) ix.

[38] See, eg V Engström, 'Deference and the Human Rights Committee' (2016) 34 *Nordic Journal of International Law* 73.

[39] Shany, 'All Roads Lead to Strasbourg?' (n 35) 191.

[40] The better position rationale was reiterated by the Court in numerous cases to support the discretion accorded to national authorities. See inter alia *Ireland v the United Kingdom*, Merits, App no 5310/71, (18 January 1978), para 207; *Brannigan and McBride v the United Kingdom*, Merits, App no 14553/89; 14554/89 (26 May 1993), para 43.

[41] S Greer, *The Margin of Appreciation: Interpretation and Discretion under the European Convention on Human Rights*, Human Rights files no 17 (Strasbourg, Council of Europe Publishing, 2000) 34.

[42] HRC, 'General Comment no 31[80]: The Nature of the General Legal Obligation Imposed on States Parties to the Covenant' (26 May 2004) UN Doc CCPR/C/21/Rev.1/Add. 13, para 7. Hence, the HRC grants some latitude to the domestic authorities with the aim to settle the scope of national executive and administrative difference while reviewing the States during the reporting procedure. However, the HRC's stance in the context of individual communications appears to be another story.

[43] *Anna Maroufidou v Sweden* (1981) UN Doc CCPR/C/12/D/58/1979, paras 6.2, 10.1. See similar pronouncements of the Committee in *G v Canada* (2000) UN Doc CCPR/C/69/D/934/2000, para 4.3; *Mansour Ahani v Canada* (2004) UN Doc CCPR/C/80/D/1051/2002, para 10.5. See also Engström, 'Deference' (n 38) 79.

[44] *RG v Denmark* (2015) UN Doc CCPR/C/115/D/2351/2014, paras 7.4–7.6; *X v Norway* (2015) UN Doc CCPR/C/115/D/2474/2014, para 7.5; *FM v Canada* (2015) UN Doc CCPR/C/115/D/2284/2013, paras 9.5–9.6.

The Geneva system has applied these standards in cases also challenging administrative measures resulting in the deportation of the authors from Canada to Pakistan. Hence, the risk of a violation of Articles 6 and 7 ICCPR is in sight when the Committee finds that the local immigration authorities have not accorded sufficient weight to serious procedural defect either omitting to consider an important risk factor or concluding to a deportation decision which is manifestly unreasonable or arbitrary in nature.[45]

It comes as no surprise that in similar cases, inconsistencies did emerge in Geneva. For instance, while, in *Masih Shakeel v Canada*, the majority reaffirmed in its own words 'the deference to be given to the immigration authorities in assessing the evidence before them',[46] and reached the conclusion that the author, if deported from Canada, would be at risk of being subjected to irreparable harm. The Committee re-examined the author's allegations with regard to the factual core of the case, slightly justifying why the evaluation of the material presented before the Canadian authorities found therein was manifestly unreasonable and which were the irregularities detected in the procedures. Distinguished members of the Committee opined in the opposite direction, observing that the latter should not have abandoned its well-established jurisprudence in this respect.[47]

In another expulsion case against Canada, Professor Ruth Wedgwood, an HRC Member, opposed the views adopted by the majority on similar grounds. In the controversial *Dauphin v Canada* case, she correctly attempted to shed light to the reasons why deferential loans from the ECtHR cannot be asserted as attacks on the universality of human rights and hence, significant room for a more flexible international scrutiny should be left pertaining to national immigration and naturalisation policies. *In casu*, the expulsion of a Haitian national, convicted in Canada for robbery with violence, was at stake since the author alleged family ties with his relatives to reverse the expulsion decision.

For Ruth Wedgwood,

> even in a globalized world, the regulation of immigration is a matter of importance to nation States. It includes not only the right to set conditions for obtaining citizenship, but also for long term residence. The Committee has never purported to suggest that the Covenant contains a detailed code for how States can regulate both matters.

While the Committee has considered in the past that a violation of the right to family life might serve as the outer boundary in these cases, since the deportation of a non-national parent would leave a citizen child without full parental

[45] *Mehrez Ben Abde Hamida v Canada* (2010) UN Doc CCPR/C/98/D/1544/2007, paras 8.4–8.6; *Ernest Sigman Pillai et al v Canada* (2011) UN Doc CCPR/C/101/D/1763/2008, paras 11.2–11.4.

[46] *Masih Shakeel v Canada* (2013) UN Doc CCPR/C/108/D/1881/2009, para 8.4.

[47] ibid Dissenting Opinion of Prof Yuval Shany et al and of Prof Iwasawa, both criticising the step-back of the HRC in this regard.

care, she recalled the jurisprudence of the ECtHR,[48] which deferred greatly to state decisions purporting to control the entry and residence of aliens convicted of criminal offences. According to this opinion, the Committee enters in troubled waters when opting for such a strict scrutiny in these cases.[49]

Naturally, greater latitude has been justified in the realm of derogations in states of emergency, particularly when fundamental second-generation rights are in question, such as freedom of expression. Besides, the birth of the conceptual construction of the margin of appreciation in Strasbourg can be first detected in the context of the derogation in emergency situations under Article 15 ECHR or under human rights provided by articles comprising limitation clauses.[50] Whereas in the relevant General Comments the HRC either abstained from referring to the margin of appreciation concept[51] or openly denied its application to its decision-making procedure,[52] the Committee has recognised in its views that for the interpretation of these clauses a certain amount of discretion could be allowed.

It was within this context of the protection of human expression that the HRC made one of its very few explicit references to margin of appreciation in these actual words while determining to what extent broadcast media can be lawfully censored on the basis of protecting public morals, within the limits of freedom of expression pursuant to Article 19 ICCPR. In its views in the famous *Leo Hertzberg et al v Finland*,[53] the Committee seems more open to adopt the Strasbourg Court's approach to permitting some latitude to states in such cases.[54]

The wide-ranging public morals play the role of the regional consensus in the CoE system and thus, constitute the basis upon which the invocation of deferential powers is made by the Committee in a handful of cases touching upon the right of states to derogate from or impose restrictions on freedom of expression[55] and the right to private life.[56] Nevertheless, the overall reserved understanding of subsidiarity and deference was, as previously stated, reiterated by the most recent General Comment no 34. Dominic McGoldrick provided in his article a

[48] *Dauphin v Canada* (2009) UN Doc CCPR/C/96/D/1792/2008, Dissenting Opinion of the Committee Member Ms Ruth Wedgwood. She actually made a perfectly good description of the way in which the ECHR is 'exported' to the Geneva system and of the inter-balance between the two architectures.

[49] ibid.

[50] ECommHR, *Denmark, Norway, Sweden and the Netherlands v Greece (I) (The Greek case)*, App nos 3321–4/67 (Commission decision, 31 May 1968), para 114.

[51] Surprisingly, no reference to any form of margin of appreciation can be found in General Comment no 29 with regard to derogations during a state of emergency. HRC, 'General Comment no 29: Article 4: Derogations during a State of Emergency' (31 August 2001) UN Doc CCPR/C/21/Rev.1/Add.11.

[52] See, eg HRC, 'General Comment no 34' (n 35) para 36.

[53] *Leo Hertzberg et al v Finland* (1982) UN Doc CCPR/C/OP/1.

[54] ibid para 10.3.

[55] *Länsman et al v Finland* (1994) UN Doc CCPR/C/52/D/511/1992, para 9.4.

[56] *Toonen v Australia* (1994) UN Doc CCPR/C/50/D/488/1992, para 8.6.

comprehensive catalogue of potential explanations for the departure taken by the HRC from deferential practices ranging from the protection of human rights' universality to anti-Eurocentrism or misunderstanding of the MoA and the lack of trust in decisions made by states.[57]

The complex and sometimes rhetorical understanding of the MoA doctrine, as documented in the ECtHR's case law, has probably contributed to the hesitation of other bodies to happily verge into the territory of this particular form of deference. Irrespective of the roots of the Committee's restraint, the path of subsidiarity and deference, if taken, might lead to the more successful universal embrace of legal plurality, as one might expect from a universal forum, to incorporate a certain flexibility in the context of its competences. Accordingly, the balanced approach of the ECtHR endorsing incrementalism together with a co-operative form of subsidiarity as institutionalised with the adoption of Protocol 15[58] expanded the strength of the regime and enhanced significantly its interrelationship with national systems, seen as parts of a united whole, not as perils for the legitimacy of the Court's adjudication *vis-à- vis* state parties.

In recent decades and despite the fact that this construction has a great future behind it under international law,[59] new fields of international law other than human rights litigation are timidly experiencing the repercussions of the application of MoA.[60]

Within the context of providing remedies, for instance, the Committee has appeared willing to take a step back from the determination of specific measures of reparation. Hence, it leaves room to the State Party to calculate the compensation to be paid to the victims of violations or on most occasions, uses a general wording according to which the state needs to provide effective remedy for the victim and to take all appropriate measures to guarantee the non-repetition of similar violations in the future.[61]

In sum, the voluminous case law of HRC providing bold pronouncements on a vast variety of human rights questions reveals the tendency of the body to restrict

[57] D McGoldrick, 'A Defence of the Margin of Appreciation and an Argument for its Application by the Human Rights Committee' (2016) 65 *ICLQ* 21, 52ff.

[58] J Gerards, 'Margin of Appreciation and Incrementalism in the Case Law of the European Court of Human Rights' (2018) 18 *Human Rights Law Review* 495.

[59] See M Iglesias Vila, 'Subsidiarity, Margin of Appreciation and International Adjudication within a Cooperative Conception of Human Rights' (2017) 15 *International Journal of Constitutional Law* 393, 403–5; S Smet, 'When Human Rights Clash in 'the Age of Subsidiarity': What Role for the Margin of Appreciation?' in P Agha (ed), *Human Rights between Law and Politics: The Margin of Appreciation in Post-National Contexts*, Modern Studies in European Law 76 (Oxford, Hart Publishing, 2017).

[60] V Dye, "Deference as Respect' in WTO Standard of Review' (2013) 12 *Journal of International Trade Law and Policy* 23; C Ragni, 'Standard of Review and the Margin of Appreciation before the International Court of Justice' in L Gruszczynski and W Werner (eds), *Deference in International Courts and Tribunals: Standard of Review and Margin of Appreciation* (Oxford, Oxford University Press, 2014); G Zarra, 'Right to Regulate, Margin of Appreciation and Proportionality: Current Status in Investment Arbitration in Light of Philip Morris v. Uruguay' (2017) 14 *Brazilian Journal of International Law* 95.

[61] G Neuman, 'Subsidiarity' in D Shelton (ed), *The Oxford Handbook of International Human Rights Law* (Oxford, Oxford University Press, 2013) 374.

the regulatory space afforded to states as to which domestic measures should be taken to align with the provisions of the Covenant. Conversely, a closer look brings to light the Committee's openness on several occasions to offer discretional powers to states without expressly adopting the MoA language. Indeed, while the Committee operates in a more complex legal landscape, in which it struggles to delineate the justiciability of the ICCPR's provisions and – by extension – reinforce the role of the body, its standing appears absolutely indicative of the fact that probably the Committee is not ready yet to engage in a more fruitful dialogue with the European Court.

III. The Vertical Dimension of the Interaction between HRC and ECtHR: Moving in Parallel, Deciding in Contrast

Measuring the extent to which the Committee has borrowed from the Strasbourg system, this section comparatively discusses the varying interpretations of human rights norms between the Committee and the Strasbourg Court with regard to three legal fields: freedom of religion, women's reproductive rights and the rights of migrants and asylum-seekers. Bearing in mind that all of the CoE State Parties are also State Parties to the ICCPR, it comes as no surprise that these legal areas are greatly touched upon by both fora, represent the types of disputes in which authors mostly invoke the European Court's level of protection before the Committee due to the – almost – identical nature of cases, and often concern the same piece of domestic legislation. They, nevertheless, remain underexplored by legal scholarship as regards the interplay between the two mechanisms.

A. The Divergence in Freedom of Religion Cases

Reaching conflicting conclusions while applying similar human rights standards does not constitute an unprecedented phenomenon within the purview of international human rights law. States with long-established constitutional values of state neutrality and secularism are repetitively confronted with the balancing act of determining whether it is possible to impose a horizontal prohibition on people wearing religious symbols in public areas as a manifestation of their religious beliefs, without interfering disproportionately with the respect for their religious expression. Both the Court and the Committee have also grappled with sensitive dilemmas emanating from the reconciliation of religious traditions with the state's quest to preserve *ordre public* within a multicultural context. The thorny issue of religious symbols, repeatedly treated by both mechanisms, instead of exemplifying the field of interaction in their case law, provided a clear illustration of their divergence in this regard.[62] The slightly different wording of the relevant articles does not seem to explain the stark conflicting application of the said right. Most often, the older Strasbourg system deals with cases in which either others' conventional rights clash with an individual's right to manifest his religious beliefs as one of the constituent elements of the freedom of religion or with the controversial concept of public safety and public order upon which state's interests are based. Amid these contrasts, conflicting interests need to be balanced in the spirit of the limitation clause of Article 9(2) ECHR.

Besides the pioneer *Kokkinakis* jurisprudence,[63] where the ECtHR was extremely protective when balancing the freedom of religion with the rights and freedoms of others, the ECtHR still affords alarming deference to national authorities to impose severe restrictions on religious expression. Since the latter has both an individual and a collective dimension, the 'necessity' for such restrictions[64] to preserve public order or public security has pointed towards a *carte blanche* given by the Court to the states. The Court has either rejected many of these cases posing sensitive questions as manifestly ill-founded, or has taken a clear and rather solid position in similar cases.

In particular, these difficult but increasingly far-reaching questions were inevitably addressed in cases in relation to the wearing religious symbols in public. Therefore, when the principle of secularism[65] is at stake, the Court feels that *ordre public* justifies the embracement of the vague 'living together' concept, which is not included in the limitation clause of Article 9 ECHR; it is encompassed nonetheless in 'the protection of rights and freedoms of others' criterion of paragraph 2. The Court, in the most controversial *SAS v France* case,[66] held that the blanket French ban pursuant to controversial French legislation which interfered with Muslim women's right to wear the *niqab* or *burqa* (full-faced Islamic veil) not systematically but in public, is in conformity with the Convention. The Court hence aligned with the argument of the French government, given the role that the face plays in social interaction.[67] However, the caution with which the Court took this path is mirrored in its flexible take on the 'living together' concept and its potential abuse, indissolubly linked to the necessity of the impugned limitation.[68] Notwithstanding its caution on the matter, the Court more recently reiterated the 'living together' concept as a legitimate justification

[62] E Brems, E Bribosia, I Rorive and S Van Drooghenbroeck, 'Le port de signes religieux dans l'espace public: vérité à Strasbourg, erreur à Genève?' (2012) 131 *Journal des Tribunaux* 602, 603.

[63] *Kokkinakis v Greece*, Merits, Series A no 260-A (1993).

[64] MT Parker, 'The Freedom to Manifest Religious Belief: An Analysis of the Necessity Clauses of the ICCPR and the ECHR' (2006) 17 *Duke Journal of Comparative and International Law* 91.

[65] The principle of secularism has the sense of strong separation between state and church.

[66] *SAS v France* [GC], Merits, ECHR 2014-III 341.

[67] ibid para 122.

[68] ibid.

of similar restrictions imposed on the religious freedom of individuals in two cases delivered on the same day concerning Belgium: *Dakir v Belgium*[69] and *Belcacemi and Oussar v Belgium*.[70]

Be that as it may, it seems that the Court felt that the 'living together' justification should be prioritised over the French republican virtues of *laïcité*.[71] The starting point of the Court's jurisprudence on religious symbols is the embracement of the role of the state as 'a neutral and impartial organiser of the exercise of various religions, faiths and beliefs, and stated that this role is conducive to public order, religious harmony and tolerance in a democratic society'.[72] Despite its overly liberal approach on freedom of religion cases and its own concerns on Islamophobic outbursts that potentially affected the adoption of the said legislation,[73] when secular ideology is on the table, the state is left with a wide margin of discretion and the Court abstains from exercising stringent review of the evidence or the necessity of the particular interference with the individual's freedom of religion.[74]

By contrast, in *Yaker v France*[75] and *Hebbadi v France*,[76] the Committee dealt with the same legislative framework and confirmed its dissonance with the Court' s approach. The HRC emphatically rejected the abstract 'living together' construction introduced by the Strasbourg Court in *SAS*, as it cannot be construed as a manifestation of the 'protection of the rights and freedoms of others', given that those rights affected are not identified in the Court's judgment.[77]

Even if the 'living together' aim is a legitimate one, the French government failed to prove that the impugned measure was actually proportionate, or that it was the least restrictive means that is protective of religion or belief.[78] The added value of the *Yaker* decision of the Committee is that the latter saw the said

[69] *Dakir v Belgium*, Merits, App no 4619/12 (ECtHR, 11 July 2017).

[70] *Belcacemi and Oussar v Belgium*, Merits, App no 37798/13 (ECtHR, 11 July 2017).

[71] French literature has strongly opposed this reform and sheds light on the alarming repercussions of this rather aggressive form of *laïcité*, especially in the context of public educational institutions. See, eg JL Debré, *La laïcité à l'école – un principe républicain à réaffirmer, Rapport de la mission de l'Assemblée nationale* (Paris, Odile Jacob, 2004); A Renaut and A Touraine, *Un débat sur la laïcité* (Paris, Stock, 2005); M Jacquemain, 'Dix arguments laïques contre l'interdiction législative du voile' in M Jacquemain and N Rosa-Rosso (eds), *Du bon usage de la laïcité* (Bruxelles, Aden, 2008).

[72] *Leyla Sahin v Turkey* [GC], Merits, ECHR 2005-XI 173, para 107.

[73] ibid para 149.

[74] SA Chaib and L Peroni, 'S.A.S. v. France: Missed Opportunity to Do Full Justice to Women Wearing a Face Veil' (*Strasbourg Observers*, 3 July 2014), www.strasbourgobservers.com/2014/07/03/s-a-s-v-france-missed-opportunity-to-do-full-justice-to-women-wearing-a-face-veil/; P Pinto de Albuquerque and A Scoseria Katz, 'Is Religion a Threat to Human Rights? Or is It the Other Way Around? Defending Individual Autonomy in the ECtHR' s Jurisprudence on Freedom of Religion' in R Uerpmann-Wittzack, E Lagrange and S Oeter (eds), *Religion and International Law: Living Together* (Leiden, Brill Nijhoff, 2018).

[75] *Sonia Yaker v France* (2018) UN Doc CCPR/C/123/D/2747/2016.

[76] *Miriana Hebbadj v France* (2018) UN Doc CCPR/C/123/D/2807/2016.

[77] ibid para 8.10

[78] ibid para 8.11.

violation also through the lens of the prohibition of discrimination pursuant to Article 26 ICCPR as it concluded that the blanket ban of *burqa* constitutes intersectional discrimination. According to the concurring opinion of five members of the HRC, less intrusive measures could be adopted so that Muslim women would not be marginalised and their individual autonomy would also be respected in the context of the manifestation of their religious beliefs.[79]

This divergence had already been boldly depicted on the occasion of the *Singh saga* adjudicated by both regimes. After having his case dismissed as inadmissible by the Court,[80] the applicant, a practising Sikh, who challenged the requirement to appear bareheaded in the identity photograph of his driving licence on religious freedom grounds, made his case all the way to Geneva. In stark contradiction with the ECtHR, for which such measures are justified in the name of public safety and public order within the limits of the state's wide margin of appreciation, the Committee decided otherwise. It acknowledged that the state's need to verify, for the purposes of public safety and order, that a person appearing in the photograph on a residence permit is, in fact, the rightful holder of that document represents a legitimate purpose. It nonetheless maintained in the context of the proportionality test that the state had failed to justify the allegation according to which the wearing of the Sikh turban particularly impedes the identification of the author, given that he constantly wears the turban.[81]

Under the same factual basis, the Committee sought a full three-stage proportionality test, which the French government failed to pass.[82] The different synthesis of the two systems might sufficiently elucidate their diametrically opposite standing: European states have predominantly Christian or secular religious traditions, in which Islamic groups are only religious minorities, whereas the Committee hears cases from a much wider range of states with diverse religious traditions.

In the same vein, the Strasbourg Court and the Committee treated differently Muslim students wearing headscarves at school on the basis of submissions

[79] *Sonia Yaker* (n 75) Joint Concurring Opinion of Committee Members Ilze Brands Kehris, Sarah Cleveland, Christof Heyns, Marcia VJ Kran and Yuval Shany, para 3. See also S Berry, 'The UN Human Rights Committee Disagrees with the European Court of Human Rights Again: The Right to Manifest Religion by Wearing a Burqa' (*EJIL:Talk!*, 3 January 2019), www.ejiltalk.org/the-un-human-rights-committee-disagrees-with-the-european-court-of-human-rights-again-the-right-to-manifest-religion-by-wearing-a-burqa/.

[80] *Mann Singh v France* (dec), App no 24479/07 (ECtHR, 13 November 2008); *Jasvir Singh v France* (dec), App no 25463/08 (ECtHR, 30 June 2009); *Ranjit Singh v France* (dec), App no 27561/08 (ECtHR, 30 June 2009).

[81] *Ranjit Singh v France* (2011) UN Doc CCPR/C/102/D/1876/2009, para 8.4; *Mann Singh v France* (2013) UN Doc CCPR/C/108/D/1928/2010.

[82] See S Berry, 'Freedom of Religion and Religious Symbols: Same Right – Different Interpretation?' (*EJIL:Talk!*, 10 October 2013), www.ejiltalk.org/freedom-of-religion-and-religious-symbols-same-right-different-interpretation/; SO Chaib, 'Ranjit Singh v. France: The UN Committee Asks the Questions the Strasbourg Court Didn't Ask in Turban Case' (*Strasbourg Observers*, 6 March 2012), www.strasbourgobservers.com/2012/03/06/ranjit-singh-v-france-the-un-committee-asks-the-questions-the-strasbourg-court-didnt-ask-in-turban-case/.

calling into question the French law of 2004 which prohibits the wearing of ostentatious religious symbols in state schools. The constitutional principle of *laïcité* has constituted one of the cornerstones of the French Republic since the French Revolution, observance of which was the first and foremost aim of the drafters of the said legislation.[83] Therefore, in its views in *Bikramjit Singh*[84] which concerned the expulsion of the Sikh applicant from state schools for refusing to remove the *keski*,[85] the Committee was called upon to strike a fair balance between the competing interests.

At the outset, the body recognised that upholding the principle of *laïcité* pursues the legitimate aim to protect the rights and freedoms of others since the latter represents 'a means by which a State party may seek to protect the religious freedom of all its population' and admitted that the adoption of the said legislative act aimed to address incidents of interference with the religious freedom of pupils and even threats to their physical safety.[86] Subsequently, the Committee exercised rigorous scrutiny to ascertain the proportionality of the measure of the author's expulsion and concluded to a violation of Article 18 ICCPR taking into account the nature of the *keski*, its mandatory character for Sikh males and the state's failure to persuade the body that the student actually posed a threat to the rights and freedoms of other pupils or to the order at school. In the Committee's words 'the State party imposed this harmful sanction on the author, not because his personal conduct created any concrete risk, but solely because of his inclusion in a broad category of persons defined by their religious conduct.'[87]

Under analogous conditions, the Strasbourg Court has reiterated its almost absolute deference to secularism in cases concerning the sensitive issue of students wearing Islamic headwear at school.[88] In the Court's decision on admissibility, the definitive expulsion of girls and boys who denied to remove their headwear was considered proportionate to the legitimate aim of protecting the public order and the rights and freedoms of others.[89] Hence, the Court found no reason to revisit its earlier case law on the matter when it was called to review the controversial French legal framework. It flows from its brief reasoning that the sole invocation of *laïcité* suffices for the Court to sacrifice the right to manifest one's religion.

[83] See *Hentrich v France*, Merits, Series A no 296-A (1994).

[84] *Bikramjit Singh v France* (2013) UN Doc CCPR/C/106/D/1852/2008.

[85] According to the ritual rules of the Sikh confession, a Sikh is not allowed to cut his hair, which is regarded as a sacred, inherent and intrinsic part of the religion, hence, the *keski* (similar to the turban, but for younger men) cannot be seen as an external religious symbol of faith but is rather intended to protect the long uncut hair of the believer.

[86] *Bikramjit Singh* (n 84) para 8.6.

[87] ibid para 8.7.

[88] See, eg *Dogru v France*, Merits, App no 27058/05 (ECtHR, 4 December 2008); *Kervanci v France*, Merits, App no 31645/04 (ECtHR, 4 December 2008).

[89] *Aktas v France* (dec), App no 43563/08 (ECtHR, 30 June 2009); *Bayrak v France* (dec), App no14308/08 (ECtHR, 30 June 2009); *Gamaleddyn v France* (dec), App no 18527/08 (ECtHR, 30 June 2009); *Ghazal v France* (dec), App no 29134/08 (ECtHR, 30 June 2009); *Mann Singh* (n 80); *Jasvir Singh* (n 80); *Ranjit Singh* (n 80).

For Stephanie Berry, what plays the most crucial role in the context of the impugned prohibitions is not the principle of the French version of state neutrality itself, but the mere fact that 'the 2004 law signalled a shift towards a hostile form of secularism that seeks to eliminate religion from the public sphere rather than upholding individual religious freedom'.[90]

At any rate, the more recent *Lachiri* judgment of the European Court of Human Rights[91] on the expulsion from courtroom of the applicant wearing the *hijab* remains in line with its prior case law on the use of religious symbols in courtrooms.[92] It further maintained that the court is not a public place compared with the street or square; yet the respect for the principle of neutrality is crucial for the impartial exercise of the judiciary in a democratic society and hence, it can prevail over the right to manifest one's beliefs as is the case of public educational establishments.[93] Notwithstanding of the fact that the Court concluded that in the mere presence of the applicant wearing in public the Islamic headgear can be considered neither disrespectful towards the judiciary nor disruptive of the proper conduct of a hearing, some of its pronouncements create severe confusion in this respect. The Court, thus, felt that it should implicitly emphasise its absolute submission to state neutrality.[94]

All that said, unlike the Strasbourg Court's approach on religious symbols in the public sphere, the Committee's understanding of religious freedom stands on the exact opposite side. It has repeatedly assessed the requirements set forth by the Court in the name of neutrality, occasionally in the exact same disputes; nevertheless, the Committee has refrained from even naming the source of inspiration of these criteria presented by the parties. In all these cases, the State Party had invoked the favourable outcome produced by the Court and the Committee seemed to have measured the arguments on the necessity of secularism. Indeed, the body opted to disregard the state's margin of appreciation in these cases and 'to interrogate the relevant issues more vigorously by displaying a fresh willingness to "stand in the shoes" of those who wish to manifest their faith through the religious attire of their choice'.[95] On the contrary, it flows from the recent case law of the Strasbourg Court that the latter remains consistent with its option of totally supporting a perception of strict secularism as an aggressive form of neutrality in the sense of complete

[90] S Berry, 'A 'Good Faith' Interpretation of the Right to Manifest Religion? The Diverging Approaches of the European Court of Human Rights and the UN Human Rights Committee' (2017) 37 *Legal Studies* 692.

[91] *Lachiri v Belgium*, Merits, App no 3413/09 (ECtHR, 18 September 2018); See also J Ringelheim, 'Lachiri v. Belgium: Headscarf Ban Imposed on a Civil Party in a Courtroom in Violation of Religious Freedom' (*Strasbourg Observers*, 23 November 2018), www.strasbourgobservers.com/2018/11/23/lachiri-v-belgium-headscarf-ban-imposed-on-a-civil-party-in-a-courtroom-in-violation-of-religious-freedom/.

[92] *Hamidović v Bosnia and Herzegovina*, Merits, App no 57792/15 (ECtHR, 5 December 2017).

[93] *Lachiri* (n 91) para 45.

[94] ibid para 46.

[95] P Cumper and T Lewis, 'Empathy and Human Rights: The Case of Religious Dress' (2018) 18 *Human Rights Law Review* 61, 63.

exclusion of religion from the public sphere, rather than neutrality perceived as a lack of coercion or absence of state preference.[96] However, reaffirming the concept of strict secularism without proposing alternatives or providing national authorities with specific standards to reconcile domestic religious tensions contradicts strikingly with the interpretation of the Convention as a 'living instrument' and can easily exacerbate these tensions. Arguably, the intensity and durability of the jurisprudential disagreement inevitably raise questions around the emerging deficit of legal certainty when it comes to the universal and indivisible application of similar fundamental rights standards. Since the dissonance between the two mechanisms often concerns the same states interfering with the freedom of religion of petitioners on the basis of the same legislation, one could argue that a more consistent approach would be proved in favour of a well-functioning human rights machinery affecting the law-making process accordingly.

B. The Dissonance Regarding Women's Reproductive Rights

Unlike religious freedom, the right to safe and legal abortion is not incorporated in mainstream human rights bills of rights.[97] Having developed an extremely nuanced case law in the field of human reproduction, the Strasbourg Court has repeatedly elucidated that a right to abortion cannot be construed as being encompassed neither in Article 2 ECHR, since it would signal a *contra legem* interpretation of the provision,[98] nor within the scope of the right to private life under Article 8 ECHR.[99] Only recently was an indicative step made which points towards the official recognition of a right to abortion since the Parliamentary Assembly of the Council of Europe adopted in 2008 a Resolution on access to safe and legal abortion in Europe.[100]

As a general rule, the Court has acknowledged a broad MoA in cases touching upon the criminalisation of abortion, so-called 'abortion tourism' and the increasing numbers of clandestine abortions, while deciding sensitive cases touching upon reproductive rights. At first,[101] there was a complete lack of consensus in this area of law; this was invoked by the Strasbourg Court as a justification for leaving

[96] J Ringelheim, 'State Religious Neutrality as a Common European Standard? Reappraising the European Court of Human Rights Approach' (2017) 6 *Oxford Journal of Law and Religion* 24, 32.

[97] Such a right is only explicitly enshrined in Art XIV of the Maputo Protocol on women's rights. Protocol to the African Charter on Human and People's Rights on the rights of women in Africa (adopted 1 July 2003, entered into force 25 November 2005).

[98] *Pretty v United Kingdom*, Merits, ECHR 2002-III 155, paras 39–40.

[99] *A, B and C v Ireland* [GC], ECHR 2010-VI 185; See also G Puppinck, 'Abortion and the European Convention on Human Rights' (2013) 3(2) *Irish Journal of Legal Studies* 142, 156–62.

[100] CoE Parliamentary Assembly, Resolution 1607(2008) on access to safe and legal abortion in Europe (16 April 2008).

[101] See A Mitra, 'We're Always Going to Argue about Abortion: International Law's Changing Attitudes towards Abortion' (2017) 1 *New Zealand Women's Law Journal* 142.

this field to the regulatory powers of the state. The general approach of the ECtHR is therefore summarised as follows: despite the domesticity of this legal field, both national and international mechanisms were – and still are – challenged to alleviate the negative repercussions for women's life and health emerging from unsafe abortions and from the criminalisation of abortion.

Testing the limits of its subsidiary character, the ECtHR managed to reconcile the right to life of the mother with the right of the unborn foetus or the rights of the partner, and prioritised the former over the latter.[102] Having recapitulated its relevant jurisprudence, the Court, in the famous *Vo v France*, maintained that 'the unborn child is not regarded as a "person" directly protected by Article 2 of the Convention and that if the unborn do have a "right" to "life", it is implicitly limited by the mother's rights and interests.'[103] The same goes for the right of the mother to decide for her own body and private life.[104]

When the lawfulness of abortion laws is under scrutiny, the diverse legal standards among State Parties have deterred the Court from pronouncing squarely on such delicate matters that fall traditionally within the sovereign powers of domestic authorities.[105] This deep-rooted reluctance of the Strasbourg Court was evinced clearly in the seminal *A, B and C v Ireland*[106] which blatantly revealed a series of controversial aspects of the Court's understanding regarding abortion-related cases.[107] The three applicants were forced to travel to the United Kingdom to get an abortion, since such an operation was illegal under Irish law. The Court found no violation of Articles 2, 8 or 14 ECHR, invoked by the applicants. It relied mostly on the democratic deliberation, and by extension, on the democratic legitimacy of the Court that preceded the adoption of the Irish law on abortions, albeit acknowledging the personal stigma and the psychological burden that the whole procedure of 'abortion tourism' entails for the applicants.

However, the focal point of the Court's judgment was the apparent lack of European consensus as regards the beginning of life[108] and the foetus's right to life, instead of taking into consideration the looming existence of consensus as regards the legal recognition of the access of the mother to a legal abortion.[109] The

[102] *Brüggemann and Scheuten v Federal Republic of Germany* (dec) (1976) 5 DR 103; *RH v Norway* (dec) (1992) 73 DR 155; *Boso v Italy* (dec) ECHR 2002-VII 451; *Tysiąc v Poland*, Merits, ECHR 2007-I 219; See *A, B and C* (n 99).

[103] *Vo v France* [GC], Merits, ECHR 2004-VII 67, para 80.

[104] See, eg *A, B and C* (n 99); *P and S v Poland*, Merits, App no 57375/08 (ECtHR, 30 October 2012).

[105] See especially C Cosentino, 'Safe and Legal Abortion: An Emerging Human Right: The Long-Lasting Dispute with Sovereignty in ECHR Jurisprudence' (2015) 15 *Human Rights Law Review* 569.

[106] *A, B and C* (n 99).

[107] E Wicks, 'A, B, C v Ireland: Abortion Law under the European Convention on Human Rights' (2011) 11 *Human Rights Law Review* 556; P Londono, 'Redrafting Abortion Rights under the Convention: A, B and C v. Ireland' in E Brems (ed), *Diversity and European Human Rights: Rewriting Judgments of the ECHR* (Cambridge, Cambridge University Press, 2012).

[108] *A, B and C* (n 99) para 237.

[109] ibid Joint Partly Dissenting Opinion of Judges Rozakis, Tulkens, Fura, Hirvela, Malinverini and Poalelung, para 2.

Court's standing was fairly criticised for not looking at the global trends settled by other international and regional human rights bodies.[110] The Court has once again opted for a pattern of 'non-interference' and only found a procedural breach of the non-implementation of the relevant legal framework. States are afforded, thus, a wide margin of appreciation in view of the lack of European consensus with regard to the highly moral and ethical questions raised.[111]

Conversely, the Committee paid particular emphasis to the detrimental results of anti-abortion legislation instead of determining whether the unborn enjoys the right to life as a subject of rights under the ICCPR. Actually, the recently adopted General Comment no 36 on the right to life (Article 6 ICCPR)[112] makes special reference to abortion.[113] Notwithstanding the critique raised with regard to the contested hesitation of the Committee to give rise to specific recommendations to State Parties, the body elucidated its standing in the *Llantoy Huamán v Peru*[114] in which it found the Peruvian state responsible for preventing a 17-year-old girl from undergoing an abortion, given the fact that she was pregnant to an anencephalic foetus (a fatal abnormality). Although Peruvian legislation provided for the possibility of lawful abortion in cases of poor maternal health, the director of the hospital feared that giving his permission for a 'therapeutic abortion' would give rise to a breach of Peruvian legislation on the matter. Since the girl was forced to give birth to her baby girl and to also breast-feed her for the four-day period of its short life, she was left in deep depression when her baby inevitably died.[115]

In casu, the HRC refrained from examining the dispute under Article 6 ICCPR on the grounds that it found a violation of the prohibition of inhuman and degrading treatment under Article 7 ICCPR. The fact that the director of the hospital and the local authorities knowingly exposed the pregnant girl to tremendous psychological suffering amounted to cruel and degrading treatment within the meaning of the aforementioned provision of the Covenant.

Although the Committee concluded to many of the breaches that the complainant alleged, namely that of the right to private life[116] and of her rights as a minor under Article 24 ICCPR, it felt profoundly unready to assess the non-discrimination dimension of the claim.[117] Mrs Llantoy Huamán stressed in her application that her different treatment in terms of reproductive rights and

[110] Cosentino, 'Safe and Legal Abortion' (n 105) 578.

[111] See also *Lambert and Others v France* [GC], Merits, ECHR 2015-III 67, para 144; *Evans v the United Kingdom* [GC], Merits, ECHR 2007-I 353, paras 54–56; *Mehmet Şentürk and Bekir Şentürk v Turkey*, Merits, ECHR 2013-II 363, paras 107–9.

[112] HRC, 'General Comment no 36: Article 6 of the International Covenant on Civil and Political Rights, on the Right to Life' (30 October 2018) UN Doc CCPR/C/GC/36.

[113] ibid para 8.

[114] *Llantoy Huamán v Peru* (2005) UN Doc CCPR/C/85/D/1153/2003.

[115] For an overview of the case see S Joseph, 'United Nations Human Rights Committee: Recent Cases' (2006) 6 *Human Rights Law Review* 361.

[116] *Llantoy Huamán* (n 114) paras 6.3–6.4.

[117] Joseph, 'United Nations Human Rights' (n 115) 362.

access to health care due to her sex and due to the well-established prejudices prevented her from the unimpeded enjoyment of her rights on an equal footing with men.[118] Nonetheless, the initially documented hesitation is clearly incompatible with the position of the Committee on the Elimination of Discrimination against Women (CEDAW), the monitoring body of the Convention on the Elimination of All Forms of Discrimination against Women.[119] The CEDAW had already declared that restrictions on abortions constitute a form of sex discrimination in its General Recommendation on Article 12[120] containing provisions for women healthcare as well as in its General Recommendation no. 19 with regard to violence against women.[121] More recently, the HRC has evolved so as to enlarge its abortion-related standards of protection including discrimination on grounds of sex on the occasion of two communications against Ireland in the *Mellet v Ireland*[122] and *Whelan v Ireland* cases.[123]

In the first of these cases, the Committee took a clear view pertaining to the Irish legal framework for abortion, which retained serious limitations. Hence, in *Mellet*, the applicant complained of being prohibited from undergoing an abortion despite the fatal abnormality of the foetus.[124] The Irish government based its reasoning on the *A,. B and C v Ireland* European Court case, and maintained that since 'Irish law permitted travel abroad for the purposes of abortion, and appropriate access to information and health care was provided, the European Court did not consider that the prohibition on abortion for reasons of health and/or well-being exceeded the margin of appreciation accorded to Member States.' The state also recalled that the ECtHR concluded to a fair balance struck by national authorities between the profound moral views of the Irish people about the nature of life as a basis for the rights of the foetus and the right to private life of the applicants.[125] Naturally, the Committee examined extensively the allegations of the claimant pursuant to Article 7 on the cruel and degrading treatment, Article 17 on the right to private and family life and Article 26 on equality before the law and prohibition of any form of discrimination.

Unlike its Strasbourg peer, the Committee took the opportunity to evince the incompatibility of Irish anti-abortion legal framework with international human rights law in and beyond circumstances of fatal foetal abnormality, and

[118] *Llantoy Huamán* (n 114) para 3.2.

[119] International Convention on the Elimination of All Forms of Discrimination Against Women (adopted 18 December 1979, entered into force 3 September 1981) 1249 UNTS 13.

[120] See CEDAW, 'General Recommendation no 24: Article 12: Women and Health' (2 February 1999) UN Doc A/54/38/Rev.1, paras 14, 31.c; See also CEDAW, *T.P.F. v Peru* (2011) UN Doc CEDAW/C/50/D/22/2009.

[121] CEDAW, 'General Recommendation no 19: Violence against Women' (29 January 1992) UN Doc A/47/38.

[122] *Amanda Jane Mellet v Ireland* (2016) UN Doc CCPR/C/116/D/2324/2013.

[123] *Siobhán Whelan v Ireland* (2017) UN Doc CCPR/C/119/D/2425/2014.

[124] See, eg F de Londras, 'Fatal Fetal Abnormality, Irish Constitutional Law, and Mellet v Ireland' (2016) 24 *Medical Law Review* 591.

[125] *Amanda Jane Mellet* (n 122) para 4.3.

to demonstrate the perennial need for a substantial constitutional reform in Ireland.[126] The Committee sought, thus, to shed light at first to the claim with regard to the cruel and degrading treatment. It emphasised the vulnerable position of the woman being aware that her pregnancy was not viable, forced to 'travel' carrying her dying unborn child without the psychological support of her family, let alone bearing the social stigma emerging from the criminalisation of abortion. On these grounds, it found the Irish state responsible for infringement of Article 7 ICCPR.[127]

As regards the right to privacy, the Committee also held that the facts *in casu* resulted in an arbitrary restriction of the author's right to private life, contrary to Article 17 ICCPR. Interestingly enough, the body went on to assess also the discrimination complaint of the author for the first time under Article 26 ICCPR. Having acknowledged that 'the State party's criminalisation of abortion subjected her to a gender-based stereotype of the reproductive role of women primarily as mothers, and that stereotyping her as a reproductive instrument subjected her to discrimination',[128] the Committee compared the situation of the claimant in the present case with similarly situated women who opt for continuing their pregnancy. It is noteworthy that some of the Committee's members have expressed their dissonance in relation with the path taken by the body in order to take the view that Article 26 of the Convention was breached. The main critique here is associated with the choice of the Committee to defend formal equality over substantial equality.[129]

In particular, for some of its members and some scholars, the Committee should have opted for comparing the unfavourable condition of pregnant women carrying a fatally ill foetus with men and not with, simply, other women, since the criminalisation imposed on a reproductive health-related option of women has no equivalent in terms of male reproduction methods and hence, results in gender-based discrimination.[130]

[126] The decisive step was taken recently following to the Irish plebiscite which took place in May 2018. Irish people were asked on the abolition of the 8th Amendment of the Constitution (Article 40.3.3) providing equal rights for the foetus's life and the pregnant woman's life. This constitutional provision, inserted in the Irish legal order after the referendum of 1983, had been enormously criticised for failing to ensure the woman's autonomy regarding reproductive rights. In the referendum held on 18 May 2018, 66.4% of the Irish electorate voted in favour of the draft legislation which purports to overturn the near-total ban on abortions.

[127] *Amanda Jane Mellet* (n 122) paras 7.4–7.6.

[128] ibid para 7.11.

[129] See also K Sękowska-Kozlowska, 'A Tough Job: Recognizing Access to Abortion as a Matter of Equality: A Commentary on the Views of the UN Human Rights Committee in the Cases of Mellet v. Ireland and Whelan v. Ireland' (2018) 26(54) *Reproductive Health Matters* 25.

[130] Yadh Ben Achour clearly stressed that the prohibition of abortion in Ireland, by its binding, indirectly punitive and stigmatising effect, targets women as such and places them in a specific situation of vulnerability, discriminatory in relation to men. On top of that, in their separate opinion (partly dissenting), Víctor Rodríguez Rescia, Olivier de Frouville and Fabian Salvioli maintained that the Committee should have given even more comprehensive responses to the discrimination questions and that the prohibition of abortion as stipulated in the Irish legal order is *per se* discriminatory since

In the same vein, similar facts led to the similar conclusions of the Committee in *Whelan v Ireland*. Its overall position on abortions[131] places in sharp relief its crystal-clear dissonance with the Court. While the latter paid particular emphasis to the blurred lines with regard to the beginning of foetal life so as to move towards a highly deferential approach of domestic limitations in terms of reproductive matters, the Committee appeared recently more determined than ever to manifest the pressing need for reading these cases from a different angle in view of a more effective protection of the women's rights. Indeed, the recent Irish plebiscite and the following reform of the contested prohibition in the country on abortions confirmed the HRC's ground-breaking pronouncements in this respect.

Divergent approaches when it comes to family planning disguise the fact that coherence with international standards can be defeated by compromise with domestic moral tensions, particularly when these tensions generate huge global debates which have not abated yet. Time and again, the Committee is called to answer such controversial questions that also trouble its European counterpart; however, it fears to respond expressly to allegations raised on the basis of the European Court's relevant case law. Even when the body opts for an enhanced level of protection that could perhaps set an example for other adjudicative mechanisms, demonising the slightest reference to other approaches fails to truly add to the self-contained character of the HRC system or to encourage further interpretative consistency. Conversely, I posit that an explicit disagreement should not be feared. Instead, it would emphasise the Committee's capacity to resolve common human rights incongruities without closing the door to a meaningful inter-judicial interaction in the foreseeable future.

C. Migration Issues before the HRC: Too Close or Too Far from Strasbourg?

Following the recent spike in migration cases brought before the Human Rights Committee, the latter is currently in the process of developing its own threshold of protection regarding the risk of migrants being subjected to torture or cruel and degrading treatment. Two classes of cases looming in this field are worthy of our attention: first, immigration detention cases, mainly against Australia, and second, expulsion and deportation cases concerning Denmark.[132]

it places the burden of criminal liability primarily on the pregnant woman. *Amanda Jane Mellet* (n 122) Partly Dissenting Opinion of Committee Members Víctor Rodríguez Rescia, Olivier de Frouville and Fabian Salvioli, para 8.

[131] See also *L.M.R. v Argentina* (2011) UN Doc CCPR/C/101/D/1608/2007.

[132] Recently, the Human Rights Committee has also pronounced on the hotly debated issue of the extraterritorial application of the duty to protect life under the Covenant in its views *A.S., D.I., O.I. and G.D. v Italy* and *A.S., D.I., O.I. and G.D. v Malta*. *A.S., D.I., O.I. and G.D. v Italy* (2021) UN Doc CCPR/C/130/D/3042/2017; *A.S., D.I., O.I. and G.D. v Malta* (2021) UN Doc CCPR/C/128/D/3043/2017.

Migrants – regular or irregular – are stuck in the middle between the state's struggle to defend its sovereign powers when regulating entry control and international human rights law bodies purporting to harmonise the applicable standards of aliens' protection. When challenging the Australian Migration Act before the HRC, the authors of the relevant complaints were often persons who had overstayed their visas or illegally entered the country. Famously, in *A v Australia*,[133] the Committee commenced formulating the necessary criteria pursuant to the proper interpretation of Article 9 ICCPR. In contravention with Article 5 ECHR, Article 9 ICCPR does not denote specifically the legitimate purposes of detention.

Australia's mandatory detention policy for unauthorised entrants was at stake, affecting also 'boat people',[134] as was the case in *A v Australia*. In practice, the Australian authorities have extensively used the measure of detention in an arbitrary and prolonged manner for all asylum-seekers arriving irregularly on the Australian shores, without offering a substantive review of their detention by any judicial forum, and without setting specific time limits to the duration of the detention.[135] The author, a Cambodian who arrived by boat in Australia without a visa, was denied asylum on the basis of the policy of the Australian government amounting to 'human deterrence', according to the allegations of the petitioner.[136]

The Committee did not oppose to the concept of immigration detention *per se*. Instead, it focused on the individual conditions of detention in the instant case and essentially, attempted to define its own understanding of the broad notion of 'arbitrariness'. Hence, having maintained that the latter 'must not be equated with 'against the law' but be interpreted more broadly to include such elements as inappropriateness and injustice',[137] it elaborated on particular factors that, if lacking, could amount to the arbitrariness of the detention. These factors are, for instance, the 'likelihood of absconding' and 'lack of cooperation'.[138] This demanding approach was also reiterated in the subsequent case law of the Committee which revolved around claims of 'boat migrants' against Australia.[139]

The added value of *C v Australia*[140] is actually the proportionality road that the Committee took, since it particularly stated that the respondent

[133] *A v Australia* (1997) CCPR/C/59/D/560/1993.

[134] Parliament of Australia, 'The Detention of Boat People' Current Issues Brief no 8 (2000–01), www.aph.gov.au/About_Parliament/Parliamentary_Departments/Parliamentary_Library/Publications_Archive/CIB/cib0001/01CIB08.

[135] See, eg C Higgins, 'The (Un-)sustainability of Australia's Offshore Processing and Settlement Policy' in V Moreno-Lax and E Papastavridis (eds), *'Boat Refugees' and Migrants at Sea: A Comprehensive Approach Integrating Maritime Security with Human Rights*, International Refugee Law Series 7 (Leiden, Brill Nijhoff, 2016) 305–6.

[136] *A v Australia* (n 133) para 3.2.

[137] *C v Australia* (2002) UN Doc CCPR/C/76/D/900/1999, para 9.2.

[138] ibid para 9.4. See also Joseph and Castan, *The International Covenant on Civil and Political Rights* (n 35) 352–54.

[139] *Shafiq v Australia* (2006) UN Doc CCPR/C/88/D/1324/2004; *Shams et al v Australia* (2007) UN Doc CCPR/C/90/D/1255,1256,1259,1260,1266,1268,1270&1288/2004.

[140] *C v Australia* (n 137).

state failed to prove the lack of less invasive measures in conformity with the domestic regulation of immigration policies (ie, reporting obligations, sureties or other conditions which would take account of the author's deteriorating condition).[141]

In sum, despite the weak non-judicial context in which the Committee operates, the latter managed to develop a 'relatively robust line of jurisprudence', in the words of Cathryn Costello.[142] Along similar lines to the Strasbourg Court as regards the lawfulness of the detention, when it comes to arbitrariness the Committee requires elements of inappropriateness, injustice and lack of predictability as well as reasonableness and necessity. Therefore, the proportionality test also applies.[143]

Crucially, the approach of the Strasbourg Court differs at some point from the HRC's perception of migrants in detention since, at the outset, the Convention has enumerated the criteria for the legitimate detention within the meaning of Article 5. The European Court thus fell short in reconciling national migration policies with the effective protection of the rights of irregular migrants in detention. The GC's well-known conclusions in *Chahal v UK*[144] in relation to prolonged detention under Article 5(1)(f) ECHR, and in *Saadi v UK*[145] on detention to prevent unauthorised entry, signalled the willingness of the latter to grant a lower level of protection pertaining to asylum and immigration which, in 'social and human terms, are the most crucial issues facing us in the years to come'.[146] Strikingly, the Court in the most recent *Rusu* case confirmed its lower standards and brought to life the *Chahal* case law, stating that the only requirement for the detention is the fact that the detention is ordered in view of the individual's deportation. Whether the impugned decision is reasonably necessary is irrelevant for the Court, whereas the due diligence requirement is present.[147] In fact, the Court felt that it should give additional attention to the potentiality of the deportation's occurrence. In this spirit, in *A v UK*[148] it decided otherwise since it concluded that the applicants were detained for being suspected terrorists, rather than in view of being deported, and clarified that a clear distinction should be drawn between the *Chahal* case and the instant case pertaining to the duration and the legality of the detention.[149]

[141] ibid para 8.2.

[142] C Costello, 'Human Rights and the Elusive Universal Subject: Immigration Detention under International Human Rights and EU Law' (2012) 19 *Indiana Journal of Global Legal Studies* 257, 273.

[143] *Samba Jalloh v Netherlands* (2002) UN Doc CCPR/C/74/D/794/1998, para 8.2.

[144] *Chahal v the United Kingdom* [GC], Merits, ECHR 1996-V.

[145] *Saadi v the United Kingdom* [GC], Merits, ECHR 2008-II 207.

[146] ibid Joint Partly Dissenting Opinion of Judges Rozakis, Tulkens, Kovler, Hajiyev, Spielmann and Hirvela.

[147] *Rusu v Austria*, Merits, App no 34082/02 (ECtHR, 2 October 2008), para 52.

[148] *A and Others v the United Kingdom* [GC], Merits, ECHR 2009-II 137.

[149] ibid para 169.

What is more, the *Saadi* standards are also 'alive and kicking', and summarised in *Suso Musa v Malta*[150] while the Strasbourg Court admitted that when the State Party has enacted legislation authorising the entry or stay of irregular migrants until their asylum application is examined, their detention might give rise to issues related to the lawfulness of the said measure.[151] It also deserves our attention that the dissenting minority in *Saadi* referred to the Committee's level of protection. Far from being an obiter dictum, the dissenters recalled that the ECHR is not applied in a vacuum and appeared open to the HRC's more protective approach towards migrants in detention as reflected in the Committee's case law. Essentially, the minority imported the position of the HRC on the concept of lawfulness as conceived in its views 'to mean that detention must not simply be lawful but must also not have been imposed on grounds of administrative expediency'. They also recalled these requirements of the Committee presented in the landmark *A v Australia* case and in *Bakhtiyari v Australia*,[152] in which (the latter) the Committee had concluded that the lack of substantive review does not meet the requirements of Article 9(4) ICCPR.

In other words, the wide perception of arbitrariness, adopted by the HRC, appears to sit comfortably with the international refugee law standards recognising the particular vulnerability that characterises migrants in an irregular situation who seek for normal and safe living conditions and for international protection. Bearing in mind that the Court has overall provided migrants and asylum-seekers with high-level protection with significant normative and practical effects,[153] taking the proportionality road in relation to the detention of migrants and endorsing specific derogations would add to the legal certainty and the consolidation of its methodology.[154] Probably, the Court is afraid of being a real trailblazer in this special category of migration/asylum cases due to the different amount of sensitivity among European states as regards immigration detention. Indeed, during recent decades, European states have extensively anchored their hard-line migration policies to the combat of terrorism. Perhaps the stringent position of some of the State Parties to the Convention led the Court to incorporate this *laissez-faire* standing, granting lower standards of protection and a certain degree of margin of appreciation, without, however, denoting it as such.

With regard to expulsion/deportation cases, the Committee has inevitably turned to the nuanced jurisprudence of the ECtHR, albeit implicitly. In a number of cases raised against Denmark, the jurisprudential trends of the Committee have

[150] *Suso Musa v Malta*, Merits, App no 42337/12 (ECtHR, 23 July 2013), para 90.

[151] ibid para 97; *O.M. v Hungary*, Merits, App no 9912/15 (ECtHR, 5 July 2016), para 47.

[152] *Bakhtiyari v Australia* (2003) UN Doc CCPR/C/79/D/1069/2002. See also *Baban v Australia* (2003) UN Doc CCPR/C/78/D/1014/2001.

[153] At this point, it is deemed necessary to recall the immediate repercussions that the bold pronouncements of the Strasbourg Court in the *M.S.S.* case had on the matter of Dublin transfers and the revision of the entire system in the light of the pioneer jurisprudence of the European Court. See *M.S.S. v Belgium and Greece* [GC], Merits, ECHR 2011-I 121.

[154] Costello, 'Human Rights and the Elusive Universal Subject' (n 142) 288.

been fleshed out drawing from the Strasbourg Court's long experience in the field. Nevertheless, the UN body still disagrees on the quality features of the human rights standards awarded to migrants or asylum-seekers.

In recent years, a whole new compendium of cases was brought before the Committee touching the pressing issues of the enormous influx of migration flows reaching the European shores. The Committee was confronted with the same challenges as the Court and thus, implicitly imported many of its values. Hence, in cases concerning deportations to a 'safe country' the Committee was called to delimit the protection afforded to aliens facing deportation who claim to face the risk of cruel, inhuman or degrading treatment within the meaning of Article 7 ICCPR.[155] Notably, both the parties have consistently invoked the same cases, used as the major argumentative tools to convince the Committee to respond accordingly. Hence, a great number of cases in which authors have sought to challenge deportation to Italy have invoked the Strasbourg Court's seminal pronouncements in *M.S.S. v Greece and Belgium*[156] and the more recent *Tarakhel v Switzerland*[157] in which the ECtHR treated in depth the constituent elements of the Italian asylum system.

Ever since the seminal *Jasin v Denmark* case[158] the Committee has replied in an almost automatic manner to the repeated argumentation of the disputants. *In casu*, a Somali national who was about to be returned to Italy relied heavily upon her vulnerable position of being a homeless single mother of three children seeking asylum, and upon her past experience in Italy. During that time, she argued that while she was granted subsidiary protection she was forced to leave the reception centre. She had remained homeless with no access to medical or social care and no funds to renew her residence permit while pregnant. Later on, she moved to Denmark and applied for asylum, but her application was rejected and she faced deportation to Italy. The author claimed that her return to that country would amount to a breach of Article 7 ICCPR, due to systemic failures of the Italian asylum system in the sense of the aforementioned jurisprudence of the Strasbourg Court. The Danish government referred to *Samsam Mohammad Hussein and Others v the Netherlands and Italy*[159] and argued with regard to the shortcomings of the Italian asylum system that 'it has not been shown to disclose a systemic failure to provide support or facilities catering for asylum seekers as members of a particularly vulnerable group of people, as was the case in *M.S.S. v Belgium and Greece*'.[160]

[155] HRC, 'General Comment no 31' (n 42).
[156] *M.S.S.* (n 153).
[157] *Tarakhel v Switzerland* [GC], Merits, ECHR 2004-VI 159.
[158] *Warda Osman Jasin et al v Denmark* (2015) UN Doc CCPR/C/114/D/2360/2014.
[159] In this case, the author also invoked *Mohammad Hussein and Others v the Netherlands and Italy* (dec), App no 27725/10 (ECtHR, 2 April 2013).
[160] ibid para 78.

In the subsequent *Tarakhel* judgment[161] the Court of Strasbourg had reiterated the distinction which needs to be drawn between the absolute deterioration of the Greek asylum procedures (*M.S.S.*) and the Italian asylum system (*Tarakhel*). However, it was the individual vulnerable position of the applicants (family with six children) and the living conditions in the Italian detention centre that mattered significantly in the instant case. The Committee agreed with the *Tarakhel* standards without, however, saying so, and emphasised that states must exercise an individual assessment of the risk[162] that the applicant is personally facing if deported to Italy, rather than examining the overall situation of the asylum system.

Although having imported some of the most crucial findings of the Strasbourg case law, the Committee's attitude remains noteworthy. It opted to refer only to the state's invocation of the Strasbourg Court's jurisprudence, and not to the convergent jurisprudence of its counterpart, also extensively invoked by the author and equally adopted by the body itself. In other words, the Committee only cites the part of Court's case law that is actually rejected, whereas it refuses to openly refer to the part of its case law underpinning the Committee's reasoning. The same arguments with the same wording were presented before the latter in a number of similar cases in which the Committee routinely reaffirmed its standards adopting also the same language.[163]

In fact, we can also trace some signs of interplay between the two mechanisms in several expulsion cases examined by the Committee revolving mostly around the proper implementation of Article 7 ICCPR.[164] Applicants who fear that expulsion would expose them to ill-treatment have often relied on the ECtHR jurisprudence to receive protection from its UN sibling institution. For instance, in *Pillai v Canada*[165] the conclusions of the latter appear to have resulted from the extensive invocation of the Strasbourg Court's abundant case law on the matter, also used by the petitioner in the present case.

[161] *Tarakhel* (n 157) para 122.

[162] The Committee recently applied the individual risk assessment test in a case against New Zealand with regard to the deportation of climate migrants. The overall findings in this decision, published in January 2020, is expected to constitute a pilot decision given the increasing number of migration flows caused by climate change. See *Ioane Teitiota v New Zealand* (2020) UN Doc CCPR/C/127/D/2728/2016; G Reeh, 'Climate Change in the Human Rights Committee' (*EJIL:Talk!*, 18 February 2020), www.ejiltalk.org/climate-change-in-the-human-rights-committee/.

[163] *Abdilafir Abubakar v Denmark* (2016) UN Doc CCPR/C/116/D/2409/2014; *Obah Hussein Ahmed v Denmark* (2016) UN Doc CCPR/C/117/D/2379/2014; *R.A.A. and Z.M. v Denmark* (2016) UN Doc CCPR/C/118/D/2608/2015; *Raziyeh Rezaifar v Denmark* (2017) UN Doc CCPR/C/119/D/2512/2014; *R.I.H. and S.M.D. v Denmark* (2017) UN Doc CCPR/C/120/D/2640/2015; *Y.A.A. and F.H.M. v Denmark* (2017) UN Doc CCPR/C/119/D/2681/2015; *M.P. v Denmark* (2017) UN Doc CCPR/C/121/D/2643/2015.

[164] See E Guild, 'To Protect or to Forget? The Human Right to Leave a Country' (*EU Immigration and Asylum Law*, 27 December 2017), www.eumigrationlawblog.eu/to-protect-or-to-forget-the-human-right-to-leave-a-country/.

[165] *Ernest Sigman Pillai* (n 45). See the Concurring Opinion of Committee Members Ms Helen Keller, Ms Iulia Antoanella Motoc, Mr Gerald L Neuman, Mr Michael O'Flahertyn and Sir Nigel Rodley.

In addition, as was the case of the *Soering* death row jurisprudence, which played a central role in the relevant jurisprudence of the Committee,[166] its conclusions were equally applied in extradition cases in an implicit manner.[167] Time and time again, the practice of the Court has sparked the attention of the UN body; however, the latter did not feel that its source of inspiration deserved an explicit reference.

Antoine Buyse commented on the impact of the use of external citations to the rise of a body's persuasiveness and quality of the case law and stressed that 'openly acknowledging existing external jurisprudence contributes to more nuanced and refined discussions and allows for new points of view, even if these are not automatically incorporated.'[168] As the previous analysis has evinced, this happens to be systematically avoided by the HRC[169] even in disputes in which the parties have solely based their argumentation on the reasoning of the Court in similar cases. Instead, the Committee prefers internal references in an attempt to fortify its own interpretative tools, even when these clearly mirror the Strasbourg Court's findings. At any rate, reading between the lines of the Committee's views and of the opinions of its distinguished Members proves that the Court's norms still provide a solid foundation for the dynamic interpretation of the Covenant.

[166] In *Kindler v Canada*, the Committee respectfully took into consideration the Strasbourg's criteria to examine whether the situation of the applicant being in a death row situation for years amounts to ill-treatment. Conversely, starting from the *Kindler* case, the Committee repeatedly found itself on the opposite side as it concluded that long periods in death row do not necessarily violate the Covenant, unless 'compelling circumstances' or psychological aspects dictate another approach, as highlighted in *Clement Francis v Jamaica*. The issue was also reconsidered by the UN body on the occasion of the *Oçalan* case law of the ECtHR. In the *Larrañaga* decision with regard to the death penalty after an unfair judicial procedure, the HRC has ostensibly imported the Strasbourg Court's standards of protection and concluded to a violation of Art 7 ICCPR, citing the judgment of the Grand Chamber. See *Soering v the United Kingdom*, Merits, Series A no 161 (1989); *Joseph Kindler v Canada* (1993) UN Doc CCPR/C/48/D/470/1991, para 15; *George Graham and Arthur Morrison v Jamaica* (1994) UN Doc CCPR/C/52/D/461/1991, para 10.3; *Clement Francis v Jamaica* (1995) UN Doc CCPR/C/54/D/606/1994; *Larrañaga* (n 4) see also *Munguwambuto Kabwe Peter Mwamba v Zambia* (2010) UN Doc CCPR/C/98/D/1520/2006, para 6.8;

[167] See the *Kindler* decision of the HRC which for the first time connected the principle of non-refoulement with the individual's risk of being subjected to cruel, inhuman or degrading treatment to Art 7 ICCPR; *Joseph Kindler* (n 166); *Chitat Ng v Canada* (1994) UN Doc CCPR/C/49/D/469/1991; *A.R.J. v Australia* (1997) UN Doc CCPR/C/60/D/692/1996; *Mohammed Alzery v Sweden* (2006) UN Doc CCPR/C/88/D/1416/2005. The latter also echoes the Strasbourg Court's standing as formulated in the *Chahal* jurisprudence in relation to the quality of assurances. See also the Joint Concurring opinion of Committee members Gerald L Neuman and Yuji Iwasawa in *B.L. v Australia* (2015) UN Doc CCPR/C/112/D/2053/2011.

[168] See A Buyse, 'Echoes of Strasbourg in Geneva: The Influence of ECHR Anti-Torture Jurisprudence on the United Nations Human Rights Committee' (2016) 59 *Japanese Yearbook of International Law* 81, 98.

[169] Indicative of the unwelcoming position of some of the Committee members towards the invocation of the European human rights standards of protection is the fact that, in his individual opinion in *Larrañaga* Committee Member Mr Nisuke Ando found regrettable the explicit reference to the Strasbourg Court's case law. See *Larrañaga* (n 4); also *S.F. v Denmark* (2019) UN Doc CCPR/C/125/D/2494/2014.

IV. Conclusion

Starting its challenging work during the Cold War, the HRC has been consistently revealed as a universally accepted forum of utmost importance in the realm of human rights adjudication. As the most experienced monitoring body at the UN level, it has managed to give extremely proactive and comprehensive responses to several topics related to the causes of deeply installed impunity and injustice in many corners of the world. Crucially, the Committee's pronouncements are of major significance, particularly for individuals living in countries not belonging to a regional system of protection of human rights, for instance Asian countries or Australia and New Zealand.

However, the well-known weakness of Geneva's non-binding views coupled with the lack of an enforcement mechanism have normally exacerbated the openness of the body to external sources of international human rights law. Yet, the HRC sometimes seems to be forced by the parties to be in a relationship with Strasbourg which has to be avoided at any cost in order to preserve its persuasiveness and the stand-alone nature of the Covenant's guarantees. In the vast majority of cases, despite the numerous references of the disputants to analogous cases decided by its European counterpart, the HRC scarcely cites the relevant case law. Without acknowledging its influence, the ECtHR's case law is still present in Geneva as reflected by the comparable style of reasoning and the concurring and dissenting opinions of distinguished Members of the Committee.[170] Notwithstanding the adverse findings in many fields of law, we can argue that the HRC has taken into account the ECtHR's practice and safeguards as developed throughout its rich jurisprudence. While it remains unknown whether explicit citing of the ECtHR's jurisprudence would serve as an effective tool by which the Committee could foster its credibility both inside and outside Europe, in practice, the transition from an on-purpose concealed conversation to an open and balanced dialogue would be proved a rather win-win solution, with manifold results. At the global level, it would enhance legal certainty in international human rights law, while at the regional level, it could put additional pressure on European states to reach the highest attainable level of human rights enforcement, and stimulate states with no regional human rights umbrella to do so.

[170] See the concurring opinion of the Committee Member Sarah Cleveland citing the ECtHR case law in relation to the rights of same-sex couples in the key judgment *C v Australia*. See also the dissenting opinion of Ruth Wedgwood in *Dauphin v Canada* in which she admits that the Convention constitutes a source of inspiration. See *C v Australia* (2017) UN Doc CCPR/C/119/D/2216/2012; *Dauphin* (n 48). However, in 2019, the Committee pronounced for the first time on the impact of environmental pollution on the enjoyment of human rights in *Portillo Cáceres v Paraguay* and considered the case law of the ECtHR – and the recent findings of the IACtHR – on the matter which is cited in the footnotes of its views. The latest attitude of the Committee echoes a more collaborationist standing as regards the external norms-related dilemma especially while the HRC is navigating uncharted legal territory. *Portillo Cáceres v Paraguay* (2019) UN Doc CCPR/C/126/D/2751/2016.

5

Concluding Remarks

The remit of international human rights protection is inevitably fragmented. A plethora of regional and supranational regimes of human rights adjudication containing normative analogies coexist often in the same region, feeding into the well-established debate between fragmentation and unity[1] in international law. The regionalisation of human rights protection as well as the proliferation of global quasi-judicial regimes with general or specialised mandates led unavoidably to the issuance of multiple decisions on the same or similar disputes that had already arisen between the Strasbourg and the Luxembourg Courts, or the Strasbourg Court and the HRC. Due to the willingness of each system to entrench its autonomy and self-contained character, this dynamic jurisprudence encouraged, in several instances, divergent interpretations of the same human rights values, highlighting the diversified needs of humans and peoples within the confines of diversified regional contexts.

The perils that fragmentation poses to the unity of the international legal order – which might be wished to function in a unified form of serene consistency as regards the application of general principles of public international law and interpretative methods of similar normative rules – have been intensely expressed by ICJ judges and within academic circles.[2] The ideal of universality gains paramount importance when it comes to international human rights protection since the structural construction of human rights system is anchored to the values and principles endorsed in the provisions of the UDHR. It is also to be kept in mind that none of the existing regional or global systems is a self-sufficient system,[3]

[1] Study Group of the ILC, 'Report on the Fragmentation of International Law: Difficulties Arising from the Diversification and Expansion of International Law' (13 April 2006) UN Doc A/CN.4/L.682; Study Group of the ILC, 'Draft conclusion of the work of the Study Group '(2 May 2006) UN Doc A/CN.4/L.682/Add.1; Study Group of the ILC, 'Report on the Fragmentation of International Law: Difficulties Arising from the Diversification and Expansion of International Law' (18 July 2006) UN Doc A/CN.4/L.702; PM Dupuy, 'A Doctrinal Debate in the Globalisation Era: On the "Fragmentation" of International Law' (2007) 1 *European Journal of Legal Studies* 25.

[2] T Buergenthal, 'Proliferation of International Courts and Tribunals: Is it Good or Bad?' (2001) 14 *Leiden Journal of International Law* 267.

[3] M Ajevski, 'Fragmentation in International Human Rights Law: Beyond Conflict of Laws' (2014) 32 *Nordic Journal of Human Rights* 87, 88; AA Cançado Trindade, 'The European Convention on Human Rights and General International Law: Concluding Reflections on the 2015 Strasbourg Conference' in A van Aaken and I Motoc (eds), *The European Convention on Human Rights and General International Law* (Oxford, Oxford University Press, 2018) 303.

since they all bear witness to their intimate connection not only with general international law[4] but also amongst each other. Hence, somehow the conceptual universality perceived as the *raison d'être* of human rights legal discourse is indicative of the fact that consistency in terms of normative and jurisprudential unity can hardly be accomplished.

The present monograph, thus, comes in support of the argument built upon the falseness of this dilemma.[5] Besides the great expectations revolving around the vague concept of the unity of international legal order which seemed to be jeopardised *in abstracto* by the ever-evolving fragmentation,[6] the risks can apparently be mitigated by other coexisting trends of international law. Judicial dialogue, in the sense of engaging with other courts' pronouncements or influencing other mechanisms can serve as an arsenal apt to empower the enrichment of traditional international law, offering new means of interpretation when common normative rules are on the table.[7]

This inter-regional judicial interaction lies thus on the flipside of the negative aspects of fragmentation in international human rights law. Therefore, putting the legal practice of the Strasbourg architecture at the centre of this research, this book has attempted to shed light on the extent to which the judicial (or quasi-judicial) institutions taking part in human rights adjudication have borrowed from the ECHR system and in particular, to discuss how the ECHR and its supervisory organ, the ECtHR, has provided a robust case law which is 'exported' to other legal orders in terms of cross-references, methodology and outcomes. At first, outlining the progressive work of the Luxembourg Court in the human rights area, the emphasis was put on the manner with which the latter makes recourse to the Convention's provisions or ECtHR's jurisprudence, either in a direct or an indirect manner. Secondly, the following chapter explored the branches of the EU law in which the CJEU used the Strasbourg Court's argumentation to revisit EU legislation touching upon human rights issues. Throughout this analysis, the overall complex relationship with both antagonistic and sympathetic features was the

[4] See L Caflisch, 'L'application du droit international général par la Cour européenne des droits de l'homme' in I Buffard, J Crawford, A Pellet and S Wittich (eds), *International Law between Universalism and Fragmentation: Festschrift in Honour of Gerhard Hafner* (Leiden, Martinus Nijhoff, 2008); See also for instance how the Strasbourg judges talk with the UN Security Council in LA Sicilianos, 'The UN Security Council, State Responsibility and The European Court of Human Rights: Towards an Integrated Approach?' in A van Aaken and I Motoc (eds), *The European Convention on Human Rights and General International Law* (Oxford, Oxford University Press, 2018).

[5] Anne Peters in her article on fragmentation emphatically observed that it is about time that we put aside the 'f' word. A Peters, 'The Refinement of International Law: From Fragmentation to Regime Interaction and Politicization' (2017) 15 *International Journal of Constitutional Law* 671.

[6] M Koskenniemi and P Leino, 'Fragmentation of International Law? Postmodern Anxieties' (2002) 15 *Leiden Journal of International Law* 553, 574–75.

[7] See A Tzanakopoulos, 'Judicial Dialogue as a Means of Interpretation' in HP Aust and G Nolt (eds), *The Interpretation of International Law by Domestic Courts: Uniformity, Diversity, Convergence* (Oxford, Oxford University Press, 2016).

key factor in this first part. Opinion 2/13 and the entire conversation that was fuelled pertaining to the future coexistence of the two institutions, coupled with the fortified role of the Charter within the EU human rights law, reshaped the interplay between the CJEU and the ECtHR. The hegemonic tendency of the CJEU prevailed in their relationship for quite some time, since in its Opinion it was felt that it should strongly defend its own normative and interpretative tools with which it is endowed, notably after the adoption of the Lisbon Treaty. Despite the heavy shadow of the 'endangered' EU supremacy that has led the CJEU to restrict itself when citing the ECHR, a more attentive look to the Luxembourg Court's case law reveals that the Strasbourg Court still has a strong say with regard to the proper realisation of human rights within the EU limits.

Hence, legal fields initially untouched by the CJEU that raise contemporary human rights concerns (ie, data protection) or areas of law giving rise to litigation under pressing conditions (ie, migration/asylum cases) are among the areas where the CJEU leveraged extensively the Strasbourg Court's guidance. The more the human rights adjudication gained ground within the EU judicial practice, the more the CJEU was confronted with the perennial need to reconcile the fundamental freedoms and common internal values serving for decades as cornerstones of the EU market and political integration with fundamental rights. Recently, the CJEU has revisited some of the thorny issues related to the autonomy of EU law, also underlined in the famous Opinion 2/13. Hence, the controversial 'mutual trust' concept in the AFSJ is better identified through the latest jurisprudential developments of the Luxembourg Court[8] in cases related to the *ne bis in idem* principle, the EAW mechanism and the Dublin system. Departing from several judgments manifesting the autonomy and supremacy of European legal order[9] when EU values are clashing with human rights under the CFR and the ECHR, the Court lately opted to cautiously step back from its rigorous perception of mutual trust when it comes to the protection of absolute rights. Lately, the ECtHR confirmed its trust in the EU system applying the 'equivalent protection' doctrine in *Bivolaru*, demonstrating that its ex post review of respect for human rights is very much needed for the effective observance of human rights in Europe.[10] In any case, the CJEU's tendency to reconcile with its Strasbourg counterpart was

[8] See, eg K Lenaerts, 'La vie apres l'avis: Exploring the Principle of Mutual (yet not blind) Trust' (2017) 54 *CML Rev* 805; S Prechal, 'Mutual Trust Before the Court of Justice of the European Union' (2017) 2 *European Papers* 75; J Cortes-Martin, 'The Long Road to Strasbourg: The Apparent Controversy Surrounding the Principle of Mutual Trust' (2018) 11 *Review of European Administrative Law* 5; See also E Gill-Pedro and X Groussot, 'The Duty of Mutual Trust in EU Law and the Duty to Secure Human Rights: Can the EU's Accession to the ECHR Ease the Tension?' (2017) 35 *Nordic Journal of Human Rights* 258.

[9] See, eg Case C-399/11 *Stefano Melloni v Ministerio Fiscal* [2013] ECLI:EU:C:2013:107; C-411/10 and C-493/10 *N. S. v Secretary of State for the Home Department and M. E. and Others v Refugee Applications Commissioner and Minister for Justice, Equality and Law Reform* [2011] ECR I-13905; Case C-394/12 *Shamso Abdullahi v Bundesasylamt* [2013] ECLI:EU:C:2013:813.

[10] For further analysis see Part I, Chapter 2 section IIIA.

also reaffirmed by President Lenaerts (CJEU) and former President Spielmann (ECtHR)[11] and can be also explained by the fact that discussions on the EU's accession to the ECHR have recommenced. This option is also embedded in the recent Copenhagen Declaration of the CoE.[12]

However, this *rapprochement* could be also conceived as a proof that the accession is no longer needed, and the requisite equilibrium is to be achieved one way or another and in any shape or form.[13] At any rate, it follows from the research at hand that, post-Lisbon, the ECtHR still provides its Luxembourg peer with useful insights and an interpretative toolkit, particularly when the latter enters uncharted territories.[14] Yet, the fact that Article 52(3) CFR establishing the ECHR as the minimum protection is, in effect, difficult to enforce coupled with the absence of this test from the judicial discourse of the CJEU, inconsistencies and discrepancies flowing from the unidentified coexistence between the two instruments inescapably remain.

The above conclusions as well as the closer nexus between the two systems that seems to be targeted *de nouveau* point towards the 'reactivation' of Article 6(2)TEU in the foreseeable future. It readily appears from the CJEU case law that accession might no longer be feared in Luxembourg or in Brussels, and the renegotiation of the accession project on a new basis is on the table. In the same vein, the ECtHR is more and more asked to rule upon human rights claims related to the enforcement of EU law. Given the state-like structure and legal philosophy of the CJEU which aims to preserve its constitutional features, as crystalised in Opinion 2/13,[15] the question remains: if the EU becomes a Contracting Party to the ECHR, is it possible for the findings of the CJEU to be excluded from the external control of Strasbourg, already operated when national acts in the context of EU

[11] K Lenaerts, 'The ECHR and the CJEU: Creating Synergies in the Field of Fundamental Rights Protection' (speech in the context of the solemn hearing at the ECtHR for the opening of the Judicial Year, 26 January 2018), www.echr.coe.int/Documents/Speech_20180126_Lenaerts_JY_ENG.pdf. See also D Spielmann, 'The Judicial Dialogue between the European Court of Justice and the European Court of Human Rights or How to Remain Good Neighbours after the Opinion 2/13' (lecture organised by FRAME and the Leuven Centre for Global Governance Studies, 27 March 2017), www.fp7-frame.eu/wp-content/uploads/2017/03/ECHRCJUEdialog.BRUSSELS.final_.pdf.

[12] CoE, Copenhagen Declaration on the reform of the European Convention on Human Rights system (13 April 2018).

[13] J Callewaert, 'Do we Still Need Article 6(2) TEU?' Considerations on the Absence of EU Accession to the ECHR and its Consequences' (2018) 55 *CML Rev* 1685.

[14] See, for instance, the *Al Chodor* case in which the CJEU relied upon the Strasbourg Court's definition of 'a significant risk of absconding' which 'if ill-defined' offers ground for unlawful detention of asylum seekers. Case C-528/15 *Policie ČR, Krajské ředitelství policie Ústeckého kraje, odbor cizinecké policie v Salah Al Chodor and Others* [2017] ECLI:EU:C:2017:213. See also the *Bougnaoui and ADDH* case on religious freedom, a new field for the EU judges. The Court based its reasoning on the well-established case law of the ECtHR and assessed that the notion of 'religion' should be perceived as including both the *forum internum* (religious belief) and the *forum externum* (manifestation of religious beliefs). Case C-188/15 *Asma Bougnaoui and Association de défense des droits de l'homme (ADDH) v Micropole SA* [2017] ECLI:EU:C:2017:204, para 30. E Bribosia and I Rorive, 'Affaires Achbita et Bougnaoui: entre neutralité et préjugés' (2017) 112 *Revue trimestrielle des droits de l' homme* 1017.

[15] J Lindeboom, 'Why EU Law Claims Supremacy' (2018) 38 *Oxford Journal of Legal Studies* 328, 356.

law are challenged for conformity with human rights obligations?[16] At the end of the day, the entire accession project was initiated so that consistency and coherence could be achieved in human rights adjudication in Europe and the necessary guidance to be offered to national judiciaries, which often strive to find the right applicable standards of protection within the context of a multi-layered model of protection with no formal hierarchy between its components. Therefore, if the original aim is to be pursued, due consideration should be given to the uniqueness of the EU legal order and its own human rights arsenal. This book takes the view that such an ambitious objective could actually add to the on-going struggle to preserve the universality and, in more practical terms, the coherent understanding of fundamental rights within the fragmented European protection of human rights.

In the second part of this book, the main objective was to discuss the echo of the ECtHR outside Europe. Unlike Europe, assessing the influence of the ECHR system to the international legal order, a distinction was drawn between the regional human rights Courts, with specific consideration to the IACtHR and the UN Human Rights Committee, while useful analogies to the case law of the African Court or the UN treaty bodies were also drawn whenever significant points of convergence or divergence with ECHR law are documented.

Initially, the echo of the Strasbourg system was evaluated in-depth through the prism of the progressive jurisprudence of the IACtHR, which operates in a continent where an international Court is forced to navigate through turbulent waters. In its attempt to entrench the democratic rule of law and to tackle the atrocities that traumatised the Americas for decades, the IACtHR relied heavily on the modus operandi of the Strasbourg Court. The analysis was thus twofold: first, it was concentrated on the examination of the areas of law in which the Latin American Court endorsed Strasbourg's norms of protection either following an analogous pattern or a different path of work. Despite the political backlash with which the Court is confronted, the latter has also accomplished a remarkable expansion of the level of protection borrowed by the Strasbourg Court. Second, the focus was thus put on the legal areas where the Inter-American Court has broken new ground to address the particular human rights challenges of the region.

At this point, the research was conferred with comparative characteristics when similar progress has not been documented across the Atlantic and it also aimed to trace signs of cross-fertilisation between the two judicial fora when such types of disputes have been also challenged before the ECtHR.

At the outset, two main external factors have encouraged and essentially, shaped the progressive jurisprudence of the Court: first, the deep-rooted impunity for the brutal human rights violations and the overall political landscape of domestic resistance to the Court's decisions. The IACtHR, thus, developed its *pro homine* principle, prioritising the most favourable interpretation for the victims

[16] Callewaert, 'Do we Still Need Article 6(2) TEU? (n 13) 1713–14.

using external legal sources varying from principles or concepts of general international law to regional soft law instruments. In stark contrast with its openness to other legal orders outside Latin America, the IACtHR was found in the middle of a storm of criticism pertaining to its reluctance to engage in a fruitful dialogue with domestic judiciaries in the region. Naturally, the long totalitarian past of most of the State Parties discouraged the San José Court from affording significant margin of manoeuvre to national jurisdictions to make the right assessment in human rights disputes. In addition, the newly institutionalised 'conventionality control', which orders national judges to review *ex officio* the compatibility of domestic provisions with the Convention, reaffirms the reserved standing of the Court.

It also goes without saying that the judicialisation of politics[17] in Latin America is one of the specificities of the region. Thus, the unimpeded function of the Court was rendered a difficult task of utmost importance in order to provide the credentials of a more harmonious process of democratisation in domestic settings. However, diversity in the legal treatment of human rights in some of the nascent Latin-American democracies dictates a rather modified approach by the Inter-American Court.

In a nutshell, in the new political environment, the Court may benefit from affording greater trust to – at least some – domestic tribunals to make the correct assessment in order to enhance their legitimacy and, by extension, the credibility of the IACtHR itself. Irrespective of the fact that the Court has its reasons to step cautiously into this field, a prudent incorporation of the MoA concept could incentivise states to enforce democratic deliberation and guarantee judicial independence, with the aim of enjoying a wider margin of manoeuvre.[18] By the same token, the reconceptualisation of the conventionality control in the sense of an inter-judicial dialogue between equals, allowing the Court to also count on domestic stakeholders for supporting a new era of human rights adjudication, might be actually a win-win solution.

Being an international tribunal whose case law takes into serious consideration the unique features of the system, the IACtHR needs the support of Latin American states to foster the rule of law over time. Besides dealing with gross human rights violations still going on in Latin America, the IACtHR is increasingly verging into new legal territories, such as gender equality, asylum and environmental protection; this shift also encourages the endorsement of more flexible standards in the case law of the Court, drawing influence from the law-making trends of its sibling institution in Europe. Along this process, the Strasbourg Court remains the

[17] See especially R Hirschl, 'The Judicialization of Politics' in G Caldeira, D Kelemen and K Whittington (eds), *The Oxford Handbook of Law and Politics* (Oxford, Oxford University Press, 2008); For Latin America see J Couso, 'The Transformation of Constitutional Discourse and the Judicialization of Politics in Latin America' in J Couso, A Huneeus and R Sieder (eds), *Cultures of Legality: Judicialization and Political Activism in Contemporary Latin America* (Cambridge, Cambridge University Press, 2010).

[18] A Follesdal, 'Exporting the Margin of Appreciation: Lessons for the Inter-American Court of Human Rights' (2017) 15 *International Journal of Constitutional Law* 359, 371.

main source of inspiration, since the IACtHR has never stopped referring to the ECtHR in the context of both its consultative and contentious jurisdiction, albeit not always consistently. By and large, the ECHR architecture offered to the Latin American system not only the paradigm but also the necessary normative and jurisprudential tools to expand its own mandate accordingly.

Ultimately, sight could not be lost of the intangible inspiration that the Strasbourg Court offered to the UN subsystems, the treaty bodies scrutinising the enforcement of their respected conventions. At the UN level, the principal analogy to the ECHR system can be drawn from the ICCPR and the body that monitors its observance in domestic settings, namely the HRC. Putting the latter mechanism into perspective, the attentive analysis of the Committee's views highlighted the blatant absence of explicit reference to the ECtHR's norms, notwithstanding the routinely repeated invocation of its jurisprudence by the disputants, both the states and the authors. Motivated by its endeavour to forge the legitimacy of its non-binding judicial production *vis-à-vis* the Parties to the Covenant, the HRC opted for taking not the same but a parallel path to the one leading to Strasbourg. As a general rule, the Committee tends to systematically overturn procedural obstacle that may impede it from pronouncing on the same matter already being judged elsewhere when it comes to disputes already been presented before the ECtHR. Along the same line, when states seek, in substance, a certain degree of discretion, the HRC appears to prefer the more stringent Inter-American understanding of the concept rather than the integrated approach of the Strasbourg Court.

Delving into the specific legal fields being adjudicated by both fora in the final chapter, conflicting approaches of human rights questions related to religious freedom, women's reproductive rights and migration policies could have not been circumvented. Nevertheless, even within the overall context of the Committee's distinct interpretative rationale, the Strasbourg Court's level of protection remains, on many occasions, the implicit point of departure. The tacit endorsement of Strasbourg norms that the HRC has so far exercised hinders the development of an extended ambit of several human rights provisions influencing, therefore, their consistent observance across the Atlantic and the legitimisation of their universal interpretation.

To conclude, the non-existence of a formal link between the ECHR and other regional or universal human rights instruments has increasingly invigorated their informal dialogue. Notwithstanding the resistance still expressed by certain systems and the divergent interpretations that inevitably occur, the paradigm of ECHR norms proves that these are, nonetheless, greatly exported to other legal systems. These systems are, hence, encouraged to increasingly endorse normative developments from outside their legal backdrop. To do so, they may tacitly take into account external norms, use them as a justification of revisiting their own rules, or even restrict them. This court-to-court conversation does not necessarily undermine the strengths of their respective systems. Conversely, should we perceive judicial dialogue not as a form of mutual and unconscious transplant of every parallel approach but as a type of collaborative engagement in a fertile exchange of legal experiences, the overall impact on human rights adjudication would be significant. As it flows from the above analysis even competitive or isolationist tendencies, expressed by some of them, may partially yield to the general interest of a more effective observance of human rights, crucially, whenever these tendencies are lacking a compelling justification. One could infer that this premise also confirms the ever-evolving idiosyncrasy of human rights instruments as living instruments constantly reinventing themselves to keep up with the multifaceted exigencies of contemporary human rights challenges.

In a world marked by rapid changes, diversity in international human rights law discourse should not be feared as emasculating the ideal of universality of human rights. Instead, it goes hand in hand with the idea of complementarity of human rights systems.[19] Thus, the judicial dialogue will not cease to flourish within this mosaic of different human rights fora, in any shape or form, both antagonistic or sympathetic, explicit or implicit, consolidating the normative force of the ECHR worldwide and its luminous interpretation by the Strasbourg Court.

[19] See inter alia with regard to the complementarity argument, J Callewaert, 'The European arrest warrant under the European Convention on Human Rights: A matter of Cooperation, Trust, Complementarity, Autonomy and Responsibility' (2021) *ZEuS-Sonderband* 105, 109

BIBLIOGRAPHY

Aaken, A van, Motoc, I and Vasel, JJ, 'Introduction: The European Convention on Human Rights and General International Law' in A van Aaken and I Motoc (eds), *The European Convention on Human Rights and General International law* (Oxford, Oxford University Press, 2018) 1–20

Ackermann, T, 'Case C-36/02, *Omega Spielhallen- und Automatenaufstellungs-GmbH v. Oberbürgermeisterin der Bundesstadt Bonn*' (2005) 42 *Common Market Law Review* 1107

AFR Cardoso Squeff, T de, and Almeida Rosa, M de, 'Jus Cogens: An European Concept?: An Emancipatory Conceptual Review from the Inter-American System of Human Rights' (2018) 15 *Revista de Direito Internacional* 123

Ajevski, M, 'Fragmentation in International Human Rights Law: Beyond Conflict of Laws' (2014) 32 *Nordic Journal of Human Rights* 87

Anagnostaras, G, 'The Common European Asylum System: Balancing Mutual Trust Against Fundamental Rights Protection' (2020) 21 *German Law Journal* 1180

Andreadakis, S, 'Problems and Challenges of the EU's Accession to the ECHR: Empirical Findings with a View to the Future' in S Morano-Foadi and L Vickers (eds), *Fundamental Rights in EU: A Matter for Two Courts*, Modern Studies in European Law 53 (Oxford, Bloomsbury, 2015) 47–68

Anghie, A, 'The Evolution of International Law: colonial and postcolonial realities' (2006) 27 *Third World Quarterly* 739

Antkowiak, T, and Gonza, A, *The American Convention on Human Rights* (Oxford, Oxford University Press, 2017)

Antonov, M, 'Conservatism in Russia and Sovereignty in Human Rights' (2014) 39 *Review of Central and East European Law* 1

Antpöhler, C, Dickschen, J, Hentrei, S, Kottmann, M, Smrkolj, M, and von Bogdandy, A, 'Reverse Solange – Protecting the Essence of Fundamental Rights against EU Member States' (2012) 49 *Common Market Law Review* 489

Arai-Takahashi, Y, *The Margin of Appreciation Doctrine and the Principle of Proportionality in the Jurisprudence of the ECHR* (Antwerp, Intersentia, 2002)

Ashworth, A, 'Self-incrimination in European Human Rights Law – A Pregnant Pragmatism?' (2008) 30 *Cardozo Law Review* 751

Attanasio, D, 'Extraordinary Reparations, Legitimacy, and the Inter-American Court' (2016) 37 *University of Pennsylvania Journal of International Law* 813

Augenstein, D, 'Engaging the Fundamentals: On the Autonomous Substance of EU Fundamental Rights Law' (2013) 14 *German Law Journal* 1917

Balfour, ADJ, 'Application of the European Convention on Human Rights by the European Court of Justice' (2005), *Harvard Law School Student Scholarship Series*, Paper 4.

Baker, S, 'How Can the U.S. Respond to Schrems II?' (*Lawfare*, 21 July 2020)

Baratta, R, 'Accession of the EU to the ECHR: The Rationale for the ECJ's Prior Involvement Mechanism' (2013) 50 *Common Market Law Review* 1305

Barcelló III, JJ, 'ECJ Review of Member State Measures for Compliance with Fundamental Rights' in JC Masclet, H Ruiz Fabri, C Boutayeb and S Rodrigues (eds), *L'Union européenne: union de droit, union des droits: mélanges em l'honneur du Professeur Philippe Manin* (Paris, Pedone, 2010) 767–774

Bard, P and van Ballegooij, W, 'Judicial Independence as a Precondition for Mutual Trust? The CJEU in *Minister for Justice and Equality v LM*' (2018) 9 *New Journal of European Criminal Law* 353

Barnard, C, 'Social Dumping or Dumping Socialism?' (2008) 67 *Cambridge Law Journal* 262

Barnard, C, *The Substantive Law of the EU: The Four Freedoms* (Oxford, Oxford University Press, 2010)

Baron, J and Poelman, E, 'The Principle of Ne Bis in Idem: On the Ropes, but Definitely Not Defeated' (2018) 46 *Intertax* 805

Bates, E, 'The Al-Adsani Case, State Immunity and the International Legal Prohibition on Torture' (2003) 3 *Human Rights Law Review* 193

Bates, E, *The Evolution of the European Convention on Human Rights: From Its Inception to the Creation of a Permanent Court of Human Rights* (Oxford, Oxford University Press, 2011)

Beduschi, A, 'The Contribution of the Inter-American Court of Human Rights to the Protection of Irregular Immigrants' Rights: Opportunities and Challenges' (2015) 34(4) *Refugee Survey Quarterly* 45

Benvenisti, E, 'Margin of Appreciation, Consensus, and Universal Standards' (1999) 31 *New York University Journal of International Law & Politics* 843

Benvenisti, E, and Downs, G, 'Democratizing Courts: How National and International Courts Promote Democracy in an Era of Global Governance' (2013) Global Trust Working Paper no 5/2013

Bergé, JS, 'Avotiņš ou le calme qui couve la tempêt' (*Réseau Universitaire Européen*, 26 May 2016)

Berry, S, 'Freedom of Religion and Religious Symbols: Same Right – Different Interpretation?' (*EJIL:Talk!*, 10 October 2013)

Berry, S, 'A 'Good Faith' Interpretation of the Right to Manifest Religion? The Diverging Approaches of the European Court of Human Rights and the UN Human Rights Committee' (2017) 37 *Legal Studies* 692

Berry, S, 'The UN Human Rights Committee Disagrees with the European Court of Human Rights Again: The Right to Manifest Religion by Wearing a Burqa' (*EJIL:Talk!*, 3 January 2019)

Bertoni, EA, 'The Inter-American Court of Human Rights and the European Court of Human Rights: A Dialogue on Freedom of Expressions Standards' [2009] 3 *European Human Rights Law Review* 332

Besselink, LFM, 'Case C-208/09, *Ilonka Sayn-Wittgenstein v. Landeshauptmann von Wien*, Judgment of the Court (Second Chamber) of 22 December 2010' (2012) 49 *Common Market Law Review* 671

Bianchi, A, 'Human Rights and the Magic of Jus Cogens' (2008) 19 *European Journal of International Law* 491

Birnhack, M, 'The EU Data Protection Directive: An Engine of a Global Regime' (2008) 24 *Computer Law & Security Report* 508

Bjorge, E, 'Been There, Done That: The Margin of Appreciation and International Law' (2015) 4 *Cambridge Journal of International and Comparative Law* 181

Björgvinsson, DÞ, 'The Role of the European Court of Human Rights in the Changing European Human Rights Architecture' in OM Arnardóttir and A Buyse (eds), *Shifting Centres of Gravity in Human Rights Protection: Rethinking Relations between the ECtHR, EU, and National Legal Orders*, Routledge Research in Human Rights Law (Oxford, Routledge, 2016) 26–45

Bleckmann, A, 'General Theory of Obligations under Public International Law' (1995) 38 *German Yearbook of International Law* 26

Bobek, M, 'Joined Cases C-92 & 93/09, *Volker und Markus Schecke GbR and Hartmut Eifert*, Judgement of the Court of Justice (Grand Chamber) of 9 November 2010' (2011) 48 *Common Market Law Review* 2005

Bockel, WB van, 'The Ne Bis In Idem Principle in EU Law: A Conceptual and Jurisprudential Analysis' (Doctoral Thesis, Leiden University 2009)

Bockel, B van, '*Krombach* Returns to Strasbourg' (*ECHR Blog*, 16 May 2018)

Bogdandy, A von, and Schill, SW, 'Overcoming Absolute Primacy: Respect for National Identity under the Lisbon Treaty' (2011) 48 *Common Market Law Review* 1417

Bonneau, K, 'La jurisprudence innovante de la Cour Interaméricaine des Droits de l'Homme en matière de droit à réparation des victimes de violations des droits de l'homme' in L Hennebel and H Tigroudja (eds), *Le particularisme interaméricain des droits de l'homme* (Paris, Pedone, 2009) 349–83

Bovend'Eerdt, K, 'The Joined Cases Aranyosi and Căldăraru: A New Limit to the Mutual Trust Presumption in the Area of Freedom, Security, and Justice?' (2016) 32 *Utrecht Journal of International and European Law* 112

Bowring, B, 'Russia and Human Rights: Incompatible Opposites' (2009) 1 *Göttingen Journal of International Law* 257

Bowring, B, 'Russian Federation, Protocol No. 14 (and 14bis), and the Battle for the Soul of the ECHR' (2010) 2 *Göttingen Journal of International Law* 589
Brems, E, 'The Margin of Appreciation Doctrine in the Case-Law of the European Court of Human Rights' (1996) 56 *Heidelberg Journal of International Law* 240
Bribosia, E, and Rorive, I, 'Affaires Achbita et Bougnaoui: entre neutralité et préjugés' (2017) 112 *Revue trimestrielle des droits de l' homme* 1017
Brown, C, 'Case C-112/00, *Eugen Schmidberger, Internationale Transporte und Planzüge v. Austria*' (2003) 40 *Common Market Law Review* 1499
Bruycker, P De, and Labayle, S, 'The Influence of ECJ and ECtHR Case Law on Asylum and Immigration' (Study of the Policy Department C: Citizens' Rights and Constitutional Affairs, European Parliament, 2012)
Buelens, J and Rigaux, M, *From Social Competition to Social Dumping*, Social Europe Series 35 (Cambridge, Intersentia, 2016)
Buergenthal, T, 'The Advisory Practice of the Inter-American Human Rights Court' (1985) 79 *American Journal of International Law* 1
Buergenthal, T, 'Interim Measures in the Inter-American Court of Human Rights' in R Bernhardt (ed), *Interim Measures Indicated by International Courts* (Berlin, Springer, 1994) 69–94
Buergenthal, T, 'Proliferation of International Courts and Tribunals: Is it Good or Bad?' (2001) 14 *Leiden Journal of International Law* 267
Burbano Herrera, C and Haeck, Y, 'Letting States off the Hook? The Paradox of the Legal Consequences following State Non-Compliance with Provisional Measures in the Inter-American and European Human Rights Systems' (2010) 28 *Netherlands Quarterly Human Rights* 332
Búrca, G de, 'The Road not Taken: The European Union as a Global Human Rights Actor' (2011) 105 *American Journal of International Law* 649
Burgorgue-Larsen, L, and Úbeda de Torres, A, 'The Right to the Freedom of Thought and Expression' in L Burgorgue-Larsen and A Úbeda de Torres (eds), *The Inter-American Court of Human Rights: Case Law and Commentary* (Oxford, Oxford University Press, 2011) 529–62
Buyse, A, 'Lost and Regained? Restitution as a Remedy for Human Rights Violations in the Context of International Law' (2008) 68 *Heidelberg Journal of International Law* 129
Buyse, A, 'Tacit Citing – The Scarcity of Judicial Dialogue between the Global and the Regional Human Rights Mechanisms in Freedom of Expression Cases' in T McGonagle and Y Donders (eds), *The United Nations and Freedom of Expression and Information: Critical Perspectives* (Cambridge, Cambridge University Press, 2015) 443–65
Buyse, A, 'Echoes of Strasbourg in Geneva: The Influence of ECHR Anti-Torture Jurisprudence on the United Nations Human Rights Committee' (2016) 59 *Japanese Yearbook of International Law* 81
Caflisch, L, 'The Reform of the European Court of Human Rights: Protocol No. 14 and Beyond' (2006) 6 *Human Rights Law Review* 403
Caflisch, L, 'L'application du droit international général par la Cour européenne des droits de l'homme' in I Buffard, J Crawford, A Pellet and S Wittich (eds), *International Law between Universalism and Fragmentation: Festschrift in Honour of Gerhard Hafner* (Leiden, Martinus Nijhoff, 2008) 627–48
Callewaert, J, *The Accession of the European Union to the European Convention on Human Rights* (Strasbourg, Council of Europe Publications, 2014)
Callewaert, J, 'Do we Still Need Article 6(2) TEU? Considerations on the Absence of EU Accession to the ECHR and its Consequences' (2018) 55 *Common Market Law Review* 1685
Callewart, J, 'Manifest deficiency in the execution of a European arrest warrant – judgment of the European Court of Human Rights in the case of Bivolaru and Moldovan v. France' (*Prof. Dr. iur. Johan Callewaert* Blog, 4 April 2021)
Callewaert, J, 'The European arrest warrant under the European Convention on Human Rights: A matter of Cooperation, Trust, Complementarity, Autonomy and Responsibility' (2021) *ZEuS-Sonderband* 105
Cançado Trindade, AA, 'Reflexiones sobre el Futuro del Sistema Interamericano de Protección de los Derechos Humanos' in J Méndez and F Cox (eds), *El futuro del sistema interamericano de proteccion a los derechos humanos* (San José, Instituto Interamericano de Derechos Humanos, 1998)

Cançado Trindade, AA, *El derecho internacional de los derechos humanos en el siglo XXI* (Santiago, Editorial Jurídica de Chile, 2001)
Cançado Trindade, AA, 'The Evolution of Provisional Measures of Protection under the Case-Law of the Inter-American Court of Human Rights (1987–2002)' (2003) 24 *Human Rights Law Journal* 162
Cançado Trindade, AA, 'Enforced Disappearances of Persons as a Violation of Jus Cogens: The Contribution of the Jurisprudence of the Inter-American Court of Human Rights' (2012) 81 *Nordic Journal of International Law* 507
Cançado Trindade, AA, 'The European Convention on Human Rights and General International Law: Concluding Reflections on the 2015 Strasbourg Conference' in A van Aaken and I Motoc (eds), *The European Convention on Human Rights and General International Law* (Oxford, Oxford University Press, 2018) 285–304
Candia, G, 'Comparing Diverse Approaches to the Margin of Appreciation: The Case of the European and the Inter-American Court of Human Rights' (2014)
Cariolou, L, 'Article 47' in EU Network of Independent Experts on Fundamental Rights, 'Commentary of the Charter of Fundamental Rights of the European Union' (July 2006) 359–71
Cassel, D, 'The Expanding Scope and Impact of Reparations Awarded by the Inter-American Court of Human Rights' in M Bossuyt, P Lemmens, K de Feyter and S Parmentier (eds), *Out of the Ashes: Reparations for Gross Violations of Human Rights* (Cambridge, Intersentia, 2006) 90–100
Cavanaugh, K, 'Policing the Margins: Rights Protection and the European Court of Human Rights' [2006] 4 *European Human Rights Law Review* 422
Celeste, E, 'The Court of Justice and the Ban on Bulk Data Retention: Expansive Potential and Future Scenarios' (2019) 15 *European Constitutional Law Review* 134
Chaib, SO, 'Ranjit Singh v. France: The UN Committee Asks the Questions the Strasbourg Court Didn't Ask in Turban Case' (*Strasbourg Observers*, 6 March 2012)
Chaib, SO, and Peroni, L, 'S.A.S. v. France: Missed Opportunity to Do Full Justice to Women Wearing a Face Veil' (*Strasbourg Observers*, 3 July 2014)
Christakis, T, 'After Schrems II: Uncertainties on the Legal Basis for Data Transfers and Constitutional Implications for Europe' (*European Law Blog*, 21 July 2020)
Cohen-Jonathan, G, 'Sur la force obligatoire des mesures provisoires: L'arrêt de la Grande Chambre de la Cour Européenne du 4 février 2005, *Mamatkulov et Askarov contre Turquie*' (2005) 109 *Revue Générale de Droit International Public* 421
Cole, M and Vandendriessch, A, 'From *Digital Rights Ireland* and *Schrems* in Luxembourg to *Zakharov* and *Szabó/Vissy* in Strasbourg: What the ECtHR Made of the Deep Pass by the CJEU in the Recent Cases on Mass Surveillance' (2016) 2 *European Data Protection Law Review* 121
Conforti, B, 'Reflections on State Responsibility for the Breach of Positive Obligations: The Case-Law of the European Court of Human Rights' (2003) 13 *Italian Yearbook of International Law* 3
Contesse, J, 'Contestation and Deference in the Inter-American System of Human Rights' (2016) 79(2) *Law and Contemporary Problems* 123
Contesse, J, 'Subsidiarity in Inter-American Human Rights Law' (2016)
Contesse, J, 'The Final Word? Constitutional Dialogue and the Inter-American Court of Human Rights' (2017) 15 *International Journal of Constitutional Law* 414
Contreras, P, 'National Discretion and International Deference in the Restriction of Human Rights: A Comparison between the Jurisprudence of the European and the Inter-American Court of Human Rights' (2012) 11 *Northwestern Journal of International Human Rights* 28
Contreras-Garduño, D, 'The Inter-American System of Human Rights' in A Mihr and M Gibney (eds), *The SAGE Handbook of Human Rights* (Los Angeles, SAGE Publications, 2014) 596–614
Cornelisse, G, *Immigration Detention and Human Rights: Rethinking Territorial Sovereignty*, Immigration and Asylum Law and Policy in Europe 19 (The Hague, Martinus Nijhof, 2010)
Cortes-Martin, J, 'The Long Road to Strasbourg: The Apparent Controversy Surrounding the Principle of Mutual Trust' (2018) 11 *Review of European Administrative Law* 5
Cosentino, C, 'Safe and Legal Abortion: An Emerging Human Right: The Long-Lasting Dispute with Sovereignty in ECHR Jurisprudence' (2015) 15 *Human Rights Law Review* 569

Costa, JP, 'Responsibility for Violations of Human Rights Obligations: European Mechanisms' in J Crawford, A Pellet and S Olleson (eds), *The Law of International Responsibility* (Oxford, Oxford University Press, 2010) 763–74
Costello, C, 'The *Bosphorus* Ruling of the European Court of Human Rights: Fundamental Rights and Blurred Boundaries in Europe' (2006) 6 *Human Rights Law Review* 87
Costello, C, 'Courting Access to Asylum in Europe: Recent Supranational Jurisprudence Explored' (2012) 12 *Human Rights Law Review* 287
Costello, C, 'Human Rights and the Elusive Universal Subject: Immigration Detention under International Human Rights and EU Law' (2012) 19 *Indiana Journal of Global Legal Studies* 257
Costello, C, 'Immigration Detention: The Grounds beneath our Feet' (2015) 68 *Current Legal Problems* 143
Cottier, T, Echandi, R, Liechti-McKee, R, Payosova, T and Sieber, C, 'The Principle of Proportionality in International Law: Foundations and Variations' (2017) 18 *Journal of World Investment & Trade* 628
Couso, J, 'The Transformation of Constitutional Discourse and the Judicialization of Politics in Latin America' in J Couso, A Huneeus and R Sieder (eds), *Cultures of Legality: Judicialization and Political Activism in Contemporary Latin America* (Cambridge, Cambridge University Press, 2010) 141–60
Craig, P, 'EU Accession to the ECHR: Competence, Procedure and Substance' (2013) 36 *Fordham International Law Journal* 1114
Croquet, N, 'The Right of Silence and not to Self-Incriminate under the European Convention on Human Rights: To Which Extent are they Qualified' (2008) 4 *Cambridge Student Law Review* 214
Cumper, P, and Lewis, T, 'Empathy and Human Rights: The Case of Religious Dress' (2018) 18 *Human Rights Law Review* 61
Curzon, S, 'Internal Market Derogation in Light of the Newly Binding Character of the EU Charter of Fundamental Rights' in G Di Federico (ed), *The EU Charter of Fundamental Rights: From Declaration to Binding Instrument*, Ius Gentium: Comparative Perspectives on Law and Justice 8 (Dordrecht, Springer, 2011) 145–59
Daskal, J, 'What Comes Next: The Aftermath of European Court's Blow to Transatlantic Data Transfers' (*Just Security Blog*, 17 July 2020)
Dauses, M, 'The Protection of Fundamental Rights in the Community Legal Order' (1985) 10 *European Law Review* 398
Davidson, S, *The Inter-American Court of Human Rights* (Brookfield, Darmouth Publication, 1992)
Davies, ACL, 'One Step Forward, Two Steps Back? The *Viking* and *Laval* Cases in the ECJ' (2008) 37 *Industrial Law Journal* 126
Davies, A, 'Radu: A case of failed dialogue' (Eutopia Law Blog, 5 February 2013) available at https://eutopialaw.com/2013/02/05/radu-a-case-of-failed-dialogue/
Debré, JL, *La laïcité à l'école – un principe républicain à réaffirmer, Rapport de la mission de l'Assemblée nationale* (Paris, Odile Jacob, 2004)
Deftou, ML, 'Fostering the Rule of Law in the Americas: Is There any Room for Judicial Dialogue between the IACtHR and National Courts?' (2020) 38 *Nordic Journal of Human Rights* 78
Dembour, MB, *When Humans Become Migrants: Study of the European Court of Human Rights with an Inter-American Counterpoint* (Oxford, Oxford University Press, 2015)
Dembour, MB, 'Ramadan v. Malta: When will the Strasbourg Court Understand that Nationality is a Core Human Rights Issue?' (*Strasbourg Observers*, 22 July 2016)
Denys, S, 'Des influences réciproques entre CJCE et CEDH:"je t'aime, moi non plus"?' (2001) 96 *Pouvoirs – Les Cours européennes:Luxembourg et Strasbourg* 31
Di Filippo, M, 'The Refugee Crisis and the Executive: on the Limits of Administrative Discretion in the Common European Asylum System' (2016) International Institute of Humanitarian Law Policy Brief
Dougan, M, 'The Treaty of Lisbon 2007: Winning Minds, not Hearts' (2008) 45 *Common Market Law Review* 617
Douglas-Scott, S, '*Bosphorus Hava Yollari Turizm Ve Ticaret Anonim Sirketi v. Ireland*' (2006) 43 *Common Market Law Review* 243
Douglas-Scott, S, 'A Tale of Two Courts: Luxembourg, Strasbourg and the Growing European Human Rights *Acquis*' (2006) 43 *Common Market Law Review* 629

Douglas-Scott, S, 'The Relationship between the EU and the ECHR Five Years on from the Treaty of Lisbon' in S de Vries, U Bernitz and S Weatherill (eds), *The EU Charter of Fundamental Rights as a Binding Instrument: Five Years Old and Growing*, Studies of the Oxford Institute of European and Comparative Law 20 (Oxford, Hart Publishing, 2015) 21–46

Duhaime, B, 'Subsidiarity in the Americas: What Room is There for Deference in the Inter-American System?' in L Gruszczynski and W Werner (eds), *Deference in International Courts and Tribunals: Standard of Review and Margin of Appreciation* (Oxford, Oxford University Press, 2014)

Dulitzky, A, 'An Inter-American Constitutional Court? The Invention of the Conventionality Control by the Inter-American Court of Human Rights' (2015) 50 *Texas International Law Journal* 46

Dupuy, PM, 'A Doctrinal Debate in the Globalisation Era: On the "Fragmentation" of International Law' (2007) 1 *European Journal of Legal Studies* 25

Dye, V, '"Deference as Respect" in WTO Standard of Review' (2013) 12 *Journal of International Trade Law and Policy* 23

Dzehtsiarou, K, 'European Consensus and the Evolutive Interpretation of the European Convention on Human Rights' (2011) 12 *German Law Journal* 1731

Dzehtsiarou, K, *European Consensus and the Legitimacy of the Strasbourg Court* (Cambridge, Cambridge University Press, 2015).

Eeckhout, P, 'The European Convention on Human Rights and Fundamental Freedoms as an Integral Part of EU Law–Some Reflections on Status and Effect' in I Govaere, E Lannon, P van Elsuwege and S Adam (eds), *The European Union in the World: Essays in Honour of Marc Maresceau* (Leiden, Brill, 2013) 87–99

Eeckhout, P, 'Opinion 2/13 on EU Accession to the ECHR and Judicial Dialogue – Autonomy or Autarky?' (2015) Jean Monnet Working Paper Series 01/15

Engström, V, 'Deference and the Human Rights Committee' (2016) 34 *Nordic Journal of International Law* 73

Ewing, KD, and Hendy, J, 'The Dramatic Implications of *Demir and Baykara*' (2010) 39 *Industrial Law Journal* 2

Fabbrini, F, 'Human Rights in the Digital Age: The European Court of Justice Ruling in the Data Retention Case and its Lessons for Privacy and Surveillance in the U.S.' (2015) 28 *Harvard Human Rights Journal* 65

Fabbrini, F, 'The EU Charter of Fundamental Rights and the Rights to Data Privacy: the EU Court of Justice as a Human Rights Court' in S de Vries, U Bernitz, and S Weatherill (eds), *The EU Charter of Fundamental Rights as a Binding Instrument: Five Years Old and Growing*, Studies of the Oxford Institute of European and Comparative Law 20 (Oxford, Hart Publishing, 2015) 261–286

Fabbrinni, F and Larik, J, 'Global Counter-Terrorism Sanctions and European Due Process Rules: The Dialogue between the CJEU and the ECtHR' in M Avbelj, F Fontanelli and G Martinico (eds), *Kadi on Trial: A Multifaceted Analysis of the Kadi Trial*, Routledge Research in EU Law (Oxford, Routledge, 2014) 137–56

Fabbrini, F and Larik, J, 'The Past, Present and Future of the Relation between the European Court of Justice and the European Court of Human Rights' (2016) 35 *Yearbook of European Law* 145

Federico, G Di (ed), *The EU Charter of Fundamental Rights: From Declaration to Binding Instrument*, Ius Gentium: Comparative Perspectives on Law and Justice 8 (Dordrecht, Springer, 2011)

Feria-Tinta, M, and Milnes, S, 'The Rise of Environmental Law in International Dispute Resolution: Inter-American Court of Human Rights issues Landmark Advisory Opinion on Environment and Human Rights' (*EJIL:Talk!*, 26 February 2018)

Florou, G and Margaritis, K, 'Article 47: Right to an Effective Remedy and to a Fair Trial' in VG Tzemos (ed), *The Charter of fundamental rights of the EU* [in Greek] (Athens, Nomiki Vivliothiki, 2015)

Follesdal, A, 'Exporting the Margin of Appreciation: Lessons for the Inter-American Court of Human Rights' (2017) 15 *International Journal of Constitutional Law* 359

Fontana, B, 'Damage Awards for Human Rights Violations in the European and Inter-American Courts of Human Rights' (1991) 31 *Santa Clara Law Review* 1127

Fontanelli, F, 'The European Union's Charter of Fundamental Rights: Two Years Later' (2011) 3 *Perspectives on Federalism* 22

Fortas, AC, *La surveillance de l'exécution des arrêts et décisions des Cours européenne et interaméricaine des droits de l'homme* (Paris, Pedone, 2015)

Frackowiak-Adamsca, A, 'Mutual trust and independence of the judiciary after the CJEU judgment in LM – new era or business as usual?' (*EU Law Analysis*, 15 August 2018)

Frommel, S, 'The European Court of Human Rights and the Right of the Accused to Remain Silent: Can it Be Invoked to Taxpayers?' (1994) *International Business Law Journal* 671

Frowein, JA, 'Provisional Measures by the International Court of Justice – The LaGrand Case' (2002) 62 *Heidelberg Journal of International Law* 55

Gaja, G 'The "Co-respondent Mechanisms" According to the Draft Agreement for the Accession of the EU to the ECHR' in V Kosta, N Skoutaris and V Tzevelekos (eds), *The EU Accession to the ECHR*, Modern Studies in European Law 48 (Oxford, Bloomsbury, 2014) 341–47

Galera, S, 'The Right to a Fair Trial in the EU: Lights and Shadows' (2013) 87 *Revista de Derecho Politico* 49

García, RA, 'The General Provisions of the Charter of Fundamental Rights of the European Union' (2002) 8 *European Law Journal* 492

Garde, A, 'The Best Interests of the Child and EU Consumer Law and Policy: A Major Gap between Theory and Practice?' in J Devenney and M Kenny (eds), *European Consumer Protection: Theory and Practice* (Cambridge, Cambridge University Press, 2012) 164–201

Gaviria, C, 'Towards a New Vision of the Inter-American Human Rights System' (1996) 4(4) *Journal of Latin American Affairs* 9

Gavouneli, M, and Bantekas, I, 'Prefecture of Voiotia v. Federal Republic of Germany, Case no 11/2000, Areios Pagos (Hellenic Supreme Court), May 4, 2000' (2001) 95 *American Journal of International Law* 198

Gerards, J, 'Margin of Appreciation and Incrementalism in the Case Law of the European Court of Human Rights' (2018) 18 *Human Rights Law Review* 495

Gill-Pedro, E and Groussot, X, 'The Duty of Mutual Trust in EU Law and the Duty to Secure Human Rights: Can the EU's Accession to the ECHR Ease the Tension?' (2017) 35 *Nordic Journal of Human Rights* 258

Gogou, K, 'The EU-Turkey Deal: Europe's Year of Shame' (Amnesty International, 20 March 2017)

Gonzalez Fuster, G, 'Fighting for Your Right to What Exactly? The Convoluted Case Law of the EU Court of Justice on Privacy and/or Personal Data Protection' (2014) *2 Birkbeck Law Review* 263

Graat, J, 'Human Rights v the European Arrest Warrant? The Legality of Surrender Detention after 90 Days' (*EU Law Analysis*, 18 October 2018)

Grabenwarter, C, *European Convention on Human Rights Commentary* (Munich, CB Beck, Hart Publishing, Nomos, Helbing Lichtenhahn Verlag, 2014)

Greer, S, *The Margin of Appreciation: Interpretation and Discretion under the European Convention on Human Rights*, Human Rights files no 17 (Strasbourg, Council of Europe Publishing, 2000)

Grossman, A, 'A Critical Assessment of the 1267 Sanctions Committee' (*E-International Relations*, 3 March 2012)

Groussot, X and Olsson, I, 'Clarifying or Diluting the Application of the EU Charter of Fundamental Rights? – The Judgments in Åkerberg and Melloni' (2013) 2 *Lund Student EU Law Review* 7

Guggisberg, S, 'The Nada Case in front of the ECtHR: A New Milestone in the European Debate on Security Council Targeted Sanctions and Human Rights Obligations' (2012) 8 *Croatian Yearbook of European Law and Policy* 411

Guild, E, 'Who is an Irregular Migrant?' in B Bogusz, R Cholewinski, A Cygan and E Szyszczak (eds), *Irregular Migration and Human Rights: Theoretical, European and International Perspectives*, Immigration and Asylum Law and Policy in Europe 7 (Leiden, Brill Nijhoff, 2004) 3–28

Guild, E, 'To Protect or to Forget? The Human Right to Leave a Country' (*EU Immigration and Asylum Law*, 27 December 2017)

Haasdijk, S, 'The Lack of Uniformity in the Terminology of the International Law of Remedies' (1992) 5 *Leiden Journal of International Law* 245

Halleskov Storgaart, L, 'EU Law Autonomy versus European Fundamental Rights Protection–On Opinion 2/13 on EU Accession to the ECHR' (2015) 15 *Human Rights Law Review* 485

Hannikainen, L, *Peremptory Norms (Jus Cogens) in International Law: Historical Development, Criteria, Present Status* (Helsinki, Finnish Lawyers' Publishing Company, 1988)

Harris, D, 'Regional Protection of Human Rights: The Inter-American Achievement' in D Harris and S Livingstone (eds), *The Inter-American System of Human Rights* (Oxford, Clarendon Press, 1998) 1–31

Harris, DJ, O'Boyle, M, Bates, EP, and Buckley, CM, *Harris, O'Boyle and Warbrick: Law of the European Convention on Human Rights*, 2nd edn (Oxford, Oxford University Press, 2015)

Hawkins, D, and Jacoby, W, 'Partial Compliance: A Comparison of the European and Inter-American Courts of Human Rights' (2010) 6 *Journal of International Law and International Relations* 35

Heffernan, L, 'A Comparative View of Individual Petition Procedures under the European Convention on Human Rights and the International Covenant on Civil and Political Rights' (1997) 19 *Human Rights Quarterly* 78

Heijer, M den, Rijpma, J, and Spijkerboer, T, 'Coercion, Prohibition, and Great Expectations: The Continuing Failure of the Common European Asylum System' (2016) 53 *Common Market Law Review* 607

Hert, P De, and Bocos, PC, 'Case of Roman Zakharov v. Russia: The Strasbourg Follow Up to the Luxembourg Court's Schrems Judgment' (*Strasbourg Observers*, 23 December 2015)

Hert, P De, and Gurtwirth, S, 'Data Protection in the Case Law of Strasbourg and Luxemburg: Constitutionalisation in Action' in S Gutwirth, Y Poullet, P De Hert, J Nouwt and C De Terwangne (eds), *Reinventing Data Protection?* (Dordrecht, Springer, 2009) 3–45

Higgins, C, 'The (Un-)sustainability of Australia's Offshore Processing and Settlement Policy' in V Moreno-Lax and E Papastavridis (eds), *'Boat Refugees' and Migrants at Sea: A Comprehensive Approach Integrating Maritime Security with Human Rights*, International Refugee Law Series 7 (Leiden, Brill Nijhoff, 2016) 303–26

Hirschl, R, 'The Judicialization of Politics' in G Caldeira, D Kelemen and K Whittington (eds), *The Oxford Handbook of Law and Politics* (Oxford, Oxford University Press, 2008) 119–41

Hoboken, JVJ van, *Search Engine Freedom: On the Implications of the Right to Freedom of Expression for the Legal Governance of Web Search Engines* (Alphen aan den Rijn, Kluwer Law International, 2012)

Iglesias Vila, M, 'Subsidiarity, Margin of Appreciation and International Adjudication within a Cooperative Conception of Human Rights' (2017) 15 *International Journal of Constitutional Law* 393

Iglezakis, I, 'The Right to Be Forgotten in the Google Spain Case (case C-131/12): A Clear Victory for Data Protection or an Obstacle for the Internet?' (2014)

Imamovic, Š, and Muir, E, 'The Dublin III System: More Derogations to the Duty to Transfer Individual Asylum Seekers?' (2017) 2(2) *European Papers* 719

Isiksel, T, 'European Exceptionalism and the EU's Accession to the ECHR' (2016) 27 *European Journal of International Law* 565

Istrefi, K, 'The Application of Article 103 of the United Nations Charter in the European Courts: The Quest for Regime Compatibility on Fundamental Rights' (2012) 5(2) *European Journal of Legal Studies* 81

Jacqué, JP, 'The Accession of the European Union to the European Convention on Human Rights and Fundamental Freedoms' (2011) 48 *Common Market Law Review* 995

Jacquemain, M, 'Dix arguments laïques contre l'interdiction législative du voile' in M Jacquemain and N Rosa-Rosso (eds), *Du bon usage de la laïcité* (Bruxelles, Aden, 2008) 75–100

Johansen, S, 'EU law and the ECHR: the Bosphorus Presumption is Still Alive and Kicking: The Case of Avotiņš v. Latvia' (*EU Law Analysis*, 24 May 2016)

Joseph, S, 'United Nations Human Rights Committee: Recent Cases' (2006) 6 *Human Rights Law Review* 361

Joseph, S, 'Trade Law and Investment Law' in D Shelton (ed), *The Oxford Handbook of International Human Rights Law* (Oxford, Oxford University Press, 2013) 841–73

Joseph, S, and Castan, M, *The International Covenant on Civil and Political Rights: Cases, Materials, and Commentary*, 3rd edn (Oxford, Oxford University Press, 2013)

Juma, D, 'Provisional Measures under the African Human Rights System: The African Court's Order against Libya' (2012) 30 *Wisconsin International Law Journal* 344

Kadelbach, S, 'Jus Cogens, Obligations Erga Omnes and Other Rules: The Identification of Fundamental Norms' in C Tomuschat and JM Thouvenin (eds), *The Fundamental Rules of the International Legal Order: Jus Cogens and Obligations Erga Omnes* (Leiden, Martinus Nijhoff, 2006) 21–40

Kammerhofer, J, 'The Binding Nature of Provisional Measures of the International Court of Justice: The 'Settlement' of the Issue in the LaGrand Case' (2003) 16 *Leiden Journal of International Law* 67

Kapotas, P, and Tzevelekos, V, (eds), *Building Consensus on European Consensus: Judicial Interpretation of Human Rights in Europe and Beyond* (Cambridge, Cambridge University Press 2019)

Karamanian, S, 'Human Rights Dimensions of Investment Law' in E de Wet and J Vidmar (eds), *Hierarchy in International Law: The Place of Human Rights* (Oxford, Oxford University Press, 2012) 236–71

Keller, H, and Grover, L, 'General Comments of the Human Rights Committee and their Legitimacy' in H Keller and G Ulfstein (eds), *UN Human Rights Treaty Bodies: Law and Legitimacy* (Cambridge, Cambridge University Press, 2012) 116–98

Koch, I, *Human Rights as Indivisible Rights: The Protection of Social-Economic Demands under the European Convention on Human Rights*, International Studies in Human Rights 101 (Leiden, Martinus Nijhoff Publishers, 2009)

Kokott, J, and Sobotta, C, 'The Kadi Case – Constitutional Core Values and International Law: Finding the Balance?' (2012) 23 *European Journal of International Law* 1015

Kokott, J, and Sobotta, C, 'Protection of Fundamental Rights in the European Union: On the Relationship between EU Fundamental Rights, the European Convention and National Standards of Protection' (2015) 34 *Yearbook of European Law* 60

Kombos, C, 'Fundamental Rights and Fundamental Freedoms: A Symbiosis on the Basis of Subsidiarity' (2006) 12 *European Public Law* 433

Koskenniemi, M, and Leino, P, 'Fragmentation of International Law? Postmodern Anxieties' (2002) 15 *Leiden Journal of International Law* 553

Kosta, V, *Fundamental Rights in EU Internal Market Legislation*, Modern Studies in European Law 58 (Oxford, Bloomsbury, 2015)

Kranenborg, H, 'Article 8: Protection of Personal Data' in S Peers, T Hervey, J Kenner and A Ward (eds), *The EU Charter of Fundamental Rights: A Commentary* (Oxford, Hart Publishing, 2014) 223–66

Kratochvíl, J, 'The Inflation of the Margin of Appreciation by the European Court of Human Rights' (2011) 29 *Netherlands Quarterly of Human Rights* 324

Kravetz, D, 'Holding States to Account for Gender-Based Violence: The Inter-American Court of Human Rights' Decisions in López Soto vs Venezuela and Women Victims of Sexual Torture in Atenco vs Mexico' (*EJIL:Talk!*, 21 January 2019)

Krenn, C, 'Autonomy and Effectiveness as Common Concerns: A Path to ECHR Accession After Opinion 2/13' (2015) 16 *German Law Journal* 147

Kuhnert, K, 'Bosphorus – Double standards in European Human Rights Protection?' (2006) 2 *Utrecht Law Review* 177

Kulk, S and Zuiderveen Borgesius, F, '*Google Spain v. González*: Did the Court Forget about Freedom of Expression?' (2014) 5 *European Journal of Risk Regulation* 389

Kuner, C, 'The Court of Justice of the EU Judgment on Data Protection and Internet Search Engines' (2014) LSE Legal Studies Working Papers 3/2015

Kuner, C, 'Reality and Illusion in EU Data Transfer Regulation Post *Schrems*' (2017) 18 *German Law Journal* 881

Kuner, C, 'Court of Justice International Agreements, Data Protection, and EU Fundamental Rights on the International Stage: Opinion 1/15, *EU-Canada PNR*' (2018) 55 *Common Market Law Review* 857

Kuner, C, 'The Schrems II Judgment of the Court of Justice and the Future of Data Transfer Regulation' (*European Law Blog*, 17 July 2020)

Kyriakou, N, 'An Affront to the Conscience of Humanity: Enforced Disappearances in the Case Law of the Inter-American Court of Human Rights (2014) 7 *Inter-American and European Human Rights Journal* 17

Lassale, M, 'Opinion 1/15: AG Mengozzi Looking for a New Balance in Data Protection' (*European Law Blog*, 18 October 2016)

Lavranos, N, 'The ECJ's Judgments Melloni and Åkerberg Fransson: Une ménage à trois difficulté' (2013) 4 *European Law Reporter* 133
Lavranos, N and Vatsov, M, '*Kadi II*: Backtracking from *Kadi I*?' in M Avbelj, F Fontanelli and G Martinico (eds), *Kadi on Trial: A Multifaceted Analysis of the Kadi Trial*, Routledge Research in EU Law (Oxford, Routledge, 2014) 108–21
Lavrysen, L, 'Less Stringent Measures and Migration Detention: Overruling Saadi v UK?' (*Strasbourg Observers*, 25 January 2012)
Lavrysen, L, 'Is the Strasbourg Court Tough on Migration?' (*Strasbourg Observers*, 5 December 2012)
Lavrysen, L, 'Positive Obligations in the Jurisprudence of the Inter-American Court of Human Rights' (2014) 7 *Inter-American and European Human Rights Journal* 94
Lenaerts, K, 'EU Values and Constitutional Pluralism: The EU System of Fundamental Rights Protection' (2014) 34 *Polish Yearbook of International Law* 135
Lenaerts, K, 'La vie apres l' avis: Exploring the Principle of Mutual (yet not blind) Trust' (2017) 54 *Common Market Law Review* 805
Lenaerts, K, 'The ECHR and the CJEU: Creating Synergies in the Field of Fundamental Rights Protection' (Speech in the context of the solemn hearing at the ECtHR for the opening of the Judicial Year, 26 January 2018)
León, G De, 'Contributions and Challenges for the Inter-American Court of Human Rights for the Protection of Migrants' Rights: The Case of Vélez Loor v. Panama' (2014) 7 *Inter-American and European Human Rights Journal* 39
Letsas, G, 'Two Concepts of the Margin of Appreciation' (2006) 26 *Oxford Journal of Legal Studies* 705
Leuprecht, P, 'Innovations in the European System of Human Rights Protection: Is Enlargement Compatible with Reinforcement?' (1998) 8 *Transnational Law and Contemporary Problems* 313
Lind, A, and Strand, M, 'A New Proportionality Test for Fundamental Rights?: The Joined Cases C-92/09 and C-93/09 Volker und Markus Schecke GbR (C-92/09) and Hartmut Eifert (C-93/09) v. Land Hessen' (2011) Swedish Institute for European Policy Studies European Policy Analysis 7/2011
Lindeboom, J, 'Why EU Law Claims Supremacy' (2018) 38 *Oxford Journal of Legal Studies* 328
Lixinski, L, 'Choice of Forum in International Human Rights Adjudication and the Unity/Fragmentation Debate: Is Plurality the Way Ahead?' (2009) 9 *University College Dublin Law Review* 23
Lixinski, L, 'The Consensus Method of Interpretation by the Inter-American Court of Human Rights' (2017) 3 *Canadian Journal of Comparative and Contemporary Law* 65
Lo Schiavo, G, 'The Principle of Ne Bis In Idem and the Application of Criminal Sanctions: Of Scope and Restrictions ECJ 20 March 2018, Case C-524/15, *Luca Menci* ECJ 20 March 2018, Case C-537/16, *Garlsson Real Estate SA and Others v Commissione Nazionale per le Società e la Borsa (Consob)* ECJ 20 March 2018, Joined Cases C-596/16 and C-597/16, *Enzo Di Puma v Consob and Consob v Antonio Zecca*' (2018) 14 *European Constitutional Law Review* 644
Lock, T, 'Walking on a Tightrope: The Draft Accession Agreement and the Autonomy of the EU Legal Order' (2011) 48 *Common Market Law Review* 1025
Lock, T, 'End of an Epic? The Draft Agreement on the EU's Accession to the ECHR' (2012) 31 *Yearbook of European Law* 162
Londono, P, 'Redrafting Abortion Rights under the Convention: A, B and C v. Ireland' in E Brems (ed), *Diversity and European Human Rights: Rewriting Judgments of the ECHR* (Cambridge, Cambridge University Press, 2012) 95–120
Londras, F de, 'Fatal Fetal Abnormality, Irish Constitutional Law, and Mellet v Ireland' (2016) 24 *Medical Law Review* 591
Lübbe, A, '"Systemic Flaws" and Dublin Transfers: Incompatible Tests before the CJEU and the ECtHR?' (2015) 27 *International Journal of Refugee Law* 135
Luchtman, M, 'The ECJ's Recent Case Law on *Ne Bis In Idem*: Implications for Law Enforcement in a Shared Legal Order' (2018) 55 *Common Market Law Review* 1717
Lundeholm, C, 'The Principle of Ne Bis In Idem: Human Rights and the Enforcement of European Union Competition Law' (Master Thesis, Lund University 2011)
Lynskey, O, 'The Data Retention Directive Is Incompatible with the Rights to Privacy and Data Protection and Is Invalid in its Entirety: *Digital Rights Ireland*' (2014) 51 *Common Market Law Review* 1789

Maiani, F, 'The Reform of the Dublin III Regulation' (Study of the Policy Department C: Citizens' Rights and Constitutional Affairs, European Parliament, 2016)

Malarino, E, 'Judicial Activism, Punitivism and Supranationalisation: Illiberal and Antidemocratic Tendencies of the Inter-American Court of Human Rights' (2012) 12 *International Criminal Law Review* 665

Mann, I, *Humanity at Sea: Maritime Migration and the Foundations of International Law* (Cambridge, Cambridge University Press, 2016)

Marin, L, 'Effective and Legitimate? Learning from the Lessons of 10 Years of Practice with the European Arrest Warrant' (2014) 5 *New Journal of European Criminal Law* 327

Martinico, G, 'The Autonomy of EU law: A Joint Celebration of *Kadi I* and *Kadi II* and *Van Gend en Loos*' in M Avbelj, F Fontanelli and G Martinico (eds), *Kadi on Trial: A Multifaceted Analysis of the Kadi Trial*, Routledge Research in EU Law (Oxford, Routledge, 2014) 157–71

Marletta, A, 'The CJEU and the Spasic Case: Recasting Mutual Trust in the Area of Freedom, Security and Justice?' (*European Law Blog*, 8 January 2015)

Mason, A, 'Interpretation of the American Convention in Latin America: The Impact of the Inter-American Court of Human Rights' Decision in *Velez Loor v. Panama* on Irregular Migrant Rights' (2012) 18 *Law and Business Review of the Americas* 71

Maulet, L, 'Le principe ne bis in idem, objet d'un «dialogue» contrasté entre la Cour de justice de l'Union européenne et la Cour européenne des droits de l'homme' (2017) 109 *Revue trimestrielle des droits de l' homme* 107

McCormick, J, '"The Last Temptation of Christ" (Olmedo Bustos et al.) v. Chile' (2016) 38 *Loyola of Los Angeles International and Comparative Law Review* 1189

McGoldrick, D, 'Affording States a Margin of Appreciation: Comparing the European Court of Human Rights and the Inter-American Court of Human Rights' in C Buckley, A Donald and P Leach (eds), *Towards Convergence in International Human Rights Law: Approaches of Regional and International Systems*, Nottingham Studies in Human Rights 5 (Leiden, Brill Nijhoff, 2013) 325–65

McGoldrick, D, 'A Defence of the Margin of Appreciation and an Argument for Its Application by the Human Rights Committee' (2016) 65 *International and Comparative Law Quarterly* 21

Mena Parras, FJ, 'From Strasbourg to Luxembourg? Transposing the Margin of Appreciation Concept into EU law' (2015) Centre Perelman de Philosophie du Droit Working Paper 2015/7

Merkouris, P, *Article 31(3)(c) VCLT and the Principle of Systemic Integration: Normative Shadows in Plato's Cave*, Queen Mary Studies in International Law 17 (Leiden, Brill Nijhoff, 2015)

Milano, L, 'Le principe non bis in idem devant la Cour de Luxembourg, vers un abaissement de la protection accordée au principe' (2019) 117 *Revue trimestrielle des droits de l'homme* 161

Milanović, M and Papić, T, 'As Bad as it Gets: The European Court of Human Rights's *Behrami and Saramati* Decision and General International Law' (2009) 58 *International Comprative Law Quarterly* 267

Milanović, M, 'European Court Decides Nada v. Switzerland' (*EJIL:Talk!*, 14 September 2012)

Milanović, M, 'Grand Chamber Judgment in Al-Dulimi v. Switzerland' (*EJIL:Talk!*, 23 June 2016)

Milanović, M, 'ECtHR Judgment in Big Brother Watch v. UK' (*EJIL:Talk!*, 17 September 2018)

Milanović, M, 'The Grand Normalization of Mass Surveillance: ECtHR Grand Chamber Judgments in Big Brother Watch and Centrum för rättvisa' (*EJIL:Talk!*, 26 May 2021)

Mitra, A, 'We're Always Going to Argue about Abortion: International Law's Changing Attitudes towards Abortion' (2017) 1 *New Zealand Women's Law Journal* 142

Mitsilegas, V, 'The Limits of Mutual Trust in Europe's Area of Freedom, Security and Justice: From Automatic Inter-State Cooperation to the Slow Emergence of the Individual' (2012) 31 *Yearbook of European Law* 319

Mock, H, 'Ne bis in idem: Strasbourg tranche en faveur de l'identité des faits' (2009) 79 *Revue trimestrielle des droits de l' homme* 867

Montoya Céspedes, MN, 'The Inter-American Court of Human Rights' Positive Obligation Doctrine: Between Unidirectional Influence and Judicial Dialogue' in Y Haeck, O Ruiz-Chiriboga and C Burbano-Herrera (eds), *The Inter-American Court of Human Rights: Theory and Practice, Present and Future* (Cambridge, Intersentia, 2015) 765–92

Morano-Foadi, S and Andreadakis, S, 'The Convergence of the European Legal System in the Treatment of Third Country Nationals in Europe: The ECJ and ECtHR Jurisprudence' (2011) 22 *European Journal of International Law* 1071

Moreno-Lax, V, and Papastavridis, E, (eds), *'Boat Refugees' and Migrants at Sea: A Comprehensive Approach Integrating Maritime Security with Human Rights*, International Refugee Law Series 7 (Leiden, Brill Nijhoff, 2016)

Motoc, I, and Volikas, M, 'The ECHR and the UN Human Rights Committee: Je t'aime plus, moi non-plus. Some Remarks on the *Correia de Matos v. Portugal* and the Right to Defend Oneself in Person' in E Decaux, I Motoc and P Gillibert (eds), *Justice et droits de l'homme: Mélanges in tribute to Judge Christine Chanet* (Paris, Pedone, 2019) 99–110

Mouzourakis, M, 'The Dublin-Strasbourg-Luxembourg Triangle: Getting the European Courts Dialogue on the Suspension of Dublin Regulation Transfers Right' (*Rights in Exile*, 1 March 2014)

Murray, D and Fussey, P, 'Bulk Surveillance in the Digital Age: Rethinking the Human Rights Law Approach to Bulk Monitoring of Communications Data' (2019) 52 *Israel Law Review* 31

Naismith, SH, 'Current Topic: Self-Incrimination Fairness or Freedom' [1997] 3 *European Human Rights Law Review* 229

Nehl, HP, 'The Principle of (Limited) Protection Against Self-incrimination in S Peers, T Hervey, J Kenner, A Ward (eds.), *The EU Charter of Fundamental Rights, A Commentary* (Hart Publishing 2014), 1278–1301

Neuman, G, 'Import, Export, and Regional Consent in the Inter-American Court of Human Rights' (2008) 19 *European Journal of International Law* 101

Neuman, G, 'Subsidiarity' in D Shelton (ed), *The Oxford Handbook of International Human Rights Law* (Oxford, Oxford University Press, 2013) 360–78

Nicolosi, S, 'Another Episode in the Strasbourg Saga on the Dublin System to Determine the State Responsible for Asylum Applications' (*Strasbourg Observers*, 20 February 2015)

O'Gorman, R, 'The ECHR, the EU and the Weakness of Social Rights Protection at the European Level' (2011) 12 *German Law Journal* 1833

Orakhelashvili, A, *Peremptory Norms in International Law* (Oxford, Oxford University Press, 2006)

Palmer, S, 'The Committee of Ministers' in S Schmahl and M Breuer (eds), *The Council of Europe: Its Law and Policies* (Oxford, Oxford University Press, 2017) 137–65

Papadopoulou, RE, '"Smart sanctions" and EC Law: Unrolling the "Ariadne's thread": The ECJ Judgment of 3 September 2008 in Kadi and Al Barakaat' [in Greek] (2009) *Efarmoges Dimosiou Dikaiou I* 21

Parker, MT, 'The Freedom to Manifest Religious Belief: An Analysis of the Necessity Clauses of the ICCPR and the ECHR' (2006) 17 *Duke Journal of Comparative and International Law* 91

Pasqualucci, J, *The Practice and Procedure of the Inter-American Court of Human Rights* (Cambridge, Cambridge University Press, 2012)

Pavageau, S, 'Les obligations positives dans les jurisprudences des Cours européenne et Inter-americaine' (2005) 6 *International Law: Revista Colombiana de Derecho International* 201

Pech, L, and Lane Scheppele, K, 'Illiberalism within: Rule of Law Backsliding in the EU' (2017) 19 *Cambridge Yearbook of European Legal Studies* 3

Pech, L and Platon, S, 'The Beginning of the End for Poland's So-Called "Judicial Reforms"? Some Thoughts on the ECJ ruling in Commission v Poland (Independence of the Supreme Court case)' (*EU Law Analysis*, 30 June 2019)

Peers, S, *EU Justice and Home Affairs Law* (Oxford, Oxford University Press, 2006)

Peers, S, 'Taking Rights Away? Limitations and Derogations' in S Peers and A Ward (eds), *The EU Charter of Fundamental Rights: Politics, Law and Policy: Essays in European Law*' (Oxford, Hart Pubishing, 2004) 141–79

Peers, S, 'The CJEU and the EU's Accession to the ECHR: a Clear and Present Danger to Human Rights Protection' (*EU Law Analysis*, 18 December 2014)

Peers, S, '*The Data Retention Judgment: The CJEU Prohibits Mass Surveillance*' (*EU Law Analysis*, 8 April 2014)

Peers, S, '*The Domino Effect: How Many EU Treaties Violate the Rights to Privacy and Data Protection?*' (*EU Law Analysis*, 25 November 2014)

Peers, S, 'The Party's Over: EU Data Protection Law after the Schrems Safe Harbour Judgment' (*EU Law Analysis*, 7 October 2015)
Peers, S, 'The Final EU/Turkey Refugee Deal: A Legal Assessment' (*EU Law Analysis*, 18 March 2016)
Peers, S, 'Human Rights and the European Arrest Warrant: Has the ECJ Turned from Poacher to Gamekeeper?' (*EU Law Analysis*, 12 November 2016)
Peers, S, 'Is Data Protection Coming Home? The CJEU on Data Protection Law and Jehovah's Witnesses – and Political Canvassing?' (*EU Law Analysis*, 11 July 2018)
Peeters, B, 'The Ne Bis In Idem Rule: Do the EUCJ and the ECtHR Follow the Same Track?' (2018) 4 *European Community Tax Review* 182
Perakis, M, *The judicial protection of fundamental rights in the European Union* [in Greek], Studies of European Law (Athens, Nomiki Vivliothiki, 2015)
Perišin, T, 'Interaction of Fundamental (Human) Rights and Fundamental (Market) Freedoms in the EU' (2006) 2 *Croatian Yearbook of European Law and Policy* 69
Peters, A, 'Targeted Sanctions after Affaire Al-Dulimi et Montana Management Inc. c. Suisse: Is There a Way Out of the Catch-22 for UN Members?' (*EJIL:Talk!*, 4 December 2013)
Peters, A, 'The Refinement of International Law: From Fragmentation to Regime Interaction and Politicization' (2017) 15 *International Journal of Constitutional Law* 671
Petkova, B, 'Towards an Internal Hierarchy of Values in the EU Legal Order: Balancing the Freedom of Speech and Data Privacy' (2016) 23 *Maastricht Journal of European and Comparative Law* 421
Phuong, C, 'Relationship between the European Court of Human Rights and the Human Rights Committee: Has the Same Matter Already Been Examined' (2007) 7 *Human Rights Law Review* 385
Piacentini de Andrade, I, 'La réparation dans la jurisprudence de la cour interaméricaine des Droits de l'Homme' (Doctoral Thesis, Université Panthéon-Assas 2013)
Pinto de Albuquerque, P, and Scoseria Katz, A, 'Is Religion a Threat to Human Rights? Or is It the Other Way Around? Defending Individual Autonomy in the ECtHR' s Jurisprudence on Freedom of Religion' in R Uerpmann-Wittzack, E Lagrange and S Oeter (eds), *Religion and International Law: Living Together* (Leiden, Brill Nijhoff, 2018) 277–93
Post, R, 'Data Privacy and Dignitary Privacy: Google Spain, the Right to Be Forgotten, and the Construction of the Public Sphere' (2018) 67 *Duke Law Journal* 981
Prechal, S, 'Free Movement and Procedural Requirements: Proportionality Reconsidered' (2008) 35 *Legal Issues of Economic Integration* 201
Prechal, S, 'Mutual Trust before the Court of Justice of the European Union' (2017) 2 *European Papers* 75
Puppinck, G, 'Abortion and the European Convention on Human Rights' (2013) 3(2) *Irish Journal of Legal Studies* 142
Pyrgakis, D, 'Article 50: Right not to be tried or punished twice in criminal proceedings for the same criminal offence' in VG Tzemos (ed), *The Charter of fundamental rights of the EU* [in Greek] (Athens, Nomiki Vivliothiki, 2015)
Ragni, C, 'Standard of Review and the Margin of Appreciation before the International Court of Justice' in L Gruszczynski and W Werner (eds), *Deference in International Courts and Tribunals: Standard of Review and Margin of Appreciation* (Oxford, Oxford University Press, 2014) 319–36
Rashkow, B, 'Immunity of the United Nations: Practice and Challenges' (2014) 10 *International Organizations Law Review* 332
Reeh, G, 'Climate Change in the Human Rights Committee' (*EJIL:Talk!*, 18 February 2020)
Reinisch, A, 'Should Judges Second-Guess the UN Security Council?' (2009) 6 *International Organizations Law Review* 257
Renaut, A, and Touraine, A, *Un débat sur la laïcité* (Paris, Stock, 2005)
Ribeiro, D, and de Oliveira Mazzuoli, V, 'The *Pro Homine* Principle as a Fundamental Aspect of International Human Rights Law' (2016) 3 *Indonesian Journal of International & Comparative Law* 77
Richards, T, '*Zambrano*, *McCarthy* and *Dereci*: Reading the Leaves of EU Citizenship Jurisprudence' (2012) 17 *Judicial Review* 272
Ringelheim, J, 'State Religious Neutrality as a Common European Standard? Reappraising the European Court of Human Rights Approach' (2017) 6 *Oxford Journal of Law and Religion* 24

Ringelheim, J, 'Lachiri v. Belgium: Headscarf Ban Imposed on a Civil Party in a Courtroom in Violation of Religious Freedom' (*Strasbourg Observers*, 23 November 2018)

Rivier, R, 'Responsibility for Violations of Human Rights Obligations: Inter-American Mechanisms' in J Crawford, A Pellet and S Olleson (eds), *The Law of International Responsibility* (Oxford, Oxford University Press, 2010) 739–61

Rizcallah, C, 'The Dublin System: The ECJ Squares the Circle between Mutual Trust and Human Rights Protection' (*EU Law Analysis*, 20 February 2017)

Robertson, AH, and Merrills, JG, *Human Rights in the World: An Introduction to the Study of the International Protection of Human Rights*, 3rd edn (Manchester, Manchester University Press, 1989)

Rodríguez Pinzón, D, 'The "Victim" Requirement, the Fourth Instance Formula and the Notion of "Person" in the Individual Complaint Procedure of the Inter-American Human Rights System' (2001) 7 *International Law Student Association Journal of International & Comparative Law* 369

Rodríguez-Pinzón, D, 'The Inter-American Human Rights System and Transitional Processes' in A Buyse and M Hamilton (eds), *Transitional Jurisprudence and the ECHR: Justice, Politics and Rights* (Cambridge, Cambridge University Press, 2011) 239–66

Roucounas, E, 'Engagements parallèles et contradictoires' (1987) 206 *Recueil des Cours de l'Académie de Droit International* 13

Roucounas, E, *Public International Law* [in Greek] (Athens, Nomiki Vivliothiki, 2015)

Rozakis, C, *The Concept of Jus Cogens in the Law of Treaties* (Amsterdam, North-Holland Publishing Company, 1976)

Ruiz-Chiriboga, O, 'The Conventionality Control: Examples of (Un)Successful Experiences in Latin America' (2010) 3 *Inter-American and European Human Rights Journal* 200

Sajfert, J, 'Bulk Data Interception/Retention Judgments of the CJEU – A Victory and a Defeat for Privacy' (*European Law Blog*, 26 October 2020)

Sandoval-Villalba, C, 'The Concepts of 'Injured Party' and 'Victim' of Gross Human Rights Violations in the Jurisprudence of the Inter-American Court of Human Rights: A Commentary on their Implications for Reparations' in C Ferstman, M Goetz and A Stephens (eds), *Reparations for Victims of Genocide, War Crimes and Crimes against the Humanity* (Leiden, Brill, 2009) 243–82

Sarkin, J, 'Why the Prohibition of Enforced Disappearance Has Attained Jus Cogens Status in International Law' (2012) 81 *Nordic Journal of International Law* 537

Sarmiento, D, 'Schipani v Italy: When Does the ECHR Require National Courts to Refer Questions to the CJEU?' (*EU Law Analysis*, 7 September 2015)

Schabas, WA, *The European Convention on Human Rights: A Commentary*, Oxford Commentaries on International Law (Oxford, Oxford University Press, 2015)

Scheeck, L, 'Solving Europe's Binary Human Rights Puzzle; The Interaction between Supranational Courts as a Parameter of European Governance' (2005) Sciences Politiques Centre d'Etudes et des Recherches Internationales Questions de Recherche no 15

Scheeck, L, 'Diplomatic Intrusions, Dialogues, and Fragile Equilibria: The European Court as a Constitutional Actor of the European Union' in J Christoffersen and M Madsen (eds), *The European Court of Human Rights between Law and Politics* (Oxford, Oxford University Press, 2011) 164–80

Scheinin, M, 'Reservations by States under the International Covenant on Civil and Political Rights and its Optional Protocols, and the Practice of the Human Rights Committee' in I Ziemele (ed), *Reservations to Human Rights Treaties and the Vienna Convention Regime: Conflict, Harmony or Reconciliation*, The Raoul Wallenberg Institute Human Rights Library 17 (Leiden, Brill Nijhoff, 2004) 41–57

Schlütter, B, 'Aspects of Human Rights Interpretation by the UN Treaty Bodies' in H Keller and G Ulfstein (eds), *UN Human Rights Treaty Bodies: Law and Legitimacy* (Cambridge, Cambridge University Press, 2012) 261–319

Schmidhauser, 'Legal Imperialism: Its Enduring impact on Colonial and Post-Colonial Judicial Systems' (1992) 13 *International Political Science Review* 321

Schutter, O De, 'The Binding Character of the Provisional Measures Adopted by the European Court of Human Rights' (2005) 7 *International Law FORUM du droit international* 16

Schutter, O De, 'The Two Lives of Bosphorus: Redefining the Relationships between the European Court of Human Rights and the Parties to the Convention' (2013) 4 *Journal européen des droits de l'homme* 584

Schutter, O De, 'Bosphorus Post-Accession: Redefining the Relationships between the European Court of Human Rights and the Parties to the Convention' in V Kosta, N Skoutaris and V Tzevelekos (eds), *The EU Accession to the ECHR*, Modern Studies in European Law 48 (Oxford, Bloomsbury, 2014) 177–98

Sękowska-Kozlowska, K 'A Tough Job: Recognizing Access to Abortion as a Matter of Equality: A Commentary on the Views of the UN Human Rights Committee in the Cases of Mellet v. Ireland and Whelan v. Ireland' (2018) 26(54) *Reproductive Health Matters* 25

Shackelford, S, 'Seeking a Safe Harbour in a Widening Sea: Unpacking the EJC's Schrems Decision and What it Means for Transatlantic Relations' (2015) Kelley School of Business Research Paper no 15–78

Shany, Y, 'Toward a General Margin of Appreciation Doctrine in International Law?' (2006) 16 *European Journal of International* Law 907

Shany, Y, 'All Roads Lead to Strasbourg?: Application of the Margin of Appreciation Doctrine by the European Court of Human Rights and the UN Human Rights Committee' (2018) 9 *Journal of International Dispute Settlement* 180

Sheeran, S, 'Reconceptualizing States of Emergency under International Human Rights Law: Theory, Legal Doctrine, and Politics' (2013) 34 *Michigan Journal of International Law* 491

Shelton, D, 'The Jurisprudence of the Inter-American Court of Human Rights' (1996) 10 *American University International Law Review* 333

Shelton, D, 'Normative Hierarchy in International Law' (2006) 100 *American Journal of International Law* 291

Shelton, D, 'Balancing Rights and Responsibilities: Human Rights Jurisprudence on Regulating the Content of Speech' in P Wahlgren (ed), *Human Rights: Limitations and Proliferation*, Scandinavian Studies in Law 55 (Stockholm, Stockholm Institute for Scandinavian Law, 2010) 211–41

Shelton, D, *Remedies in International Human Rights Law* (Oxford, Oxford University Press, 2015)

Shelton, D, 'Sherlock Holmes and the Mystery of Jus Cogens' (2015) 46 *Netherlands Yearbook of International Law* 23

Shelton, D and Gould, A, 'Positive and Negative Obligations' in D Shelton (ed), *The Oxford Handbook of International Human Rights Law* (Oxford, Oxford University Press, 2013) 562–83

Sicilianos, LA, 'Preventing Violations of the Right to Life: Positive Obligations under Article 2 of the ECHR' (2014) 3 *Cyprus Human Rights Law Review* 117

Sicilianos, LA, 'The UN Security Council, State Responsibility and The European Court of Human Rights: Towards an Integrated Approach?' in A van Aaken and I Motoc (eds), *The European Convention on Human Rights and General International Law* (Oxford, Oxford University Press, 2018) 213–29

Simonato, M, 'Ne Bis In Idem in the EU: Two Important Questions for the CJEU (Opinion of the AG in C-486/14 KUSSOWSKI)' (*European Law Blog*, 12 January 2016)

Simonato, M, 'Two Instruments but a Difficult Relationship? Some Upcoming Decisions of the CJEU on the Ne Bis In Idem' (*European Law Blog*, 15 November 2017)

Skandamis, N, Sigalas, F and Stratakis, S, 'Rival Freedoms in Terms of Security: The Case of Data Protection and the Criterion of Connexity' (2007) Challenge, Liberty and Security Research Paper No.7

Skouris, V, 'Fundamental Rights and Fundamental Freedoms: The Challenge of Striking a Delicate Balance' (2006) 17 *European Business Law Review* 225

Slaughter, AM, 'A Typology of Transjudicial Communication' (1994) 29 *University of Richmond Law Review* 99

Slaughter, AM, 'A Global Community of Courts' (2003) 44 *Harvard International Law Journal* 191

Smet, S, 'When Human Rights Clash in 'the Age of Subsidiarity': What Role for the Margin of Appreciation?' in P Agha (ed), *Human Rights between Law and Politics: The Margin of Appreciation in Post-National Contexts*, Modern Studies in European Law 76 (Oxford, Hart Publishing, 2017) 55–70

Soley, X, and Steininger, S, 'Parting Ways or Lashing Back? Withdrawals, Backlash and the Inter-American Court of Human Rights' (2018) 14 *International Journal of Law in Context* 237
Spielmann, D, 'Allowing the Right Margin: The European Court of Human Rights and the National Margin of Appreciation Doctrine: Waiver or Subsidiarity of European Review' (2012) 14 *Cambridge Yearbook of European Legal Studies* 381
Spielmann, D, 'The Judicial Dialogue between the European Court of Justice and the European Court of Human Rights or How to Remain Good Neighbours after the Opinion 2/13' (lecture organised by FRAME and the Leuven Centre for Global Governance Studies, 27 March 2017)
Staes, D, 'Correia de Matos v. Portugal: Fragmented Protection of the Right to Defend Oneself in Person' (*Strasbourg Observers*, 24 May 2018)
Steiner, E, 'Some Reflections on the Process which Led to the Preparation of the European Convention on Human Rights (ECHR)' in D Spielmann, M Tsirli and P Voyatzis (eds), *La convention européenne des droits de l'homme, un instrument vivant: Mélanges en l'honneur de Christos Rozakis* (Brussels, Bruylant, 2011) 597–623
Sudre, F, Milano, L, Surrel, H, and Pastre-Belda, B, *Droit européen et international des droits de l'homme*, 8th edn (Paris, Presses Universitaires de France, 2006)
Swire, P, '"Schrems II" backs the European Legal Regime into a Corner – How Can it Get Out?' (*Privacy Perspectives*, 16 July 2020)
Tavernier, P, 'L'identification des règles fondamentales un problème résolu?' in C Tomuschat and JM Thouvenin (eds), *The Fundamental Rules of the International Legal Order: Jus Cogens and Obligations Erga Omnes* (Leiden, Martinus Nijhoff, 2006) 1–20
Tigroudja, H, 'L'autonomie du droit applicable par la Cour interaméricaine des droits de l'homme: en marge d'arrêts et avis consultatifs récents' (2002) 49 *Revue trimestrielle des droits de l' homme* 69
Tigroudja, H, 'La force obligatoire des mesures provisoires indiquées par la Cour européenne des droits de l'homme: Observations sous l'arrêt Mamatkulov contre Turquie' (2003) 3 *Revue Générale de Droit International Public* 601
Tomuschat, C, 'Individuals' in J Crawford, A Pellet and S Olleson (eds), *The Law of International Responsibility* (Oxford, Oxford University Press, 2010) 985–91
Torres Pérez, A, 'Too Many Voices? The Prior Involvement of the Court of Justice of the European Union' (2013) 4 *Journal européen des droits de l'homme* 565
Torres Pérez, A, '*Melloni* in Three Acts: From Dialogue to Monologue' (2014) 10 *European Constitutional Law Review* 308
Torres Pérez, A, 'Too Many Voices? The Prior Involvement of the Court of Justice of the European Union' in V Kosta, N Skoutaris and V Tzevelekos (eds), *The EU Accession to the ECHR*, Modern Studies in European Law 48 (Oxford, Bloomsbury, 2014) 29–44
Tzanakopoulos, A, 'Kadi Showdown: Substantive Review of (UN) Sanctions by the ECJ' (*EJIL:Talk Blog!*, 19 July 2013)
Tzanakopoulos, A, 'The Solange Argument as a Justification for Disobeying the Security Council in the Kadi Judgments' in M Avbelj, F Fontanelli and G Martinico (eds), *Kadi on Trial: A Multifaceted Analysis of the Kadi Trial*, Routledge Research in EU Law (Oxford, Routledge, 2014) 121–34
Tzanakopoulos, A, 'Judicial Dialogue as a Means of Interpretation' in HP Aust and G Nolt (eds), *The Interpretation of International Law by Domestic Courts: Uniformity, Diversity, Convergence* (Oxford, Oxford University Press, 2016) 72–94
Tzanou, M, 'Case-note on Joined Cases C-402/05 P & C-415/05 P *Yassin Abdullah Kadi & Al Barakaat International Foundation v. Council of the European Union & Commission of the European Communities*' (2009) 10 *German Law Journal* 123
Tzanou, M, 'Balancing Fundamental Rights: United in Diversity? Some Reflections on the Recent Case Law of the European Court of Justice on Data Protection' (2010) 6 *Croatian Yearbook of European Law and Policy* 53
Tzanou, M, 'Data Protection in EU Law: An Analysis of the EU Legal Framework and the ECJ Jurisprudence' in C Akrivopoulou and A Psygkas (eds), *Personal Data Privacy and Protection in a Surveillance Era: Technologies and Practices* (Hershey, IGI Global, 2010) 273–97

Tzevelekos, V, 'The *Al-Dulimi* Case before the Grand Chamber of the European Court of Human Rights: Business as Usual? Test of Equivalent Protection, (Constitutional) Hierarchy and Systemic Integration' (2017) 38 *Questions of International Law* 5

Úbeda de Torres, A, 'Freedom of Expression under the European Convention on Human Rights: A Comparison with the Inter-American System of Protection of Human Rights' (2003) 10(2) *Human Rights Brief* 6

Uruena, R, 'Double or Nothing: The Inter-American Court of Human Rights in an Increasingly Adverse Context' (2018) 35 *Wisconsin International Law Journal* 398

Vedaschi, A and Graziani, C, 'PNR Agreements between Fundamental Rights and Natural Security: Opinion 1/15' (*European Law Blog*, 23 January 2018)

Veldman, A, 'The Protection of the Fundamental Right to Strike within the Context of the European Internal Market: Implications of the Forthcoming Accession of the EU to the ECHR' (2013) 9(1) *Utrecht Law Review* 104

Veldman, A and Vries, S de, 'Regulation and Enforcement of Economic Freedoms and Social Rights: A Thorny Distribution of Sovereignty' in T van den Brink, M Luchtman and M Scholten (eds), *Sovereignty in the Shared Legal Order of the EU* (Cambridge, Intersentia, 2015) 65–92

Vermeulen, J, 'Big Brother May Continue Watching You' (*Strasbourg Observers*, 12 October 2018)

Vervaele, J, 'The Transnational *Ne Bis In Idem* Principle in the EU: Mutual Recognition and Equivalent Protection of Human Rights' (2005) 1(2) *Utrecht Law Review* 100

Vervaele, J, 'Ne Bis In Idem: Towards a Transnational Constitutional Principle in the EU?' (2013) 9(4) *Utrecht Law Review* 211

Vervaele, J, 'Schengen and Charter-Related *Ne Bis In Idem* Protection in the Area of Freedom, Security and Justice: *M* and *Zoran Spasic*' (2015) 52 *Common Market Law Review* 1339

Vesterdorf, B, 'Legal Professional Privilege and the Privilege against Self-Incrimination in EC law: Recent Developments and Current Issues' (2004) 28 *Fordham International Law Journal* 1179

Vetzo, M, 'The Past, Present and Future of the Ne Bis In Idem Dialogue between the Court of Justice of the European Union and the European Court of Human Rights: The Cases of Menci, Garlsson and Di Puma' (2018) 11(2) *Review of European Administrative Law* 55

Vicini, J, 'The Dublin Regulation between Strasbourg and Luxembourg: Reshaping *Non-Refoulement* in the Name of Mutual Trust?' (2015) 8(2) *European Journal of Legal Studies* 50

Voorhoof, D, et al, *Freedom of Expression, Media and Journalists: Case-law of the European Court of Human Rights*, IRIS Themes Vol III (Strasbourg, European Audiovisual Observatory, 2015)

Voorhoof, D, 'ECtHR Accepts Strict Application of Data Protection Law and Narrow Interpretation of Journalistic Activity in Finland' (*Strasbourg Observers*, 12 August 2015)

Voorhoof, D, 'Freedom of Expression versus Privacy and the Right to Reputation: How to Preserve Public Interest Journalism' in S Smet and E Brems (eds), *When Human Rights Clash at the European Court of Human Rights Conflict or Harmony*? (Oxford, Oxford University Press, 2017)

Vries, S de, 'Balancing Fundamental Rights with Economic Freedoms According to the European Court of Justice' (2013) 9(1) *Utrecht Law Review* 169

Vries, S de, 'The EU Single Market as "Normative Corridor" for the Protection of Fundamental Rights: The Example of Data Protection' in S de Vries, U Bernitz and S Weatherill (eds), *The EU Charter of Fundamental Rights as a Binding Instrument: Five Years Old and Growing*, Studies of the Oxford Institute of European and Comparative Law 20 (Oxford, Hart Publishing, 2015) 235–60

Vosyliute, L, 'The ECtHR and the ECJ Overlapping Jurisdictions on Common EU Asylum Policy Issues: What Matters?' (*Academia*, March 2011)

Waisman, V, 'Human Trafficking: State Obligations to Protect Victims' Rights, the Current Framework and a New Due Diligence Standard' (2010) 33 *Hastings International and Comparative Law Review* 385

Walker, S, 'International Human Rights Law: Towards Pluralism or Harmony? The Opportunities and Challenges of Coexistence: The View from the UN Treaty Bodies' in C Buckley, A Donald and P Leach (eds), *Towards Convergence in International Human Rights Law*, Nottingham Studies on Human Rights 5 (Leiden, Brill Nijhoff, 2017) 491–515

Watt, E, 'Much Ado About Mass Surveillance: the ECtHR Grand Chamber "Opens the Gates of an Electronic "Big Brother" in Europe" in Big Brother Watch v UK' (*Strasbourg Observers*, 28 June 2021)

Weatherill, S, 'From Economic Rights to Fundamental Rights' in S de Vries, U Bernitz and S Weatherill (eds), *The Protection of Fundamental Rights in the EU after the Lisbon Treaty*, Studies of the Oxford Institute of European and Comparative Law (Oxford, Hart Publishing, 2013) 11–36

Weatherill, S, 'Protecting Internal Market from the Charter' in S de Vries, U Bernitz and S Weatherill (eds), *The EU Charter of Fundamental Rights as a Binding Instrument: Five Years Old and Growing*, Studies of the Oxford Institute of European and Comparative Law 20 (Oxford, Hart Publishing, 2015) 214–34

Wet, E de, 'From Kadi to Nada: Judicial Techniques Favouring Human Rights over United Nations Security Council Sanctions' (2013) 12 *Chinese Journal of International Law* 787

Wet, E de, 'Jus Cogens and Obligations Erga Omnes' in D Shelton (ed), *The Oxford Handbook of International Human Rights Law* (Oxford, Oxford University Press, 2013) 541–61

White, S, 'Accession of the European Union to the European Convention on Human Rights' (2011) 86 *Amicus Curiae* 7

White, M, 'The New Opinion on Data Retention: Does it Protect the Right to Privacy?' (*EU Law Analysis*, 27 July 2016)

Wicks, E, 'A, B, C v Ireland: Abortion Law under the European Convention on Human Rights' (2011) 11 *Human Rights Law Review* 556

Woods, L, 'Facebook Fan Pages and EU Data Protection Law: the Implications of Unabhängiges Landeszentrum für Datenschutz Schleswig-Holstein v. Wirtschaftsakademie Schleswig-Holstein GmbH' (*EU Law Analysis*, 3 July 2018)

Wyngaert, C van den, and Stessens, G, 'The International *Non Bis In Idem* Principle: Resolving Some of the Unanswered Questions' (1999) 48 *International and Comparative Law Quarterly* 779

Xanthopoulou, E, *Fundamental Rights and Mutual Trust in the Area of Freedom, Security and Justice-A Role for Proportionality?* (Bloomsbury Publishing 2020)

Yourow, HC, *The Margin of Appreciation Doctrine in the Dynamics of European Human Rights Jurisprudence*, International Studies in Human Rights 28 (Dordrecht, Martinus Nijhoff Publishers, 1996)

Zamboni, M, 'Romeo Castaño v Belgium and the Duty to Cooperate under the ECHR' (*EJIL:Talk!*, 19 August 2019)

Zarra, G, 'Right to Regulate, Margin of Appreciation and Proportionality: Current Status in Investment Arbitration in Light of Philip Morris v. Uruguay' (2017) 14 *Brazilian Journal of International Law* 95

Ziegler, KS, 'Strengthening the Rule of Law, but Fragmenting International Law: The *Kadi* Decision of the ECJ from the Perspective of Human Rights' (2009) 9 *Human Rights Law Review* 288

INDEX

www.ingramcontent.com/pod-product-compliance
Ingram Content Group UK Ltd.
Pitfield, Milton Keynes, MK11 3LW, UK
UKHW020240290926
15470UKWH00002B/645

9 781509 952434